AF449144

ALBERT TAYLOR BLEDSOE

Copyright secured
A.B. Walter engd

ALBERT TAYLOR BLEDSOE

Defender of the Old South
and Architect of the Lost Cause

TERRY A. BARNHART

LOUISIANA STATE UNIVERSITY PRESS
BATON ROUGE

Published by Louisiana State University Press
Copyright © 2011 by Louisiana State University Press
All rights reserved
Manufactured in the United States of America
First printing

Frontispiece: Albert Taylor Bledsoe, ca. 1859. Engraving by A. B. Walter. Virginia Historical Society, Richmond, Virginia (1999.161.1003). Used by permission.

DESIGNER: Michelle A. Neustrom
TYPEFACE: Whitman, text; Black Widow, display
PRINTER: McNaughton & Gunn, Inc.
BINDER: Dekker Bookbinding

LIBRARY OF CONGRESS CATALOGING-IN-PUBLICATION DATA

Barnhart, Terry A., 1952–
  Albert Taylor Bledsoe : defender of the old south and architect of the lost cause / Terry A. Barnhart.
    p. cm. — (Southern biography series)
  Includes bibliographical references and index.
  ISBN 978-0-8071-3724-6 (cloth : alk. paper)
1. Bledsoe, Albert Taylor, 1809–1877. 2. Intellectuals—Southern States—Biography. 3. Slavery—Southern States—Justification. 4. Southern States—Intellectual life—19th century. 5. Secession—Southern States. 6. United States—History—Civil War, 1861–1865—Causes. I. Title.
  E449.B646B37 2011
  973.7'13092—dc22
  [B]
                                                                                    2010038031

Portions of Chapter 2 appeared previously as "Albert Taylor Bledsoe: The Political Creed of an Illinois Whig, 1840–1848," *Journal of Illinois History* 3, no. 1 (Spring 2000): 3–30. Used by permission.

The paper in this book meets the guidelines for permanence and durability of the Committee on Production Guidelines for Book Longevity of the Council on Library Resources. ∞

CONTENTS

ACKNOWLEDGMENTS   ix

INTRODUCTION
Albert Taylor Bledsoe and the Intellectual History of the Old South   1

1. EDUCATION AND VOCATION
The Origins of a Southern Intellectual   10

2. PUBLIC ORDER AND PRIVATE LIBERTY
The Political Creed of an Illinois Whig   22

3. SOUTHERN EDUCATION AND POLITICS
The Making of a Sectionalist   39

4. A PHILOSOPHY OF THE WILL
Metaphysical and Theological Speculations   57

5. SOUTHERN SLAVERY JUSTIFIED
A Watchman's Response to Abolitionism   75

6. A SOUTHERN DISCOURSE
Replies to Liberty and Slavery   101

7. BROKEN FAITHS AND COVENANTS
Sectionalism, Secession, and War   125

8. WRITING THE REVOLUTION
A Confederate Interpretation of the Civil War   146

9. THE JUDGMENT OF HISTORY
The Right of Secession and the Lost Cause   169

10. RISING UP FROM THE ASHES
The Mission of the Southern Review   188

WRITING A LIFE: *A Note on Sources*   211

NOTES   217

INDEX   263

Illustrations follow page 100

ACKNOWLEDGMENTS

I FIRST ENCOUNTERED Albert Taylor Bledsoe, many years ago now, as a graduate student. My initial inquiries into Bledsoe's life and thought occurred in a seminar on the American Civil War and Reconstruction era taught by the late John N. Dickinson at Miami University in Oxford, Ohio. Dr. Dickinson suggested that Bledsoe deserved more attention than he had received, challenged me to think more expansively about his place as a southern intellectual, and encouraged me to persist in my research. Other historical interests and activities intervened along the way, but I have endeavored to remain faithful to that charge by probing more deeply into the experiences and sources of ideas that shaped his worldview. Convinced that his body of work merited serious attention, I never lost sight of one day writing his biography. That quest at length brought me here.

My obligations to those who helped me along the way are many. My foremost debt is to Bertram Wyatt-Brown. Bert believed in this project and gave the manuscript several critical readings at various stages in its development. I owe him much. Thanks is likewise due to Rand Dotson, senior acquisitions editor at Louisiana State University Press, who finally convinced me that less about Bledsoe could actually be more, and to Andrew Burstein, the incoming editor of the Southern Biography Series, for his meticulous and discerning reading of the penultimate draft of the manuscript. The manuscript further benefited from the comments and recommendations of the anonymous outside reader and from the scrupulous copyediting of Grace Carino.

I am likewise obliged to the History Department at Eastern Illinois University for the assignment of a research sabbatical that enabled me to get this project off the ground after years of chronic neglect. Colleagues at EIU subsequently meted out equal parts encouragement and constructive criticism on my preliminary thoughts about Bledsoe and my approach to his career in a departmental colloquium. I further benefited from the generous time and attention given this endeavor by Debra A. Reid of the History Department at EIU, who made substantive comments on an earlier draft of the manuscript. Janet Sue Ebel and Christine Merllié-Young of the Interlibrary Loan Department of

ACKNOWLEDGMENTS

Booth Library at EIU and Stacey L. Knight-Davis and Bradley P. Tolppanen of the Reference Department all assisted me in this enterprise by making the fugitive sources relating to Bledsoe and his contemporaries far more accessible.

Acknowledgment is also due to several others who likewise helped me in the prosecution of these investigations. Janet H. Stuckey, Betsy Butler, Suzanne Haag, and Jim Bricker at the Walter Havighurst Special Collections Library at Miami University in Oxford, Ohio, together with their predecessors Frances D. McClure and Helen Ball, have all contributed to this undertaking in various ways. Thanks also to Dr. Robert Schmidt, university archivist at Miami, and Stephen C. Gordon, curator at the William Holmes McGuffey Museum in Oxford, Ohio. Sarah C. Barr and Karen Clift, formerly of the Interlibrary Loan Department of King Library at Miami, have done me many courtesies—more certainly than I can now remember. Dr. Richard L. Aynes of the University of Akron and Judge C. Ellen Connally of Cleveland answered questions regarding the federal government's legal proceedings against Jefferson Davis. Dr. John M. Coski, historian and library director at the Museum of the Confederacy in Richmond, accommodated me by supplying copies of Bledsoe materials within that repository.

Rebecca Starr at the University of Gloucester clarified details relating to the life, writings, and family papers of Bledsoe's eldest daughter, Sophia Bledsoe McIlvaine Herrick, whose life is the subject of a forthcoming biography by Starr. John Ayres Greenlee of Fairfax Station, Virginia, generously provided me with transcripts of the diary of Thomas Eldridge Ayres Sr., a Baltimore schoolteacher, relating to his friendship with Bledsoe and his family. Thanks also go to several of the staff at the Abraham Lincoln Presidential Library in Springfield, Illinois: Daniel W. Stowell, director, and John Lupton, associate director, the Abraham Lincoln Legal Papers; Cheryl Schnirring, manuscripts manager, and Glenna Schroeder-Lein, librarian, special collections; Thomas Schwartz, state historian; and Kathryn Harris, director of library services.

Several archivists, manuscript curators, and librarians at other repositories have similarly eased my way. Frances Pollard, director of library services at the Virginia Historical Society, provided me with copies of the society's manuscript holdings relating to Bledsoe, while Meg Eastman, visual resources manager, and Jeffrey Ruggles, a curator in the Museum Department, provided images from the society's photographic collections. Similar services were received from Ann L. S. Southwell, manuscripts cataloger; Margaret Downs Hrabe, reference coordinator; and Sharon Defibaugh, technical services assistant at the

Albert and Shirley Small Special Collections Library at the University of Virginia in Charlottesville. Ann Southwell in particular did me many kindnesses by sorting out the provenience of the miscellaneous Bledsoe manuscripts at the University Virginia. Equally helpful were the services rendered by Diana Carey and Jacalyn R. Blume of the Arthur and Elizabeth Schlesinger Library at Harvard University's Radcliffe Institute for Advanced Study.

Research and writing are solitary pursuits, but they do not occur in a vacuum. If doing history removes one from the here and now in one sense, it directly impinges upon it in many other senses—obligations to family being the most conspicuous among them. The support and understanding of family enable all and deserve far more than the token acknowledgment given here. My wife, Jo Ellen Asher Barnhart, to whom my endless hours of preoccupation with this project must have at times seemed misplaced, was nonetheless encouraging and tolerant in equal measure. I can only hope that our children, Adrian and Andy, will one day understand why their father has dwelled so long among the catacombs of the past. My late mother and father, Helen Hanks Barnhart and Russell Allen Barnhart, provided the means of acquiring an education, which was but one of many gifts given as loving parents.

ALBERT TAYLOR BLEDSOE

INTRODUCTION

*Albert Taylor Bledsoe and the Intellectual History
of the Old South*

WRITING IN THE AUTUMN of life, Albert Taylor Bledsoe lamented that his solitary devotion to intellectual pursuits had largely alienated him from the world about which he so earnestly thought and wrote. Bledsoe grappled with several perplexing problems connected with causality, Christian theology, moral philosophy, political theory, and mathematics. He was the author of *An Examination of President Edwards' Inquiry into the Freedom of the Will* (1845) and *A Theodicy; Or, Vindication of the Divine Glory, As Manifested in the Constitution and Government of the Moral World* (1853)—works that earned him a respectable reputation as a metaphysician and speculative theologian. Yet Bledsoe is best remembered today as a stalwart vindicator of southern slavery, the constitutional right of secession, and the "Lost Cause" of southern independence. He assailed egalitarianism and defended the southern institution of slavery in *An Essay on Liberty and Slavery* (1856), justified the contested right of secession in *Is Davis a Traitor; Or Was Secession a Constitutional Right Previous to the War of 1861?* (1866), and upheld the sanctity of the Lost Cause as the editor of the *Southern Review* between 1867 and his death in 1877. He was also an accomplished mathematician, both as a teacher and as a theoretician. His major contribution in this field was *The Philosophy of Mathematics, with Special Reference to the Elements of Geometry and the Infinitesimal Method* (1868).

Students of Bledsoe's life have invariably commented on his unusual abilities, the breadth and depth of his intellectual attainments, and the force of his personality and writings. As he was at various times a soldier, mathematician, clergyman, lawyer, journalist, theologian, political theorist, and historian, his career has been called "a remarkable example of American versatility of character."[1] John Wilson Townsend, the literary historian and author of *Kentucky in American Letters*, described Bledsoe's intriguing qualities and diverse accomplishments in this manner: "Consider him from a dozen angles and one will not find his like again in the whole range of American history."[2] Perhaps Townsend exaggerates, but by no means did Bledsoe live an idle or aimless life.

He treasured the companionship of his wife, Harriet, and their four daughters but was largely a prisoner of his manifold pursuits. He spent much of his life lost in thought and controversy—communing with the great minds of the past and formulating his own ideas about the great issues of time and eternity. "*I have lived apart from the world. Its pleasures have been unknown to me. They have, indeed, never entered into my imagination till these life-long labors were completed. Would that I had never dreamed of them! Those who have tried them say they are full of vanity and vexation of spirit, and no doubt they say truly.*"[3] Vanity and vexation were, indeed, constant companions in Bledsoe's embattled life. He was, and remains, a complex and engaging figure.

Bledsoe's wide-ranging interests and disputatious nature embroiled him in many of the theological and political debates of the mid- and late nineteenth century. He was first and last a controversialist, who, in a very real sense, lived for the fight. While Bledsoe's larger significance is as a "southern" intellectual, he did not emerge as a spokesperson for the South until the height of the sectional crisis. After leaving his native Kentucky in his fifteenth year to attend West Point, Bledsoe spent most of his early adult life in the North. His interests and activities cut across sections, disciplines, religion, and politics, even though he exclusively and ardently identified himself as a southerner after 1856. Yet Bledsoe's previous educational and vocational experiences in Ohio and Illinois as a teacher, clergyman, and attorney shaped his attitudes, propensities, and talents as a polemicist in significant ways. Bledsoe spoke of sectional issues in muted tones as a Whig newspaper editor in the 1840s. But during the sectional crisis of the following decade, he resolutely aligned his own destiny with that of the South—its self-conscious conservatism, its educational and cultural aspirations, and its social and political imperatives as a slaveholding society.

The seedtime in the development of Bledsoe's sectionalism occurred during his tenures at the University of Mississippi and the University of Virginia. He served as chair of mathematics and astronomy at the University of Mississippi from 1848 to 1854 and as chair of mathematics at the University of Virginia from 1854 to the outbreak of the war. The mounting controversy over slavery immersed him and other southern academicians in the ideology of slavery and the doctrine of states' rights. And those concerns were further reflected in a defensive movement by southerners to educate themselves as a means of containing the spread of northern ideas regarding slavery and the nature of the federal Union. Most southerners placed a premium upon orthodoxy regarding slavery and the doctrine of states' rights and expected southern academicians to validate prevailing attitudes and accepted beliefs regarding the rectitude of both causes. As the slavery controversy intensified over northern resistance to the enforcement of the new Fugitive Slave Law, the repeal of the Missouri Compromise under the Kansas-Nebraska Act, and the birth of the Republican Party, southern academicians as well as southern politicians were called upon to defend southern rights and interests. Bledsoe's initial response to those events was *An Essay on Liberty and Slavery*.

Eugene D. Genovese has ranked Bledsoe alongside John C. Calhoun as one of America's ablest political theorists. And in a similar vein Joseph L. Blau recognized *Liberty and Slavery* as the best of the philosophical defenses of slavery. Even more clearly than Calhoun, Douglas Ambrose has observed, Bledsoe demonstrated "the dramatic departure of southern social thought from that of mainstream Western culture, including the North."[4] Bledsoe's defense of slavery, while conventional in many of its arguments, also possessed elements of distinctiveness. His attempt to rationalize natural rights theory with southern slavery was exceptional. Some of his contemporaries, indeed, found it puzzling and even troubling. Bledsoe was also altogether silent about the northern system of free labor. He manifested none of the antipathy toward free labor espoused by Henry Hughes and George Fitzhugh. Nor did he make overdrawn claims regarding the supposed moral and social superiority of slave labor as the basis of an ideal society. He defended the ethics of southern slavery and berated the alleged fallacies of abolitionists. Yet he did not assault free labor or northern society en mass. Bledsoe spent many years in the North during the early part of his life. Those experiences restrained his views on the alleged virtues and vices of northern versus southern society and their contrasting systems of labor. His defense of slavery was comprehensive and stoutly argued yet comparatively moderate.

Defending slavery and subscribing to states' rights doctrine did not necessarily make one an ardent secessionist in 1860 and early 1861—at least not *initially*. It only imparted a predisposition to side with the cause of southern independence under the right set of circumstances. Union sentiment died a lingering death among most southerners, particularly in the Upper South, no matter how unswerving their loyalty to the Confederacy became afterward. Only the most doctrinaire welcomed the advent of secession. John McCardell has noted that most southerners "were sectionalists, but not Southern nationalists" before the commencement of the war.[5] Bledsoe is a prime example. His hopes for sectional reconciliation led him to endorse the Constitutional Union Party in the presidential election of 1860, at which time he rejected the extremism he attributed to both the Republican Party and the southern wing of the Democratic Party. He beheld the groundswell of the secessionist tide and cautiously moved with it. Bledsoe was a moderate on secession before 1861 despite his earlier defense of slavery and his later vindication of the right of secession both during and after the war. There were many moderate southerners —especially in Virginia, North Carolina, and Tennessee—who, like Bledsoe, became radicalized only in the eleventh hour of the Union. He was at no time a southern fire-eater before the war, even though he has sometimes been incorrectly described as an ardent secessionist.

The secession of Virginia in April 1861 forced the issue with Bledsoe as it did for many Virginians. He cast his lot with the cause of southern independence and never looked back in doubt. Colonel Bledsoe spent a contentious and frustrating fourteen months in the Confederate War Department at Richmond from May 1861 to September 1862—first as the chief of the Bureau of War and then as the assistant secretary of war—before resigning his position and briefly returning to the University of Virginia. He next embarked on a new mission in the cause of southern independence, and one for which he was much better suited. As a Confederate publicist in London from October 1863 until the fall of Richmond in April 1865, Bledsoe joined other Confederates in their faltering efforts to influence British public opinion in favor of recognizing the sovereign independence of the Confederate States of America, negotiating an end to the hostilities, and possibly even intervening in the conflict as an ally of the Confederacy. The fourth estate was an important theater of the war both at home and abroad. Bledsoe's quixotic literary mission to London, however ineffective in saving the Confederacy, was nonetheless an essential period in elaborating his creed as a southern nationalist and formulating his historical and constitutional defense of the right of secession. It was, indeed, his most important contribution to the Confederate cause.

The publication of *Is Davis a Traitor?* in the fall of 1866 placed Bledsoe in the front ranks of those who championed the Lost Cause. He was determined to write the history of the war from the Confederate perspective and continued to do so until the end of his days. As David W. Blight has noted, Bledsoe "led the diehards in the defense of secession." Charles Reagan Wilson recognized *Is Davis a Traitor?* as the most important constitutional defense of the South's right to secede, while Douglas Southall Freeman described it as "that brief classic of American political argument."[6] It is more closely argued than either Alexander Hamilton Stephens's two-volume *A Constitutional View of the Late War* (1868, 1870) or the equally discursive two volumes of Jefferson Davis's *The Rise and Fall of the Confederate Government* (1881), although both works are better known. Bledsoe's exegesis into the history of the Constitution, what he called the "northern" (nationalist) and "southern" (states' rights) constructions of the Union, demonstrates the significance of those rival theories of American federalism from the founding of the Republic through the Civil War. Nowhere are the divergent views on the origin, nature, and meaning of the American Union and the causes of the Civil War more clearly delineated than in the meticulously argued pages of *Is Davis a Traitor?* The work still bears reading for its philosophical acumen and the thoroughness of its legalistic arguments regardless of whether one agrees with Bledsoe's premises and conclusions regarding the constitutionality of secession. Nor does one have to accept his audacious and oft-repeated claim that the book prevented Davis from being brought to trial for treason to still appreciate the prominence of Bledsoe's place within the pantheon of Lost Cause apologists.

The same determined resolve to discuss the causes, consequences, and meaning of the war from the perspective of the vanquished led Bledsoe and William Hand Browne to establish the *Southern Review* at Baltimore in 1867. Bledsoe was the sole editor and proprietor of the *Southern Review* from January 1869 until January 1875, when his daughter Sophia Bledsoe Herrick joined him as coeditor. Bledsoe's writings in the *Southern Review* epitomize obstinacy in the face of change. He promoted the cause of southern literature; wrote jeremiads on a multitude of literary, educational, scientific, and religious subjects; and continued to vigorously champion the Lost Cause. His offerings on the origin and meaning of the war in the *Southern Review*—together with the arguments advanced in *Is Davis a Traitor?*—represent a Confederate history of the Civil War according to Bledsoe. His animus toward the North softened somewhat after he affiliated the *Southern Review* with the Methodist Episcopal Church, South, in October 1870 and entered the Methodist clergy. Yet on the whole Bledsoe typified the irreconcilable ex-Confederate. He continued to write on the war as late as 1876. But after 1870 he increasingly wrote on theological subjects—his first and last passion.

Bledsoe's life and thought are by no means unique even if his trajectory and essence are somewhat distinctive. His experiences and views signify something larger than himself. The triangulations of self-interest, opportunity, and changing circumstances that centered in Bledsoe's life are not the mere eccentricities or inconsistencies of an individual. If they are this to one degree or another, they also represent something far more significant. The demons of personal conscience and loyalty with which he wrestled afflicted others too. His interests and activities exemplify a broad spectrum of American thought and experience. Even the more unorthodox and peculiar aspects of his speculative theology are rooted within a much broader discourse about causality, moral philosophy, and divinity that demonstrates the diversity of opinion among liberal and conservative theologians in both the North and the South. And nowhere is his representativeness more important than in his writings on slavery, secession, and the Civil War. His writings on those subjects speak directly, and sometimes eloquently, to the issues that divided the Civil War generation. Bledsoe's significance as an architect of the Confederate interpretation of the conflict is second to none. His exonerations of the Lost Cause did much to shape collective memory about the war among former Confederates and were an indelible part of Bledsoe's own identity. Historically and historiographically he is a very representative figure, which provides a useful measure for appraising the significance of his life and thought.

The degree of continuity and change that centers in an individual life is attributable to many variables and contingencies. Political affiliations and personal loyalties are not immutable. What individuals espouse at an earlier phase of what Peter Knupfer has instructively called their "civic life cycle" may or may not coincide with later convictions. Intervening events and changes in personal circumstances often challenge earlier assumptions and understandings, our own and those of the historical figures whose lives we presume to reduce to the pages of history and biography. Affiliations and loyalties, Knupfer reminds us, often "undergo significant and permanent alterations in response to critical historical circumstances."[7] The sectional crisis of the 1850s and the coming of the war presented precisely such conditions. Bledsoe underwent a gradual but certain process of accommodation, adjustment, and rationalization after 1848 from which he emerged as a defender of southern slavery in 1856 and of the contested right of secession both during and after the war. His positions on the tariff, the issue of slavery in the territories, and the value of the Union notably changed, yet in other regards he remained remarkably faithful to the conservative social and political views he first espoused in the 1840s as an Illinois Whig. He remained an old-line Whig, by his own testimony, as late as the presidential election of 1860. But once Virginia seceded from the

Union, Bledsoe became a committed southern nationalist. He continued to defend the unrequited aspirations of Confederate nationalism after the war and took great exception with anyone who implied that he should perhaps let the issue go.

The American Civil War calls into to question any single definition of national identity and purpose as has no event before or since. As Robert Penn Warren so tellingly commented, "The Civil War is, for the American imagination, the great single event our history." So far from fading from our memory, the conflict "grows in our consciousness." Later generations of Americans continue to make personal connections with the war because of its epic nature and pathos. The war, said Penn, presents "a gallery of great human images for our contemplation." David R. Goldfield has explored the legacy of the conflict and issues of national identity to equally good purpose: "The Civil War is like a ghost that has not yet made its peace and that roams the land seeking solace, retribution, or vindication. It continues to exist, an event without temporal boundaries, an interminable struggle."[8] Bledsoe knew that ghost and sought that same absolution. As the author of *Is Davis a Traitor?* and numerous contributions as the editor of the *Southern Review* he personified the unrepentant and unreconstructed southerner. The judgment of history to which Bledsoe so fervently and frequently appealed in his writings has not been kind to him or to the causes that he espoused. His defenses of slavery and secession have placed him, as his perspicacious daughter Sophia once so telling observed, on the wrong side of history. She was not wrong. Bledsoe rethought several of the first principles of American democracy in the 1850s and 1860s and found them wanting. And in equal measure with which he and likeminded southerners did so, that democracy returned an equally negative judgment against them.

Southern intellectuals who defended slavery created a conservative political ideology that challenged equalitarian assumptions and assertions. It was a commentary on society, politics, and culture that ranged well beyond the slavery issue itself. Proslavery thought was part of broader philosophical discourse about human nature, race, natural law, natural rights, the inherent tension between personal liberty and public order, and the aspirations of the South as a self-conscious region. As Eugene D. Genovese observes in the *Slaveholder's Dilemma*, "We could, if we would, profit greatly from a reasoned engagement with the thought of Calhoun, Dew, Bledsoe, Thornwell, and others. . . . The finest aspects of their thought, shorn of the tragic commitment to slavery and racism, constitute a searing critique of some of the most dangerous tendencies in modern life." Yet it is just as daunting a challenge to leave our own cultural baggage and time-bound understandings behind when dealing with proslavery thought as it was for those who confidently and assertively defended slavery as a positive good. Bertram Wyatt-Brown has stated the problem of historicism thusly: "But to label slavery a crime is to insist that its white beneficiaries should have known what we know, should have done as we do (or at least pretend to do). The philosophy of history could explain the fallacy involved. Recapturing the mood of the past is hard enough without indulging in the should-have-beens." A similar caveat by Drew Gilpin Faust addresses the same difficulty: "We have too long regarded the proslavery argument either as an object of moral outrage or as a contributing cause of the Civil War. For those who elaborated its details, it had a different meaning."[9]

Endeavoring to comprehend proslavery thought as its advocates understood it, however, is hardly the same as excusing or condoning its racist assumptions and claims. Bledsoe defended southern slavery in the abstract. His idealized representations conveniently ignored many of the institution's harsher realities—human injustices about which he surely knew even though he was not himself a slaveholder. He defended slavery not as it was actually practiced but as he needed it to be to advance the premises of his arguments. Bledsoe was noticeably mute, for instance, about the buying and selling of families at the auction house—such a conspicuous part of the abolitionists' moral condemnation of slavery. Yet the domestic slave trade was an integral part of the peculiar institution. By defending the system as a whole, Bledsoe also defended the aspects he chose to overlook—if not explicitly, at least implicitly. It matters little whether he ignored the more pernicious features of the institution as a rhetorical convenience or because he could not in good conscience defend them. His silence regarding the effects of the slave trade on individuals and families is, in effect, a complicity of silence.

Yet the life of the mind in the antebellum South ranged much further afield than the slavery controversy. There was nothing static, isolated, banal, or deviant about the intellectual history of the Old South, once commonplace assumptions to the contrary notwithstanding. Few historians today would accept the condescending assertion made by Samuel Elliott Morison in 1927 that "the cultivation of cotton and the neglect of men" adequately explained the abysmal fact that "by 1850 the cotton kingdom had killed practically every germ of creative thought, had excluded every means of purifying discipline."[10] Southern thought, quite to the contrary, was creative, disciplined, and ccomposed of transatlantic as well as indigenous elements—a significant juxtaposition that made southern intellectuals both cosmopolitan and self-consciously provincial. Michael O'Brien has ably demonstrated in his two-volume *Conjectures of Order* and related writings that intellectual life in the antebellum South was a differentiated province of Western thought but by no means an aberrant detour. And Eugene D. Genovese has similarly described the tradition of southern conservatism as a "variant of transatlantic traditionalism."[11] Southerners refashioned that intellectual heritage into expressions of regional identity and common purpose. Bledsoe is again a significant case in point. The authorities to which he makes appeal in his theological and political writings are European more times than not. His works are samplings of Western thought applied to American concerns and contexts. Bledsoe and other southern intellectuals who wrote in the conservative tradition delineated by Genovese placed a premium on maintaining hierarchy in social relations, often perceived political issues in religious and moral terms, and were hostile to egalitarian reform movements.

Determining the degree to which intellectuals speak for others besides themselves is a perilous endeavor. Those who dominated the literary culture and processes of self-definition in the antebellum South existed within a multifaceted and conflicted society. Speaking for the region as a whole was a presumptive though common practice. Southern intellectuals positioned themselves within a discourse about southern identity and culture that in large measure defined them without altogether eradicating their individuality. Yet identities, as Bledsoe's life and thought so readily attest, are complex social and cultural landscapes, and their constructions have been as problematic in the South as in any other region of the nation. Southerners, indeed, have not infrequently found it necessary to explain the distinctiveness of their region both to themselves and to others.[12] Socially, culturally, and geographically there was not one South but several, and the monolithic "southern mind" has proven more elusive than real.[13] Southern intellectuals shared many assumptions, fears, and beliefs through which they individualized and affirmed their "southernness," yet orthodoxy regarding the ideologies of slavery and states' rights channeled without entirely precluding divergent opinions.[14] It is not to be supposed, however, that Bledsoe entirely spoke for himself alone in his writings on slavery, secession, and the Civil War. His works are forceful reminders that American identity has often been contested ground and that appeals to the verdict of history in the defense of sacred causes seldom constitute a final judgment.

1

EDUCATION AND VOCATION
The Origins of a Southern Intellectual

ALBERT TAYLOR BLEDSOE WAS a Kentuckian by birth yet spent much of his early adult life in the North. The social and cultural contexts in which he was raised, educated, and first pursued a durable vocation represent a little-known but important period in his life. Between 1825 and 1839 he attended the United States Military Academy at West Point, New York; briefly read law at Richmond, Virginia; studied divinity at the Theological Seminary of the Protestant Episcopal Church at Kenyon College in Gambier, Ohio; and cast about for a profession as a teacher and clergyman in Ohio. His education and early experiences did *not* predict his later life and thought. Yet they do make them far more intelligible. Notable continuities exist between his early years at West Point and the Kenyon theological seminary and his later writings on theology, moral philosophy, mathematics, and education. Those years of intellectual and spiritual awakening proved profound. They provide important insights into the leading traits of his mind and character, incipient intellectual interests, and the beginnings of important lifelong associations. Many West Pointers, moreover, later found their allegiances and sense of duty at cross-purposes. They struggled with the sectional crisis of the 1850s, fought the Civil War, and spent the rest of their lives coming to grips with the conflict's personal meaning and the verdict of history as to the sanctity of their respective sides. Bledsoe was prominent among them.

Albert Taylor Bledsoe was born in Frankfort, Kentucky, on November 9, 1809. He was the eldest of the five children of Moses Owsley Bledsoe (1788–1851) and Sophia Childress Taylor (1792–1879). His parents had four other children: Emily (1811), Eliza (1813), Samuel Taylor (1815), and William (1817). Albert's father began his versatile career in the state capital of Frankfort. Moses was briefly associated from 1808 to 1809 with Willard Gerard in publishing the *Argus of Western America*, an "Independent Republican" newspaper published weekly in Frankfort. Moses subsequently became the proprietor, editor, and publisher of the *Commentator*—another weekly paper first published on January 3, 1817.[1] He later became a Whig, but his political affiliation before the 1840s is uncertain. It is likely, however, that he remained an "Independent Republican" during his years in Kentucky. The *Commentator* identified itself in 1828 as a paper of the National Republican Party, a short-lived party that joined other anti-Jackson groups in forming the Whig Party in 1834. Moses was a community leader and man of some means. He owned a large amount of land, a small number of slaves, and had political connections. His childhood friend Robert Perkins Letcher served in the U.S. House of Representatives from 1823 to 1833. Recognizing the intellectual abilities of Moses's son, Albert Taylor Bledsoe, Congressman Letcher nominated him in 1825 for admission to West Point.[2]

Moses married Sophia Childress Taylor in Frankfort, Kentucky, on January 4, 1809. She too was a Kentuckian and a daughter of Samuel and Elizabeth Taylor, a Virginia lawyer, planter, and slaveholder who moved his family to Harrodsburg, Kentucky. A member of the Virginia gentry class, Samuel represented Mercer County in the Virginia legislature and later served as a delegate to the Kentucky constitutional conventions of 1792 and 1797. Sophia had a distinguished lineage that included Chancellor Creed Taylor (1766–1836), a judge of the Superior Court of Chancery for Richmond, Virginia, and the founder of the Needham Law School (1821–42). Albert Taylor Bledsoe would later read law in the Richmond law office of Sophia's brother Samuel Taylor Jr. in preparation for a vocation as an attorney.[3] Little more is known of Sophia other than that she inherited a small number of slaves whom she allowed to purchase their freedom with a portion of the money earned from hiring them out to work for other families.[4] The manumissions probably occurred sometime prior to the removal of Sophia and her family to Carrollton, Illinois, around 1826. Sophia outlived her husband and eldest son, Albert, and died in Chicago in 1879 at eighty-seven years of age.

Bledsoe was a precocious and curious boy who reportedly manifested an indomitable will at an early age. We know virtually nothing about his education before his admission to the United States Military Academy. His daughter Sophia attests that before entering the academy he possessed only the rudiments of an education.[5] When the young Kentuckian entered West Point on July 1, 1825, he was only fifteen years old. Yet such an early age for entrance into the academy was not uncommon. Four of his classmates, indeed, had yet to reach their fifteenth birthday, and several other fifteen-year-olds in his class were even younger in months than he. Entering West Point at that tender age nonetheless proved a challenge. While Bledsoe's previous education and native talents were sufficient for passing the entrance exam, his lack of a formal education disadvantaged him relative to his older and better-prepared classmates. The West Point examiners had him enter the next incoming class (the Class of 1830) in January 1826 owing to a deficiency in French. His disappointment, however, spurred his later accomplishments.[6] Bledsoe ranked only seventy-first out of a class of eighty-seven in 1826 but held his own in the class standings each year thereafter. He ranked eighth in a class of sixty-three in 1827, tenth out of fifty-five in 1828, and eighth out of forty-five in 1829. He graduated from West Point on July 1, 1830, standing sixteenth in a class of forty-two and second in his class in mathematics. Years later he informed his friend and colleague William Holmes McGuffey that he would have finished first in his class in math except that the cadet who stood ahead of him, William Nelson Pendleton, had studied advanced mathematics for several years before entering West Point.[7]

The course of study at the United States Military Academy stressed the sciences and mathematics, along with military tactics, artillery, swordsmanship, French, belles lettres, moral philosophy, and rhetoric. Bledsoe received a thorough grounding in moral philosophy at West Point. It awakened an intellectual interest he continued to cultivate. The primary text was William Paley's *Principles of Moral and Political Philosophy* (1785)—an influential work widely adopted in American colleges.[8] While mathematics was his strongest subject and French his weakest, he overcame his deficiency in the latter subject by the end of his second year. Indeed, he later either taught French or tutored in the subject at Kenyon College in addition to teaching mathematics. Even so mathematics, the most rigorous subject in the curriculum, was the only subject in which Bledsoe distinguished himself. Charles Davies taught mathematics at the academy from 1816 to 1837. Under Davies's instruction and that of his assistants, Bledsoe mastered the principles of algebra, geometry, and trigonometry. Davies translated several French textbooks in the simpler and higher mathematics that were widely adopted in American colleges. Bledsoe later used them in his own classes. The training he received in mathematics at West Point was probably the best then available in the United States.

Bledsoe's aptitude for the study of higher mathematics first appeared in 1826. At the age of sixteen, he solved a problem in geometry first identified by Archimedes (287–212 BC). The ancient geometer indicated the corollaries or consequences that would follow the solution of the problem, but instead of solving it himself he bequeathed its solution to posterity. Adrianus Romanus and later Descartes also failed to solve it. Newton was more successful but figured out the solution by using two mechanical curves instead of the right line and circle prescribed by Archimedes. Cadet Bledsoe successfully applied the method stipulated by Archimedes. Professor Davies praised the result as the perfect solution. Bledsoe understandably took great pride in this feat. Yet he did not publish his discovery until the final year of his life.[9] He greatly valued his early training in mathematics and would demonstrate his mastery of the subject over a long and distinguished career as a teacher. "To the mind without mathematics, the great volume of nature is, in no small measure, a sealed book; for it is the science of number and magnitude alone, which teaches the very rudiments of the language in which its most sublime lessons are written. The mind trained in mathematics is far superior to the mind trained in any other field of mental endeavor."[10] Bledsoe's training in mathematics influenced his views on causality (what was necessitated and what was not) and his logical approach to tackling difficult metaphysical questions. He made many mathematical analogies in his writings and attempted to attain the same precision in presenting the logic of his arguments as in solving a problem in math.

Bledsoe's years at the United States Military Academy were crucial not only in terms of his education but also for the establishment of lifelong associations with fellow cadets and faculty. Several of those early acquaintances had profound influence on his intellectual interests and character. The West Point experience was a bond between Bledsoe and his fellow cadets, several of whom remained intimately involved with the circumstances and events of later life. The cadets in his own class and those ahead of him were also destined to play conspicuous roles in the Civil War. At West Point Bledsoe came to know Jefferson Davis, Robert E. Lee, Joseph E. Johnston, Albert Sidney Johnston, Leonidas Polk, and William Nelson Pendleton. At one time he and Leonidas Polk of North Carolina were roommates and remained cherished friends.[11] Bledsoe and Jefferson Davis likewise kept in touch in later years. Those warm attachments no doubt influenced Bledsoe's later strong advocacy for the Confederacy notwithstanding the oath of loyalty that West Pointers had pledged to uphold. He respected the character of those southern cadets and in time defended their honor as well as his own against the charge of treason and rebellion.

The chaplain at West Point during Bledsoe's first three years as a cadet was the Episcopal clergyman Charles Pettit McIlvaine (1799–1873). The Reverend McIlvaine taught ethics and belles lettres during Bledsoe's first two years and rhetoric and moral philosophy his last year. A gifted orator, McIlvaine possessed a commanding presence at the pulpit. According to his memorialist, Alfred Lee, "The physical man corresponded well with the intellectual, and the lovers of oratory found his discourses a rich treat." He preached with an "unwonted fervor." His chapel services and prayer meetings made a strong impression on the cadets. McIlvaine's ministry at West Point from 1825 to 1827 would be a turning point in Bledsoe's life and also in the life of Leonidas Polk, who later became the bishop of Louisiana. When McIlvaine baptized Polk before the entire corps of cadets and officers, others soon followed in making confessions of their faith. Bledsoe's own expression of faith occurred soon after Polk's. The conversion of Polk and the religious revival at West Point that followed were events that McIlvaine continued to fondly recall.[12] Bledsoe's and Polk's associations with McIlvaine continued long after their years together at the academy.

McIlvaine received cadet Bledsoe into communion as a member of the Protestant Episcopal Church in 1826.[13] The piety of the young cadet made a distinct impression upon James Milnor, the rector of St. George's Parish in New York, who visited West Point in June 1826 in the midst of McIlvaine's revival. Milnor met with McIlvaine's new converts, and some of them (Bledsoe apparently among them) traveled with McIlvaine to visit Milnor in New York. Milnor later asked McIlvaine to "tell dear little Bledsoe" [he was smaller than his older classmates] that the declaration and promise of the Lord that "I love them that love me; and they that seek me early shall find me" were most assuredly his if he truly believed in the teachings of the Redeemer. Little Bledsoe did, indeed, persist in the convictions of his newfound faith. Many years later he remembered his days at the United States Military Academy as "the very dawn of our Christian life."[14] Further testimony to the efficacy of McIlvaine's ministry at West Point is the fact that cadets Leonidas Polk of North Carolina, Francis Vinton of Rhode Island, William Nelson Pendleton of Virginia, and Albert Taylor Bledsoe of Kentucky all became clergymen in the Protestant Episcopal Church.

After graduating from West Point in July 1830, Bledsoe received the commission of brevet second lieutenant in the Seventh Infantry. Although he greatly valued his West Point education and relationships with fellow cadets and faculty, he did not find army life after the academy to his liking. He completed the two years of service required of West Point graduates at Fort Gibson in the Indian Territory (present-day Oklahoma) and resigned his commission on August 31, 1832.[15] Bledsoe's quest for a vocation next took him to Richmond, Virginia, to study law under the tutelage of his maternal uncle Samuel Taylor Jr. The legal profession was a tradition on both sides of his family. His great-uncle Jesse Bledsoe had a distinguished career at law and in politics before teaching law at the University of Transylvania.[16] Albert's father, Moses Owsley Bledsoe, is also said to have practiced law, although when and where is uncertain.

Nothing is known of Bledsoe's legal studies at Richmond. Yet young men who prepared themselves for careers at law—whether in law schools or as apprentices to practicing attorneys—studied the principles of English common law codified in Edward Coke's *Institutes of the Laws of England* and William Blackstone's *Commentaries on the English Common Law.* Bledsoe would have gained a working knowledge of these authorities along with the legal and political principles set forth in William Rawle's *A View of the Constitution of the United States* (1825) and the state, federal, and international law and the law of personal and property rights contained in Chancellor James Kent's *Commentaries on American Law* (1826–30). It is likely that Bledsoe first encountered the states' rights jurisprudence and constitutional theory advocated by St. George Tucker in his *Blackstone's Commentaries: With Notes of Reference* (1803) under his uncle's tutelage as well. Tucker's views influenced the political theory of many Virginians and were well known to all who taught, practiced, or studied law within the close-knit legal circles of Virginia.[17] It certainly would have been a part of the legal education of Bledsoe's legal mentor Samuel Taylor Jr., who was himself a product of Creed Taylor's Needham Law School in Virginia.

Bledsoe delayed his career at law, however, to pursue a new opportunity offered by the Reverend Charles Pettit McIlvaine. As the newly consecrated bishop of Ohio, McIlvaine became the president of Kenyon College and the head of the Episcopal theological seminary there in October 1832. Sometime before Bledsoe's arrival in July 1833, McIlvaine invited him to teach at Kenyon. Bledsoe's name appears in the Kenyon College *Catalogue* for 1833–34 and in the *Laws of Kenyon College and Theological Seminary* for 1833 simply as a tutor. Bledsoe himself, however, said he was an adjunct professor of mathematics and a teacher of French at Kenyon for the academic year 1833–34. He also entered the seminary. His fellow seminarians were Samuel Buell, Joshua T. Eaton, Abraham Edwards, Mansfield French, and Sherlock A. Bronson. Bledsoe once reported that he resigned his teaching position when he entered the seminary. Yet it appears from the college records that he continued to teach math while pursuing his theological studies.[18]

Bledsoe initially accepted the teaching position at Kenyon as a means of furthering the education of his sixteen-year-old brother William. He was intellectually gifted and aspired to be a physician but lacked the formal instruction that would be required by medical schools. Soon after his appointment at Kenyon, Bledsoe wrote William proposing that he join him at Gambier. There he would assist him financially in the completion of his studies. Sadly, William never received the letter. He died in July 1833, only a day or two before its arrival, during an outbreak of Asiatic cholera that swept through Carrollton, Illinois. His death prompted his grief-stricken elder brother to take up an ecclesiastical career. Intellectually it was the beginning of a difficult but rewarding journey. Bledsoe later recalled the profound impact of his brother's death on his nascent interest in theology. That heartrending event "seemed to extinguish in us the very light of life. But it led in the end to our entrance into the Theological Seminary, connected with Kenyon College under the Presidency of Bishop McIlvaine, and to our becoming a candidate for orders in the Protestant Episcopal Church. . . . Thus, by one afflictive dispensation of Providence, was changed the whole color and complexion of our moral life, and also, perhaps, our destiny for eternity."[19]

McIlvaine formalized the curriculum at the seminary soon after his arrival at Kenyon.[20] The required areas of study included evidences of Christianity, systematic divinity or theology, ecclesiastical history, Oriental and Greek literature, interpretation of the scriptures, church government, and the duties of the pastoral office. It would be difficult to overestimate the impact of those subjects on Bledsoe's social and political views. Bledsoe held a theistic view of society and government that emphasized human depravity and the need for the restraining hand of the law—moral as well as civil. He regarded the authority and majesty of the law not merely to be the handiwork of humans but rather as a divine dispensation. Natural law to Bledsoe was not a secular construction merely. It was only when political principles conformed to the precepts of divine law and the lamp of experience that they were trustworthy. It was a conviction that became firmly fixed during his early studies of moral philosophy and theology as a seminarian. Such a view of the world was by no means peculiar to Bledsoe but one to which he rigidly adhered. Many others who formally prepared themselves for the ministry had to similarly reconcile the sources of secular and divine authority.

Bledsoe had the good fortune to study under the direction of Dr. William Sparrow (1801–74). Sparrow served as vice president of Kenyon College, professor of moral philosophy, and the Milnor Professor of Ecclesiastical History and Systematic Divinity. Bledsoe considered him his greatest intellectual benefactor. "We have always regarded it as one of the most blessed events of our life that a kind providence placed us under the influence of such a teacher. He was at once the father, the mother, and the midwife of our intellectual being." Sparrow, like McIlvaine, was an evangelical or low-church Episcopalian. He was oriented toward the free will doctrine advocated by the Dutch Calvinist Jacobus Arminius (1559–1609) and later adopted by John Wesley and the Methodists. Sparrow's views on human nature, the problem of evil, and his Arminian sympathies deeply imprinted themselves upon the conscience of his precocious pupil. They were seminal influences in the development of Bledsoe's philosophy of the will.[21] Sparrow left Kenyon College in 1841 to become the professor of systematic divinity and Christian evidences at the Episcopal Theological Seminary at Alexandria, Virginia, where continued to extend the sphere of his liberal theology until his death in 1874. Bledsoe and Sparrow renewed their friendship after Bledsoe joined the faculty at the University of Virginia in 1854.

The years spent as a theological student at Kenyon were also important to Bledsoe for reasons other than his intellectual growth and spirituality. It was then that he first made the acquaintance of Harriet Coxe (1811–87) of Burlington, New Jersey. Harriet was the tenth child and youngest daughter of William Coxe and Rachel Smith Coxe. On October 8, 1822, Harriet's older sister Emily Coxe married Charles Pettit McIlvaine, whom Emily had known since their childhood together in Burlington, New Jersey. Harriet was a frequent visitor to the McIlvaine home in Gambier during Bledsoe's studies as a seminarian. Albert and Harriet and fell deeply in love and were married in Gambier on April 15, 1836. They had seven children, three of whom died in infancy or early childhood. The surviving children, all sisters, were named Sophia, Emily, Elizabeth, and Anna.[22]

Bledsoe completed his theological studies at Kenyon in September 1835. He received deacon's orders in the Protestant Episcopal Church at Christ Church in Cincinnati that same year and was admitted to presbyters' orders on September 11, 1836, at the Trinity Church in Cleveland, Ohio.[23] But Bledsoe did not begin parish work immediately. In October 1835, he accepted a teaching position in mathematics at Miami University in Oxford, Ohio. The new professor heard three recitations of mathematics a day from the freshman, sophomore, and part of the junior classes. Reverend Bledsoe also heard a Sabbath recitation from the freshman class, where they studied as closely as possible the greater part of the Epistle of Saint Paul to the Romans in the original—an exercise he deemed "useful both to the cultivation of the head and the heart."[24] He also introduced the Episcopal Church service into the chapel at Miami and occasionally conducted services at St. Matthew's Church in neighboring Hamilton.[25] His prospects at Miami seemed fair at first but soon turned sour.

The keynote of Bledsoe's brief tenure at Miami was controversy. Soon after his arrival in Oxford he unwisely became embroiled in an ongoing feud between President Robert Hamilton Bishop and Professor William Holmes McGuffey. Bishop, a native of Scotland, was educated at Edinburgh as a Presbyterian minister. He had held the office of president at Miami since the beginning of the first classes in 1824 and also taught history and the philosophy of social relations. As the founding president of Miami he had decided opinions as to how the fledging institution should be run and shaped its early culture in significant ways. McGuffey, a professor of ancient languages and other subjects, became President Bishop's leading antagonist on the faculty. Ambitious and outspoken, McGuffey denounced the president for his alleged laxity in the enforcement of discipline. Bledsoe's habits of firm discipline acquired at West Point drove him into the McGuffey camp, while his impulsiveness and fiery temper helped bring the Bishop-McGuffey affair to a head.[26]

The quarrel between Bishop and McGuffey centered on how disruptive students should be disciplined. The issue adversely affected faculty morale and personal relations by dividing the faculty into opposing camps. The climax came in March 1836 when the board of trustees invited faculty members to state their views. John Witherspoon Scott, professor of natural philosophy and chemistry at Miami since 1828, gave testimony that Bledsoe stated his opposition to Bishop's disciplinary policies to the trustees with so much candor that he came perilously close to demanding Bishop's impeachment.[27] When the board of trustees supported Bishop, both Bledsoe and McGuffey resigned their positions the following summer. The trustees accepted Bledsoe's resignation on September 26, 1836, and McGuffey's the following day. Bledsoe was bitter about his experience at Miami and regarded his friendship with McGuffey as the only redeeming quality of that former connection.[28] Nearly two decades later Bledsoe and McGuffey renewed their friendship as faculty members at the University of Virginia.

Bledsoe resigned his professorship at Miami to become the rector of Grace

Church in Sandusky, Ohio. His friend and brother-in-law Bishop Charles Pettit McIlvaine helped Bledsoe secure the appointment. His fellow professor John Witherspoon Scott informed the board of trustees that Bledsoe had left Miami with a jaundiced view of the college and everything connected with it. Scott described him as honest, candid, and upright but also reckless. Bledsoe was "too honest and candid perhaps for his prudence or at least for his own comfort."[29] The lack of restraint and tact manifested by Bledsoe in the McGuffey-Bishop affair remained leading traits of Bledsoe's character. He often acted too rashly for his own good. Bledsoe, indeed, admitted as much to his then fiancée and future wife, Harriet Coxe, in February 1835: "the most frequent error of my life," Bledsoe confessed, was that he could not help himself from "being carried away by an impetuous ardour of feeling."[30]

It has sometimes been speculated that President Bishop's antislavery sentiments might have been another reason for Bledsoe's opposition to his administration. But the postulate is de facto conjecture that receives no support from the record of Bledsoe's tenure at Miami. The supposition is based upon the plausible though dangerous assumption that the views that Bledsoe expressed in his later defense of slavery reflected his earlier position on the subject as well. Yet no evidence exists to document Bledsoe's views on slavery during his tenure at Miami. His later views on slavery changed significantly in response to events and his own personal circumstances after he moved to Oxford, Mississippi, in 1848. Bishop's antislavery sympathies and activities eventually resulted in conflict with the Miami University Board of Trustees and led, according to his biographer, to his stepping down as president in 1841. But they did not prompt Bledsoe to oppose the administration of Bishop or influence his decision to resign from the faculty. Surviving evidence indicates that Bledsoe opposed Bishop and resigned his position at Miami over matters of disciplinary policy and a desire to become a full-time clergyman and nothing more.[31]

Bledsoe spent the next two years following his resignation from Miami as a clergyman. He met with far more disappointment, frustration, and financial hardship in that undertaking than success. His position at the Grace Church in Sandusky, which he obtained through the recommendation of McIlvaine, lasted less than a year. He suffered with "fever and ague" throughout the fall and winter of 1836. The affairs of the new church were in such a state of disarray, moreover, that he had been unable to recoup the seven hundred dollars promised him in salary. When Bishop McIlvaine learned of Bledsoe's plight, he was positively furious. He wrote to the wardens and vestry of Grace Church in January 1837 stating his displeasure. "It is with no little pain and mortification that I have seen the absolute necessity that the Rev. Mr. Bledsoe was under of relinquishing his charge of your parish." It was McIlvaine who had persuaded Bledsoe to resign his professorship at Miami University—where he had received a much higher salary (eight hundred dollars), had fewer living expenses, and had a much lighter assignment of duties—in order to accept the position at Sandusky. "Had I dreamed of what has since taken place as to his support, I would sooner have lost my right hand."[32]

Bledsoe resigned his position at Sandusky in the early part of 1837 and accepted another at St. Paul's Church in Lexington, Kentucky. He also assisted Bishop Benjamin B. Smith of the Diocese of Kentucky and at some point served as the assistant minister of Christ Church at Cincinnati headed by the Reverend John T. Brooke.[33] He resided in Lexington and Cincinnati separately from his wife and recently born daughter Sophia, who still lived at the McIlvaine home in Gambier, Ohio. He grew weary over the lengthy periods of separation from his family and impatient over disputes arising from an unspecified problem within the Diocese of Kentucky involving Bishop Smith and his opponents. Whether the difficulty was one of church doctrine or governance is unclear. But Bledsoe did not doubt that the religious convention he was about to attend at Danville, Kentucky, would be disagreeable and stormy. The restless clergyman resigned his positions at Lexington and Cincinnati and next briefly served at St. John's Church in Cuyahoga Falls in northeastern Ohio. Yet that arrangement still kept him separated from his family. It was a taxing situation that he no longer wished to tolerate. He resigned his position at St. John's Church in October 1838 and was now without any means of supporting himself and his family.[34]

Besides those problems Bledsoe also began to question several points of church doctrine. He no longer subscribed to the Calvinistic assumptions that he believed lay behind some of the Thirty-nine Articles of Religion. He thought Article 17 was predicated upon the doctrine of predestination and that Article 9 presupposed the concept of original sin. He regarded both doctrines to be "utterly inconsistent with the teachings of Christ, as well as with the eternal and immutable dictates of reason." He objected to Article 9 because in his estimation it taught that newborn infants were somehow deserving of God's wrath and damnation.[35] If he did not agree with the doctrine of the church on so fundamental a principle, he could not in good conscience remain in the ministry. The Ohio Diocese displaced Bledsoe from the Episcopal clergy at his own request in 1839 for causes not affecting his moral character. He remained a communicant in the Protestant Episcopal Church until 1870 but found himself increasingly drawn to the doctrines of Methodism. He made an unsuccessful application for admission into the ministry of the Methodist Episcopal Church either at the time of his resignation from the clergy of the Protestant Episcopal Church or a few years later.[36] He had come to accept the Methodist version of the Thirty-Nine Articles as enunciated by John Wesley. He did not endorse all aspects of the Methodist scheme of church governance but for the most part remained in sympathy with Methodism for the rest of his life.

Wearied of poverty, separations from his family, and doctrinal disputes Bledsoe resigned his orders in the Protestant Episcopal Church and set out for greener pastures. The year 1839 found him reunited with his family in Carrollton, Illinois, after an absence of twelve years. Bledsoe left the family circle at age fifteen to attend the United States Military Academy and returned to it as a graduate of West Point, a former Episcopal clergyman, and an experienced college teacher of mathematics. Yet the restive young man was still in search of a durable vocation. Bledsoe experienced nothing but hardships as a minister, which, quite apart from his crisis of conscience, would adequately explain his decision to join his family in Illinois and take up the practice of law. Bledsoe had earlier prepared himself for that profession at his uncle's law office in Richmond, Virginia, and it may well have been the career urged upon him by his parents. The history, logic, and ethics of the law appealed to Bledsoe's scholarly cast of mind, while the practice of law at Springfield, Illinois, led him, naturally enough, into the arena of politics. In this new venture, he would enjoy more success than he had as a peripatetic and intellectually troubled clergyman.

2

PUBLIC ORDER AND PRIVATE LIBERTY

The Political Creed of an Illinois Whig

BLEDSOE'S YEARS AT SPRINGFIELD, Illinois, were a decisive period in the development of his political thought. There he first declared his conservative principles in a partisan eulogy of William Henry Harrison delivered in May 1841. Bledsoe's tribute voiced the Whig Party's pledge to redeem the Republic and restore it to its "purer days." He joined Abraham Lincoln, Stephen Trigg Logan, and other Whigs in July 1842 in organizing the Springfield Clay Club. Bledsoe again united with Lincoln and Logan in coauthoring an "Address to the People of Illinois" in March 1843. The campaign circular explained the Whig Party platform and outlined the party's formula for national prosperity. As coeditor of the *Illinois Journal* in 1847 and 1848, Bledsoe opposed the Polk administration's conduct of the Mexican War, supported the Wilmot Proviso, and endorsed Zachary Taylor for president. Those were certainly not positions that a proslavery Kentuckian would have embraced. Instead, he adopted the same positions that Lincoln and many northern Whigs held on the issue of slavery in the territories. Bledsoe's political writings between 1841 and 1848 are embryonic expressions of ideas and arguments to which he returned in several of his later writings. Notwithstanding notable changes in his later views on slavery, states' rights, and protective tariffs, his nascent political philosophy first emerged in Illinois.[1]

Bledsoe joined his mother and father in Carrollton, Illinois, after resigning from the clergy in 1839. His parents moved to Carrollton from Kentucky within a few years after their son's admission to West Point in 1825. Moses established himself as a prominent member of the community soon after his arrival. He first served as clerk of the circuit court in Greene County, Illinois, in 1829. His name also appeared in the "Courier Extra" campaign circular at Springfield on July 26, 1830, as an opponent of John Reynolds during the gubernatorial contest of that year. Moses appears to have considered running for governor himself in that election, or at the very least allowed his name to be brought forward in consideration for the office by his supporters, but nothing ever came of it.[2] Apart from serving as clerk of the circuit court in Greene County from 1829 to 1848, he served as justice of the peace, clerk of the county court from 1834 to 1837, and commissioner of the county school lands from 1838 to 1840. Moses's years as a clerk of the circuit and county courts suggest a legal background. He may have practiced law in Kentucky at some point, but there is no record that he ever practiced law in Carrollton or elsewhere in Illinois.[3]

Bledsoe was admitted to the Illinois bar on March 15, 1839, and initially practiced law in Carrollton.[4] The new state capital at Springfield, however, offered far greater opportunities for an aspiring attorney. Consequently, Bledsoe established himself there in December 1839. His law notice in the *Sangamo Journal* announced his intention of practicing before the judges in the District Court of the United States at Springfield, the Illinois Supreme Court, and the circuit courts of Sangamon, Morgan, Greene, and neighboring counties. In February 1840 he formed a short-lived partnership in Springfield with a more established attorney and jurist, Jesse Burgess Thomas Jr. Bledsoe soon practiced as a member of the firm before the federal court, the Illinois Supreme Court, and several circuit courts.[5] Yet for reasons unknown Thomas and Bledsoe parted company in August 1840. Bledsoe formed a more successful partnership in May of the next year with his father's onetime protégé at Carrollton—Edward Dickinson Baker (1811–62). Baker was an able attorney and a close friend and political crony of Abraham Lincoln's.[6]

The partnership of Baker and Bledsoe appears to have lasted at least until the fall of 1844, during which time they appeared together in several cases before the Illinois Supreme Court. Baker was well connected in both legal circles and the Whig Party, which included a place on the influential Whig State Central Committee with Lincoln and a seat in the Illinois Senate from 1840 to 1844. He was one of the "Springfield Junto"—a clique, according to the Democratic *Illinois State Register*, that was led by Lincoln and which allegedly dominated the Whig Party in Illinois.[7] Presumably Baker and Bledsoe remained friends after their years together at the Springfield bar. Yet the erstwhile partners failed to share the same loyalties during the Civil War. Baker remained a close friend and political supporter of Lincoln's and a staunch Unionist. As a U.S. senator from Oregon, Baker denounced the legitimacy of secession in the first speech he ever made upon the floor of the Senate in January 1861. When the war began, he served as a colonel in the Union army while still retaining his seat in the Senate. Baker died at the Battle of Ball's Bluff on October 21, 1861.[8] Baker's steadfast loyalty to Lincoln and the Union is but one of several ironies regarding the war that runs like a leitmotif throughout Bledsoe's life.

Bledsoe proved himself an abler advocate before the bar than he had been as a preacher at the pulpit. He and Lincoln appeared together in numerous cases, though usually as opponents. Baker and Bledsoe were co-counselors with Lincoln and Logan in only three cases heard before the Sangamon County Circuit Court in the spring of 1842. Bledsoe won thirty-seven of sixty-four cases in six years of practice before the Illinois Supreme Court, opposing Lincoln in a dozen of those legal actions. He won at least seven out of twelve cases in which he opposed Lincoln in the state court. According to family tradition, Bledsoe customarily brought home a basket of champagne annually awarded by his peers at the Springfield bar for conducting the most successful cases. Those accomplishments, however, did not always translate monetarily. His practice enabled his family to live more comfortably in Springfield than during his prior years as an impoverished minister, but there were few windfalls. More philosopher than businessman, Bledsoe showed little aptitude or patience for finances.[9]

By all accounts Bledsoe mastered the art of legal pleading. His intellectual qualities as an attorney made a particular impression upon Samuel Willard, who visited the law office of Baker and Bledsoe in 1843.[10] Willard described him as a man "of logical mind, acute, learned, versatile, able and even powerful in any field of thought except natural science, in which was untried." Many years later he speculated that Bledsoe might have had a more brilliant legal and political career than either Lincoln or Baker. Instead, though, he sank "his splendid powers in the hum-drum life of a professor of mathematics." He followed his own interests and inclinations and authored two books: "one, a theodicy, to defend the glory of God, which was needless; the other to defend the glory of slavery, which was vain." Willard affirmed that no one who knew Lincoln, Logan, and Bledsoe as Springfield attorneys could possibly have guessed their futures, not even someone with the wildest imagination. If one were asked to predict which of those talented prosecutors would one day be president of the United States, said Willard, "Bledsoe must be the man!" John Todd Stuart, Lincoln's first law partner and a U.S, congressman, was similarly impressed with Bledsoe's legal acuity. Stuart reportedly declared that in terms of logic Bledsoe was the strongest lawyer at the Springfield bar. "But contentment was not with him a cardinal virtue. He could remain in one position but a short time."[11]

If the second American party system came of age during the pageantry and rhetoric of the presidential elections of 1840 and 1844, so too did the political and social consciousness of Albert Taylor Bledsoe. He was affiliated in those histrionic campaigns with Simeon Francis, the Connecticut-born editor of the *Sangamo Journal.* Francis moved to Springfield in 1831 and launched the *Journal* in November of that year. He declared the paper's endorsement of William Henry Harrison in 1838. After that the *Sangamo Journal* became the voice of Springfield Whigs. Francis printed the *Old Soldier,* an extra campaign paper, at the office of *Sangamo Journal* under the direction of the Whig State Central Committee. The committee included Bledsoe's law partner Edwin Dickinson Baker, Joshua Fry Speed, Anson G. Henry, Richard F. Barrett, and Lincoln. Bledsoe's father was also active in Whig politics. Such personal associations rooted Bledsoe in the political culture of the Whig Party. American Whigs invoked the English country-party tradition of opposing executive authority to protect the Constitution, shared a conception of republican virtue and a sense of redemptive or regenerative mission, and concerned themselves with controlling basic human passions and licentiousness in the political life of the nation.[12] Bledsoe articulated all of those convictions in public addresses at Springfield and as editor of the *Illinois Journal.*

Bledsoe worked diligently as both a campaigner and a journalist to promote party principles and policies. He and other Springfield Whigs turned out in full force to support their nominee, William Henry Harrison, at the Young Men's Whig Convention and Old Soldiers' Meeting held at the capital in June 1840. Bledsoe, one of the assistant chief marshals, was mounted and paraded down the street wearing a pink scarf with white rosettes and carried a white baton. Delegations came from Missouri, Indiana, and Iowa as well.[13] The log cabin and hard cider doggerel, the mass barbecues, and the grand parades held on that noisy occasion had their counterpart throughout the nation during the presidential election of 1840. Those rallies heralded the rise of a new kind of electioneering. Every effort was made to engage the popular mind and emotions, particularly by means of mass demonstrations. Later in life Bledsoe denounced such campaigning as humbuggery. He would lament that the Whigs had been so power-hungry that they forfeited their presumptive claim to being the most intelligent and virtuous party by adopting the very political tactics they once denounced as demagoguery. The mass meetings and celebrations in which he once participated later appeared to him as nothing more than "shams" and "carnivals of folly and madness" designed to win over the passions of the people to the Whig cause. "An intelligent observer might have supposed, indeed, that the tremendous contest which then convulsed the country, was intended to establish the great principles that log-cabins are the best of all houses, that coon skins are the finest of all furs, and that hard cider is the most delicious of all drinks."[14]

Despite the delirium of the campaign, the Whigs did not carry Illinois in 1840. But the election of Harrison as president lifted their spirits as never before. Now the Whig agenda of reform could finally move forward. Those hopes instantly dissipated, however, when Harrison died of pneumonia only one month after his inauguration. It was a solemn moment when a group of citizens gathered themselves at memorial services held for the late president at the Second Presbyterian Church of Springfield on May 1, 1841. Bledsoe delivered a partisan eulogy on the life of Harrison for the occasion. He declared the principles that made him a Whig and expressed some of the fears he harbored for the Republic's future.[15] He dwelled on cherished Whig principles: restraint in federal-state relations, a limitation on presidential power, and the preservation of both majority and minority rights. He lauded Harrison's heroism, statesmanship, and republican virtues and delivered a panegyric to American exceptionality and the sagacity of the founders of the Republic. Bledsoe's public address on Harrison is the earliest known statement of his political principles. It delineates concerns relating to human nature and government that became canons of his political theory.

Bledsoe's extravagant praise of the spirit and principles of the American Revolution—the ideology of which both Harrison and his father had faithfully adhered to—was conventional Whig oratory. He venerated the main beliefs of the American Revolution by accentuating how that event in many respects differed from other revolutions. Other nations had likewise resisted tyranny, but the legacy of many of those revolutions had been one of destruction and anarchy only. They lacked the spirit of moderation that Bledsoe extolled as the leading characteristic of the American Revolution. "All that is most sacred and dear to man has been exposed to the fierce and raging domination of unchained passion. . . . The prospect of liberty, so bright at first, has been converted into scenes of licentiousness and crime, the most terrific and appalling." Bledsoe distrusted any revolution or scheme of government that disrupted "the deep foundations of society." The American Revolution, he declaimed, had not done that, whereas the French Revolution had. Maddened by centuries of oppression, the votaries of that mighty upheaval soon became the oppressors of others and delighted in the spilling of human blood in the name of liberty. Denouncing the French Revolution and it frenetic cry of liberty, equality, and fraternity remained a set piece in Bledsoe's antiegalitarian rhetoric from that day forward. He would inveigh, much in the tradition of Edmund Burke, against the erroneous ideas he attributed to the eighteenth-century Enlightenment—delusions that had spawned the tyranny and terror of the French Revolution. Fifteen years later he would censure those same egalitarian notions in his assault upon the American abolition movement.

The same spirit of moderation that had animated the American Revolution, Bledsoe continued, also formed the basis of the political principles enunciated by William Henry Harrison. Bledsoe endorsed the president's formula of reconciliation, concession, and forbearance in federal-state relations. "I believe it to be the duty of a representative to conciliate, by every possible means, the members of our great political family, *and always to bear in mind that as the Union was effected only by a spirit of mutual concession and forbearance, so only can it be preserved.*" Harrison had learned "the great lesson of national fraternity" that seemed lost on those who embraced the common cause of nationhood with much less ardor than he. He pledged himself to the principle of supporting all measures that promised to promote the greater good at the expense of "any local or inferior interests." Yet it was also Harrison's regard for the good of the whole nation, not just the greater part of it, that at the same time taught him "to respect the rights—nay, the very prejudices of the minority." Such a moderate and conciliatory attitude was necessary to mitigate the extremes of party spirit and wrath "which have shaken the foundations of the republic." Bledsoe at that juncture of his life was impatient with zealots among the advocates of states' rights. He steered a middle course between the extremes of states' rights and national consolidation while seeking a further balance between majority and minority rights. He believed that such equilibrium could be maintained through mutual forbearance and restraint, although he would later lose that faith entirely.

Bledsoe's eulogy established his credentials as a spokesman for the Whig Party. He was among the fifty or so Whigs who met at the statehouse in July 1842. The disgruntled partisans condemned President John Tyler's abandonment of Whig policies and nominated Henry Clay as the standard-bearer of the party. They organized the "Clay Club" of Springfield in an effort to secure his election as president in the election of 1844. Bledsoe, Baker, Lincoln, and Stephen Trigg Logan were among those attending. Bledsoe and Lincoln were appointed to the nine-member Executive Committee of the Clay Club on July 15, 1842. The committee's chief business was to ensure that Clay's principles and policies would constitute the Whig Party platform in the forthcoming election. Bledsoe joined Lincoln and Logan in preparing a declaration of the Clay Club's position.[16] An "Address to the People of Illinois" endorsed a tariff for the protection of American industry, opposed direct taxation, advocated a national bank, and championed the Clay Land Bill for the distribution of revenues from the sale of public land.[17] Bledsoe's enthusiasm for the American System of Henry Clay faded in time; Lincoln's did not. Bledsoe denounced protective tariffs in 1863 as a perpetual system of tribute that impoverished the South and enriched the North. He came to view the American System he once so ardently supported as a grand delusion and counted himself among the duped. Yet in 1842 he was as a Henry Clay Whig through and through.

Bledsoe's activities in the Whig Party continued through the presidential election of 1844. He and Lincoln were among the delegates and speakers from Sangamon County at the Whig Convention held in Vandalia, Illinois, on July 17, 1844. Between five thousand and six thousand animated Whigs gathered there in the hope of redeeming Illinois from "the thrall of Locofocoism." The pageantry of the occasion rivaled that of the Whig convention at Springfield in 1840. A barbecue fed the assembled multitude, "live coons" added further interest to the festivities, and eloquent addresses were delivered beneath the liberty pole throughout the afternoon and evening. Among those speaking were Usher F. Linder, Lincoln, and Bledsoe. The delegates ratified the nomination of Henry Clay of Kentucky for president and Theodore Frelinghuysen of New Jersey for vice president. They recommended the establishment of Clay Clubs in every county and every precinct of the state. When the delegates returned to Springfield, they made their way to a Whig "Cabin," where Lincoln and Bledsoe delivered an "animating speech" before dismissing their fellow delegates and returning home.[18]

The relationship between Bledsoe and Lincoln also extended beyond their association in law and politics. The Bledsoe and Lincoln families both lived at the Globe Tavern during the years 1843–44. Harriet Bledsoe and her daughter Sophia reportedly attended upon Mary Todd Lincoln during the birth of the Lincolns' eldest son, Robert Todd Lincoln.[19] Bledsoe also played a part in the celebrated Lincoln-Shields affair—a comic but potentially tragic opera in which James Shields, the state auditor and a leading figure in the Democratic Party, challenged Lincoln to a duel. Much has been written about this incident, and the details bear repeating only to the extent that they further document Bledsoe's personal relationship with the future president. The episode sprang from Lincoln's habit of writing anonymous letters that ridiculed political opponents. Lincoln, Mary Todd, and Julia M. Jayne wrote anonymous satires, the "Rebecca Letters," which appeared in the *Sangamo Journal*. Lincoln wrote the first Rebecca letter under the date of August 27, 1842, and Mary Todd and her friend Julia M. Jayne wrote the second dated September 8. The letters made sport of Shields through the persona of a poor widow named "Becca" who lived in the "Lost Townships." Becca spoke in an upland southern dialect and expressed dissatisfaction with Shield's financial policies. She lamented the fact that she could no longer use paper money to pay her taxes.[20]

After learning that Lincoln was involved in the authorship of the letters, Shields demanded that he write a retraction. When Lincoln refused, he challenged him to a duel. Lincoln, as the challenged party, exercised the right to choose weapons. He selected cavalry broadswords of the largest size.[21] Broadswords were unconventional dueling weapons but were potentially effective for a man of Lincoln's stature and strength. Since dueling was illegal in Illinois, the would-be combatants and their respective parties lighted out for the Missouri shore. Elias H. Merryman, William Butler, and Bledsoe joined Lincoln at Jacksonville, Illinois, around midnight on September 20, 1842. As the "friends of Lincoln," Merryman, Butler, and Bledsoe crossed the Mississippi to Missouri with him at sunrise on September 22, 1842. Meeting with their counterparts in Shields's party, the trio acknowledged Lincoln's authorship of the first "Rebecca" letter that appeared in the *Sangamo Journal* but denied that he had written any of the others. They assured Shields that Lincoln "had no intention of injuring the personal or private character or standing of Mr. Shields as a gentlemen or a man."[22] Shields accepted the explanation as an adequate apology, and the principals and their respective parties sheepishly retuned to Springfield.

Despite a successful law practice in Springfield, Bledsoe again succumbed to wanderlust. In the fall of 1844 he moved to Cincinnati, where he opened a law office. Soon afterward, however, Harriet was stricken with an acute case of inflammatory rheumatism that left her permanently impaired in one knee. Hoping for improvement, she sought a more congenial climate and specialized medical treatment. Albert and Harriet went first to White Sulphur Springs in Virginia in the hope that taking the mineral waters there would help relieve her condition. They next traveled to Washington, D.C., and Philadelphia to consult with physicians and visit relatives. During their sojourn, the couple left their eight-year-old daughter Sophia in a boarding school conducted by her aunt Margaret Coxe (1805–55) in Cincinnati and afterward at Dayton, Ohio. The time that Bledsoe spent in Philadelphia between 1844 and 1845 appears to have been brief, although it is possible that he and Harriet divided their time between Philadelphia and Washington seeking medical treatments for Harriet's rheumatism. It was in 1845 that the Philadelphia publisher H. Hooker brought forward Bledsoe's *An Examination of President Edwards' Inquiry into the Freedom of the Will*. And in a review contributed to the *Biblical Repository and Classical Review* in January 1846 he is identified as "A. T. Bledsoe, Esq., Philadelphia, Pa."

Yet presumably Bledsoe spent most of his time in Washington, where he briefly joined his brother-in-law Richard Smith Coxe in the practice of law. Coxe attended the Burlington Academy and graduated from the College of New Jersey (later Princeton) in 1808. He moved in December 1822 to Washington, where he established a successful legal practice in the Circuit Court of the District of Columbia and before the Supreme Court of the United States. Bledsoe would be briefly associated with Coxe's law office in 1845 and 1846. He appeared in at least three cases with Coxe before the U.S. Supreme Court: one case in January 1845 and two others during the winter of 1845–46. The Court's decision in all three cases went against the appeals of the plaintiffs represented by Coxe and Bledsoe. Yet neither the nation's capital nor its highest tribunal seems to have held much attraction for Bledsoe. He ended his partnership with Coxe and left Washington just as abruptly as he arrived. "We were a nomadic gens," his daughter Sophia recalled, because her father always expected better things ahead.[23]

The Bledsoe caravan returned to Springfield in 1847. Bledsoe continued to work occasionally as an attorney but now devoted most of his time to journalism. He became coeditor with Simeon Francis of the *Illinois Journal* (formerly the *Sangamo Journal*) in September 1847. Francis and Bledsoe changed the name of the paper because they wanted it to be more than a local concern and one better suited for the capital city. The prospectus of the *Illinois Journal* declared it to be an organ of the Whig Party and noted that Bledsoe would conduct the editorial department in association with Francis, who was the former editor of the *Sangamo Journal*. The editors would be further assisted in that enterprise "by some of the most distinguished Whigs in the State."[24] The editorials appearing in the *Illinois Journal* are unsigned, but internal and collateral evidence clearly identifies Bledsoe as the author of several. The *Illinois State Register*, the principal organ of the Democratic Party, consistently upbraided "the new editor" of the *Illinois Journal* in its editorials and not Simeon Francis. It was Bledsoe, moreover, who invariably replied in retaliation. Bledsoe's chief nemesis was Charles Henry Lanphier (1820–1903), editor and publisher of the *Illinois State Register*. Lanphier was an accomplished journalist and formidable opponent who needled Bledsoe incessantly.

The most acerbic and significant exchanges between Bledsoe and Lanphier concerned the Mexican-American conflict. The *Illinois State Register* charged that the Whig Party, and the *Illinois Journal* in particular, were "the friends of Mexico" and traitors to their own country. Bledsoe questioned the motives of those who made such accusations and defended the patriotism of the leaders of the Whig Party as well as his own.[25] Yet notwithstanding the seemingly united position of the Whigs, they were deeply divided over the Mexican War and Clay's position on the annexation of Mexican territory. Clay opposed the war and annexation in a speech given in Lexington, Kentucky, on November 13, 1847, especially if acquiring new territories from Mexico meant extending the institution of slavery. Clay was himself a slaveholder but knew how divisive the issue of expansion would be in the free states. While some Whig editors, Bledsoe among them, supported that position, others feared it would cost Clay the nomination of his party in the next election. Anson G. Henry— editor of the *Pekin (Ill.) Whig* and an associate of Baker and Lincoln on the Whig State Central Committee—voiced that very concern. Henry confided to Lincoln that he did not like the strong stand taken against the acquisition of Mexican territory by his close friend and Bledsoe's former law partner Edward Dickenson Baker. Henry took it upon himself to report a softer version of Baker's speech on the subject, since he feared that his harder line would do neither the Whig Party nor Baker any good.[26]

Questions concerning the justice of the war were seldom discussed dispassionately. Democratic papers roundly denounced Senator Thomas Corwin of Ohio, a Whig and an opponent of the war, as a traitor for his antiwar speech in the Senate. The best-known and most controversial line in Corwin's speech was that "if he were a Mexican, he would meet the American army with bloody hands and hospitable graves." Bledsoe confessed that he did not approve of that sentiment. But he did not think that Corwin's unfortunate remark provided grounds for charging him with treason. "We have some little acquaintance of Mr. Corwin, and whatever may be the errors of his judgment, we believe him to be as true a patriot as ever lived." Corwin wrote Bledsoe thanking him for his support. Bledsoe published the letter in the *Illinois Journal* as the best defense he could give of Corwin against the "slanders" of the *Illinois State Register*. Corwin's letter restates his contention that the Mexican War was unnecessary and on our part unjust and that Congress, the sole authority under the Constitution to declare war, must necessarily have the power to end it. He saw no good reason for continuing the war and asserted that justice to both belligerents required an immediate end to hostilities.[27]

If the Union was to endure, and if the Whigs themselves were to survive as a viable national party, they would have to concurrently maintain two distinct and difficult positions on the slavery issue. Existing constitutional protections of slavery had to be maintained to placate southern Whigs, while the extension of slavery into new territories had to be opposed to conciliate the sensibilities of antislavery Whigs in the North. Nor was this a strictly party or sectional issue. Some Democrats, like U.S. congressman David Wilmot of Pennsylvania, also opposed the extension of slavery. The Wilmot Proviso, which would have excluded slavery from the territory acquired from Mexico, was approved by the House in August 1846 but rejected by the Senate. An editorial on Secretary of State James Buchanan's opposition to the Wilmot Proviso that appeared in the *Illinois Journal* attributed that position to his political aspirations to the presidency and the need for southern votes to get there. "Did Mr. Buchanan believe that the extension of slavery by our legislature, into regions where it now does not exist, is required by the great interests of freedom and humanity, or by his desire to be President of the United States? For our part, we cannot resist the conclusion, that Mr. Buchanan sacrificed the convictions of his own soul, when he put in this bid for southern influence. . . . Alas! What costly sacrifices are made on the altar of an unholy ambition!"[28]

The prospect of acquiring New Mexico and California from Mexico reopened the divisive issue of extending slavery into federal territories. It also raised questions in the minds of those who opposed the war as to the motives behind the Polk administration's determination to wage such an aggressive campaign against Mexico. Bledsoe's editorial entitled "Republicanism," for example, argued that those who considered it America's duty to extend the blessings of free institutions by the sword forfeited their moral authority and abandoned the first principles of republicanism. That was also the position of Daniel Webster and many other Whigs. The moral fervor that Whigs expressed on that score, however, was at times tinged with ethnocentrism. Some argued that Mexicans were not intelligent or virtuous enough to live happily under American institutions of government. Polk, charged Bledsoe, had shown himself to be "disgracefully ignorant of the very first elements of political philosophy," for he had not considered whether Mexican society was suited to a republican form of government. Bledsoe maintained that it was not.[29] Nine years later in *Liberty and Slavery* he affirmed that slaves were not suited for the blessings of liberty on precisely the same grounds.

One of Bledsoe's more revealing contributions in the *Illinois Journal* commented on the political career of John C. Calhoun. Internal evidence in this instance leaves no question that Bledsoe wrote the unsigned editorial on Calhoun.[30] He noted that Calhoun's blind devotion to the rights of his state had been misplaced in the nullification crisis. His almost exclusive devotion to states' rights, moreover, often made him inconsistent in the positions he had taken in his earlier political career as a nationalist. Where national and state interests were in apparent conflict, said Bledsoe, Calhoun had been on every side of almost every issue that had distressed the nation. He had been for internal improvements and then against them. He initially favored a national bank and then opposed it. He advocated the protective tariff and then denounced it. Bledsoe drew attention to Calhoun's inconsistencies but respectfully added that they "lie merely on the surface; they all meet and harmonize at the centre." Such men as Calhoun, said Bledsoe, were often seen as being insincere and hypocritical because insufficient allowances were made "for their power of self-deception, for the wonderful facility with which they can delude themselves." Bledsoe himself was not invulnerable to the power of self-deception and self-delusion, as his unqualified defense of slavery so amply attests. And witness further the related comment that "the sophistries of other men he [Calhoun] can snap and rend asunder with infinite ease. But he can easily bind himself with his own." It might well be said, as Willard Murrell Hays has appropriately noted, that within the fullness of time that statement would apply equally to Bledsoe himself.[31]

According to Bledsoe, such a man as John C. Calhoun was to be both admired and feared. "The very intensity of his convictions renders him an object of terror. . . . We have admired him as a huge comet whose portentous glare threatens to dash the globe from its centre, and shed disastrous influence over the nations. It was thus that we admired the career of the great luminary during the dark and fearful period of nullification." That crisis had passed, but the nation now faced another equally portentous predicament regarding the issue of slavery in the territories. The power, respect, and influence commanded by South Carolina and its great spokesman could not fail to exert "a more benign influence on the cause of humanity,—*Provided always*, that these powers be not exerted to extend the dominion and the curse of slavery." It should be noted that Bledsoe is referring to "the curse of slavery" only as it relates to the issue of extending it into the territories where it did not exist. So far as is known, he at no time during his years as a Whig editor denounced slavery as a domestic institution of the South. Even so, the statement is hardly a friendly one for the interests of slavery.

The Democratic press exploited Whig opposition to the war and the extension of slavery at every turn. The *Illinois State Register* accused Henry Clay of changing his position on slavery to attract the support of the antislavery, antiwar, and antiterritory factions of the country in his bid for the presidency. The *Illinois Journal* refuted the accusation. Clay's position on slavery was precisely the same as it had always been, even at the beginning of his illustrious political career. The ground upon which Clay stood regarding the question of slavery was where "every true patriot and lover of his kind should stand with a firm and unalterable determination to maintain it." Clay, himself a slave owner, did not favor immediate emancipation and never had. But as early as 1797, when he had first arrived in Kentucky from Virginia, he supported a measure that would have abolished slavery in Kentucky through a means of gradual emancipation. The legislature never adopted the measure, which would have required slaves already in bondage to remain so for life while all their children would become free after arriving at a certain age. A further provision required masters to provide their slaves with such instruction as was necessary for making the transition from slavery to freedom.

Embracing the goal of gradual abolition and rejecting immediate emancipation was a moderate position assumed by many of Clay's contemporaries. Nor were its supporters by any means confined exclusively to the South. Thus it was, affirmed the *Illinois Journal,* that Clay had once endorsed a plan for abolishing "the odious and desolating system of slavery from his own State." And even though that measure never became law, he had at least publicly supported it. "Is it any inconsistency in him, at present, to oppose the extension of that system, and the fastening of it upon soil now free? Does he descend from the lofty position which he then occupied, by raising his voice against the acquisition of any more territory in order to plant slavery upon it? He does not." Those who opposed Clay by arguing that slavery should be extended into territories that were then free "will have to ascend several degrees above their present low and despicable doctrines before they can place themselves on a level with him." Clay had not changed his view to secure the votes of the "antislavery party," even though that was the party "to which all good men belong."[32] Assuming that Bledsoe was the author of that anonymous editorial, which seems likely, it was a sentiment he would never again utter—at least not in public.

Bledsoe's interests as the coeditor of the *Illinois Journal* ran more toward political philosophy and criticism and less toward contentious issues like slavery. What most intrigued him were prevailing ideas about the nature of civil liberty and what those different meanings suggested for public order and good government. As Montesquieu stated in his *Spirit of the Laws* (1748), "There is no word whatsoever that has admitted of more various significations, and has made more different impressions on the human mind, than that of *Liberty*." Bledsoe acknowledged the wisdom of "that pregnant passage," which was a point of departure in his own investigation of the subject. Liberty, he contended, was too often confused with licentiousness. "Almost every man, it seems, adopts a notion of liberty to suit his own taste and inclination: he deems himself free, only when he can gratify and enjoy all his own fancies, and feelings, and prejudices, and follies." Since the cry of liberty had been the basis of revolutions, constitutions, and all manner of political creeds, its principles and authority ought to be a subject of profound interest to the statesman and the philosopher, yet such was not the case. "No subject is more talked about, or less understood, than the subject of liberty."[33]

A false conception of liberty begot the abomination of the French Revolution and likewise explained the contagion of reform movements that swirled about American society as the genius and glory of his own age. Bledsoe's disdain for those movements provides a further glimpse of the conservative nature of his social and political thought and the dark view of human nature upon which it rested.

> Of all political dreamers, those are the wildest, who fondly imagine that the manifold disorders of the world proceed almost exclusively from bad organizations of society. Hence the mania, so prevalent in various quarters, for new forms of society. Hence all your new harmonies, which only require to be reduced to practice to end in discord. Hence your Fourierism, and your Chartism, and the whole swarms of *isms* which are continually buzzing in our ears. . . . These reckless schemers have yet to learn that human affairs will go on smoothly under no

> system of polity that can possibly be invented. They have yet to learn
> the great lesson, so impressively taught by all history, that there is a
> fountain within,—in the profoundest depth of man's nature,—which
> is continually sending forth its streams, unless purified, to disturb the
> free actions of every good thing on earth.[34]

Abolitionists are notably absent from Bledsoe's list of political dreamers. But less than a decade later he applied the same strictures to them in *Liberty and Slavery,* where he indicted abolitionists as the most reckless and dangerous reformers of all.

Bledsoe elaborated his political philosophy in a three-part editorial entitled "The Nature of Civil Liberty."[35] According to the English jurist William Blackstone, civil liberty is but natural liberty duly restrained by law for the good of all. Locke and numerous other jurists and political thinkers had rendered similar opinions. When individuals entered into society, they presumably gave up a portion of their natural liberty in exchange for the protection and security provided by civil law and government. Hobbes likewise observed that "each individual has, in a state of nature, a right to all things." Bledsoe challenged that conception of natural liberty and the confusion about natural rights that arose from its general acceptance. "If so, then each and every man has a right to all things, and consequently to the same things! If so, then lawless anarchy is the legitimate result of natural liberty!—Robbery and murder and outrage are its legitimate fruits. But this is a flagrant caricature of natural liberty, designed by Hobbes to render it odious in the estimation of mankind, that we might see it sacrificed as an offering to despotic power, without indignation or regret."

Bledsoe believed that Locke, Blackstone, and Hobbes had erred in their explanations of the relationship existing between civil liberty and natural rights. He dissented from Blackstone's assertion that laws restraining individuals from doing harm to fellow citizens diminished their natural liberty. As Bledsoe reasoned, "No man has a natural right to do mischief; and hence the law which restrains him from doing it, does not diminish his natural liberty. The law which restrains a man's disposition to do mischief, does not restrain his *liberty,* but his *depravity.* That learned authors should thus include the enjoyment of liberty, and indulgence of depravity, in one and the same definition, is an error of which we feel constrained to complain as an offence against sound philosophy and an outrage against all political ethics. It is to confound the source of all tyranny with the fountain of all freedom." Such false notions

inflamed minds with the idea that they were "struggling and fighting for liberty, when, in reality, they are only struggling and fighting for the gratification
of their own lawless passions. No error is fraught with more tremendous and
desolating consequences."

Civil society was not a restraint on theoretical natural rights but on the
natural brutishness of humankind. That opinion is an amalgam of Bledsoe's
theological and legal training. His theological tenets influenced his understanding of human nature, the origin and authority of the law (it was divinely
sanctioned), and his views on various schemes of social and political organization. Bledsoe expressed the synergy between the theological and legalistic
strains of his moral philosophy in the following words: "We are bound by the
law of nature and the law of God to love our neighbor as ourselves." It was the
duty of everyone, even in a state of nature, to protect the rights and ensure
the well-being of all. "Thus it is that the law of man comes into contact with
the law of God, and rests upon it." The source of natural law and the authority
of political institutions and civil law in Bledsoe's worldview were not entirely
secular matters. It is a theme to which Bledsoe later returned in his attack on
the principles of abolitionism.

The exercise of natural rights, however, also entailed certain obligations. It
was the duty of all living in civil society to promote the common good. Only
then could private rights be called into existence, and only then could society
fulfill its obligation to honor natural law and the law of God. The authority of
law was the guardian of liberty and not its adversary. *"Thus, it is that civil society
arises, not from a surrender of individual rights, but from a right originally possessed by all, and which is upheld and supported by the will of all in the enactment
of law.* God himself has laid its foundations deep in the moral nature of man.
It is an ordinance of heaven which no human decree can reverse or annul. It
is not a thing of compacts, bound together by promises and paper; it is formed
in the moral law; it is ratified and confirmed by the necessities of man. Social
compacts may give us one form or another; but, in one form or another, it
must exist."[36]

The organization of civil society did not demand the surrender of individual rights but only that individuals work in concert to establish and protect
them for the benefit of all. "No good law is, indeed, a restraint upon our natural liberty." Good laws called natural liberty forth and protected it from the rav-
ages of human depravity and the natural tyranny of humankind. "It is because
men are prone to transcend the law of nature, and thereby inflict injury on

their fellow men, that legal enactments and restraints are necessary." There was no discord between liberty and law, only between liberty and license. "Liberty and law could never be dissevered. Liberty, robed in law, and radiant with love, is the best and brightest gift of God to man. But liberty despoiled of law, becomes a dark and fierce licentiousness." The very idea that humankind had more rights before entering into a state of society than they did afterward was preposterous—a convenient figment of the imagination among those who explained the origin of society, government, and rights by inventing an antithetical state of nature. A free government was one that restrained the passions and propensities of humans to do harm to the extent necessary to promote the general good but *no farther*.[37] One of Bledsoe's favorite maxims, first stated in the *Illinois Journal*, was that "there must be public order, or there can be no private liberty."[38]

Bledsoe never again practiced law or actively participated in the ballyhoo of political campaigns and journalism. He later came to disdain electioneering, distrust politicians, and reject the egalitarian assumptions and extreme individualism he attributed to American democracy in general. But his legal training and experiences as a Springfield attorney and Whig partisan remained with him always. They shaped his views on the nature of civil liberty, the conservative principles of his political philosophy, and the leading political and constitutional issues that agitated the nation during the sectional crises of the 1850s. His later defenses of slavery and secession were solidly grounded in constitutional law and presented in the spirit of a public prosecutor. His legal training and experiences in the courtroom augmented his skills as a polemicist. Bledsoe was ever the advocate in pleading his causes.

3

SOUTHERN EDUCATION AND POLITICS
The Making of a Sectionalist

THE THIRTY-EIGHT-YEAR-OLD BLEDSOE arrived at Oxford, Mississippi, in the fall of 1848 as professor of mathematics and astronomy. Except for a brief sojourn as an Episcopal clergyman in Lexington, Kentucky, in the spring and summer of 1837, it was the first time he had permanently resided in a slave state since leaving Kentucky for West Point at age fifteen. Bledsoe taught at the University of Mississippi from 1848 to 1854 and occupied the chair of mathematics at the University of Virginia from 1854 until the coming of the Civil War. The struggle for southern identity and cultural autonomy that occurred during Bledsoe's years in Mississippi and Virginia was a crucible of change—a process of accommodation and adjustment from which he emerged as a defender of the social, political, and cultural imperatives of the South. Given Bledsoe's earlier educational and vocational experiences in the North, such a prospect could not have occurred to him at any time before his arrival in Oxford. Yet southern academicians were expected to instill "right thinking" on the subjects of states' rights and the institution of slavery. Southerners place a premium on orthodoxy in education, and there was no tolerance for dissent. As education and politics made common cause during the sectional crisis, Bledsoe aligned his interests and fortunes with those of the South and never looked back.

The board of trustees met at Oxford, Mississippi, in July 1848 to elect a president and a faculty. According to John Newton Waddel, a faculty member and former trustee, it was "a rather stormy meeting." The trustees selected Bledsoe as chair of mathematics and astronomy from more than sixty applicants. He credited his appointment to the strength of his references, his reputation as an attorney, and the recognition he received as the author of *An Examination of President Edwards' Inquiry into the Freedom of the Will* and for his contributions to journals on other theological subjects. Those accomplishments had nothing to do with the teaching of mathematics and astronomy. Yet they certainly distinguished him as a well-rounded applicant with a breadth of learning. When considered alongside his experience as a teacher of mathematics at Kenyon College and Miami University and his standing as second in his class in mathematics at West Point, his credentials were indeed impressive. The same day the board members elected Bledsoe, they chose the twenty-eight-year-old George Frederick Holmes (1820–97) as president.[1] Holmes, who was then a faculty member at the College of William and Mary, was a prolific writer and a frequent contributor to southern periodicals.

The board assigned Bledsoe additional duties as a professor of natural philosophy in 1850. He continued to teach the sciences until his resignation in July 1854. Bledsoe's math and astronomy classes included lectures on the history of those sciences that were innovative for the time. His *Three Lectures on Rational Mechanics; Or, The Theory of Motion* and *A Brief Sketch of the Rise and Progress of Astronomy, in Three Lectures* were published in Philadelphia in 1854.[2] Those lectures, quite apart from demonstrating Bledsoe's grasp of those subjects and interest in the history of science, also provide clear evidence of his belief in the compatibility of religion and science—his twin faiths. As the most senior faculty member he shouldered many responsibilities besides those involved in teaching his own classes. The piling up of tasks for a teacher was the general rule of nineteenth-century college life given the limited resources. He inspected the conditions of dormitory rooms and campus buildings, served as librarian in 1850 and 1851, and as secretary of the faculty deliberated in matters concerning academic policies and disciplinary actions. He also accepted the duties of acting president in 1849 when Holmes went on leave due to illness in his family and disciplinary problems on campus. The academic life was a vocation for which Bledsoe was better suited than any of his previous callings.

Earlier generations of southerners willingly sent their sons to northern colleges, but that became less common with the heightening of sectional tensions in the 1840s and 1850s. The earlier the educational experiences of southerners in the North, Michael O'Brien has observed, the fewer the cultural tensions. But attitudes hardened in the South and the mood changed with the rise of the abolitionist movement in the 1830s.[3] Southerners began to insist that southern youth be educated at home. Impressionable southern minds had to be protected from contamination by radical northern ideas, and especially from the heresy of abolitionism. The founding of the University of Mississippi in 1844 clearly reflected that increasingly defensive attitude. There was a general movement throughout the southern campuses to inculcate orthodox social and political views.[4] At the opening of the University of Mississippi in 1848 Jacob Thompson, a trustee, declared it "a sin against our children" to send them North for an education. Holmes struck a similar note of guardianship. There was a discernible need to inoculate southern youth against the influence of dangerous ideas: "We believe that true patriotism and a well founded State pride, no less than high considerations of policy[,] will induce the gentlemen of the South to prefer to trust the education of their sons to a Southern institution, [than] to the hazardous, expensive, and humiliating experiment of sending them abroad, to imbibe at the North delusive views which will infect their minds during their whole life."[5]

The American South was hardly an intellectual desert. Yet southerners themselves recognized that they were educationally disadvantaged relative to the North. Alexander M. Clayton, president of the board of trustees at the University of Mississippi, argued that the South should follow the examples of Scotland and Massachusetts in providing a common school education to their young. Otherwise the region would continue to suffer a galling intellectual and economic dependence upon the North. It was precisely because southerners had devoted too little attention to common schools and to training their own teachers, Clayton continued, that "we often see the enterprising Yankee, formed in the Yankee school-house, bearing away in our midst, the richest rewards, from the more luxurious and indolent sons of the South." The world depended on the South's staples, but the profits, he protested, enriched others and built the "marble palaces" and "granite store-rooms" of the northeastern states. "What England could not do in the days of Lord Chatham by force, our brethren do by insinuation.—They scarcely let us make a hob nail for ourselves." The only solution to the problem in Clayton's view was the urgent advancement of southern education. "We must build school-houses."[6]

The new university at Oxford opened in November 1848 amidst numerous problems. Bledsoe and other faculty members more than earned their salaries that first year. Most of the eighty students constituting the first freshman and sophomore classes were ill prepared for their studies. The faculty found itself in scarcely better circumstances. Neither a library nor a laboratory yet existed, and classes began without the trustees having made any provisions for purchasing textbooks. The personal books and laboratory equipment of the faculty were the only resources initially available. John Newton Waddel, the professor of ancient and modern languages, purchased some schoolbooks and supplies from a defunct academy at Holly Springs, but beyond that instructors were left to their own devices. John Millington used his own scientific apparatus to teach his chemistry classes. His appointment, indeed, may have been largely determined by the fact that he offered to make his instruments available to the university should he be the successful candidate. Opening the university without a library was a particularly embarrassing deficiency. As President Holmes apologetically observed in his inaugural address, "The University without a library is like Polyphemus without his eye." Holmes later recalled that when classes began scaffolding and the stumps and limbs of felled trees framed the buildings of the new campus, some of which had yet to be fitted with outer doors and porches.[7]

Academic life at the University of Mississippi was far from uneventful. The morals and gentlemanly deportment of the students left much to be desired. Discipline problems occupied much of faculty's time during that first year. Only forty-seven of the eighty students in the original freshman and sophomore classes completed their first year of study. Expulsions, suspensions, and withdrawals reduced their ranks at an alarming rate. Bledsoe observed in the commencement address he delivered as acting president in July 1849 that many of the students labored under the notion "that College life is a sort of farce or comedy in which each actor is expected to display the brilliancy of his parts, and to signalize his genius in freaks of mischief and scenes of dissipation." His colleague John Newton Waddel seconded that opinion. A large number of students had come to Oxford merely for "fun and frolic." They were on the whole "disorderly and turbulent" and a large number "idle, uncultivated, viciously disposed, and unconquerable." The strong liquor smuggled into Oxford made matters even worse. It was natural under such conditions that disorderliness and dismissals of ungovernable students would weaken faculty morale. The conduct of college students at the University of Mississippi was hardly less riotous than that of students at other campuses throughout the nation during this time—a reality that Bledsoe knew firsthand from his own brief tenure at Miami University. Nonetheless it was a serious concern.[8]

Meeting with the faculty, a troubled group of trustees insisted that they adopt a more rigid form of discipline. Compounding the problem in the opinion of some of the faculty was President Holmes's liberal views on student discipline. Waddel was one of those who believed that Holmes needed to be stricter in the manner in which he dealt with miscreants. His philosophy of student discipline made too great an appeal to their sense of "true honor and gentlemanly manhood" and too little to the tried and true means of maintaining an orderly campus. When Bledsoe served as acting president during Holmes's absence, the board of trustees implemented a much harsher policy for dealing with unmanageable students. Bledsoe sent a clear message to future malefactors. There was no place at the university for any who wasted their time in idleness or squandered their parents' money in acts of debauchery. They would not be permitted "to fix a stain upon the character of this infant Institution." He warned that regardless of their parents' social and financial standing they would not be permitted "to enact their obscene comedies in this holy temple of learning." The University of Mississippi would not become a haven for "the incorrigibly vicious and worthless."[9]

The close of the first session at the new temple of learning marked the end of a critical and trying period—one that naturally gave rise to reflections on what had been accomplished under difficult circumstances and what remained to be done. Since the problem of discipline occupied so much of the faculty's time that first year, Bledsoe largely confined his commencement address to a discussion of the subject. He attributed the source of those disorders to the frailties of human nature, which necessarily beset any scheme of education or government. Yet the difficulties arising from the infirmities and shortcomings of human nature were too often underrated by those who believed in human perfectibility and innate goodness. A proper understanding of the imperfect character of humankind was essential for the maintenance of order, said Bledsoe, yet too often the friends of education entertained an overly generous estimation of human nature that was altogether self-defeating. "No greater mistake, we humbly conceive, can be made in any kind of government or discipline, whether it be parental, collegiate, civil, or ecclesiastical, than to proceed on the supposition of the inherent rectitude and purity of the human mind."[10]

Taking a page from his earlier editorial "The Spirit of Liberty" in the *Illinois Journal*, Bledsoe again warned against the visionary schemes and self-delusions of reformers. Statesmen and educators too often ignored or minimized the "internal source" of social problems and placed entirely too much emphasis on changing "the external arrangements" of society as a corrective. The organic structures of societies were not so tractable, nor were evanescent schemes of social reform so efficacious. Holmes fully shared that sentiment. At the opening of the University of Mississippi on November 6, 1848, Holmes likewise made reference to "the delusive hope of removing social ills which cannot be reached by political innovations."[11] Holmes, Bledsoe, and many other conservatives in the mold of Edmund Burke were in accord on that opinion. Those who wished to revolutionize and remodel a particular form of government, Bledsoe proclaimed, forgot the great lessons of history and philosophy, which taught that the best form of any government was of little value unless human nature was elevated and adapted to it *first*. It was a profound error that historically had led reformers to demolish sects and repudiate creeds when instead they should have concentrated on reforming "the weakness and depravity of the human heart, from which both sects and a sectarian spirit inevitably proceed."[12]

Human nature was obstinate, and history's litany of failed attempts to reform it should never be forgotten or minimized. If philanthropists and statesmen were to ameliorate social conditions and perfect political arrangements, they needed to concern themselves with "the inner machinery, and not its external operations." They had to elevate and purify the human mind and shape human will "aright" to that purpose. That good but difficult work could not be accomplished without the aid of the Christian religion, which for Bledsoe was intimately connected with all that was good and glorious in the destiny of humanity. Christianity for Bledsoe was civilization itself. No purely secular solutions to social and political ills could answer its purpose. If experience showed anything, it was that whenever human nature was left to its own devices it "invariably fades away amid the thickening mists of superstition and idolatry." Christianity was the great benefactor of the intellectual, moral, social, and political condition of humankind and the only true guide for human affairs. It was the purifying influences of Christianity to which philanthropists and statesmen should look in order to safeguard "the perpetuity and glory of our free institutions."

Bledsoe was not a secularist. He maintained that should the light of revelation ever be extinguished from the citizenry the time would most certainly come when the glory and promise of the American Republic would pass away "like a bright vision of the night" and join the other vanished glories of humankind. "The great republic under which we live is good enough. It is, beyond all question, the most magnificent and beautiful political structure the world has ever seen. If, under such a frame of government, liberty shall perish, it will not be for the want of better institutions, but for the want of better men and better Statesmen." It should never be assumed, he cautioned, that the American Republic was somehow exempt from the problems that beset other kinds of governments. "We must remember, that the spirit of tyranny exists under every form of government, and dwells in every human breast. . . . The spirit of tyranny is, indeed, the electric fire of the passions, which, to a greater or less extent, pervades all ranks and conditions of society. . . . Can we control an untamed power like this with mere human laws? We might as well read the riot act to a thunderstorm, or seek to bind the roaring Hellespont in chains. There is but one voice and one power, that can say, '*Peace, be Still*,' and in that power is our hope." That single voice and power was the moral authority vested in the word of God. Even the most enlightened laws, constitutions, and institutions were no match for "the electric fire of the passions."

Sectional issues other than the South's perceived educational dependence on the North also intensified during Bledsoe's years at the University of Mississippi. The development of states' rights doctrine and Bledsoe's eventual embrace of it took a significant step forward when California applied to Congress for admission to the Union as a free state in December 1849. The Mississippi legislature passed several resolutions opposing the admission of California and rebuked U.S. senator Henry Stuart Foote of Mississippi for voting in favor of admission as part of the Compromise Measures of 1850. His fellow senator Jefferson Davis and all Mississippi congressmen, in contrast, followed their instructions from home by opposing admission. The compromise measures admitted California to the Union as a free state in September 1850; established the territories of New Mexico and Utah with no mention of the issue of slavery, thus leaving open the question of whether the future states created in those territories would enter the Union as slave or free states; prohibited the slave trade in the District of Columbia; and as a concession to the South implemented a new Fugitive Slave Law that was more stringent than the Fugitive Slave Law of 1793.

The issues surrounding the Compromise Measures of 1850 continued to be debated during the rancorous Mississippi gubernatorial election in November 1851. Mississippians were of neither one mind nor one voice in the matter. Those differences of opinion, indeed, led to the formation of new political parties. The supporters of Senator Foote formed themselves into the Union Party, which included many former Whigs and a smaller number of Democrats, and nominated Foote for governor. He was opposed in that election by former governor John Anthony Quitman, who was supported by the State Rights Party. The Union Party obtained a majority of delegates for the state convention and legislature, which prompted Quitman to resign his candidacy. His supporters then asked Senator Jefferson Davis to enter the contest as the gubernatorial candidate of the State Rights Party. Davis resigned his seat in the U.S. Senate and stood for the office of governor. It was a bitterly divisive election between Unionists and the more extreme elements within the State Rights Party who loosely spoke of secession. The attorney Reuben Davis of Aberdeen, Mississippi, remembered those days as extremely trying ones. "Mississippi was in a blaze." Partisans in both the State Rights Party and the Union Party "were pervaded by a spirit of intolerance, and the presence of ten men at any one point involved the possibility of serious trouble."[13]

Shortly after that contentious election Foote received an invitation to speak at the University of Mississippi. Most of the students and faculty members at Oxford vigorously supported Davis and states' rights. They asked the twenty-six-year-old Lucius Quintus Cincinnatus Lamar (1825–93)—a graduate of Emory College, an attorney, and Bledsoe's assistant in the Mathematics Department—to represent the views of the State Rights Party against Foote in a debate about his role in the passage of the Compromise of 1850. Lamar, who had recently emerged from the shadows as a political speaker, accepted the invitation. The occasion launched the young Mississippian's political career as a states' rights conservative. Lamar was the son-in-law of Augustus Baldwin Longstreet, who became president of the University of Mississippi in July 1849 following the resignation of Holmes. Lamar worked with Bledsoe as an adjunct professor of mathematics from 1850 to 1852. The pair remained lifelong friends and held each other in the highest esteem.[14]

It was during his debate with Foote that Lamar reprimanded his opponent for joining "his Northern allies" against the interests of the South, particularly with the admission of California to statehood. Foote insisted during that election that the only issue before the people of Mississippi was union or disunion and that by voting for the Compromise of 1850 he had justly and wisely voted for the Union. Yet Lamar charged that by so doing he had acted in bad faith. He insisted that Foote explain the "gross inconsistency" in word and deed that resulted in his support of "the miscalled compromise measures." He had voted for the compromise measures against the express instructions of the Mississippi legislature. Lamar's position leaves little to imagination as to why he later drafted the Mississippi ordinance of secession. He was particularly agitated at the refusal of northern legislatures to repeal their personal liberty laws, notwithstanding the fact that in 1842 the U.S. Supreme Court declared them unconstitutional in *Prigg v. Pennsylvania*. He also had no faith that northerners would honor the new Fugitive Slave Law any more than they had the old one. There were no tangible gains in southern rights and interests under the Compromise of 1850, charged Lamar, only substantial losses.[15]

We do not know whether Bledsoe supported the Unionist ticket led by Foote or the State Rights ticket led by Davis or whether he even cast a ballot during the Mississippi gubernatorial election of 1851. Many Mississippi Whigs and pro-Union Democrats supported Foote in that election, placing concern for the Union above all other considerations. Supporting the Union Party in Mississippi in 1851 would be consistent with Bledsoe's later decision to support the Constitutional Union Party in the presidential election of 1860. But on a personal level it would have been difficult for him not to support his old friend Davis and his new friend Lamar, both of whom sang from the same states' rights hymnal. However Bledsoe cast his ballot in 1851, many of the sentiments expressed by Lamar and Davis later became his own. He and other Whigs in Mississippi could feel the political terrain shifting beneath their feet in 1850 and 1851, and it was not a comforting sensation. Yet direct testimony as to Bledsoe's views and opinions on the sectional controversy during his tenure at the University of Mississippi is entirely wanting. The influence of those events must be inferred—with due prudence—from his later loyalties and writings as a committed southern partisan. Bledsoe, however, had clearly entered into a critically important period in his odyssey from Unionism to southern nationalism.

The sentiments expressed by Jefferson Davis in his address to the Phi Sigma and Hermean literary societies at the University of Mississippi on July 15, 1852, also spoke directly to the worsening sectional crisis. The framers of the Constitution, said Davis, had purposefully construed the distribution of powers, jurisdictions, and rights between the national and state governments as a means of protecting the sovereignty and independence of the states. The intent of the founders had been "to perfect the union of the states, not to destroy their existence."[16] Davis also echoed the sentiments expressed by Jacob Thompson and George Frederick Holmes at the opening of the university in November 1848. He affirmed that the South could derive certain advantages by educating southerners at home among the institutions and popular opinions that would surround them in later life. Southern students could better defend the region against the calumnies of its detractors. "An unholy crusade" had been directed against a domestic institution of the South under the pretext that African slavery was a "holy horror"—an institution that ended at the North only after "it ceased to be profitable among our assailants." Davis affirmed that all Americans had a duty to concern themselves with politics but it was especially incumbent upon students attending southern universities and colleges that they understand the duties, obligations, and character of citizenship. They were "the future guardians" of southern rights and interests and would soon be entrusted with resisting "the dangers of consolidation" and protecting the rights of the "the minority sections and assailed party."

That Bledsoe was one of Davis's attentive auditors and hosts on the occasion of his commencement address is confirmed by the *Democratic Flag*, which noted that upon the completion of the address Davis left Oxford for Holly Springs in the company of Bledsoe and others.[17] He and Davis renewed their acquaintance during Bledsoe's tenure at the University of Mississippi, as Bledsoe's eldest daughter, Sophia, later recalled. She remembered Davis visiting the Bledsoe home on several different occasions and that her father maintained his relationship with him with great cordiality. Davis's influence was unquestionably a boon to Bledsoe's budding career as a southern academician. During his tenure at the University of Mississippi, for example, Davis recommended to Joseph Henry, the secretary of the Smithsonian Institution, that Bledsoe and Jeremiah Chamberlain, president of Oakland College, be placed on the list of Smithsonian correspondents.[18] Davis and Bledsoe continued to pass in and out of each other's lives. His uncritical fealty toward Davis and the cause of southern independence that he eventually came to personify trumped all other considerations and previous loyalties. Few of Davis's friends proved themselves more loyal to him during the war or more skilled at defending him afterward than Bledsoe.

Political events during Bledsoe's six years in Mississippi exacerbated sectional tensions and tried the loyalties of many southerners. The unwillingness of antislavery justices in the North to enforce the new Fugitive Slave Law, the refusal of northern legislatures to repeal their personal liberty laws, and the publication of *Uncle Tom's Cabin* in 1852 continued to weaken intersectional goodwill. The appeals made by abolitionists to the higher law of conscience regarding constitutional protections of slavery and the controversy surrounding the repeal of the Missouri Compromise under the Kansas-Nebraska Act in March 1854 spawned a new militancy among defenders of state sovereignty and the peculiar institution. The University of Mississippi was not immune from the heightened sectional animosity. The board of trustees petitioned the state legislature in 1854 for the creation of a department of law and government so that these important subjects could be taught from a southern point of view. "We live in a Confederacy of States," the petition reminded the legislators, the founding principles of which were matters of vital interest to all concerned. It was dangerous for southerners to study law and government at colleges outside their section where "the relations of the states to each other are looked at in somewhat different lights."[19] The very nature of the Union, what it had been at its founding and what it had since become, was being rethought in some quarters of the South and reargued as a matter of fundamental importance.

Bledsoe's years at the University of Mississippi had been as challenging as they were rewarding. He established his credentials as a southern academician amidst numerous difficulties. Those achievements brought him a new and unexpected opportunity. He reluctantly resigned his position at the University of Mississippi on July 12, 1854, to accept the chair of mathematics at the University of Virginia. For Bledsoe, who had held one of the chairs of the University of Mississippi since its inception, the decision to sever that connection was an emotional one. In tendering his resignation, he expressed appreciation for the many kindnesses and courtesies paid him during his tenure. The board accepted Bledsoe's resignation and the following day conferred upon him the honorary Doctor of Laws degree in appreciation for his six years of service. The honor was particularly gratifying because it was the first such degree ever awarded by the University of Mississippi: "it was conferred, unsolicited on my part, by noble men, or a Board of Trustees, whom I had served for six long years, and who I had learned to love and honor. I have always been proud of their friendship." That same year he received the same honorary degree from Kenyon College at the behest of Charles Pettit McIlvaine, which was again unsolicited.[20] Bledsoe had made his mark as an academician and would remember his connection with the University of Mississippi fondly.

Bledsoe arrived at the University of Virginia in the fall of 1854 to fill the vacant chair of mathematics created by the death of Edward H. Courtenay. Courtney was a West Point graduate and professor of natural and experimental philosophy at the academy during Bledsoe's years as a cadet. One of the applicants competing with Bledsoe for that prestigious position was another West Pointer, Thomas Jonathan Jackson (later known as "Stonewall Jackson"). Jackson was then teaching at the Virginia Military Institute in Lexington. A third candidate was William Nelson Pendleton, who graduated from West Point the same year as Bledsoe. Pendleton ranked first in his class in mathematics at the academy to Bledsoe's second. Pendleton's religious awakening also occurred during McIlvaine's ministry at West Point, which led him to become an Episcopal clergyman in 1837. According to Bledsoe's wife, Harriet, when Pendleton learned that Bledsoe had also applied for the chair of mathematics at the University of Virginia he withdrew his name from consideration and requested that the letters submitted in support of his own application be used on behalf of his former classmate.[21]

Yet Bledsoe had obtained testimonials from two West Pointers that carried considerable weight in their own right. Jefferson Davis, who was then secretary of war, and Robert E. Lee, who was then the superintendent at West Point, both wrote letters of recommendation for Bledsoe. Lee recommended Bledsoe in June 1854 and in January had also submitted a letter of endorsement for Jackson. Lee testified to the character, merit, and academic accomplishments of both applicants. He regarded both candidates as eminently qualified for the position and stated a preference for neither. Davis was even more accommodating in the matter. Bledsoe wrote his old friend William Holmes McGuffey (who was then professor of moral philosophy at the University of Virginia) that if the testimonial that Davis submitted in support of his candidacy was not satisfactory Davis would gladly write another. McGuffey aided Bledsoe's candidacy by keeping him informed of developments and gathering the letters of recommendation written on his behalf for submission to the board of visitors. McGuffey no doubt supported Bledsoe's application himself.[22]

The board of visitors elected Bledsoe as the chair of mathematics in June 1854. He reunited not only with McGuffey at the University of Virginia but also with Holmes. Bledsoe, indeed, appears to have been instrumental in securing Holmes's appointment. He wrote Holmes in May 1856 informing him that there would soon be two vacancies on the faculty: one in ancient languages and the other in history and general literature. He advised Holmes to visit the campus before the next meeting of the board of visitors as a show of serious interest. Bledsoe further counseled Holmes to apply for both of the available positions, believing it would increase his chances of securing at least one of them. Bledsoe sincerely hoped that Holmes would be the successful candidate and did what he could to smooth the way. "I should rejoice to be associated with you again."[23] Holmes also learned from Bledsoe that unidentified parties had misrepresented him as a Swedenborgian and that he was objected to by still others as being a Roman Catholic—incongruous associations based entirely upon rumor and innuendo. Such difficulties did not make Holmes overly optimistic at his prospects of success.[24] He must have been as surprised as pleased when he learned in February 1857 that the board of visitors had unanimously selected him professor of history and general literature. Holmes secured the position on his own merits, but Bledsoe definitely did him a good turn at the critical moment by defending him with the trustees and dispelling their unfounded reservations: "*I have done nothing for you, except blow prejudice to atoms.*"[25]

The colleague at the University of Virginia with whom Bledsoe was the closest, even more so apparently than McGuffey and Holmes, was James Lawrence Cabell (1813–89), professor of anatomy, physiology, and surgery and a faculty member since 1837. Bledsoe described Cabell to Holmes as his most intimate friend and "one of noblest men that ever lived—and you will like him beyond measure." Bledsoe joined with Cabell and McGuffey and other faculty members in establishing a Sunday school at the University of Virginia, which was sponsored and run by the Young Men's Christian Association.[26] Cabell, like Bledsoe, was a man of both faith and science. His knowledge of human anatomy and physiology naturally led to an interest in anthropology. His *Testimony of Modern Science to the Unity of Mankind*, published in 1859, appeared at the height of the monogenesis-polygenesis controversy over whether the different types of humankind were a single species with a single origin (monogenesis) or different species with separate origins (polygenesis).[27] Cabell defended the monogenesist position, arguing that the different races of humans had a common origin as related in the biblical account of creation. Blacks and whites were not separate species but different types of the same species and shared a common origin. Both were of one blood and origin.

Succeeding so eminent a figure as Edward H. Courtney as the chair of mathematics was no easy matter for Bledsoe—much was expected of him. But his mathematical abilities so impressed his students and fellow faculty members that during his tenure as chair mathematics at the University of Virginia maintained its prestige. Bledsoe developed and taught a formal course of lectures entitled "The History and Philosophy of Mathematics" apart from teaching the usual courses in higher math. It was an interest he carried forward from his years at the University of Mississippi, as evidenced in his earlier lectures on rational mechanics and the history of astronomy, but he first formalized those investigations as an area of study within the mathematics curriculum at the University of Virginia. Bledsoe taught the history and philosophy of mathematics to seniors only. Yet evidence provided by the notebooks kept by two of Bledsoe's math students indicates that he also integrated the subject into lower-level math courses. The philosophy of mathematics at that time received little or no attention in American colleges and universities. It appears to have been entirely neglected at West Point, which for several decades was unquestionably the most influential mathematical school in the country. It most certainly formed no part of the mathematics curriculum when Bledsoe studied there with Davies. His later interest in the subject is at least an implicit suggestion that Bledsoe considered it a deficiency in his own training as a mathematician. The history and philosophy of mathematics continued to be taught at the University of Virginia for many years after Bledsoe's departure.[28]

Direct testimony of Bledsoe's accomplishments as a mathematician at the University of Virginia comes from one of his closest friends and colleagues, Francis Henry Smith (1829–1928), the professor of natural philosophy. According to Bledsoe's grandson William Dinwiddie, he and the younger Smith became "great cronies."[29] Smith had assisted Courtenay with the teaching of math before becoming the professor of natural philosophy. He knew Bledsoe's interests and capabilities as well as anyone. It was because of Bledsoe's "life-long addiction to metaphysical studies," Smith accurately observed, that he entered into the philosophy of mathematics with such ardor. "In this field I think Dr. Bledsoe won a place by the side of Bishop [George] Berkeley and Auguste Comte." That was high praise truly. Berkeley presented a critique of the foundations of infinitesimal calculus in *The Analyst* (1734) that holds a conspicuous place in the history of mathematics, while Comte formulated a positivist philosophy of mathematics, astronomy, physics, chemistry, biology, and sociology in his six-volume *Course on Positive Philosophy* (1830–42) that has earned him recognition as the first true philosopher of science.

But Smith recognized Bledsoe's limitations as well as his strengths. Strictly as a manipulator of mathematical formulas and solver of mathematical problems, he observed, Bledsoe was not particularly adept. Smith had known many mathematicians of less intellectual strength and knowledge who were Bledsoe's superior in algebraic dexterity. But few grasped the logic of their work as well as Bledsoe. Smith was convinced that if Bledsoe had devoted his life to science "he would have left the pure mathematics simplified in statement and improved in form. His originality and force were obvious to me, to whom he freely communicated his difficulties and successes, during his entire residence here."[30] Those exertions led Bledsoe to begin work on a manuscript that explicated the intricacies of the infinitesimal calculus of Newton and Leibnitz. He informed Leonidas Polk in October 1860 that his philosophy of calculus was nearly ready for publication, but he made no further progress in completing the work until after the war. That manuscript eventually made its appearance as *The Philosophy of Mathematics,* published in 1868—a work that clearly traces its origin to Bledsoe's earlier lectures on the history and philosophy of mathematics at the University of Virginia.

The sectional crisis that had so troubled Mississippians in the fall of 1851 only intensified after Bledsoe's arrival at the University of Virginia in the fall of 1854. The political maneuvering and violence in Kansas hardened attitudes in both sections of the country, while the slaveholding interests of the South beheld the rise of the Republican Party with great foreboding. Yet the sectional issues in education were much the same at Charlottesville as they had been at Oxford. The attitudes toward southern education earlier expressed by George Frederick Holmes, Jacob Thompson, and Jefferson Davis at the University of Mississippi were similarly voiced in Virginia and elsewhere in the South. Opposition to the influence of northern ideas and northern teachers in southern schools, John McCardell has noted, was widespread and became a distinct province of sectional consciousness from the 1840s onward.[31] Resolutions adopted at the southern commercial conventions held in Memphis, Tennessee, in 1853; Charleston, South Carolina, in 1854; and Savannah, Georgia, in 1856 expressed the desire that southern youth should not only attend southern colleges and universities but should be taught from textbooks written and published expressly for use on southern campuses.[32] Trustees, faculty members, and students expected southern academicians to inculcate proper views on the subjects of slavery and states' rights. There was no tolerance for dissent and no academic freedom within that climate of opinion.

The resolutions concerning education and schoolbooks adopted by the Southern Convention in Savannah in December 1856 gave clear voice to the expectation that southern intellectuals were to inculcate orthodox views. One of those resolutions identified nineteen academicians, clergymen, and men of letters who had the convention's confidence as suitable custodians of southern education. Among the nineteen were Bledsoe and William Holmes McGuffey at the University of Virginia. The resolution asked whether those scholars would not enlist themselves in the cause of southern education, as a kind of ad hoc committee at large, by selecting and preparing a series of books for use in southern schools. According to the resolution, educational materials should be prepared in every department of knowledge, from the earliest primer to the highest branches of literature and science, which would "elevate and purify the education of the South." When the proposed series of books was completed, southern state legislatures should be requested to require their use in all public schools within their respective states and an appeal made to the trustees of private academies to follow suit. Parents and guardians could further promote the cause of southern education if they ceased neglecting the claims of their own seminaries and colleges by patronizing and enriching those in the North. Sending southern students to be educated outside the South was a practice "fraught with peril to our sacred interests, perpetuating our dependence on those who do not understand and cannot appreciate our necessities and responsibilities, and at the same time fixing a lasting reproach upon our own institutions, teachers, and people."[33]

The concerns expressed at the southern commercial conventions over the presumably corrupting influences of northern teachers and textbooks were also a matter of complaint in Virginia. And as the most prominent and important educational center of the South, the University of Virginia led the movement for achieving the region's intellectual and cultural independence. The minds of its students were shaped and molded according to orthodox views on southern rights, institutions, and manners and on the nature of the federal government. The *Kanawha Valley Star* approvingly reported on December 2, 1856, the very week in which the Southern Convention met in Savannah, that in the past ten years Virginia had undergone a great change in attitude regarding the presence of northern schoolteachers. Whereas "indifferent Yankee school teachers" were once common in the state, it had become almost impossible for anyone in eastern Virginia to gain employment as a teacher unless he or she was born, raised, and educated in Virginia.[34] Yet that was far from an exclusively Virginian concern. It was shared by many southerners in the 1850s, who were assuming increasingly defensive postures against the introduction of hostile ideas regarding slavery and states' rights that were presumably being instilled by northern teachers and northern textbooks.

Leonidas Polk—Bledsoe's former schoolmate at West Point and the Episcopal bishop of Louisiana—fully shared the educational anxieties and issues expressed at the southern commercial conventions. Polk spearheaded a movement to address those problems in an open letter on July 1, 1856, to his fellow bishops and clergymen in Tennessee, Georgia, Alabama, Mississippi, Florida, Arkansas, Texas, and North and South Carolina. He identified the educational needs existing within their respective dioceses and parishes and challenged them to join him in constructing a plan to meet those requirements. He proposed the establishment of a new seat of higher learning to be called the University of the South that would rival the prestige of Harvard, Yale, and the

University of Virginia. He declared that "a movement of some kind is indispensable, to rally and unite us to develop our resources, and demonstrate our power." Polk pressed the matter with Bishop Stephen Elliott of Georgia, a close friend, in a long and urgent letter written in August 1856. It was imperative that impressionable southern minds be "protected from the taint of northern fanaticism"—which he characterized as a danger of growing and portentous magnitude. Southerners had to train their own teachers and ministers, Polk contended, since they could no longer be safely educated in the North. He further alleged that the difference in feeling and sympathy in the North and South was simply too great to bridge.[35]

Polk also took the lead in raising an endowment for the proposed University of the South in 1859, and the following year he and Elliot drafted a constitution and set of bylaws. Bishop Richard H. Wilmer of Alabama later recalled that the ideological nature of the enterprise was readily apparent. "It [the sectional controversy] was at first a conflict of ideas, and ideas could only be met by ideas." The object of the University of the South, said Wilmer, was "to educate in harmony with Southern ideas." Polk's biographer, Glenn Robins, has similarly observed that the proposed University of the South was a self-conscious sectional endeavor from the start. Polk and his supporters wanted to create a university tailored to the educational and ideological needs of a slaveholding society. He made a strong appeal to conservative white southerners like himself who wished to immunize their society against the dangerous ideas that were generally believed to be emanating from the North. Such cultural concerns, educational and literary, became a mainstay of southern nationalism.[36]

Had the war not intervened, Bledsoe might well have joined the faculty at the University of the South. Polk solicited his views and those of his colleague James Lawrence Cabell in the fall of 1860 on how the faculty should be appointed and the curriculum organized.[37] Polk also made overtures to Bledsoe about the possibility of filling the chair of moral philosophy and evidences of Christianity. Bledsoe informed Polk that he would be inclined to accept the position should it be offered him. He regretted that he could not attend the laying of the cornerstone ceremony because he was hard at work on completing two manuscripts: the first a work on the philosophy of calculus, which he hoped to have published in January, and the second a work on moral philosophy that was also in an advanced stage of preparation. He asked Polk whether it would be wise to delay publication of these manuscripts until such time as he might be chosen as a faculty member at the University of the South. He also solicited his opinion as to whether he should formally apply with supporting letters of recommendation first or wait to do so after Polk had formally presented his name to the trustees as a candidate.[38] Whether Bledsoe would have accepted the position at the University of the South were it actually tendered is far from certain. The prestige of being a faculty member at the University of Virginia could not be easily discarded, especially since the proposed University of South at that time only existed on paper. Yet given the testimony of his letter to Polk, one must conclude that he gave the matter serious consideration.

There is no evidence to suggest that Bledsoe was not relatively happy at the University of Virginia. But he was more than willing to pursue new opportunities with his friend Polk and elsewhere too. It appears that he either applied for the vacant position of president at the University of Missouri in Columbia in 1859 or at least allowed his name to be brought forward in consideration. It is possible that he was nominated for the position without aggressively seeking it. Whatever the circumstances, the board of trustees at the University of Missouri was sufficiently impressed with his reputation as an academician to offer him the position. The board, on the nomination of Caleb S. Stone, elected Bledsoe president of the University of Missouri on August 22, 1859. Curiously, however, Bledsoe showed little, if any, ardor for the position. He delayed his answer to the board and subsequently declined the appointment.[39] We know as little about why he applied for the presidency, assuming that he actually did, as we do about why he declined the appointment once it was tendered. It is one of many unanswered questions concerning Bledsoe's life that perhaps will never be adequately addressed given the paucity of his surviving correspondence.

Bledsoe's years at the University of Mississippi and the University of Virginia represent a noteworthy period of change in his life and thought. The common political ground he once shared with Lincoln as a Henry Clay Whig steadily diminished after his return to the South in 1848. Precious little is known about his years at the University of Mississippi and the University of Virginia. But what we do know greatly augments our understanding of his later loyalties and the causes he chose to champion. Bledsoe had assumed a nationalist attitude and posture toward sectional issues as a Whig editor in 1847 and 1848. Yet his sympathies and loyalties clearly changed during the sectional crisis of the following decade. As a southern educator, Bledsoe heard the siren song of southern nationalism and understood its aspirations. He became a sectionalist but was not yet a southern nationalist.

4

A PHILOSOPHY OF THE WILL
Metaphysical and Theological Speculations

BLEDSOE'S INTERESTS IN METAPHYSICAL and theological inquiries consumed him throughout his diverse career. He periodically wrote on these subjects between 1837 and his death in 1877. His works were original, learned, and well-argued treatises that earned him something of a following among advocates of free will who shared his disdain of Calvinism. By far his most significant contributions to American philosophy, however, were *An Examination of President Edwards' Inquiry into the Freedom of the Will* (1845) and *A Theodicy; Or, Vindication of the Divine Glory, As Manifested in the Constitution and Government of the Moral World* (1853). Bledsoe probed deeply in these works and related minor writings into the problems connected with free will and determinism, moral accountability, original sin, the problem of evil, and the attributes of divinity and human nature—subjects strenuously debated by theologians since the beginning of Christian thought. He had struggled with these subjects since his days as a seminarian and ultimately formulated his thoughts into a philosophy of the will. As an advocate of free will, Bledsoe was, apropos, a controversialist. He became entangled in many theological disputes. Bledsoe's writings on moral philosophy and speculative theology, moreover, typify several of the leading trends in American philosophy in the early and mid-nineteenth century.

Bledsoe's philosophy most closely aligned with the free will doctrine first advanced by the Dutch Calvinist Jacobus Arminius (1559–1609). Arminius declared that human free will existed without limiting God's sovereignty or contradicting the Bible. The Synod of Dort in 1619 affirmed the doctrines of John Calvin and denounced those of Arminius as heresy. Yet the appeal of Arminianism lived on among the critics of orthodox Calvinism. The Methodist theology of John Wesley owed much to the Arminian doctrine of free will, as did Bledsoe's philosophy of the will. Bledsoe offered a systematic critique of the central tenets of orthodox Calvinism, although he was not uncritical of the inconsistencies and errors he also attributed to Arminianism.[1] Bledsoe's theological positions were not in strict accordance with the doctrine of any church.

He rejected predestination, baptismal regeneration, close communion, and the idea that original sin applied to infants. Because of his heterodoxy the late Elizabeth Fox-Genovese and Eugene D. Genovese have aptly described him as "an unchurched theologian."[2] Yet on balance Bledsoe was far more comfortable with the principles of Methodism and its Arminian message of hopefulness than with any other systematic body of Christian thought. His advocacy of self-agency and moral accountability clearly places him within the Wesleyan tradition of Protestant thought.[3] And the appeal of Methodism is clearly reflected in the articles that Bledsoe contributed to Methodist periodicals during the 1840s and 1850s.[4]

According to John Newton Waddel, one of Bledsoe's colleagues at the University of Mississippi, mathematics was not his primary interest. "I have heard him say that he regarded theology as the queen of sciences, metaphysics her hand-maiden, and mathematics next in rank." Bledsoe's daughter Sophia likewise noted that "he really greatly preferred metaphysical to mathematical study." Teaching mathematics was his sinecure and an intellectual endeavor that disciplined his mind. Yet metaphysics and theology remained his ruling passions. The study of theology as a practical matter, however, was as difficult for Bledsoe as its intellectual claims were compelling. Making a living and supporting a family came first and his intellectual interests second. His wife, Harriet, recognized that his far-ranging interests created an inner conflict or tension regarding his true calling in life. She implored him in February 1836, when he was still an Episcopal clergyman and a professor of mathematics at Miami University, not to allow his interests in mathematical science and literature to divert him from that higher calling upon which he had embarked. Bledsoe's service an ordained churchman was brief, but he never abandoned his love of theology or his interest in the ministry.[5]

Bledsoe's abiding passion for religious studies dates from his days as an Episcopal seminarian in 1834 and 1835. William Sparrow, the professor of systematic divinity at Kenyon College, had been his inspiration. The first fruit of Bledsoe's indebtedness to Sparrow appeared as *An Examination of President Edwards' Inquiry into the Freedom of the Will* (1845). Sparrow greatly admired Jonathan Edwards's great treatise but nonetheless objected to his negation of a self-determined will. He encouraged Bledsoe to scrutinize Edwards's work closely. He did so over the next ten years. Bledsoe initially replied in a letter to Sparrow, the substance of which later constituted eleven pages of *An Examination*. He eventually composed eighteen letters to Sparrow. He never sent any of those letters, but in them he developed ideas and arguments that were the basis of *An Examination*. Bledsoe appropriately dedicated the work to Sparrow "as a token of admiration for his genius, and affectionate regard for his virtues." His response to Sparrow's challenge gave direction to his later metaphysical and theological interests.[6]

Jonathan Edwards, the subject of Bledsoe's attack upon Calvinism, was the most eminent theologian of America and an uncompromising opponent of Arminianism. Edwards glorified God by emphasizing human dependence upon divine sovereignty; Bledsoe exalted God by stressing the divine gift of human freedom. Edwards's *Enquiry* has often been recognized as one of the most original and important works in American philosophy. His views on the free will–determinism debate were rooted in the doctrines of predestination, election, original sin, and divine sovereignty. His theology became a bulwark of orthodox Calvinism and the power of his logic a standing challenge to advocates of free will. Many of Edwards's numerous admirers believed the arguments advanced in support of his philosophy of determinism were unanswerable. Yet the self-assured and audacious Bledsoe was prepared to challenge Edwards's major premises and conclusions. He acknowledged Edwards's learning and respected his powerful style of dialectical argument, but he rejected his views on causality. Bledsoe argued that Edwards based his necessitarian thought solely upon logical inference, not upon empirical evidence.

Empirical observation was a better means of reasoning than reliance upon a priori assumptions, or what Francis Bacon called the "idols of the tribe." Edwards did not base his assumptions and conclusions on the inductive method of reasoning outlined by Bacon in his *Novum Organum; or, Indications Respecting the Interpretation of Nature* (1620) but rather on his own preconceived ideas or "idols." Edwards, charged Bledsoe, had not studied human consciousness and volitions as they could actually be observed but rather as he supposed them to be and needed them to be given his necessitarian assumptions. Bledsoe concurred with Bacon's insistence that if truth was to be arrived at it was necessary that all prejudices and preconceived ideas be abandoned. The preconceptions common to all classes of thinkers, or the *mentalités* of humans in general, Bacon called the "idols of the tribe," while the ideas peculiar to individuals were the "idols of the cave"—thoughts conceived in relative isolation from notions that passed as common currency. Bacon's "idols of the tribe" metaphor perfectly explained for Bledsoe how Edwards's ideas on free will had established themselves as unanswerable truisms among his acolytes. His necessitarian assumptions were idols of the tribe. If the strength of Edwards's system was to be truly tested, even the most plausible and widely received opinions had to be abandoned and the ground retraced anew.

The Baconian tradition of American theology had many exponents in the early and mid-nineteenth century. E. Brooks Holifield has noted that "*the patron saint of evidential Christianity, at least in its American Protestant forms, was Francis Bacon, whose advocacy of inductive science in his Novum Organum furnished an ideal that sustained theologians in America for half a century.*" Bruce Kuklick, Mark A. Noll, and Theodore Dwight Bozeman have similarly commented in their respective works on the importance of Baconian methodology in American theology. Kuklick has observed that "Baconian empiricism supplied the chief argument for God, the argument from design. Science exhibited a harmonious universe, governed by a pleasing order and regularity that implied a benign creator. Baconian philosophers believed that science led toward religious understanding."[7] Bledsoe well exemplified the Baconian paradigm in his theological writings. The intellectual framework in which he cast his metaphysical and theological speculations owed a great deal to Bacon—a debt he freely and appreciatively acknowledged.[8]

Bledsoe structured his *Examination* around the central question that divided determinists and libertarians: What actually determined the will? Was the will governed by the strongest motive acting on an individual at any given moment as Edwards's maintained? Was the will, in fact, determined at all? Why did individuals will themselves to do one thing as opposed to another? Was the will self-determined as an action of the mind at a given moment or predetermined by a previous volition or series of volitions? Edwards used the word *cause* to mean any antecedent, either natural or moral, upon which an event was dependent. The cause determined why that event must necessarily be one thing and not another. An *effect* to Edwards was the consequence of something else, which was either its occasion or its actual cause properly speaking. An act or volition could have an occasion or condition that produced it, yet it would still be connected and dependent on another antecedent action or event that was its true cause and not merely its occasion. But the principle to be maintained in necessitarian thought is that all things that come to pass are dependent upon some anterior cause. That view disallows the existence of a self-determined will that originates as an independent act of consciousness and owes nothing to antecedent causes. Acts under the supposition of a self-determined will are not *effects* of antecedent causes but are themselves determinations or originating *causes.*

What Bledsoe adamantly denied in *An Examination* is the idea that the strongest motive is *the* determining cause of human volition. He was clear in making that distinction lest he be accused of being an indeterminist, even though some of his Calvinist critics, either by misunderstanding him on key points of argument or by design, unfairly charged him with closing out causality. Bledsoe had, in fact, anticipated that very criticism. *"I contend against no other kind of necessity but this moral necessity, just as it is explained by Edwards himself."* Bledsoe the mathematician and astronomer understood that the laws of force and motion were observable, immutable, and necessitated phenomena. But Bledsoe the metaphysician denied that the moral necessity propounded by Edwards operated on the same rational principles. Since humans beings were free agents, the notion of moral necessity was a contradiction in terms. He opposed "so monstrous a system" because he could reconcile Edwards's scheme of necessity neither with the moral agency and accountability of humans nor with the purity of God. He rejected Edwards's views on the will because he believed them to be groundless. Yet he still recognized that motive, circumstance, prior experience, belief, passion, and reason all came to bear upon the will as influences, inducements, and necessary conditions for volition. But that did not mean that those factors determined the will in any true sense of the term or that they were connected with a series of antecedent causes. Motives and prior experience conditioned volition but did not necessarily determine them. They did not cause action but might explain its occasion.[9]

Bledsoe conceded nothing to Edwards's idea of moral necessity. Morality could not be necessitated because virtue and vice were conscious choices. Individual actions or volitions were expressions of an unfettered will and were not the effects of antecedent causes or determinants. The human will was the sole agent of causality—a self-actuated, self-directed faculty of the mind. A volition or act was not caused by anything other than itself. It was not the *effect* of anything but its actual *cause* properly speaking. Bledsoe certainly believed that the testimony of personal consciousness (perception) and conscience (one's moral sense) influenced human choice—which desires and actions one decides to gratify and those one resolves to inhibit in accordance with one's ethics and sense of duty. Yet the dictates of one's conscience were not adequate safeguards against immoral behavior. Bledsoe distrusted the passions inherent in human nature too much to believe that a sense of right and wrong alone could adequately restrain human nature within proper bounds. It was a conviction shared by many of his contemporary philosophers as well. Bruce Kuklick has stated the free will assumptions that informed the moral philosophy of the period thusly: "But conscience could not dictate to a perverted will. At the same time, although directly perceiving duty, conscious could be trained and educated. Its enlightenment intimated that cognition might influence the will."[10] The entire premise of moral philosophy in colleges and universities, indeed, was predicated upon that very assumption. Public ethics, in fact, demanded an instructed conscience.[11]

The necessitarian doctrine presented in Edwards's *Enquiry* created a vicious circle based upon an insignificant truism or tautology: the will is determined by the strongest motive, and the strongest motive determines the will. What is this, Bledsoe asked, but to say that an act of the will is caused by its cause? The proposition is undeniable because obviously true yet says nothing about the true nature of causality. "The matter will not be mended, by alleging that the strongest motive is not defined to be that which actually determines the will, but that which has the greatest degree of previous tendency or advantage, to excite or move it; for we cannot know what motive has this greatest degree of previous tendency or advantage, except by observing what motive actually does determine the will." There was no escape from Edwards's circular logic unless one challenged the assumption that volition was an effect of an antecedent cause. "If volition is an *effect*, it has a *cause*, then most unquestionably the cause of volition is the cause of volition. Admit that volition is an effect, as so many libertarians have done, and then his [Edwards's] definition of motive, which included every cause of volition, places his doctrine upon an immutable foundation." Bledsoe was unwilling to engage in the hopeless task of assuming that volition was an effect and at the same time attempt to break out of the determinist's iron chain of causes and effects.[12] Bledsoe maintained that an act of will does not proceed from the mind, or from motive, or from anything else in the same manner that an effect, properly understood, proceeds from its efficient cause.

The pivotal question in the free will–determinism debate was whether an act of the will is an effect in the same sense that the motion of the body is an effect. Bledsoe answered in the negative. The nature of the will could only be understood by observing the actions of the human mind: *"by simply looking at it and seeing what it is,"* not as an abstraction or theory but as an observable phenomenon of nature. When one observed the thing itself, instead of reasoning from a priori assumptions about its antecedent causes, it could clearly be seen that a volition was not an effect at all but a cause. A volition or act of the will, unlike the passive motion of the body, was not the effect or the result of anything. In the latter case, the mind willed the body to move and it moved. But volition originated in the mind without a prior cause; it was an *active principle* and not a passive effect of anything. "It is not the result of action; it is action itself. The mind is not passive as to its production; it is in and of itself an action of the mind. It is not *determined*; it is a *determination*. It is not a produced effect, like the motion of the body; it is itself an original producing cause." Free agency could not be rationally explained upon any other grounds. It could not exist as an effect but only as a cause.

Whether volitions were determined freely or by necessary causes was a question that could be adequately determined only by submitting it to "the testimony of consciousness." Inferences were to be made from "observed phenomena of the mind" and not from transcendental abstractions external to it, whose existence could be logically inferred but could be neither observed nor demonstrated. Bledsoe the mathematician and Baconian empiricist distrusted any theory of knowledge that transcended the limits of experience and observation. He believed that if the problem of liberty and necessity was ever to be adequately addressed it would require investigations into the faculties and functions of the mind, which would have to be conducted according to the inductive method of reasoning. Edwards's metaphysics, in contrast, was "altogether a thing of definitions and words." He had not observed the intellectual world just as it had been created by the Almighty. Edwards had only reasoned about it from his a priori assumptions. "We hope for better results, not from better minds, but from better methods."[13]

Supporters and detractors of Bledsoe's *Examination* predictably divided themselves into Arminian-Calvinist camps. An anonymous reviewer in *Methodist Quarterly Review* for October 1845 hailed the work as decisive, strong, and conclusive. "It is a masterly effort, and the friends of the great New England necessitarian will have to try again or give up their idol." A second review of the work in the same periodical for October 1846 followed suit. "We deem the work of Mr. Bledsoe to be a full, direct, and incontrovertible refutation of the celebrated Inquiry of President Edwards." He was, the reviewer declared, "the only writer who has placed the doctrine of the freedom of the will upon its proper foundations." Bledsoe was so pleased that he reprinted the laudatory review in the *Southern Review* during the final year of his life. E. Brooks Holifield recognized Bledsoe's *Examination* as one of the strongest attempts to refute Edwards written in the nineteenth century and further noted that Methodists by and large considered the work "a denominational victory."[14]

While Methodists hailed the work as the ultimate refutation of Edwards's necessitarian thought, Calvinists, of course, took a different view. Presbyterian reviewers could not accept his theory of volition without abandoning the Calvinist doctrine of predestination, election, divine foreknowledge, and unrestricted divine sovereignty. An orthodox Calvinist perspective appeared in the *Princeton Review* for October 1845 in a short but insightful notice of *An Examination*.[15] The reviewer claimed that Jonathan Edwards's work on the difficult and perplexing subject of freedom of the will had justly earned him a reputation for profound research and conclusive reasoning. Yet as great as Edwards's reputation was, it could not be said that "public sentiment" had ever acquiesced in his conclusions. His theory was received in many quarters "with the same suspicion and incredulity, as the logical argument of [George] Berkeley, to prove that no external world existed." Samuel Johnson, James Beattie, Thomas Reid, and Dugald Stewart regarded Edwards's theory of volition to be "absurd" and in no way compatible with the "common sense" realism to which they subscribed. The author of *An Examination* was clearly of the common sense school as well. He successfully demonstrated that Edwards was confused in his views on the nature of the will in relation to "the desires and affections of the mind; which our author, in accordance with some other writers, calls 'sensibilities.'"[16]

Yet Bledsoe's critic in the *Princeton Review* dissented entirely from two of Bledsoe's most fundamental positions. The contention that human volitions could not properly be called "effects" is rejected out of hand, as is Bledsoe's other main position that our desires and passions (the sensibility or feelings) had no causal influence on acts of volition. The reviewer also criticized Bledsoe's attempt to answer the argument from divine foreknowledge, which was "a curiosity" that failed to convince the reader. "We never saw a stronger case of a man striving against evidence; he is like a strong man in water over his depth and unable to swim, catching objects which cannot aid him. Yet he acknowledges everything that Edwards considers important. He acknowledges the absolute certainty of all events as being foreknown by God, and admits that there is some kind of necessity that they should come to pass. And Edwards's argument requires nothing more."[17] Yet his argument most certainly did require something more for Arminians who rejected Edwards's idea of an infinite regression of antecedent causes to a primordial first cause. That remains one of Bledsoe's most convincing criticisms.

An even more probing review by the Reverend Benjamin Nicholas Martin (1816–83) of New York City appeared anonymously in the *New Englander and Yale Review* in July 1847.[18] Martin graduated from Yale in 1837, Yale Divinity School in 1840, and became a frequent contributor to theological reviews. He and Bledsoe knew each other from a previous encounter. Martin wrote an unfavorable review of Henry Philip Tappan's *A Review of Edwards's "Inquiry into the Freedom of the Will"* (1839–41) that appeared in the *American Biblical Repository* in January 1843. Bledsoe made no reference to Tappan's earlier work in *An Examination* but vigorously defended him in the *Biblical Repository and Classical Review* for January 1846.[19] Bledsoe was convinced that some of the unfavorable comments made in Martin's appraisal of his own work on Edwards were motivated by his earlier controversy with Bledsoe regarding Tappan. "Wounded and sore, angry and resentful, under the effects of his recent conflict [with Bledsoe], he did not spare our 'Examination of Edwards on the Will.'" Bledsoe did not think that Martin's review of *An Examination* had in all instances done him justice, but he nonetheless admitted that Martin was "capable *at times* of real candor and magnanimity."[20]

Martin found Bledsoe's *Examination* to be a work of "mingled merits and defects." It was "the work of an ingenious and vigorous mind" whose familiarity with psychological writers added further value and originality to his arguments. But the admitted virtues of the work were not augmented by the author's presumptive attitude, sarcasm, and ungracious tone. "The confidence with which he asserts the correctness of his views of Edwards—the sensitiveness with which he seems to resent any doubt of it, resemble more the spirit of a man who is resolved that his opinions *shall* stand scrutiny, than the calm reliance of one who is assured that they *will*." Bledsoe's argumentative posture toward Edwards was utterly incompatible with his professed claims of impartiality. "If Mr. B. were a professed controversialist, content to acknowledge that he had the prejudices and prepossessions of other men," his attitude and tone toward his subject would neither be a matter of surprise nor a reason for censure. He foreswore "all partisan warmth" and eschewed the "vulgar impulses" of the polemicist even as he gave ample evidence of both in his treatment of Edwards. "We are not for so unscrupulous an exercise of belligerent rights, on the part of one who professes entire neutrality." The author's insolent spirit toward Edwards was also as ironic as it was misplaced. "This asperity is the more ungracious in Mr. B., inasmuch as whether he is, or is not, conscious of it, no recent writer is so largely indebted to Edwards as himself."[21]

Bledsoe was prone to overstatement and selective memory. Like other sensitive authors, he grumbled about his severest critics and smiled upon those who praised him. He valued most of all the words of his mentor William Sparrow. According to Bledsoe, "He pronounced it a complete refutation of President Edwards; and expressed great surprise at the 'intellectual indolence' of the world, which had so long permitted such a 'system of metaphysical shadows' to challenge and defy the reason of mankind. This was more than reward for our labors. But, after all, the labor itself, with the discipline it imparted to our intellectual powers, was it own best reward." However much vanity and conceit are present in that statement, the last part of it is unquestionably true. Answering Edwards honed Bledsoe's reasoning and strengthened his abilities as a polemicist. As Martin had so truly said in his review, no one was more indebted to Edwards than the author of *An Examination* himself. It was an intellectual obligation, moreover, that Bledsoe himself acknowledged many years later: "For twenty years, after we began our [theological] studies, Edwards was our table companion at home, and our traveling companion abroad."[22]

The sequel to Bledsoe's *Examination* was *A Theodicy; Or, Vindication of the Divine Glory, As Manifested in the Constitution and Government of the Moral World* (1853). The two works are intimately related, as Bledsoe himself noted. "The studies connected with our work on the Will, and the ideas they clearly fixed in our mind, led naturally, not to say necessarily, to the conception of 'A Theodicy.'" Not only did *An Examination* provide the foundation for *A Theodicy*, but it also provided much of its material. "Above all, the leading idea of our Theodicy, that a necessary holiness is no holiness at all, was evolved by those studies, and stood out in our mind as 'the one bright particular star' of the whole system."[23] Bledsoe made a case in *A Theodicy* that the scheme of moral necessity advanced by Edwards was based upon "a false psychology." Bledsoe's criticisms are based upon the "faculty psychology" then in vogue in colleges and seminaries. His treatment of the subject is heavily indebted to the writings of the Scottish realists and especially to the philosophy of Sir William Sterling Hamilton (1788–1856). Psychology for Hamiltonians was the investigation of the distinct mental faculties associated with cognition, which was based entirely upon the authority or testimony of consciousness. The characteristics of consciousness were universal and primal and like any other natural phenomenon were to be observed in nature as they actually occurred.[24]

The phenomena of thinking, feeling, and acting possessed distinct characteristics that had to be separately delineated "if we would extricate the philosophy of the will from the obscurity and confusion in which it has so long been involved." It was only necessary "to interrogate our consciousness" to understand instinctively and implicitly how each of these different mental faculties functioned in relation to each other. Human intelligence and sensibility were *necessitated* phenomena because their powers were *passive,* but it was otherwise with the will. The will was the only *active* faculty of the mind and owed nothing to necessity. It was a self-actuating cause and not an effect of anything else. Bledsoe demonstrated the three different properties of the mind with an illustration of how the mind perceives an apple (the intelligence), desires to eat the apple (the sensibility), and finally determines to act in the matter by eating the apple (volition). The conscious decision to eat the apple was an entirely voluntary act. It was influenced and conditioned by many things—hunger, the prior experience of eating apples, and the opportunity to do so again. But it was not determined by a chain of antecedent causes.[25]

The psychological attributes of the will are what make it the sole agent of human liberty and moral responsibility. It is the foundation of Bledsoe's philosophy of the will and his rejection of determinism. He arrived at that conclusion after many years of investigating the workings of the human mind. One of his most influential authorities was the French philosopher and educator Victor Cousin (1792–1867). Cousin's lectures on psychology and the history of philosophy were major sources of ideas and arguments that Bledsoe drew upon in justifying his philosophy of the will. Like many students of philosophy in the early and mid-nineteenth century, Cousin was particularly influenced by the philosophy of common sense realism developed by the Scottish philosopher Thomas Reid (1710–96), professor of moral philosophy at the University of Glasgow. Reid argued that the judgments of the mind (consciousness) regarding the causality of phenomena are true and reliable sources of knowledge. His *Inquiry into the Human Mind on the Principles of Common Sense* (1764), *Essays on the Intellectual Powers of Man* (1785), and *Essays on the Active Powers of Man* (1788) exerted great influence upon European and American theologians, especially after they were popularized in Cousin's lectures.

Bledsoe first encountered Cousin's lectures on psychology either during his days as a seminarian or shortly thereafter. Caleb Sprague Henry (1804–84), an Episcopal clergyman and professor of moral and mental science at New York University, translated and edited Cousin's *Elements of Psychology* in 1834, which appeared in four editions.[26] Henry's work is a translation of ten lectures contained in the second volume of Cousin's *History of Philosophy in the Eighteenth Century*. Henry believed that the conclusions presented in Cousin's *Elements of Psychology* demolished the foundations of Lockean philosophy and that Cousin made the existence of God more than a belief—he made it a "positive cognition."[27] Bledsoe fully shared that opinion. It was in Henry's edition of the *Elements of Psychology* that Bledsoe first read Cousin's lectures on Locke, which never ceased to impress him for their clarity, precision, and exhaustive philosophical analysis and criticism. "It has ever been to us a mine of precious gems. No writer on 'the philosophy of religion,' especially of the Arminian school, is furnished for his work who has not mastered the Psychology of Cousin." Cousin's treatment of the threefold distinction between the *intelligence*, the *sensibility*, and the *will* remained a conspicuous feature of Bledsoe's philosophy thereafter. No distinction was more indispensable to his scheme of free agency. "It became a light to us then; and ever since it has been a light to us, in all our studies."[28]

Equally influential was Cousin's later *Course of the History of Modern Philosophy* translated by Orlando Williams Wight and published in New York in 1852. It was that edition of Cousin's *History of Modern Philosophy* that Bledsoe cites in *A Theodicy* as the authority for his discussion of the three distinct faculties of the human mind. Bledsoe again freely acknowledged his debt to Cousin, saying that the last chapter of the second volume of the *History of Modern Philosophy* contained by far the best exposition of the threefold division of mental faculties with which he was familiar. Sir William Sterling Hamilton, the Scottish philosopher and professor of logic and metaphysics at the University of Edinburgh, made the same distinction in his *Metaphysics*, crediting its origin to the German philosopher Immanuel Kant. Yet Bledsoe took issue with that attribution. He credited Aristotle as being the first philosopher to make the distinction between these three faculties of the mind in his *Nicomachean Ethics* (350 BC).

The great question of why God permits sin in the world receives due attention in *A Theodicy*. It is an intellectual problem that has puzzled theologians over the centuries and has direct bearing on the subjects of free will, moral accountability, and divine sovereignty. Yet Bledsoe maintained that it was "a most idle and insignificant inquiry" as the question was usually framed. The only real question was why God created human beings at all and not why he created them as he did and then permitted them to sin. The problem with the question of why God created humans and then permitted them to sin was an unmeaning one because it seeks to know "the *reason why* God has permitted a thing, which, in reality, he has not permitted at all." Since God created men and women as morally responsible agents, it was just as necessary that they could will themselves to be reprobates as it was that they could will themselves to be paragons of virtue. "Having created a world of moral agents, that is, a world endowed with the power to sin, it was impossible for him [God] to prevent sin, so long as they retained this power, or, in other words, so long as they continued to exist as moral agents." The existence of sin and evil in the world was a necessary consequence of moral free agency. God could not create humankind as moral agents and then deny them the power of moral choice. "He could no more deny peccability to such creatures than he could deny the properties of the circle to a circle; and if he could not prevent such a thing, it is surely very absurd to ask why he permitted it. On the supposition of such a world, God did not permit sin at all; it could not have been prevented."[29]

Bledsoe contended that the question of why God tolerated evil was just as absurd as asking why God allowed two and two to equal four and not something else, or why he permitted the three angles of a triangle to be equal to two right angles. Could an omnipotent God change the rational principles of mathematics into something else just to prove to skeptics that he was in fact omnipotent? Bledsoe answered no. God was a rational being who created the universe and set it in motion on logical principles. So it was also in the moral realm of human existence. A rational God could not have created humans any differently than they were found in nature and *still* allow them to be morally responsible for their actions. God could be said to have permitted sin *only* in the sense that he created creatures capable of sinning and doing evil. And without that capability they could in no sense exist as free agents. It was for that reason that the idea of moral necessity or a necessary virtue is "a contradiction in terms, an inherent and utter impossibility." As moral beings individuals were endowed with the ability to sin and transgress the laws of God. Human liberty, indeed, required it. And to expect God to prevent sin in a world based upon moral choice was to ask a rational being to do an irrational thing: "to expect him to cause a thing to be what it is, and not what it is, at one and the same time."

Advocates of free will rejected the doctrines of predestination, election, and original sin because they denied that individuals were masters of their own fate. And none did so more thoroughly than Bledsoe in *A Theodicy*. The strain of Calvinism advocated by Jonathan Edwards had always been a hard sell, and its hopelessness ultimately led to its demise. It was difficult to rationalize such pessimism with the rising tide of optimism and belief in the perfectibility of humanity. Evangelists in the early and mid-nineteenth century made Calvinism more palatable to the masses by softening its severity. They made it yield to the democratic predilections and expectations of their own day. What Mark A. Noll calls "the Americanization of Calvinism"—a process of adaptation that had been at work for some time—exploded in the early and mid-nineteenth century.[30] Those who found no promise of salvation in the determinism of high Calvinism took comfort in Bledsoe's philosophy of the will. God was not an arbitrary and capricious being but loving, good, and just. Bledsoe's God empowered individuals to control their destinies through moral choice. It was a welcome and comforting message.

The Calvinist belief that Bledsoe abhorred above all others, however, was the doctrine of infant damnation. He categorically refused to justify the suffering of infants on the ground that original sin was imputed to them as well. "A sentiment so dark and appalling but ill accords with the sublime and beautiful spirit of the gospel. It partakes more of the weakness and infirmity of human nature than of the divine nature of Him who 'spake as never man spake.'" Saint Augustine was the first Christian theologian to apply the doctrine of original sin to newborns. He contended that infants sinned in Adam like the rest of humanity and could justly experience pain, death, and damnation. Bledsoe denounced the doctrine as a blasphemy against the goodness of God and a corruption of scripture. It was a notion entirely at war with reason itself. Many churchgoers and ministers who believed in sanctification in the present life had similar difficulty with accepting so harsh a doctrine. Lyman Beecher, Charles Grandison Finney, Nathaniel William Taylor, Horace Bushnell, and others emphatically rejected the doctrine of infant damnation. It had no place within an evangelical religion that emphasized personal salvation through the acceptance of Jesus Christ and the authority of the Gospels.

While some Methodists objected to certain aspects of Bledsoe's *Theodicy,* more often than not they spoke of it reverentially. A rare dissenting opinion appeared in a three-part review in the *Quarterly Review of the Methodist Episcopal Church, South.*[31] The reviewer echoes some of the objections raised against the work by Presbyterian critics, such as his observation that "our author lacks, we think, the reverence and modesty of a profound and devout philosopher." The reviewer preferred the two-volume *Essays in Theodicy on the Goodness of God, the Liberty of Man, and the Origin of Evil* (1710) by the German rationalist and polymath Gottfried Wilhelm Leibnitz to the *Theodicy* of Albert Taylor Bledsoe. Leibnitz, said the reviewer, did not place as many restrictions on God's sovereignty. It was a criticism more in keeping with Calvinism than Methodism, yet the reviewer, like Bledsoe, thought for himself. He asked whether it might not be possible for Omnipotence to create a universe free of all moral evil and maintain that state through the ongoing influence of divinity acting upon the moral agency of individuals without denying free will. "Who will dare to say that it might not?"[32] Bledsoe had dared to say that it might not, much to the displeasure of his reviewer.

Majority opinion among Methodists, however, ran in the direction of praise. An anonymous review in the *Methodist Quarterly Review* in January 1854 hailed *A Theodicy* as a valuable contribution to theology that gave a heightened understanding and appreciation of divine government.[33] Another Methodist writer pronounced the work to be one of "transcendent merit," which delivered a mortal blow against the canons of Calvinism. The author made a clear and convincing exposition of the grounds for the Arminian belief in free will. Methodists should "thank him, for having gone down among the dark foundations of Calvinism, and, Samson-like, for having grasped the pillars therefrom, and upheaving the dingy, gloomy superstructure from its very basis, tumbled it into ruins."[34] E. Brooks Holifield has acknowledged that Bledsoe's arguments were well received by most advocates of free will, while Robert Eugene Chiles has noted that Methodists generally embraced Bledsoe's *Theodicy* "with enthusiasm and quoted it profusely for fifty years." John Boyce Bennett offers further testimony of the influence of *A Theodicy* among Bledsoe's contemporaries, noting that one finds marginal notes in nineteenth-century Methodist and Presbyterian periodicals that mention "Bledsoeism" alongside "Calvinism" and "Arminianism."[35]

A Theodicy predictably fared less well at the hands of Calvinist reviewers. Thomas Ephraim Peck—a Baltimore clergyman and a former theological student of James Henley Thornwell's—roundly condemned the work in the *Presbyterial Critic and Monthly Review* in January 1855.[36] The greatest thinkers, fumed Peck, had always been those who were "the readiest to acknowledge the insoluble difficulties" involved in contemplating the plans, attributes, and dispensations of divinity. "They know by many painful experiments, the very narrow sphere in which the human faculties have been ordained and constituted to move." But not so with the impudent author of *A Theodicy,* who recklessly presumed to reveal the hidden majesty of God. Wiser men were content to let the subject alone. They "prostrate themselves in adoring faith." Peck acknowledged that Bledsoe displayed "metaphysical acumen." Yet he complained of the arrogant tone that pervaded his discussions of intractable problems that had humbled the greatest minds. "It is very edifying and pleasant to be told, for example, that the mystery which baffled the powers of Plato and Leibnitz, not to mention a host of smaller luminaries, is no mystery at all, but only 'the sophism of the atheist.'"[37]

Peck complained that the author of *A Theodicy* presented himself as the Christopher Wren of the universe. He discerned "proportion, harmony, and order" where no other "mortal" had been able to see them. It would be the better part of humility and sound philosophy had he chosen "to be restive under real difficulties, than deny their existence." Peck found nothing new in Bledsoe's theology (it was but another reaffirmation of Arminianism) and regretted that Methodists so greatly admired the work. Bledsoe made too little appeal to the scriptures for Peck's taste, preferring his own speculative constructions of divinity to the testimony of the Gospels. Peck compensated for the deficiency by quoting several passages from the Bible that in his judgment altogether refuted Bledsoe's Arminianism. It would better for the author, Peck suggested, if he walked more by faith and the authority of the scriptures and less by the light of his own consciousness and rationality.

The most substantive Calvinist response to *A Theodicy* came from the Virginia clergyman and Old School Presbyterian John Holmes Bocock. Two anonymous reviews by Bocock appeared the *Southern Presbyterian Review*.[38] He admitted the merits of the work, which he found superior to the usual anti-Calvinist polemics written by Methodists. Yet he nonetheless lamented that one still found "the same hot and half-frenzied antipathy to the theology of the apostle Paul." Apparently not knowing of Bledsoe's grounding in theological studies, Bocock found it strange that a professor of mathematics would take it upon himself to write a book touching upon some of the deepest moral and theological questions of all time. Nor was the critic satisfied with Bledsoe's assaults on Edwards's conception of free will. Bocock offered up an old chestnut in defense of Edwards: "No man would undertake to refute Edwards if he understood him." What troubled Bocock most about Bledsoe's *Theodicy* was the author's "peculiar mode of mental philosophy" concerning moral free agency, one that Bocock believed "removes the human soul from under Divine influence, which necessarily goes along with his theory."[39]

Bocock's second essay on *A Theodicy* drew attention to similarities in the personal theologies of Bledsoe and Nathaniel William Taylor.[40] Taylor, a professor of divinity at Yale, was an influential Congregationalist thinker with sympathies for revivals during the Second Great Awakening. Bocock noted that, while Bledsoe developed his theology outside the Presbyterian Church, his fellow traveler Taylor incubated his within the dissenting principles of New School Presbyterianism. Taylor and Bledsoe arrived at their respective positions independently of each other, yet both had cut themselves loose from the traditional moorings of orthodox Christianity. They were both were guilty of hubris, charged Bocock, since they placed their own personal convictions and speculations regarding divinity above the received authority of the scriptures—the only true source of Christian faith. Taken together, the ideas of Taylor and Bledsoe constituted "a new theology." Bocock, a dedicated Old School Presbyterian, had no sympathy for either Taylorisms or Bledsoeisms. He considered each to be kindred in spirit though distinct in origin. Both were equally dangerous to the traditional authority of the Christian faith. Bocock was convinced that, if followed to their logical conclusions, the new theologies of Taylor and Bledsoe would encourage the very skepticism and atheism that each writer had set out to refute.[41]

Bledsoe received many gratifying notices of his *Theodicy* and regretted that he had not made more of an effort to ensure their survival. As he observed in his Memorandum Book, "If I had preserved all the letters and papers which I have received on the same subject they would fill a large volume. But I did not sufficiently value them." Yet it always gave him great comfort and delight in knowing that his metaphysical musings had delivered many tortured spirits from their "bondage beneath the awful mysteries of the universe, and made them send forth shouts of joy and deliverance." One such thankful soul was William Henry Harrison of Wigwam, Virginia. Harrison wrote Bledsoe in September 1854 that reading *A Theodicy* had been nothing less than a revelation. He rejoiced to see the light and rhapsodized, "Thanks, thanks, a thousand times thanks." Bledsoe claimed to have received many such expressions of "everlasting gratitude." For some he had made "the providence of God forever beautiful and holy in their eye."[42] However inflated the praise of *A Theodicy*, and of Bledsoe's own estimation of its value, the number of editions in which the work appeared establishes its importance beyond question. *A Theodicy* appeared in at least seven American editions, and possibly as many as sixteen, and an English edition was published in London in 1864. The first three editions were issued within four months of its publication in 1853. Bledsoe's daughter Sophia said that thirty thousand or more copies were sold, a truly remarkable number for a treatise on speculative theology.[43]

Subsequent opinion of what Bledsoe attempted to accomplish in *A Theodicy* has remained respectful. The *Methodist Review* of New York said of *A Theodicy* in September 1893 that "it is a work through which the dead author still lives and speaks. It has power in purpose, plan, and execution." Methodist clergyman Samuel Augustus Steel—formerly of Virginia and later of Columbia, South Carolina—regarded Bledsoe's work to be the greatest vindication of Arminian theology he had ever read. The severity of Bledsoe's attacks on determinism led Steel to refer to him as "the Arminian sledge hammer." He "pulverized the errors of Calvinism as a sledge hammer crushes rock." One could not read *A Theodicy* without being impressed with the force of Bledsoe's argument that "God could not work impossibilities, cannot make two and two equal five, cannot make an inside without an outside, or a straight line the longest distance between two points. A rational God could not do anything irrational." The Reverend J. M. Hawley, a Methodist minister in Hamilton, Virginia, and himself the son of a Methodist preacher, echoed Steel's flattering opinion. Hawley pronounced Bledsoe's *Theodicy* one of the greatest productions of the human mind he had ever read. "As a piece of destructive criticism it is simply overwhelming."[44] Orthodox Calvinists bestowed no such laurels upon the work, yet most Methodists continued to pay it homage.

The influence of Bledsoe's metaphysical and theological interests on the entire range of his thought should not be underestimated. His views on human nature, natural rights and equality, the social contract, civil liberty, democracy, slavery, and the sanctioning authority of law and government were essentially theistic conceptions and should be examined within that context regardless of their more secular bearings. Intersections between Bledsoe's theological, social, political, legal, and scientific thought are numerous and significant. If Bledsoe's contributions to American philosophy were modest, they are nonetheless essential to understanding the operative assumptions of his worldview. Indeed, Bledsoe would devote a good portion of his later life to elaborating and defending his philosophy of the will as the editor of the *Southern Review*. His interests in metaphysics, theology, and moral philosophy were constant companions.

5

SOUTHERN SLAVERY JUSTIFIED
A Watchman's Response to Abolitionism

IN 1856, BLEDSOE EMERGED as a propagandist of slavery with the publication of *An Essay on Liberty and Slavery*. The treatise was arguably one of the most erudite and thorough apologies written in defense of that dubious cause. His arguments were part of a conservative counterrevolution in social and political thought that challenged the egalitarian assumptions of abolitionism and other social reforms. That movement was by no means an exclusively southern occurrence. Yet from the 1830s onward the antiegalitarianism argument, together with the indispensable biblical defense of slavery, provided the grounds upon which southerners attempted to answer the abolitionists. Bledsoe attempted to vindicate slavery by revising received opinion on the nature of civil liberty and natural rights and by repudiating seventeen alleged "fallacies" promulgated by the abolitionists. He advanced arguments in defense of slavery from the scriptures and the perspective of the public good and warned that an increasingly aggressive abolitionist movement was imperiling the Union by failing to enforce the Fugitive Slave Law. *An Essay on Liberty and Slavery* encapsulates the fears and anxieties of a social order in crisis. Together with Henry Hughes's *Treatise on Sociology* (1854) and George Fitzhugh's *Sociology for the South* (1854) and *Cannibals All! Or Slaves without Masters* (1857), Bledsoe's defense of slavery represents the high watermark of proslavery thought. Even so it remains one of the least studied of the major proslavery texts.

Much of the social and political theory that Bledsoe draws upon in justifying southern slavery originated in other contexts. He first described the social compact theory of government as "a splendid fiction" in an article on capital punishment. The essay appeared in the *Methodist Quarterly Review* for July 1846 and advanced the argument that individual rights, as in the case of the death penalty, could be denied if the public good required it.[1] Even more important, the editorials on the nature of civil liberty that Bledsoe contributed to the *Illinois Journal* in 1847 and 1848 reappear in the first chapter of *Liberty and Slavery* with only slight modification and elaboration. He initially made those arguments entirely without reference to the slavery controversy but pressed them into service in *Liberty and Slavery* in the hope of discrediting the principles of abolitionism. The philosopher Herbert Wallace Schneider observed that Bledsoe's defense of slavery was a broad-ranging philosophical discourse with "a general discussion of social theory only indirectly related to slavery."[2] Schneider's statement is essentially accurate, but it is far from an adequate appraisal of the work as a whole. Bledsoe's polemic spoke directly to various facets of the slavery controversy. *Liberty and Slavery* is a reasonably comprehensive index of the attitudes, apprehensions, and arguments embodied in proslavery ideology.

Bledsoe responded in *Liberty and Slavery* to the ethical indictments of slavery set forth in the respective writings of Francis Wayland and William Ellery Channing (both moderates in the antislavery movement) and to organized opposition to the enforcement of the Fugitive Slave Law. William Henry Seward, Charles Sumner, and Salmon Portland Chase led the movement as the political arm of abolitionism. Bledsoe leveled his criticisms solely at those whom he described as "the more decent, respectable, and celebrated" of the abolitionists. The more "scurrilous writers" who engaged in the "wholesale abuse of Southern character" he deemed altogether unworthy of notice: "no educated gentlemen will tolerate them." Theodore Parker received but a passing execration as a political preacher unfit for the performance of his sacred trust, while the firebrand William Lloyd Garrison, Lucretia Mott, Lucy Stone, and members of the American Antislavery Society received no mention at all.[3] The hard-edge rhetoric adopted by the more extreme wing of the abolitionist movement made southerners ill disposed to discuss emancipation and invited an equally belligerent response. Elizabeth Fox-Genovese and Eugene D. Genovese have well said regarding the agitations of the more zealous abolitionists: "The militantly proslavery Albert Taylor Bledsoe of Virginia and a good many other Southerners recognized a declaration of war when they were handed one."[4]

Bledsoe made no apology for his use of strong language. He asked only that the reader judge if he had spoken justly. "We have certainly not spoken without provocation. For even these men, the lights and ornaments of abolitionism, have seldom condescended to argue with us as equals." Instead, the enemies of slavery "habitually address us as if nothing but a purblind ignorance of the very first elements of moral science could shield our minds against the force of their irresistible arguments." Abolitionists took "pity of our most lamentable moral darkness, and graciously condescend to teach us the very A B C of ethical philosophy!" Yet in making that charge Bledsoe took pains to distinguish between the abolitionists—"our accusers"—and northerners in general. "We have only assailed those by whom we have been assailed; and we have held each and every man responsible only for what he himself has said and done." It would be a "monstrous injustice" to denounce the majority of northerners because of the words and deeds of the few. "We had infinitely rather suffer such injustice—as we have so long done—than practice it toward others."[5]

The burden of Bledsoe's argument is "that the institution of slavery, as it exists among us at the South, is founded in political justice, is in accordance with the will of God and the designs of his providence, and is conducive to the highest, purest, best interests of mankind."[6] Slavery was the "great problem of our social existence and national prosperity, upon the solution of which the hopes and destinies of mankind in no inconsiderable measure depend." No remedy existed in appeals to "passion or to sordid interest" but only to reason. "And if justice, or mercy, or truth, be found at war with the institution of slavery, then, in the name of God, let slavery perish. But however guilty, still let it be tried, condemned, and executed according to law, and not extinguished by a despotic and lawless power more terrific than itself." Whatever qualms Bledsoe might have privately entertained about the justice of slavery, his dread of immediate abolitionism was far greater.[7]

According to Bledsoe, the practical solution of the problem of liberty and slavery in the South "imperatively demands" the institution of slavery, without which neither "a sound public order" nor "a decent private liberty" could exist. "We shall endeavor to show, that the very laws or institution which is supposed by fanatical declaimers to shut out liberty from the Negro race among us, really shuts out the most frightful *license* and disorder from society." He charged that abolitionists did great mischief by "preaching up liberty *to and for* the slaves of the South." Southern slaves could "neither comprehend the nature, nor enjoy the blessings, of the freedom which is officiously thrust upon them." Should the black race ever be moved by the abolitionists' "fiery appeals," it would only imperil "the fair fabric of American liberty, which, with all its shortcomings and defects, is by far the most beautiful ever yet conceived or constructed by the genius of man."[8]

Defenders of slavery denied the charge that slavery was always and everywhere a moral wrong and a transgression against the law of God. The Baptist clergyman and president of Brown University Francis Wayland (1796–1865) took the position in his influential *Elements of Moral Science* (1835) that holding men and women in bondage and obliging them to work for the benefit of others was immoral. Slavery disregarded the law of God regarding our duty to our own kind. Human bondage stood in defiance of the Christian teaching that *"thou shalt love thy neighbor as thyself"* and the related precept of doing unto others as you would have them do unto you. Wayland further charged that by forbidding slaves the right to read—even to study the Bible—the dominion of slavery crushed the intellectual, social, and moral development of those it held in servitude. It was another evil at variance with the duty of all Christians toward humankind. If the slaves were to be held in slavery only so long as they remained in a lower intellectual state, that gave their masters little incentive to bring them along. Wayland objected that such a circumstance gave the master the right to control the intellectual development of the slave "just as far as may be necessary to secure entire subjection."[9]

Wayland elaborated his views on the issue of slavery and the Bible in his published correspondence with the Baptist minister Richard Fuller of Beaufort, South Carolina, which appeared in 1845 as *Domestic Slavery Considered as a Scriptural Institution*. Fuller (1804–76) was a slave owner who ministered to some 200 white and 2,400 black parishioners as the pastor of the Beaufort Baptist Church. He took a deep interest in the spiritual instruction of slaves during the fifteen years of his ministry at Beaufort and took great exception to Wayland's interpretation of the scriptures as an indictment of slavery. He challenged Wayland's assertion that slavery stood condemned because it violated the most fundamental principles of natural justice, conscience, and the teachings of Christianity. Wayland attributed the universal existence of slavery at the time of Christ to "the moral darkness of the age," which was in no way compatible with the law of universal love expounded in the New Testament. He reaffirmed the conviction that the institution of slavery, whether at the time of Christ or in the American South, could never be rationalized with the instruction to love thy neighbor as thyself and to do unto others as you would have them do unto you.[10]

Advocates of slavery found it difficult to deflect the force of Wayland's moral condemnation of slavery. Yet they countered by arguing that slavery was a beneficent institution of social progress, which was little understood by those who denounced it. If the morals and behavior of slaveholders were as depraved as abolitionists represented them to be, argued Bledsoe, he would himself be among the first to condemn their transgressions. But he insisted that such was not the case. Slaveholders generally regarded it as their duty to promote both the earthly and eternal good of their slaves in return for service.

The *right* to own slaves came with the corresponding *duty* of looking to their well-being. And so far from debasing the intellectual, social, and moral condition of slaves, Bledsoe contended, the southern institution of slavery actually improved their situation. Slavery could be defended against the charge of turpitude only if it benefited both the master *and* the slave—and great emphasis was placed upon the duties of masters.[11] The ideal of moral stewardship examined in Clifford Stephen Griffin's *Their Brothers' Keepers* informed the political and religious aspects of the abolitionist crusade, but defenders of slavery also appealed to the concept by portraying masters as the moral stewards of the race that providence had presumably entrusted to their care.[12]

Bledsoe maintained that the African race was already so degraded as to be unfit for freedom or a higher position within southern society. Yet when abolitionists spoke of the intellectual and moral oppression of southern slaves by their master, they spoke and reasoned "just as if we had caught a bevy of black angels as they were winging their way to some island of purity and bliss here upon earth, and reduced them from their heavenly state, by the most diabolical cruelties and oppressions, to one of degradation, misery, and servitude." The abolitionists had to be reminded "that Africa is not yet a paradise, and that Southern servitude is not quite hell." They forgot in the heat and haste of their declamations "that the institution of slavery is designed by the South not for the enlightened and the free, but only for the ignorant and the debased. They need to be constantly reminded that the institution of slavery is not the mother, but the daughter, of degradation." It was "the legitimate offspring of that intellectual and moral debasement which, for so many thousand years, has been accumulating and growing upon the African race." If the abolitionists would only invent some means by which "all this frightful mass of degradation may be blotted out *at once*, then will we most cheerfully consent to 'the *immediate* abolition of slavery.'"[13]

The crucial question in the debate over slavery was whether the institution was harmful or beneficial to slaves. Wayland argued in *Elements of Moral Science* that slavery injured its victims in many ways. It should be abolished immediately, since there was never an acceptable reason for doing wrong and inflicting harm. Yet Bledsoe refused to accept Wayland's assumption. "If a state of slavery be a greater injury to the slave than a state of freedom would be," he replied, "then are we willing to admit that it should be abolished. But even in that case, not *immediately*, unless it could be shown that the remedy would not be worse than the evil." Even if it could be shown that the institution of slavery was a curse to the slave, it should not be abolished "suddenly" like "a whirl-wind." Considerations of the public good dictated that "the counsels of wise, cautious, and far-seeing statesmen" work gradually toward a plan of emancipation that took into account "all the diversified and highly-complicated interests of society."[14]

That statement leaves the door open to the possibility that Bledsoe might have embraced a self-directed program of gradual emancipation under the right set of circumstances. Yet he says nothing about how gradual emancipation might be accomplished as an alternative to immediate abolition. Thus the assertion made by James Royce Bennett that Bledsoe actually favored gradual emancipation may be true, but it gets no support from anything said in *Liberty and Slavery* or any of Bledsoe's other writings. Nor, indeed, does Bennett himself provide any supporting evidence for his claim. Bledsoe clearly believed that southern slavery had a future. He showed no interest in discussing how and why it might one day end.

Bledsoe's opposition to immediate emancipation was entirely predicated upon the unproven and self-serving claim that slaves were not competent to govern themselves. If individuals were "cut from pasteboard" each one exactly like the other, the arguments of the abolitionists would be unassailable. But Bledsoe maintained that no such equality existed. Men and women were quite different in terms of their characters, habits, and propensities. Some, Bledsoe wrote, were intellectually and morally brutes while others were intellectually cultivated and well versed in the moral teachings of religion. The former set was not capable of self-government and should be held by the law of society in a state of servitude while the latter should enjoy the blessings of liberty in the fullest. "There is a difference between a Hottentot and a Newton. The first should no more be condemned to astronomical calculations and discoveries, than the last should be required to follow a plough." The question in every instance was where individuals or groups were situated within "the scale of being."[15] Such differences among humankind found no place within the egalitarianism of the abolitionists but a prominent one in the ideology of slavery. Slaves under that view were lumped together with children, the indigent, and the mentally incompetent—entirely dependent persons who were allegedly incapable of managing their own affairs and needed a protector and friend to guide them.

Bledsoe's assault on egalitarianism was aggressive and unyielding. He dismissed the assertion that each individual, simply by being a part of humanity, is equal in rights to all others as one of the greatest and most dangerous sophistries bequeathed by the eighteenth century. He believed that inequalities in the human condition were to be found everywhere—disparities that no political theory or human laws could change. However inconvenient those dissimilarities might be to the egalitarian, the political architect could no more overlook them than the mathematician could disregard magnitude. "The man, the political dreamer, who pays no attention to them, may be fit, for aught we know, to frame a government out of moonshine for the inhabitants of Utopia; but, if we might choose our own teachers in political wisdom, we should decidedly prefer those who have an eye for facts as well as abstractions." Bledsoe further observed, borrowing a metaphor from Thomas Babington Macaulay, that "the legislator who sees no difference among men, but proposes the same kind of government for all, acts about as wisely as a tailor who should measure the Apollo Belvidere to cut clothes for all his customers—for the pigmies and well as for the giants."[16]

Bledsoe argued that those who failed to acknowledge inequalities in the human condition had no business lecturing southerners on their ethics in the matter of slavery. The majority of southern blacks lived in a state of servitude not because they were "guilty of a skin" that differed in color from that of their white masters but because they were purportedly different in their capabilities. If skin color were the only foundation of southern slavery, said Bledsoe, he could never defend it. "Shame and confusion seize the man, we say, who thus dooms and devotes his fellow-man [to servitude], because he finds him guilty of a skin!" If skin color were the only difference between the black and white races of the South, he would himself gladly join William Henry Seward in advising all men to be born white. For if all men were born white, the only supposed difference existing between them would be abolished. All men would be equal in fact and entitled to the same political rights, powers, and conditions. But if skin color was *not* the only difference existing between southern whites and blacks, "then neither philosophy nor paint can establish an equality between them."

Equality of rights had to be based upon the capacity for self-government and not on the abstractions of visionary reformers. Liberty should be conditional and should never be limitless. Unrestricted liberty threatened public order and the common good because it encouraged license and disorder, whereas constrained liberty protected them. "An equality of conditions, of political powers and privileges, which has no foundation in an equality of capacity or fitness, is one of the wildest and most impractical of all Utopian dreams." And should such a state of social and political equality ever prevail, its lawless reign would be brief. "Indeed, to aim at an equality of conditions, or of rights and powers, except by first aiming at an equality of intelligence and virtue, is not to reform—it is to demolish—the governments of society." Aristotle maintained that it was the striving for equality that caused sedition. The truth of that axiom was as self-evident to Bledsoe as the maxim of equality and inalienable rights was to the abolitionist. Like many of his conservative predecessors and contemporaries, he believed that inequalities in the human condition were part of the natural order. God created humankind in his own image but did not endow individuals with the same intellectual and moral capabilities. All men were not created equal in fact, the assumptions of egalitarians to the contrary notwithstanding. Differences in men quite naturally translated into social classes and hierarchies.[17]

Whether the disparities in capability, intelligence, and virtue that Bledsoe ascribed to blacks and whites were innate and immutable or merely conditional and remedial was an open question he never addressed. Indeed, he dodged the issue entirely. But his argument that liberty would actually be harmful to slaves because they were unfit for freedom begged further questions as to why. Were slaves inherently unfit for liberty or only provisionally so? If the answer was that slaves were only conditionally unfit for freedom, how would the circumstances of southern servitude ever change so that they would be fit for freedom in the future? Southern slave codes were expressly designed to perpetuate existing social conditions among slaves and free blacks in the South. There was no apprenticeship to freedom under the slave codes. They were designed to control every aspect of a slave's behavior and gave little incentive for assuming any role other than that of being a slave. Those questions were implicit in the slavery debate, but it did no part of Bledsoe's defense of slavery any good to introduce them, since they played directly to the strength of the abolitionists' condemnation of slavery.

Bledsoe's defense of southern slavery drew upon assumptions regarding the supposed inferiority of the African race that were deeply embedded in Western thought. Yet they owed nothing to the scientific theories of racial inferiority and human origins that agitated the religious and scientific communities at the time he wrote *Liberty and Slavery*. There were those like Dr. Josiah Clark Nott of Mobile and Dr. Samuel A. Cartwright of New Orleans who argued upon presumably scientific grounds that blacks were congenitally inferior to whites, but their views were extreme.[18] Bledsoe, indeed, passed over in contemptuous silence the racial theory advanced by Nott and coauthor George Robins Gliddon in their celebrated *Types of Mankind* (1854), even though their arguments were serviceable in the defense of southern slavery.[19] Seventeen years later in the *Southern Review*, however, Bledsoe stated his disdain for the anthropology of Nott and Gliddon in no uncertain terms. Who did not remember, he asked, the recent reign of Nott and Gliddon "and the great noise, as of a mighty, rushing wind, they made in the so-called learned world?" He gave no credence to their leading idea that all the races of men, with all their physical diversities, could not possibly have descended from a single pair of progenitors. Nott and Gliddon and their enraptured followers, said a dismissive Bledsoe, had confidently declared "that God, as his *pretended* word declares, did not make of one blood all the nations of the earth." The Bible was invalidated and the Christian religion deposed.[20]

Bledsoe shared the opinion of James Lawrence Cabell—professor of anatomy, physiology, and surgery at the University of Virginia and Bledsoe's closest friend—that science was on the side of the monogenists (those who argued for a single or common origin for humankind) and against the polygenists (those who argued for separate origins for each of the human races).[21] Nott and Gliddon's skeptical attitude toward the Mosaic account of creation and biblical chronologies and their advocacy of polygenesis alienated many southern clergymen, many of whom upheld the righteousness of southern slavery based upon the authority of the Old Testament. Such an infidel view of human origins presented Christian scholars like Bledsoe and Cabell with too many problems.[22] For them, the Bible provided the definitive answer to the vexed question of human origins. The apostle Paul affirmed in Acts 17:26 that God "made of one blood all nations of men for to dwell on all the face of the earth." That passage, together with the account of human origins given in Genesis, led most Christians to regard the separate origins doctrine as blasphemy, however convenient it might be as a defense of slavery upon other grounds.

What Larry E. Tise has called the retreat from liberty and Joseph L. Blau "a failure of nerve" concerning the egalitarian principles of the American Revolution was a national and not a sectional phenomenon. It predated the slavery controversy and was not confined exclusively to the South.[23] Yet defenders of slavery recoiled from the ideology of the American Revolution even further after the rise of the abolition movement. Gone were the ambivalent and apologetic attitudes of Thomas Jefferson that rationalized slavery as a necessary evil—a notion that gradually vanished during the cotton boom and its southwestern expansion after the introduction of the cotton gin. Jefferson never adequately resolved the conflict between liberty and slavery within his own life, as evidenced by his tortured explanations and regrets on the subject.[24] Slavery could not be justified within the Jeffersonian framework of liberty, which defenders of slavery jettisoned and replaced with a more restricted and provisional idea of liberty. They rationalized slavery as being necessary for the maintenance of public order within the racially heterogeneous society of the South—precisely the ground assumed by Bledsoe in *Liberty and Slavery*. Bledsoe had this to say about those, such as himself, who had at one time been of two minds on the subject of slavery but had rethought the issue due to the assumptions, claims, and tactics of the abolitionists: "We owe at least one benefit to the Northern abolitionists. Ere the subject of slavery was agitated by them, there were many loose, floating notions among us, as well as among themselves, respecting the nature of liberty, which were at variance with the institution of slavery." But the agitations of the abolitionists had forced southerners to look more closely into the grounds of slavery, as well as into the arguments by which it is assailed. They had found "the first as solid as adamant, the last as unsubstantial as moonshine."[25]

Jefferson became something of an apostate among defenders of slavery who rejected both his apologies for slavery and the egalitarian assumptions of his political philosophy. He categorically stated in *Notes on the State of Virginia* (1782), for example, that the existence slavery in Virginia exerted "an unhappy influence" upon the manners of Virginians. He described the master-slave relationship as one based upon "the most unremitting despotism on the one part, and the most degrading submission on the other." Yet Thomas Roderick Dew, the architect of the slavery as a "positive good" argument, suggested that the injustices and evils that Jefferson attributed to slavery were not supported by the facts. Most masters, said Dew, were not tyrants but exemplars of the true interests of morality and religion. It was in their own best interests that their behavior be actuated by the noblest and most elevated sentiments and the most humane and virtuous feelings. Dew did not deny that cruel masters existed but maintained they were not typical. Masters who were malicious toward their slaves were reprobates who deserved to be scorned. Dew implied that Jefferson had allowed his philanthropy and egalitarian ideas to cloud his better judgment in his representations of slavery, an institution that was not despotic but beneficent.[26]

Nowhere was the retreat from the liberal humanitarian principles of Jefferson (notwithstanding his own contradictory exclusion of slaves) more evident than in Bledsoe's response to the argument from the Declaration of Independence. "We do not mean to play upon these words; we intend to take them exactly as they are understood by our opponents." He did not reject natural rights doctrine entirely but rather pruned and corrected it to suit his argument in defense of slavery. It was, indeed, a distinguishing characteristic of his proslavery thought. The supposedly self-evident truth set forth in the Declaration, Bledsoe argued, did not mean that all men had an equal right to political power and positions of honor. Such a conception of equality was altogether alien to those who fought the American Revolution and founded the Republic. It was as absurd a notion as it was impractical. "The man, for example, who has no capacity to govern himself, but needs a guardian, has no right to superintend the affairs of a great nation." Only those qualified to exercise the right of the elective franchise in a manner consistent with the public good should be permitted to have it. It was often necessary to restrict the rights of some members of society in order to promote the greater good of the community as a whole. "And if the public good required that any class of men, such as free blacks or slaves, for example, should be excluded from the privilege [of citizenship and voting] altogether, then no doubt can remain [that] the law excluding them would be just. It might not be equal, but would be *just.*"[27]

Bledsoe's idea of ordered liberty subordinated the rights of slaves to the supposed requirements of the public good. He placed great emphasis on the duty of all to maintain public order. Individual rights were always subordinate to the security of the community. Moreover, a right of self-defense was "inseparably linked to a sacred duty" to promote the greatest good. "Surely we can have no right which is adverse to duty." If the general good required that individuals relinquish both their rights and liberties, both could be rightfully taken from them. "We have, it is true, inherent and inalienable rights, but among these is neither liberty nor life." These could be sacrificed as required by the public good. The only inherent and inalienable rights were "conscience, truth, and honor." These alone "may not be touched by man."

Bledsoe asserted that inalienable rights were too often misunderstood and misapplied. "In a certain sense, or to a certain extent, all men have equal rights. All men have an equal right to the air and light of heaven; to the same air and the same light. In like manner, all men have an equal right to food and raiment, though not to the same food and raiment." Natural rights were conditional and not absolute. Likewise, all have a right to worship and serve God "according to the dictates of their own consciences. The poorest slave on earth possesses this right—this inherent and inalienable right; and he possesses it as completely as the proudest monarch on his throne." Ignoring the actualities of slave management regarding churchgoing, Bledsoe claimed the slave "may choose his own religion, and worship his own God according to his own conscience, provided always he is seen not in such service to interfere with the rights of others." Servants had the right "to worship the Creator of all men in all ways not inconsistent with the moral law." Bledsoe said he had never known a slave owner who denied that right. But if such a person could be found, let the abolitionists hunt him down: "he is not fit to be a man, much less a Christian master."[28]

The real issue was not whether slaves received religious instruction but whether they were allowed to *read*. That right was not denied blacks in the North. "But here lies the difference—here lies our peculiar sin and shame. This great primordial right is, with us, denied by law. The slave shall not be taught to read. Oh! That he might be taught! What floods of sympathy, what thunderings and lightnings of philanthropy, would then be spared the world!" And why, Bledsoe asked, should the slave be taught to read? "That he might read the Bible, and feed on the food of eternal life, is the reply; and the reply is good."[29] The reply was good but in direct conflict with both the law of slavery and southern fears. Southern slave codes forbid slaves to assemble for religious instruction, except under controlled conditions, or to be taught to read and write. Virginia's slave code, for example, made the assembly of both slaves and free blacks for the purpose of religious worship unlawful if blacks conducted those meetings instead of whites, while the gathering of blacks for the purpose of instruction in reading and writing was banned under any circumstances.

Discouraging slaves from reading the Bible was difficult for any Christian to defend. But it was particularly problematic for those who based their defense of slavery on the duty of Christian stewardship. Nothing was more fundamental to Protestantism than the belief that the word of God should be accessible to everyone and that biblical literacy promoted order, civility, and morality.[30] Bledsoe understood that argument implicitly and felt its justice acutely. His regret that the slave codes proscribed literacy was sincere because such a ban violated the convictions of his own conscience. But his position on the issue of slave literacy was not entirely philanthropic. He hastened to add that southerners clearly perceived the "dangers" confronting them regarding the issue of slave literacy as well as their duties. It was generally feared in the South that teaching slaves to read would make them more susceptible to the appeals of the abolitionist press. Along with many other apologists, Bledsoe claimed that the agitations of northern emancipationists prevented a change in southern laws. They wrote and preached from the Declaration of Independence instead of the Bible and advocated "resistance" instead of "submission."

Slave owners had long expressed concern over the issue of slave literacy, and Bledsoe fully shared their trepidation. "Let all incendiary publications be destroyed. Let no conspiracies, no insurrections, and no murders be instigated. Let the pure precepts of the Gospel and its sublime lessons of peace be everywhere set forth and inculcated." When that day arrived, southerners might well be expected to teach their slaves to read. "But until then we shall refuse to head a conspiracy against the good order, the security, the morals, and against the very lives of both the white and the black men of the South."[31] A menacing dread of slave conspiracies and insurrections trumped all other considerations. Concern over the issue did not subside and only heightened after John Brown's raid on Harpers Ferry in 1859. Fear of a slave insurrection fomented by outside agitators, it has been argued, was one of the causes of the secession of Virginia in 1861.[32]

A cornerstone of proslavery ideology was the argument from the scriptures —a subject that receives considerable attention in *Liberty and Slavery*. The New School Presbyterian theologian Albert Barnes, a moderate in the antislavery crusade, stated the problem of slavery and the Bible succinctly in his *Inquiry into the Scriptural Views of Slavery* (1846): "There is no power *out* of the church that could sustain slavery an hour, if it were not sustained *in* it." Biblical criticism or interpretation informed a wide cross section of thought in antebellum America. Yet nowhere did it have greater utility and polemical value than in the debate over the righteousness or iniquity of slavery.[33] Abolitionists contended that slavery violated the first principles and teachings of Christian ethics, and defenders of slavery countered that the institution was not everywhere and always wrong by pointing to the existence of slavery among the Hebrews. The patriarch Abraham (the friend of God) was a slaveholder. Moses, furthermore, enacted laws regulating the relationships between Hebrew masters and slaves.

Antagonists in the slavery debate quoted the authority of the scriptures to support their opposing positions. Hermeneutical debates among biblical scholars about the actual contexts and meanings of scriptural texts relating to slavery and the rules of biblical interpretation used in discussing them were an important component of the slavery debate. That portion of the Mosaic code contained in Deuteronomy 23:15–16, for example, was what Bledsoe called "a precious morsel" with those who opposed the Fugitive Slave Law. "Thou shalt not deliver unto his master the servant that is escaped from his master unto thee: He shall dwell with thee, even among you, in that place which he shall choose in one of the gates [towns] where it liketh him best: thou shalt not oppress him." Wayland cited that proscription as evidence that Moses intended to abolish slavery because slavery could not indefinitely continue in a society where it was forbidden to surrender fugitive slaves. That same passage from Deuteronomy also formed the basis of an antislavery petition from the citizens of Albany, New York, that Senator William Henry Seward presented to the Senate in March 1850. The petition prayed that Congress pass no law regarding fugitive slaves that did not contain the passage from Deuteronomy forbidding the delivery of servants who had escaped from their masters.[34]

But Bledsoe argued that in their eagerness to appeal to the moral authority of Deuteronomy the opponents of slavery had misconstrued the actual context and meaning of the verses in question. He enlisted the learned opinion of the biblical scholar Moses Stuart to show that abolitionists had little understanding of the law of Deuteronomy relating to fugitive slaves or its relationship to other laws within the Mosaic code concerning slavery. Stuart, who died in 1852, had been the professor of sacred literature at the Andover Theological Seminary in Massachusetts. He was an authority on Hebrew, and his commentaries on the books of the Old Testament were widely received in matters of scriptural interpretation. Stuart was no friend of slavery, but his *Conscience and the Constitution* (1850) urged northerners to comply with the new Fugitive Slave Law.[35] He was also highly critical of what he believed was the abolitionists' misrepresentation of the attitude toward slavery in the Old Testament. In regard to the meaning of the passage from Deuteronomy, for example, Stuart contended that the first question to be asked was where did the master live? Was it among the Hebrews or among foreigners?

The language of the text made it clear that the law prohibiting the restoration of fugitive slaves did not relate to Hebrew slaves owned by Hebrew masters. It concerned only servants who had escaped from heathen masters and fled to Israel seeking asylum. Since those slaves were not Hebrews themselves and had not previously lived among them, they were not subject to the same laws in the Mosaic code that regulated the relationship between Hebrew masters and slaves. If the fugitive slaves had been Hebrews belonging to Hebrew masters, the injunction in question would not apply. The circumstances of the case mattered because the laws relating to Hebrew slaves were different from those pertaining to refugee slaves from outside Israel. Bledsoe believed that Stuart's interpretation of the law of Deuteronomy was the only acceptable one, since it harmonized one portion of the Old Testament with another regarding the status of slaves within Israel. It should not be supposed that the same legal code that upheld the right of Hebrews to own slaves would also encourage them to flee their masters. Bledsoe contended that the Albany petitioners and Seward had deceived themselves in believing that the return of fugitive slaves was contrary to the word of God. "But if we are not heathen idolaters, if the God of the Hebrews be also the God of Southern masters, then the Northern States do not violate the precept in question." There was nothing in Deuteronomy or any other part of the Mosaic code that prevented northerners from discharging "the solemn constitutional obligation" of remanding fugitive slaves.[36]

Charles Sumner held a different opinion. Contrary to the teachings of the gospel, charged Bledsoe, Sumner had decided for himself that the first duty of slaves was not obedience to their masters but to escape from them. In his speech against the Fugitive Slave Law delivered in the U.S. Senate in August 1852, Sumner approvingly quoted a verse from the American poet Sarah Wentworth Apthorp Morton (1759–1846) that urged slaves to flee their masters. A prominent Bostonian and early abolitionist, Morton regarded slavery to be incompatible with the founding principles of the American Republic. She gave voice to that conviction in her popular poem "The African Chief" (1792), which urged slaves to reclaim their natural rights by taking flight.

> Does not the voice of reason cry,
> Claim the first right that nature gave,
> From the red scourge of bondage fly,
> Nor deign to live a burdened slave."[37]

Sumner pronounced Morton's poem "a truthful homage to the inalienable rights" of bondsmen to break the chains of servitude. It was the necessity of that struggle against oppression that made fugitive slaves "the heroes of the age." Bledsoe stood amazed. He complained that, instead of acknowledging the divine instruction that slaves were to be obedient to their masters, Sumner had the effrontery to give them the nod to become runaways. "He appeals from Christ and his apostles to Sarah W. Morton."[38]

Sumner further avowed in an antislavery address given at the Metropolitan Theatre of New York in May 1855 that he saw no need to reconcile the texts of the Old Testament regarding slavery. Regardless of their significance, they were all allegedly absorbed or superseded in the New Testament, the tone and spirit of which were categorically hostile to slavery. Nor was he disposed to consider the exact meaning of the oft-quoted phrase "*Servants, obey your masters.*" He believed that "imperfect injunction" did not outweigh the greater Christian duty and commandment to love thy neighbor as thyself. That principle, he maintained along with Wayland, was entirely inimical to slavery. No degree of "ingenuity" or "apology" countenanced an institution that "tramples on man,—which defiles woman,—and sweeps little children beneath the hammer of the auctioneer." The only part of the scriptures that Sumner noted in his speech at the Metropolitan Theatre was the Epistle of Saint Paul to Philemon, in which Paul sent the slave Onesimus back to his Christian master, Philemon. Sumner introduced that missive with the remark that in the support of slavery "it is the habit to pervert texts and invent authority. Even St. Paul is vouched for a wrong which his Christian life rebukes."[39]

Those were fighting words. Bledsoe was determined to show that it was Sumner and other abolitionists, and not southern slaveholders, who distorted texts and concocted authority. He specifically responded to Sumner's claim that "when truly interpreted" the epistle to Philemon was actually "a protest against slavery, and a voice for freedom." Paul on another occasion had condemned "man stealers" or slave traders, which Sumner maintained was his real opinion regarding the evil of slavery. But Bledsoe affirmed that in defending southern slaveholders he was not defending man stealers or slave traders but rather vindicating the characters of masters and mistresses who lived by Christian precept and example against the aspersions of their detractors. "To take any free man," said Bledsoe, "whether white or black, by force, and sell him into bondage, is man stealing." Man stealing or slave trading was an "odious traffic" for which there could be no defense, but he denied that such was southern slavery. Bledsoe conveniently made no mention of the domestic slave trade of the South, which Sumner had so passionately condemned in his antislavery speech at the Metropolitan Theater.

Sumner also contended that, while it appeared that Onesimus was the servant of Philemon, it was by no means certain that Philemon had ever held him as a slave in the true meaning of the term. He further implied that if Onesimus was in fact a slave, it seemed likely that Paul had sent him back to Philemon with the request that he be emancipated.[40] Sumner's interpretation, though, was shared by the eminent theologian Albert Barnes, who was likely Sumner's authority in the matter. Barnes did not hesitate to state his conviction that the teachings of Christ and the apostle Paul were opposed to slavery and if acted upon would lead to its universal abolition.[41] And he specifically addressed the controversial question surrounding the Pauline injunction for Onesimus to return to his master, Philemon, in his *Notes, Explanatory and Practical on the Epistles of Paul to the Thessalonians, to Timothy, to Titus, and to Philemon* (1845) and in *An Inquiry into the Scriptural Views of Slavery* (1846). It was possible, Barnes speculated, that Onesimus might not have been the slave of Philemon but rather a hired servant or an apprentice. He argued that the Greek word used to describe Onesimus denoted a "servant of *any* kind," regardless of whether such an individual was a hired servant, an apprentice, or a slave. Since it was uncertain whether Onesimus was actually owned by Philemon, it should never be taken for granted that he was a slave proper. He might just as easily have been a hired servant or an apprentice.[42]

Bledsoe disagreed. He severely criticized Barnes's translation from the Greek and his subtle semantic distinctions regarding what the apostle Paul had actually meant in his epistle to Philemon. Barnes's interpretation, said Bledsoe, was nothing more than an attempt to confuse the obvious fact that the apostle had sanctioned slavery. If the word in question referred to a hired servant or a servant of any kind, as Barnes maintained, it was truly extraordinary that Greek lexicographers had not yet made the discovery. The Greek word used to identify Onesimus was the same word that invariably appeared in other passages of the New Testament in reference to slaves and in contexts that were altogether unambiguous. Thus it appeared that Onesimus was a slave of Philemon after all. The return of Onesimus was a concession of duty on the part of Paul that slaves should be returned to their masters—one entirely in keeping with the New Testament injunction for slaves to be obedient to their masters. However abstruse these quarrels might appear to us, they were taken very seriously at the time, since they related directly to the question of whether slaveholding was a sin.[43] Thus Bledsoe's exegesis into biblical criticism served an important purpose for those who denied that slaveholding was a transgression against divine law.

While it is most certainly true that abolitionists never convinced a majority of white southerners that they were living lives of iniquity, the question of whether the abolitionists or the defenders of slavery had the better part of the biblical argument has resulted in divergent opinions. Elizabeth Fox-Genovese and Eugene D. Genovese affirmed in the *Mind of the Master Class* that "to speak bluntly, the abolitionists did not make their case for slavery as a sin—that is, as condemned in the Scriptures. The proslavery protagonists proved so strong in their appeal to the Scriptures as to make comprehensible the readiness with which southern whites satisfied themselves that God sanctioned slavery." Eric L. McKitrick earlier arrived at the same conclusion, noting that the argument from the Bible in proslavery thought was "something more than an exercise in equivocation; it is strong historical exegesis, and on this plane the Southern divines clearly had the better of their Northern counterparts."[44] Nonetheless, those who believed it a Christian duty to state their indignation against the oppression and wrongs of American slavery did not feel constrained from doing so by the biblical sanction of slavery. An unidentified writer in the English literary and theological periodical the *Prospective Review* for November 1852, for example, dismissed those who defended slavery at the pulpit as "orthodox liars for God."[45] Stephen R. Haynes in *Noah's Curse* has challenged the Genoveses' opinion that the defenders of slavery had the better part of the biblical argument and also takes issue with their contention that race and slavery were largely unconnected in proslavery thought.[46]

Nor were the majority of white southerners the only ones who remained unconvinced that slaveholding was a sin. Many conservative northerners also distanced themselves from the doctrine that slavery was immoral. The *Princeton Review,* a conservative Presbyterian journal edited by Charles Hodge in Princeton, New Jersey, made a scathing indictment of abolitionists for allegedly placing themselves above the word of God in regard to slavery. And it is significant to note that Bledsoe ended his argument from the scriptures with the "just and impressive testimony" of the *Princeton Review* on the subject of abolitionism and the Bible: "The mass of the pious and thinking people in this country are neither abolitionists nor the advocates of slavery." They stood apart from the abolitionists because they disapproved of their principles. "As nothing can be plainer than that slaveholders were admitted to the Christian church by the inspired apostles, the advocates of this doctrine are brought into direct collision with the Scriptures." Since abolitionists seemed to consider themselves above the law of God, it was no wonder that they would likewise disregard "the laws of men."[47] While some northern clergy opposed slavery openly and supported antislavery political measures, the majority did not. No major denomination endorsed immediate emancipation before the war, much to the outrage of the abolitionists. John R. McKivigan has noted that "applying strict, evangelically defined standards of moral responsibility, the abolitionists believed that the northern as well as the southern churches were guilty of sanctioning slavery and should be branded as exponents of a proslavery religion."[48]

The great practical problem of slavery in the United States would not be decided by the abstractions of the abolitionists, said Bledsoe, but by consideration of the public good. The test of experience and the "sober lessons of history" were the only sure guides. "The Question" was to determine whether the practical results of emancipation would promote public order in the South or disrupt it. The problem at hand was not whether slavery should be introduced in the first place but what was the best social arrangement for communities in which the institution was customary and had taken deep root. "We are eternally told that Kentucky has fallen behind Ohio, and Virginia behind Pennsylvania, because their energies have been crippled, and their prosperity overclouded, by the institution of slavery." Bledsoe neither denied nor affirmed the charge, but it seemed to him to be an irrelevant consideration. "If the question were, whether slavery should be introduced among us, or in any other non-slave holding State, then such facts and explanations would be worthy of our notice." But, he continued, such was not the question. "We are not called upon to decide whether slavery shall be established in our midst or not." The matter had been decided long ago. Slavery was introduced under British rule "and that, too, against the earnest remonstrances of our ancestors."[49]

Even Bledsoe must have recognized, however, that the argument from inheritance was an inadequate defense of slavery. It begged the question as to why southerners had not made more of an effort to end an institution that had been "forced" upon them as an alleged matter of complaint. It did not absolve southerners of responsibility for perpetuating an institution that had become even more firmly entrenched since the achievement of American independence. The past was beyond the control of southerners but not the present and future. But the argument from inheritance, however hypocritical, shows in its own telling way that the prospect of abolishing slavery simply conjured up too many uncertainties and fears to be seriously considered by most white southerners. The assumptions were all against it. What assurances did southerners have that ending slavery would promote the public good? That question had to be answered first, said Bledsoe, before any scheme of immediate emancipation could be undertaken. If abolitionists were to convincingly speak to that point, they would have to go beyond moral condemnation and provide a practical example of a country in which the experiment of abolition had actually promoted instead of harmed the public good.

According to Bledsoe, one needed to look no further than the experience of emancipation in the British colonies to see its likely consequences in the American South. "Here we may see and taste the fruits of abolitionism, ere we conclude to grow them upon our own soil."[50] American abolitionists greeted the advent of emancipation in the British colonies with enthusiasm and joy. But what, asked Bledsoe, were the actual results of British emancipation? Defenders of slavery regarded emancipation in the British West Indies to be a reckless experiment that had resulted in decay, desolation, and distress. Bledsoe saw it as a tragic example of what happened when reformers and legislators allowed misguided philanthropy to overturn the lessons of experience. That the abolition of slavery in the British West Indies had been an unmitigated disaster was a trope commonly encountered in proslavery thought. Emancipation in the West Indies, moreover, continued to inform discussion of race relations in the United States during Reconstruction, as both southerners and the federal government were forced to come to terms with the difficulties associated with making the transition from slavery to freedom. An explicitly racist ideology regulated social relations between whites and blacks in both the British and the American emancipation experiences in response to what Thomas C. Holt has called "the problem of freedom" in former slave societies.[51]

The divergent responses of American abolitionists and defenders of slavery to emancipation in the British West Indies are most instructive of how ideology formed opinions on whether emancipation had been a successful experiment or a disaster. Ultimately it came down to whether one's sympathies were with the emancipated slaves or with the British planters who now had to pay wages and operate their businesses on a different footing. What was the greater human injustice: the perpetuation of slavery as a profitable concern or the economic difficulties attending the transition from slave to free labor? Were advances in human rights to be measured solely against the profits and losses of counting houses? The English banker, religious writer, and Quaker philanthropist Joseph John Gurney made no effort to disguise his empathy and compassion for the emancipated West Indian laborers in his *Familiar Letters to*

Henry Clay of Kentucky, Describing a Winter in the West Indies (1840). Gurney was active in the antislavery and prison reform movements in England, and his views were well known to likeminded reformers in the United States.[52] Given his longstanding commitment to emancipation, Bledsoe questioned the trustworthiness of his account of the conditions existing in the West Indies after emancipation. He characterized Gurney's glowing descriptions of the rising prosperity of Jamaica as the misrepresentations of an abolitionist who had closed his eyes to the signs of economic decline and social disarray that were everywhere to be seen.[53]

Bledsoe considered Robert Baird, John Bigelow, and Henry Charles Carey to be more impartial observers than Gurney, or least found their opinions better suited to his own argument that American abolitionists had deluded themselves in believing that West Indian emancipation had been a success. Drawing upon statistics and observations made by those British and American authorities, Bledsoe painted a bleak picture of what emancipation had wrought in the West Indies. He quotes testimony from Baird's *Impressions and Experiences of the West Indies and North America in 1849* (1850), Bigelow's *Jamaica in 1850; Or, The Effects of Sixteen Years of Freedom on a Slave Colony* (1851), Carey's *The Slave Trade, Foreign and Domestic* (1853), and the findings of three different British commissions sent to the West Indies in 1842, 1848, and 1850. Jamaica, the largest and once the most valuable of those colonial possessions, had reportedly become a land of closed ports, abandoned estates, and uncultivated sugarcane and coffee plantations that were rapidly reverting to a state of nature. Bledsoe made no concession to the justice and humanity of emancipation, arguing that the miseries resulting from that event unerringly marked it as an act of injustice and inhumanity that blighted the prosperity, hopes, and moral well being of an entire society—black and white.

The slaveholding interests of the American South were determined not to repeat the British experiment in freedom at home. Emancipation would most certainly lead former slaves to demand a full share of the rights and privileges enjoyed by white southerners based upon their claim of natural rights and equality. Bledsoe minced no words in stating his objection to granting southern blacks, be they bondsmen or freemen, equal rights and privileges. "For the government of these Southern States was, by our fathers, founded on the VIRTUE and the INTELLIGENCE of the people, and there we intend it shall stand. The African has neither part nor lot in the matter." The determination to maintain white privilege and power, so candidly confessed by Bledsoe, made the antebellum South what George M. Fredrickson has called "a *Herrenvolk* democracy"—a white man's republic whose existence was entirely dependent upon the suppression of black rights. Yet such attitudes toward blacks were not solely restricted to the South, as Bledsoe well knew from his years of residence in Ohio and Illinois. The idea of a *Herrenvolk* republic also had appeal in the North. Senator Thomas Corwin of Ohio, for example, supported African colonization as a means of removing the growing number of free blacks in the North through colonization.[54]

Defenders of southern slavery attempted to counter the abolitionists' charge that it was a degrading institution by advancing the argument that it both improved the conditions of blacks and promoted the common good. They attempted to blunt that indictment, H. Shelton Smith has noted, by favorably comparing the supposed condition of southern slaves to that of their African brothers and ancestors.[55] Bledsoe maintained precisely that position in response to an anonymous writer in the *Edinburgh Review* for April 1855 who made a wholesale indictment of American slavery. The master-slave relation "degraded the other into a brute," while the internal or domestic slave trade was "the worst of all the abominations" connected with American slavery. The writer did not believe that such "oppression" existed anywhere else in the world or had ever existed before. Yet that same author further observed that American slaves bore but slight resemblance to those who were brought to America from Africa in the days of the foreign slave trade. "Their dispositions have been softened, their intellects sharpened, and their sensibilities excited, by society, by Christianity, and by all the ameliorating but enervating influences of civilization." It seemed that what the writer called "the civilized Virginian," jeered Bledsoe, had somehow benefited from American slavery after all, even though it was the most "oppressive" form of subjugation that had ever existed.[56] It was Bledsoe's contention that southern slavery was a "school of correction" that elevated and improved the condition of slaves, which is similar to the representation of slavery made by Richard Fuller in his response to Francis Wayland. It is a depiction of slavery that would, moreover, have a long life in American historiography.[57]

There were many in the southern clergy, Bledsoe's good friend Leonidas Polk among them, who opposed abolition yet were committed to improving the conditions of slaves. It was an evangelical movement that Bledsoe sanctioned as evidenced by his qualified endorsement of slave literacy. He sincerely believed that slaves should be encouraged to read the Bible for the good of their souls. But he also wanted to deny the abolitionists such a potent and damaging argument against what defenders of slavery touted as being a benevolent and morally uplifting institution. He embraced the evangelical mission to the slaves advocated by Polk of Louisiana, James Henry Thornwell of South Carolina, James Hervey Otey of Tennessee, Charles Colcock Jones of Georgia, and other southern clergyman, even though he took no direct part in it himself.[58] It was that evangelical movement that for Bledsoe made the institution of southern slavery a "school of correction."

Defenders of slavery could represent slaves as happy, loyal, and contented children or as debased savages depending upon the requirements of their arguments. And it is equally true that opponents of slavery could be just as selective in their facts and representations as its defenders, as Bledsoe hastened to note. "The truth is, the abolitionist can make the slave a brute or a saint, just as it may happen to suit the exigency of his argument." If slavery degraded its subjects into brutes, as the writer in the *Edinburgh Review* maintained, then one would suppose that slaves were brutes. "But the moment you speak of selling a slave, he is no longer a brute,—he is a civilized man, with all the most tender affections, with all the most generous emotions." If the abolitionist's intention was to incite indignation against slavery, then slaves were brutes. But if the purpose was to arouse righteous anger against the slaveholder, "then he holds, not brutes, but a George Harris—or an Eliza—or an Uncle Tom—in bondage.[59] Bledsoe, of course, was equally adept at shaping facts and truths as best suited his own arguments. He could portray slaves as civilized Christians who greatly benefited from servitude or as a degraded segment of southern society that was unfit for freedom. His depictions of slaves reflect more on the observer than the observed.

The political and constitutional dimensions of the slavery controversy were its most intractable and divisive. Those issues are the subject of Bledsoe's concluding chapter on the Fugitive Slave Law of 1850. The topic brought his narrative within the realm of recent events. "It cannot be disguised that the Union, with all its unspeakable advantages and blessings, is in danger." Bledsoe described that measure as "that great constitutional guarantee of our rights." It was a protection that southerners were "the most inflexibly determined to maintain." He deprecated the "higher law" doctrine advocated by Senator William Henry Seward of New York. Seward declared that when the "higher law" of God and personal conscience were at odds with the Constitution and the laws of the country, it was the duty of all to reject them. Seward stated in a

Whig political rally in Cleveland, Ohio, on October 26, 1848, that the Fugitive Slave Clause of the Constitution violated "divine law" regarding the surrender of fugitives who sought refuge from slave catchers—another allusion to Deuteronomy 23:15–16. The requirement of that clause and the Fugitive Slave Law of 1793 that enforced it should be resisted. He exhorted northerners to "extend a cordial welcome to the fugitive who lays his weary limbs at your door, and defend him as you would your paternal gods."[60]

Senator Charles Sumner of Massachusetts took a similar position. Sumner supported the repeal of the Fugitive Slave Law of 1850 in his "Freedom National; Slavery Sectional" speech delivered in the U.S. Senate in August 1852.[61] Bledsoe assailed him as fiercely as he had Seward. While acknowledging the electrifying power of Sumner's address, he had nothing positive to say about the uncritical manner in which his assertions were accepted. Senator Samuel Portland Chase of Ohio, however, voiced the conviction that logically and historically Sumner's speech was "impregnable—entirely impregnable." It marked a new era in American history. Sumner himself asserted in supporting another motion to repeal the Fugitive Slave Law in February 1855 that the arguments made in his "Freedom National; Slavery Sectional" speech had never been answered. But Bledsoe retorted that the points made in that speech could be easily refuted. Sumner's history was "half fiction" and his logic "wholly false." His recital contained just enough truth to deceive and his logic just enough plausibility to convince those who were "waiting, and watching, and longing to be convinced."[62]

Bledsoe described Sumner's "Freedom National; Slavery Sectional" address as "distressingly disjointed," illogical, and devious. "Mr. Sumner," he wrote, "deems it necessary to refute the position that slavery is national, in order to set the world right with respect to the relations of the Federal Government to slavery." Sumner claimed that even though the relations of the national government to slavery were plain and obvious they were constantly misunderstood. "A popular belief at this moment," said Sumner, "makes slavery a national institution, and, of course, renders its support a national duty. The extravagance of this error can hardly be surpassed." Bledsoe accused Sumner of flailing at a straw man, for he and other southerners fully conceded that slavery was *not* a national institution. Slavery was not national but local, being restricted to certain states and exclusively established and perpetuated by them through state laws. "The question," said Bledsoe, "is not whether slavery is a national institution, but whether the National Government does not recognize slavery as a local institution, and is not pledged to protect the master's right to reclaim the fugitive from justice."[63]

Bledsoe suspected that Sumner's assertion that freedom was national and slavery sectional might possibly mean that it was the duty of the federal government to exclude slavery from the territories and admit no new slave states into the Union. "If this be his meaning, we should reply, then it is as foreign from the merits of the Fugitive Slave Law, which he proposed to discuss, as it is from the truth. The National Government has, indeed, no more power to exclude, than it has to ordain, slavery; for slavery or no slavery is a question which belongs wholly and exclusively to the sovereign people of each and every state or territory." It was a dubious statement. Congress had, in fact, banned slavery in the Northwest Territory and its future states in 1787 and restricted its extension by a geographical line under the Missouri Compromise of 1820. But Bledsoe had apparently convinced himself that in both instances Congress had exceeded its authority. His former support of the Wilmot Proviso as an Illinois Whig in 1847 must have been an inconvenient and perhaps even an unsettling memory. But Bledsoe now warmly seconded the opinion stated by President Franklin Pierce in his third annual message to Congress in December 1855. "If the friends of the Constitution are to have another struggle," said Pierce, "its enemies could not present a more acceptable issue than that of a state, whose Constitution clearly embraces 'a republican form of government,' being excluded from the Union because its domestic institutions may not, in all respects, comport with the ideas of what is wise and expedient entertained in some other state."[64]

The legal aspects of the slavery controversy were just as thorny as its political bearings and Bledsoe's grasp of them just as substantive and partisan. Northern legislatures passed personal liberty laws that prevented local authorities from remanding alleged fugitive slaves for trial in the South without first granting them due process within their own courts. Bledsoe argued that southern courts protected the rights of southern slaves and that the Fugitive Slave Law did not impair the right of trial by jury for fugitives. Those rights were upheld in southern states, he affirmed, and it was impertinent that the justice of southern courts should be gainsaid in the North. Bledsoe agreed that fugitive slaves had rights and were entitled to their day in court should they want it, but those trials should be in the courts of the states *from which* they had fled and not in those of the states *to which* they had fled. The presumption that fugitive slaves should be tried in northern instead of southern courts was a galling insult. Bledsoe acknowledged that the intent of the liberty laws was to protect free blacks from being kidnapped or wrongly accused of being fugitive slaves. Yet he was certain that the number of instances in which such abductions and indictments had actually occurred was greatly exaggerated.

The Supreme Court of the United States ruled in *Prigg v. The Commonwealth of Pennsylvania* (1842) that the personal liberty laws were unconstitutional because they in effect nullified the Fugitive Slave Law of 1793, thus denying slave owners their constitutional rights of recapturing fugitives in the free states. Yet Justice Joseph Story further ruled in the case that the Fugitive Slave Law applied only to the federal government and that it alone was responsible for helping slave owners recover fugitives. The states were not bound in the matter. Yet despite that decision more liberty laws were passed after the ruling in *Prigg v. Pennsylvania* and still more enacted after the Kansas-Nebraska Act in 1854.[65] Bledsoe and many other southerners regarded the personal liberty laws as northern nullification of the Fugitive Slave Clause, the Fugitive Law, and the rulings of Supreme Court—nothing more or less.

Salmon Portland Chase maintained that so long as the decision of the Supreme Court in *Prigg v. Pennsylvania* prevailed the nation would encounter serious difficulties, to which Bledsoe responded: "If it must be so, then so be it." If sectional comity within the Union could not be found under the Constitution and the decisions of the U.S. Supreme Court, said Bledsoe, it could not be found at all. "If the question be whether the decisions of the Supreme Court, or the dictation of demagogues, shall rule our destinies, then is our stand taken and our purpose immovably fixed. We have a right to peace under the decisions of that august tribunal." It was neither right nor proper that either party in the great controversy over slavery should decide the matter for itself. "Hence, if the abolitionists will not submit to the decisions of the Supreme Court, we shall most assuredly refuse submission to their arrogant dictation." Those in high places within the federal government who counseled resistance to the Constitution and the laws of the Republic were "guilty of a high misdemeanor."[66] Opposition to the Fugitive Slave Law weakened goodwill in the South and threatened the prosperity and perpetuity of the Union. Bledsoe was becoming more militant when he made that indictment but was still a Unionist. He still spoke sincerely about the advantages and blessings of the Union in 1856 but was deeply concerned about its future. He was watchman of southern rights and interests and a defender of slavery, but not yet a southern nationalist.

Portrait of Albert Taylor Bledsoe, ca. 1870. Albumen print, cartes de visite. Kuhn and Cummins, Photographers, Baltimore, Maryland. The Schlesinger Library, Radcliff Institute, Harvard University

Harriet Coxe Bledsoe with her children, 1845. Daguerreotype. Harriet, her
unidentified son (who did not survive childhood), and her daughter Sophia
Bledsoe. The Schlesinger Library, Radcliff Institute, Harvard University

Harriet Coxe Bledsoe, ca. 1880. Silver gelatin print. The Schlesinger Library, Radcliff Institute, Harvard University

Sophia Bledsoe Herrick, ca. 1875. Albumen print, cartes de visite. W. Kurtz, Photographer, New York, New York. The Schlesinger Library, Radcliff Institute, Harvard University

6

A SOUTHERN DISCOURSE

Replies to Liberty and Slavery

An Essay on Liberty and Slavery was Bledsoe's most important work. The treatise is the most comprehensive statement of his social and political theory he ever made. It launched his career as a southern spokesperson, for which undertaking he remains a key figure in southern intellectual history. Bledsoe's major reviewers hailed his exertions in defense of slavery as superior to all other previous efforts. It was a high compliment indeed given their erudition and the prominence of their own writings on the subject of slavery. Such discerning analysts as George Fitzhugh, Robert Lewis Dabney, and George Frederick Holmes praised Bledsoe's ingenuity, learning, and powerful style of argument. Other southern voices, some of them anonymous, replied to Bledsoe as well. The appraisals of those commentators are important cultural texts that place *Liberty and Slavery* within an expanded frame of reference. Reactions to *Liberty and Slavery,* moreover, spoke to the intersectional dimension of the slavery debate, the motives of proslavery authors, and the audiences they hoped to reach. About these subjects historians have disagreed. An analysis of the reviews of *Liberty and Slavery* together with a consideration of the divergent interpretations of proslavery writers by historians is the subject of the present chapter.

Most southern reviewers of *Liberty and Slavery* bestowed superlatives in recommending the work to the attention of their readers. That was not a unanimous opinion but certainly the prevailing one. Northern commentators, in contrast, virtually ignored the work. Brief notices appeared in northern periodicals, but formal reviews appear to have been entirely wanting. George Fitzhugh's writings received the same chilly reception, about which treatment Fitzhugh shrilly complained. Bledsoe must have been disappointed that his own work occasioned so little comment in the northern press. He had made a conscious effort to reach a conservative northern readership, even though he surely knew that proslavery literature was as unwelcome in the literary circles of the North as abolitionist literature was in the South. Yet such indifference is still somewhat surprising. Bledsoe's publisher, J. B. Lippincott and Company, a major Philadelphia publishing house, sold enough copies of *Liberty and*

Slavery to warrant a second printing in 1857.[1] One must conclude either that southerners purchased most of those two editions or that northern reviewers found the premises of the work so objectionable that they simply dismissed it out of hand. The abolitionist press, tit for tat, appears to have dismissed Bledsoe much as he had dismissed the Garrisonians in *Liberty and Slavery*. Bledsoe may have reached more northern readers than we know, but the sparse notice given *Liberty and Slavery* in the North would seem to suggest otherwise. The favorable judgments made about the work in the southern press, however, mitigated any annoyance that it did not merit more attention in the North.

A congratulatory assessment of *Liberty and Slavery* originally written for the *Southern Planter* simultaneously appeared there and in the *Southern Literary Messenger* in May 1856. Both periodicals were published in Richmond, and the review appeared by the joint arrangement of Frank G. Ruffin, editor of the *Southern Planter,* and John Reuben Thompson, editor of the *Southern Literary Messenger*. Ruffin solicited the appraisal from an unidentified friend who identified himself only as "R." Ruffin introduced R.'s review to the readers of the *Southern Planter* with the confident assertion that Bledsoe had placed the defense of slavery upon an unshakeable foundation. The author's attempt "to reconcile the dogmas of the Declaration of Independence with property in man" was a crowning success. Southerners could now maintain that the principles of the Declaration of Independence were true and also affirm "that negro slavery is in entire accordance with them without contradiction, and that it never was either a moral or political wrong, but a divine necessity." *Liberty and Slavery* was destined to become "the standard of its class."[2]

Bledsoe's reviewer "R." concurred in that opinion. He commended *Liberty and Slavery* as "the best fruit of the slavery controversy" and a triumphant vindication of the righteousness of southern slavery. The author ranged beyond the bothersome question of slavery itself and ventured into the field of political theory, where he closely investigated the relative rights of society and individuals. "The result of his enquiry is the best treatise on Government extant. Indeed, the publication of his book may well be considered an era in the history of political philosophy, inaugurating new principles and establishing them on a basis equally permanent with truth itself." Bledsoe's treatment of "the time honored fiction" of a social compact, whereby individuals purportedly give up certain rights originally held outside society in a theoretical state of nature, is credited with redefining the very grammar of political discourse. He had masterfully shown that "man is formed for society and society is reciprocally designed for man." The purpose of civil law and institutions was to protect the natural rights that were derived from the law of God. Bledsoe critiqued conventional ideas of rights and liberties and supplanted them with a theistic view of society and government that stressed duty and obedience to the rule of law.[3]

Yet R. also believed that Bledsoe made a statement that inadvertently subverted his argument against the abolitionists' interpretation of inalienable rights. Bledsoe held that if the general good required an individual to give up life and liberty, society could rightfully deny both. He acknowledged that all individuals possessed certain inherent and inalienable rights but that neither life nor liberty was among them. Yet the author had previously said that it was an error to define inalienable rights as those over which society had no control. He had defined inalienable rights as either those that individuals could not themselves alienate or transfer or those that society itself does not have the power to deny them. "According to the import of the terms," said Bledsoe, "the first would seem to be what is meant by an inalienable right." It seemed to the reviewer that by taking that position Bledsoe had actually adopted the abolitionists' view of an inalienable right as one that society itself could not deny an individual without doing wrong. "Was it necessary for his argument in behalf of slavery, to maintain that man has a right to alienate his life and his liberty? Had he not previously stated that 'society arises not from a surrender of individual rights,' and hence, need not appeal to the alienation of such rights in support of its powers? Was it wise to abandon this impregnable position for the purpose of maintaining that slavery is justifiable, because life and liberty are alienable rights?"[4]

Bledsoe responded to his reviewer in the next numbers of the *Southern Planter* and *Southern Literary Messenger*.[5] He wrote to thank the writer for his strictures no less than for his praise. Yet he regretted that so able a critic had charged him with self-contradiction and capitulation to the abolitionists regarding the inalienable rights affirmed in the Declaration of Independence and the Virginia Bill of Rights. The contradiction complained of by the reviewer, said Bledsoe, was more apparent than real. Nothing had been further from his intention than to suggest that it was an error for the abolitionists to define inalienable rights as those over which society had no control. Quite to the contrary, it had always appeared to him to be a perfectly legitimate interpretation of inalienable rights and one he had repeatedly used himself. Inalienable rights by definition were those that individuals cannot relinquish or transfer to society and which society cannot take from them. "Most assuredly, if we mean to combat the proposition of an adversary, we should take its terms as he intends them to be understood." But accepting the abolitionists' definition of inalienable rights was hardly the same as agreeing with their construction of them regarding the slavery controversy. "I adopt none of their views. I declare eternal hostility to them." He did not deny the correctness of their definition of inalienable rights, only that life and liberty were not everywhere and always inalienable. Both could be sacrificed if the public good required it. Slaves were entitled to the kind of government that best suited them and that also promoted the public order of southern society as a whole. And such, said Bledsoe, was the institution of southern slavery.[6]

Bledsoe's discussion of inalienable rights in relation to the slavery controversy confused others too. His position on the Declaration of Independence did not satisfy Edmund Ruffin. Ruffin noted in his diary on July 20, 1857, that he did not think Bledsoe's views were acceptable from what he called a southern point of view. "I objected to Prof. Bledsoe's book in defense of slavery, because it defends the indefensible passage in the Declaration of Independence, that asserts that 'all men are created equal,' instead of admitting it to be both false & foolish." That is not an altogether fair appraisal of Bledsoe's actual views. Nonetheless, his attempt to reconcile natural rights doctrine with the institution of slavery was unacceptable to Ruffin. After reading *Liberty and Slavery* a second time, he again noted in his diary that despite the reputation of the work it was in his opinion "much inferior to some of the earlier works of much less pretension."[7] Ruffin would have preferred less debate and more denunciation. He read and reread the works of Dew, Fitzhugh, Fletcher, Armstrong, Stringfellow, and Bledsoe, borrowing from them the arguments with which he agreed and rejecting those with which he did not. Adding his own thoughts on the slavery versus free labor debate into the mix, Ruffin authored several proslavery pamphlets between 1853 and 1860.[8]

George Fitzhugh held a much higher opinion of *Liberty and Slavery*. Fitzhugh favorably reviewed Bledsoe's work in the *Daily Richmond Enquirer*.[9] He particularly approved of Bledsoe's views on the origin of society and government and his strictures against Lockean notions of natural rights. "Man and society are congenital," said Fitzhugh. "He is born in society, [and] does not originate and form it. He may change, modify, improve and adapt it, but cannot make it, out and out." Individual rights owed nothing to an imagined state of nature but everything to the organic nature of society itself and the most fundamental wants and needs of human nature. That theory of society dated from Aristotle. But it had largely been forgotten after being replaced with Locke's theory of the social contract. "Locke's doctrine begins with disintegrating society, and then bringing the separate monads or human atoms together by a social contract, under which, each one surrendering equal amounts of rights, all would continue in a state of equality." Fitzhugh judged Bledsoe's organic concept of society to be the correct one and Locke's artificial notion a great and dangerous deception. Lockean theory was the progenitor of political revolutions—a doctrine that now also threatened to unleash a social revolution in the form of Mormonism, infidelity, free love, and anarchy. It would be far better if social and political arrangements were based on the trustworthy precepts of Aristotle's *Politics* than the dangerous ideas of John Locke.

Fitzhugh was impressed with the strength of Bledsoe's responses to the arguments against slavery advanced by the abolitionists. "He is modest as he is learned and ingenious, and does not push his theories to their ultimate but legitimate consequences. Probably his course is the most prudent and wise one for the time. He carries on no offensive warfare." Bledsoe laid down principles that justified southern slavery in general "and leaves their application to the exigencies of time, circumstances, and race." He defended the institution of southern slavery only and addressed himself to the alleged failure of emancipation in the West Indies. "He has probably left that offensive warfare which the starving, riotous, infidel and revolutionary state of free society invites, to other hands, or reserved it for the subject of another book. His work is '*totus, teres, et rotondus.*' It attempts enough, and does thoroughly what it attempts." Bledsoe did, indeed, leave the indictment of free society to others, most notably to Fitzhugh himself. He attacked the ideology of individualism he attributed to abolitionism but did not attack the system of free labor. He defended southern slavery against its accusers, but, unlike Fitzhugh and Henry Hughes, he neither touted slavery as an ideal social arrangement nor deprecated free labor.

An equally insightful review by Robert Lewis Dabney appeared in the *Presbyterial Critic and Bi-Monthly Review* for May 1856. Dabney was professor of ecclesiastical history at the Union Theological Seminary of Hampden-Sydney College. He and Bledsoe were complete opposites in their theology (Dabney was an Old School Presbyterian and a defender of Calvinism), yet both shared the conviction that southern slavery was just and sanctified by the scriptures. Dabney himself had defended the institution in a seven-part series entitled "The Moral Character of Slavery," which appeared in the *Richmond Enquirer* between April and May 1851. He argued that slaveholding was neither intrinsically immoral or unjust nor opposed to the authority of the scriptures.[10] Dabney's review of *Liberty and Slavery,* moreover, speaks directly to the intersectional dimension of the proslavery argument. Defenders of slavery, he affirmed, ran the risk of alienating conservative opinion in the North by taking extreme positions in the defense of slavery. The characteristic of Bledsoe's work that most appealed to Dabney was its relative moderation, which was precisely the quality that presumably would recommend his views to the attention of fair-minded readers in the North.

Dabney was an astute observer. He noted that Bledsoe's arguments reflected his background and previous experiences. He was born in Kentucky, where emancipation sentiment had once flourished, and spent several of his early years in Ohio and Illinois before moving to Mississippi. At no time during his residence in the North was he in any way directly connected with the institution of slavery or its interests. Bledsoe could be fairly regarded as "a man who has seen both sides, and who stands in an intermediate post of observation."[11] Having made that remark, however, Dabney anticipated the criticism that not being a slaveholder, or not being connected with an occupation involving slave labor, did not necessarily make Bledsoe an objective observer, especially after his years in Mississippi and Virginia. Abolitionists were likely to answer that the author of *Liberty and Slavery* spoke in the language of "self-interest" because he held a faculty position at a state university in a "'slave-breeding commonwealth.'" Dabney understood the argument implicitly but took exception to its underlying assumptions. Such accusations were yet another means by which abolitionists impugned the character of all southerners and not just the slaveholders they directly assaulted. Such charges were "offensive to public morality," for they seemed to take it for granted that candor, public virtue, and moral courage were dead in the South. It was an opinion that Bledsoe had expressed himself.

Dabney affirmed that if the debate about slavery was to produce any good for the country at large the propositions advanced in its defense "must be marked by a wiser moderation" and sounder arguments than had sometimes been the case. "The Southern cause does not demand such assertions, as that the condition of master and slave is the normal condition of human society, in such a sense as to be preferable to all others, in all times, and under all circumstances." Fitzhugh had made such arguments in defense of slavery, but Bledsoe had not. Assuming such a position disadvantaged the proponents of slavery by placing them in the position of being "the propagandists, instead of the peaceful defenders of an institution, which is, and will continue very naturally [to be] distasteful to their opponents; and they array the self-esteem of those opponents against them, by placing the discussion in an attitude, where the acknowledgement of the Southern cause must be a confession of Northern inferiority." Northerners would find such characterizations just as objectionable as southerners did those of the abolitionists. Fitzhugh's offensive campaign was problematic and disturbing, Bledsoe's defensive stance straightforward and reassuring.

The best policy for the South, declared Dabney, was to "take no ultra positions" on slavery and advance no unnecessary and invidious comparisons between the virtues of northern and southern society. If compromise and conciliation on the issue of slavery were to be found anywhere, it would be at the center and not at the extremes of debate. Dabney was content to argue, as Bledsoe had done, that the Old Testament sanctioned the existence of slavery among the Hebrews beyond a reasonable doubt. The southern institution of slavery was warranted because of the differences in social conditions existing between the white and black races, a position based upon the widespread presumption of racial inferiority shared by many white southerners: "That for the African race, *such as it is in fact,* such as Providence has placed it here, this [slavery] is the best, yea, the only tolerable relation." Bledsoe in Dabney's estimation had made that argument well and several others besides. And it was precisely because *Liberty and Slavery* was "marked by this just moderation in its positions" that he was willing to recommend it to the public.

By far the most incisive and substantive analysis of *Liberty and Slavery* was that written by George Frederick Holmes—Bledsoe's colleague at the University of Virginia. Holmes reviewed *Liberty and Slavery* in *De Bow's Review* for August 1856 and spoke of it in the most positive terms.[12] Bledsoe's treatise in his opinion redefined the terms of debate about slavery in a most satisfactory manner. Holmes fully agreed with him that the agitation of the slavery issue had produced at least one positive development. It had prompted southerners to inquire more deeply into the social and political principles upon which the institution of slavery was based, as well as the tenets of those who so acrimoniously assailed it. They compared the systems of slave and free labor and weighed the effects of each upon society. The eyes of the southern people had been opened to "the delusion and sophistry" of the abolitionists. Southerners (Holmes, like Bledsoe and Fitzhugh, confidently spoke in the aggregate) were now convinced of the complete propriety and justice of slavery as a domestic institution of the South. "Notwithstanding the speculative doubts by which the slave-owners were troubled, the general sentiment among them . . . has always tenaciously maintained the sanctity and inviolability of slavery." But the problem in the past had been that in making that claim they had not adequately understood or articulated the reasons that justified slavery and proved that it was both "right and expedient."

That situation had greatly changed. The necessities of southern society in regard to the question of slavery had called forth a new literature: "We shall be indebted to the continuance and asperity of this controversy for the creation of a genuine southern literature—in itself, an inestimable gain to our people. For out of this slavery agitation has sprung not merely essays on slavery, valuable and suggestive as these have been, but also the literary activity, and the literary movement which have lately characterized the intellect of the South." Southern society was self-consciously distinctive, and its imperatives demanded its own literature. Proslavery ideology intersected with a larger desideratum for the South to declare its literary independence from the North. The defense of slavery in Holmes's judgment was well calculated to do that, not as an isolated genre of controversial literature but as an integral part of a larger cultural movement based upon the distinctiveness and conservative nature of southern society. Thus the slavery controversy both reflected and fed a larger desire for cultural independence that, it was hoped, would one day be embodied in a distinctively southern literature.

Holmes had no criticisms or complaints to register in his review of *Liberty and Slavery,* which he declared a tour de force. He did, however, strike a note of disappointment. He regretted that Bledsoe did not draw more fully upon his years of experience as a resident of Ohio and Illinois in comparing the relative advantages and disadvantages of northern and southern society. "Professor Bledsoe has the further advantage of being equally at home at the North and at the South. Of Southern parentage and Southern birth, his education and his residence have been distributed between the two dissimilar sections of the Union." Those experiences had given him the opportunity of studying the institutions of the free states and those of the slave states in situ and comparing their respective effects on society. "It may be a matter of regret that he has not deemed it expedient to draw more largely on the private stores of information which he must possess in regard to this contrast; but it is manifest that this avoidance of all digression, and this unusual abstinence from all collateral topics, add to the cogency of the sole argument which he has undertaken to evolve."

Liberty and Slavery was "the most lucid" work that had yet been published on the subject. It was controversial yet animated by a "spirit" and "temper" that raised it "far above the level of ordinary polemics." The author "revels in the metaphysical conflicts and dialectical subtleties of philosophical controversy. He is acute, ingenious, and perspicacious." Holmes approved of the great severity and savor with which Bledsoe leveled his broadsides against Wayland, Channing, Seward, and Sumner. "We are not aware of any person in our country more accomplished or more dangerous in a logical encounter than Prof. Bledsoe." He credited him with having refuted the arguments of the abolitionists in the most complete and conclusive manner. "Prof. Bledsoe's essay is perhaps the most remarkable contribution which has been added to the literature of slavery. . . . He performs his office with the coolness as well as with the logical precision of a mathematician engaged in the solution of a geometrical problem." It was an apt analogy on Holmes's part and one that doubtless reflected how Bledsoe himself believed he was approaching the problem of liberty and slavery.

Bledsoe's views on the nature of liberty, said Holmes, furnished the elements of a more comprehensive political philosophy. Holmes had remarked in some of his previous writings that an adequate investigation of the slavery question would necessitate the creation of a new political science. The received maxims of political philosophy were riddled with "fallacies" that would have to be discredited, since they strengthened the representations of the abolitionists. Such popular misconceptions had to be discarded through "the careful re-examination and purification of political principles." Holmes affirmed that the respective works of Fitzhugh and Bledsoe confirmed the correctness of his earlier views. "They both rebel against the antiquated political doctrines; they both propound dogmas completely at variance with them, and inaugurate a new school of political speculation." The arguments and views advanced by Fitzhugh and Bledsoe had great utility for those like Holmes who saw the need for a new social and political ideology if the southern institution of slavery was to be successfully defended against its critics.[13] Holmes understood that it was only by inverting the assumptions and shibboleths of American political discourse, by rethinking American democracy in effect, that the defenders of slavery could bring forward new arguments and change the parameters and dynamics of the debate.

Holmes delighted in the dexterity with which Bledsoe turned the positions of his adversaries "like clay in the hands of the potter." He was relentless in ferreting out the supposed sophistries of his opponents and laying them bare. "Mr. Sumner did not receive a more complete or overwhelming castigation corporeally from the cane of Col. Preston Brooks than he sustains intellectually from the dialectical tortures of Prof. Bledsoe." Holmes appreciated the work's potential usefulness for ideological indoctrination: "No treatise could be more happily adapted to the function of implanting correct doctrines on the slavery question in the minds of students, and of guarding them in advance against the subterfuges and lubricities of the abolitionist sentiments and reasonings." He was particularly pleased with the way in which Bledsoe handled the antislavery biblical interpretations of Albert Barnes, which he endorsed as a complete refutation. Holmes was joined in that opinion by the English traveler James Stirling, who was no friend of slavery. Stirling believed that the southern institution was irreconcilable with "the common sense and moral sentiments of mankind" and that its days were numbered. Yet he was struck by the force of the metaphysical arguments advanced by its leading defenders. Stirling was far from uncritical in his comments on *Liberty and Slavery* yet believed that Bledsoe's handling of the scriptures in response to the abolitionists was "perfectly triumphant" and would be difficult to answer.[14]

Not all southerners were enthusiastic about *Liberty and Slavery*. A dissenting voice was that raised by Charles Brion Shaw, an instructor of civil engineering at the University of Virginia. Shaw had formerly worked as the engineer on the survey of the Covington and Ohio Railroad and as the engineer and superintendent on the South-Western Turnpike Road. His strictures against the innervating effects of slavery on southern character and institutions were those of a practical and well-educated man with firsthand experience in the use of slave labor in the building of roads and bridges. Writing anonymously as "A Citizen of the South" Shaw responded to Bledsoe in *Is Slavery a Blessing?*—a 120-page rebuttal published in Boston in 1857.[15] There are points of agreement between Shaw and Bledsoe regarding some of the alleged misrepresentations of the abolitionists and the dire consequences that would follow immediate abolition. Nonetheless, Shaw challenged several of Bledsoe's basic premises and conclusions. He endorsed the idea of voluntary, gradual emancipation as being in the best interests of both white and black southerners. Shaw's well-argued response to Bledsoe is a reminder that not all white southerners were fond of slavery. And the fact that he found it necessary to publish his reply anonymously in Boston says equally as much about the stifling of dissent in the South on the subject of slavery. As Shaw himself observed, the existence of that climate of opinion was yet another appalling price that southerners paid for their darling institution of slavery. There was no absence of Virginians and other southerners who disliked slavery, but few were willing to speak against it publicly without the cloak of anonymity.[16]

Shaw was not impressed with many of Bledsoe's arguments. He knew what all students of logic know: if one permits a disputant to make his or her own premises, the disputant can prove anything. He was convinced that southerners would be better served if they weaned themselves from the "fusillade" of proslavery arguments espoused by Calhoun, McDuffie, Dew, Stringfellow, Fitzhugh, and Bledsoe, to say nothing of the puerile offerings of county courthouse lawyers and politicians in the southern press. "The Paixhan gun of the whole battery is understood to be Prof. Bledsoe's 'Liberty and Slavery.'" He and his supporters touted the work as a "final and conclusive response" to the antislavery views of Wayland and Channing and their less moderate allies who contended for immediate emancipation. "In this inky contest, each section seems to read the arguments of its own advocates and no other. Fitzhugh and Bledsoe are denied a perusal in the North, as are Wayland and Channing in the South. The question, nevertheless, has a right and a wrong side. If truth has not been utterly prostrated and overwhelmed in the mire of controversy, she must have votaries in both the North and South, who are willing to hear an argument which is not, like and advocate's plea, wholly on one side."[17]

Shaw dismissed the staple argument that slavery was a blessing because slaves were incapable of governing themselves as an untested proposition. Given the restricted circumstances under which slaves lived, how were we to know? The present condition of slaves did not necessarily determine their future situation should the circumstances of their existence be altered. What was conditional was not inherent and irremediable, even though that very assumption had been advanced upon presumably scientific grounds within the racial theory of the master class. Shaw was unwilling to suppose that slaves were incapable of improving the state of their existence if given the chance. It was inconceivable to him that—contrary to the evidence of "progress toward millennial perfection" found throughout the globe—it was "the Creator's will to *perpetuate* the subjugation of man to man by means of the moral inferiority of one race to another." Slavery was at war with the attitude and mood of an age seeking enlightenment and progress. Before slavery could be entirely abolished, however, the slaves had to be prepared for freedom, for a premature abolition would find both blacks and whites unprepared for the event. There was no disagreement between Shaw and Bledsoe on that point. The circumstances in which numerous generations of slaves had been forced to live would have to change before slavery was abolished. Not only would the law of slavery have to change, but the attitudes and assumptions of white southerners would have to be altered too. Both southern whites and blacks would have to be progressively acclimatized to change. As an unidentified observer in the *North American Review* once commented, and Shaw approvingly quoted, the institution of slavery enslaved the entire South: "The white race is as much fettered to one end of the chain as the slave to the other."[18]

A means of effecting such fundamental change, Shaw argued, would be to hire free laborers from the North to introduce much-needed industrial skills into the South. It would take time to change the orientation and inclinations of southern society given its long dependence on slave labor. It would also take time to fit slaves with new industrial skills, since the mass of them were employed as agricultural workers or domestic servants. It would be more efficient to import these new skills from the North and, just as important, the new attitudes toward manual labor that would come with them. Free laborers would work for purpose (the self-interest of wages). The incentives and rewards were all wrong under slave labor—the dogmas of proslavery writers to the contrary notwithstanding—and the disparities in the industrial and educational capabilities of the North and South reflected that underlying problem. Slave labor was unquestionably profitable and produced great wealth, but it supported the prosperity of the few against the rights and interests of the many. Shaw's observations were by no means mistaken though certainly profane.

It should not be supposed, however, that Shaw was necessarily correct in his opinion that the introduction of free labor into the South would naturally and efficiently wean southerners from slavery. There were other scenarios. Southerners were so accustomed to the institution that, even if they could be brought around to embrace the use of increasing amounts of free labor, that did not mean that slavery would be abolished as a matter of course. Even though Shaw was adamant that slavery was an anachronistic and retrograde institution that hindered every aspect of southern society, culture, and prosperity, there were proslavery advocates who saw things differently. They did not regard the institution as an antiquated vestige of the past but as a work in progress. The conception of slavery as a static or stagnant institution was an altogether foreign one to those who defended it as a positive good. Southern slavery had changed much over the years. It would likely continue to evolve in responses to changes afoot in southern society just as it had since its distant colonial beginnings. Proslavery advocates maintained that the institution on the whole had become more humane and less brutal and that it performed a valuable civilizing mission. Henry Hughes, for example, believed that with the help of an authoritarian state the institution of slavery would accommodate itself to new exigencies and opportunities and would become a more and not a less important underpinning of southern society.[19]

Shaw spoke other heresies too. He showed no deference but only contempt toward the "privilege of caste" and the status conferred in southern society by owning property in slaves. He lamented that joining the slaveholding class, even among white mechanics, was a desideratum, even though he insisted that the perpetuation of slavery was directly opposed to their true interests. Although comparatively few white southerners would ascend to the ranks of slaveholders, they nonetheless devalued manual labor. Manual labor was slaves' work. Slavery under that view resulted in a self-imposed dependence on the North because it precluded the possibility of a more balanced and competitive economy developing in the South. The disproportionate influence of slaveholders in Virginia—and by extension the entire South—meant that the propertyless classes or needy poor whose interests were opposed to slavery were still dependent upon the patronage and influence of slaveholders for much of their livelihood. Concern over that issue, indeed, led some southerners to fear that they might one day have to defend slavery from *within* as well as from *without*.[20] There was a nagging anxiety that a significant number of southern whites might one day reject the leadership of the slaveholding elite and the social institution that gave them their wealth and power.

Shaw was uncertain how much slavery had affected the ministry of the gospel. He believed southern ministers to be as "single-minded and self-sacrificing" as any others in fulfilling their spiritual obligations. He would not sit in judgment on them regarding the issue of slavery, but he was troubled by the willingness of so many men of the cloth to defend the institution on moral grounds. He treaded lightly here but did not absolve the southern clergy of a duty he believed was theirs to fulfill. "We do wish, however, that whilst so many of them have suddenly discovered Divine authority in the existence, in some form, of slavery, they had been as zealous in enforcing such Gospel principles as seem to us to discountenance its perpetuity. Their situation is

one of difficulty, however. Public opinion will sometimes leaven the very purest characters, without their being conscious of it."[21] Ministers in the South
were under the same scrutiny regarding their orthodoxy on the slavery issue
as everyone else. It was a hard reality that confronted them at the pulpit and as
members of their communities at large.

Shaw did not single out southerners alone for his criticisms. He shared
Bledsoe's disdain for the demonization of slaveholders in the abolitionist press.
Southerners would have to recognize the pervasive and detrimental influences
of slavery on their society for themselves. They could not be browbeaten or
shamed into reform or dictated to regarding the manner in which slavery
might one day end. Emancipationists who assumed an imposing attitude in
the matter did their just cause no favors. It was high time for northerners and
southerners to ease sectional distrust and animosity by abstaining from their
mutual deprecations. It would be helpful if more northerners understood that
most southerners were polite, generous, hospitable, and God-fearing people—
qualities possessed by slaveholders and non-slaveholders alike. And it would
be equally advantageous if southerners appreciated that most northerners
were not callous, money-worshipping idolaters and were not abolitionists of
the "ultra school." It was a matter of profound regret that northerners and
southerners—"scions of a common stock"—had drifted so far apart that they
considered each other as dangerous foreigners. Sectional bigotry was the curse
of all and had brought the nation to the brink of disaster. "Fanaticism at the
North first begot the sophistry which defended slavery." Defenders of slavery
responded to the persistent abuse of the institution by the abolitionists until
the proclaimed beneficence of slavery assumed in the South the semblance of
a "religious truth."[22]

Proslavery ideology in the South was no more virtuous in Shaw's opinion
than the more extreme manifestations of abolitionism in the North. He was
certain, however, that the ideology of slavery was far more detrimental to the
South's true interests and future. And for Shaw that was the key point. His
comments were primarily directed at the manner in which southerners had
closed ranks behind the dogma that slavery was a positive good. He acknowledged that they had done so in reaction to the uncertainties and apprehensions occasioned by the prospect of immediate abolition. Southerners had
been pushed to "the brink of a precipice from which they may wildly leap if
urged too far." Mutual forbearance was the only acceptable course for ameliorating sectional rancor over slavery and saving an imperiled Union. "To the

North then we would say, 'hold back!' and to the South, 'go not on!'" He asked southerners to carefully consider their situation and whether their own peace and prosperity, the preservation of the Union, and "the obligations of humanity" did not require them to revise their institutions and laws so as "to make your slaves partakers of the universal progress of mankind." He rejected immediate abolition but believed that southerners should begin the necessary and difficult task of preparing slaves for freedom the soonest possible. They should do so not because abolitionists demanded it but because it was in their own best interests to do so. Shaw's forceful reply to Bledsoe deserves a wider reading than it received in his own day or since.

The absence of major reviews of *Liberty and Slavery* in the North indicates that most northern reviewers regarded the work as deserving no lengthy appraisal at all but only brief notices. *Putnam's Monthly Magazine*, for example, took only a few words to repudiate Bledsoe's elaborate defense of slavery. The author of *Liberty and Slavery* maintained "that the subjugation of one race of men by another is the very essence of human liberty, sanctioned explicitly by the moral law of the Bible, and amply sustained by the inductions of experience." The only thing more surprising than the speciousness of the argument was that it was so uncritically accepted by many southerners. "Strange as it may seem, it is still a fact that the interests involved in a particular culture, and the prejudices which it engenders, are able to mislead minds of some degree of original force, and of learning, into such a systematic perversion of all the dictates of nature, good sense, and religion." Everyone the world over knew that slavery still existed in the United States simply because it was believed to be the most efficient and profitable means of cultivating cotton. But since slavery was attacked upon moral grounds, southern writers were compelled to defend it in like manner. "It is a sorry exemplification of the facility with which the mind will often persuade itself that what it wants to be right is right. Professor Bledsoe writes with earnestness, and, now and then, eloquently; but his logic is very much out at the heels."[23]

Nor could Bledsoe have been pleased with, if he even knew, the harsh judgment rendered against him in the *Leader*—a political and literary review published in London. Copies of *Liberty and Slavery* were on hand in London through Trubner and Company almost as soon as the work became available in the United States, if not simultaneously, suggesting that Lippincott and Grambo had sent Trubner advance copies. The anonymous English reviewer found the work to be "triumphant in tone" but weak in logic. More was to be expected of a professor of mathematics whose mind had been trained in the logic of mathematical relations and solutions. "We have seldom met with propositions more feebly supported or handled, or deductions more illogically drawn." The author assumes and asserts the degradation of the African race and then proceeds to justify southern slavery because slaves are unfit for any higher or nobler state. "Who told him they are unfit for a higher state than slavery?" The reviewer found Bledsoe's selective use of facts equally unconvincing. "Facts, Professor Bledsoe? Tearing children from their parents, parents from their children; forcing them to labour beyond their strength, cruelly scourging and torturing them—are these not facts?" The reviewer summarily dismissed the book as "a mass of declamatory verbiage."[24]

Historians have sometimes been at cross-purposes in explaining the intentions of proslavery authors and identifying the audiences for whom they wrote. Did the advocates of slavery write primarily, if not exclusively, for other southerners? Whereas William Sumner Jenkins viewed proslavery literature as an unapologetic justification of southern slavery submitted to "the world tribunal," Ralph E. Morrow questioned the validity of that interpretation. He saw proslavery propaganda as being aimed at a local constituency to ensure orthodoxy on the subject at home.[25] David Donald seconded Morrow's opinion regarding the motives and intended audience of proslavery writers and stated the case with even greater assurance. "The motives of these proslavery writers were less evident than their industry. It is by no means clear to whom their treatises were addressed or just what results they expected to produce through their circulation." Donald was fairly certain, however, that the proslavery writers of the 1840s and 1850s entertained no hope of reaching or convincing a northern audience. "It is evident from even a sampling of the proslavery writings in the last two decades before the war that southerners were not writing for a northern audience."[26]

Yet in making those declarations Morrow and Donald failed to make the critically important distinction between northern abolitionists and northerners generally, especially among the conservative members of the Democratic Party, the Democratic press, northern churches, African colonization societies, and, most important of all, northern merchants, whose economic interests were directly tied to the lucrative cotton trade.[27] Abolitionists were reviled as disturbers of the peace and prosperity of the nation in those circles as well. There was no absence of northern Democrats who were willing to make common cause with southerners in the defense of slavery, especially within the

Buchanan wing of the party. Southerners were perceptive enough before 1860 to see that some northerners shared their concerns regarding abolitionism and other "isms" that had supposedly infected northern society.[28] Defenders of slavery appealed directly to their conservative counterparts in the North who they had good reason to believe would be open to at least some of their claims regarding the principles of abolitionism. The *Princeton Review*, for example, denounced the abolitionists' "anarchical opinions" on civil and ecclesiastical government and especially those pertaining to the rights of women. "Let these principles be carried out, and there is an end to all social subordination, to all security for life and property, [and] to all guarantee for public or domestic virtue." The writer considered the "disgusting and disorganizing opinions" of the abolitionists on the role of women in society to be just as abhorrent as did many conservative southerners.[29] These were, indeed, the very sentiments to which Bledsoe made direct appeal at the close of his argument from the scriptures in *Liberty and Slavery*.

Defenders of slavery knew their potential allies as well as their enemies. Fitzhugh made a conscious effort at appealing to those in the North who also feared the potential results of "immediate emancipation." He knew that abolitionists appeared to some northerners as fanatics whose views on the rights of blacks and women were just as disquieting to them as to their counterparts in the South. Fitzhugh exhorted southern writers in 1857 to make common cause with the conservative element of northern society by affirming shared values and launching an offensive campaign against the dogmas of northern fanaticism. Every charge of the abolitionists had to be answered at the lectern and in the press, as well as in books and essays. The cause of conservatism, he affirmed, was that of government against anarchy, religion against infidelity, private property against agrarianism, and of "female virtue" and Christian marriage against the doctrine of "free love."[30] Concern over such issues, although exaggerated, was nonetheless real and not exclusively confined to the South. Most certainly defenders of slavery wanted to convince southerners of the justice of the institution they so often found it necessary to explain. A significant portion of proslavery literature was unquestionably intended for local consumption. Yet it is unwarranted to assert that by the 1840s and 1850s defenders of slavery had "abandoned" all hope of reaching a northern audience. They most certainly had not forsaken the conservative elements of northern society to which they made direct appeal.

Ignoring the abolitionists accomplished nothing. Defenders of slavery knew it would be utterly self-defeating if they preached only to southern choirs. The fact that they understood the burden under which they labored in defending slavery did not mean that they had forfeited the North to the abolitionists, who, however vocal and influential, were still a minority. Chancellor William Joseph Harper of South Carolina stated his displeasure at the "indisposition of the rest of the world to hear anything more on this subject." Northerners, Harper further complained, seemed oblivious to the fact that there was even an argument to be made in defense of slavery. George Fitzhugh similarly expressed anger over "the silent contempt" with which northern periodicals ignored his works—a cool treatment also accorded Bledsoe's *Liberty and Slavery*. But it does not follow that Harper, Fitzhugh, and Bledsoe had not made a conscious effort to reach northern readers or to *directly* answer the abolitionists. Fitzhugh's willingness to debate Wendell Phillips in New Haven, Connecticut, in 1855, indeed, suggests that he wished to be heard in the North, even in the hostile environs of New England. He was not writing and speaking exclusively for southerners.[31] Proslavery apologists like Fitzhugh and Bledsoe were still debating the rectitude of southern slavery with the abolitionists, since that was the only way they could reach a larger northern audience.

It is likewise true that George Frederick Holmes did not believe that the defense of slavery would change the hearts and minds of abolitionists. But again it is just as important to note that the majority of northerners were *not* abolitionists. Holmes spoke directly to this very point in the *Southern Quarterly Review* for January 1843. "We trust that they [the proslavery pamphlets under discussion] may be of service in convincing the North of the folly and impropriety of Abolitionism; but, for our own part, we think it is hardly to be expected that anything which can be said at this late date, in defense of slavery, as an institution, will at all diminish the wrongheaded fanaticism and perverse intolerance of the Northern Abolitionists." Holmes considered the disease of abolitionism to be "past the cure of argument." He further believed that proslavery literature was "capable of doing good service within our own borders, by bringing forward other arguments besides the plea of necessity, which, if they be not as strong as the latter, are less likely to be disputed." But Holmes made that comment in reference to northern abolitionists only. It should not be inferred that he believed that northern society as a whole was beyond reach. Indeed, he trusted that defenses of slavery would be helpful in convincing northerners of "the folly and impropriety of Abolitionism."[32]

Nor was Holmes alone in adopting such an attitude. Dr. Samuel Cartwright of New Orleans highly recommended John Fletcher's 637-page *Studies on Slavery, in Easy Lessons* (1852) to the readers of *De Bow's Review* because of the salutary effect it would likely have on northern readers. "The lessons will be doubly useful to the North, as they untie the knots and meshes of that web of sophistry which has entangled the intellectual and moral faculties of northern people, and made them the *slaves* of false doctrines."[33] Seldom has the truism that one person's faith is another's heresy stood in bolder relief than in the debate over slavery. Northerners and southerners, it is true, often talked past each other on the issue of slavery, but they did not ignore each other in any meaningful sense. The slavery debate, indeed, makes little sense on any other supposition.

Bertram Wyatt-Brown has suggested that much of what has been written on proslavery and antislavery intellectuals has failed to recognize the social realities of that broader intersectional conversation. "Had both sides spoken only to the broad ranges of their respective regional classes, they could have ignored the counterthrusts of distant opponents. As it was, however, proslavery and antislavery writers wrote for a common, generally well-read, and civically engaged public, North *and* South. . . . To treat the causes as if their spokesmen had only discrete, local constituencies in mind would miss the major point of sectional, literary controversy." Larry E. Tise has in much the same way drawn attention to the significance of the interregional aspects of proslavery thought and the importance of thinking of it in an expanded geographical and chronological context.[34] Bledsoe is a conspicuous case in point. Like other proslavery propagandists, he most assuredly wrote for southerners but not only for them. He also hoped to reach those in the North who he knew from his years of residence in Ohio and Illinois were less than enamored of abolitionists and free blacks. Neither Bledsoe nor other proslavery writers were disposed to forfeit the arena of public opinion in the North to the abolitionists without a contest.

Defenders of slavery wrote for an intersectional audience regardless of whether they chose northern or southern presses to bring forward their works. Publishing in the North, however, at least promised a potentially larger audience. The major publishing firms were in the North, as well as most of their agents and distributors. Bledsoe chose to have *Liberty and Slavery* published in Philadelphia by J. B. Lippincott and Company instead of a southern press for precisely that reason. Likewise, Henry Hughes chose to have his *Treatise on Sociology* published in Philadelphia by Lippincott, Grambo and Company. Yet even southern publishers who found it difficult to compete with the resources of northern publishing houses and markets did not want their defenses of slavery to be read by southerners *only*. The Augusta, Georgia, publisher M. P. Abbott of Pritchard, Abbott, and Loomis, for example, expressly stated that the company wanted to secure a wide readership for E. N. Elliott's *Cotton Is King, and Pro-Slavery Arguments* (1860) in the North as well as the South. It was a plan of which Bledsoe heartily approved and that he personally recommended to the attention of Jefferson Davis.[35]

Historians have similarly struggled to comprehend why southern intellectuals could be so ardent in the defense of so objectionable a cause. The fact that most white southerners did notthemselves view the institution as being abhorrent has fallen short of an adequate explanation of their motives. According to some historians, validations of slavery had to be based on feelings of angst, guilt, or ulterior motives. These scholars have suggested that defenders of slavery were attempting to convince themselves of the righteousness of the institution as a means of mitigating feelings of guilt and shame over its deviation from America's democratic principles. And perhaps, indeed, they were. David Donald, however, has posited an alternative explanation. Donald concluded that the social contexts of the defenders of slavery he investigated (Bledsoe was not among them) suggested that these ambitious writers "all were unhappy men who had severe personal problems relating to their place in southern society. . . . Most looked back with longing to an earlier day of the Republic when men like themselves—their own ancestors—had been leaders in the South." Frustration and failure are keynotes in Donald's interpretation. Defending slavery was a means of proving a writer's worth and elevating his standing within a conservative society that placed a premium on orthodoxy regarding the subject of slavery.[36]

Drew Gilpin Faust has argued that the relationship of southern intellectuals to the defense of slavery is perhaps best characterized as a stewardship, the understanding of which lies in how intellectuals perceived their roles in southern society generally and in reference to the slavery issue specifically. Southern intellectuals defended slavery as a means of articulating their values and defining themselves within a society that by and large did not set great stock in intellectuals. Faust's thesis is more helpful in explaining the aims or objectives of these writers. It allows intellectuals from a variety of social backgrounds to embrace the defense of slavery for multiple reasons without attributing their motives to the guilt thesis (psychological "guiltomania" as Faust has called it), anxiety, or maladjustment. Yet Faust also argues that many of the more puzzling aspects of proslavery thought are best understood as expressions of alienation: the special psychological needs of an estranged southern intellectual class concerned with questions that ranged well beyond the rights and wrongs of slavery.[37] Bledsoe was certainly part of the southern intelligentsia, and his varied interests extended well beyond the slavery controversy. Like his colleague George Frederick Holmes at the University of Virginia, he clearly viewed his role in southern society as being that of a steward. Bledsoe was certainly not immune from the desire to be honored by his community, and in a slaveholding society that required something more than a token bow to orthodoxy on the subjects of slavery and states' rights. Nor should it be supposed that he did not possess his share of special needs and aspirations as a southern academician. It may well be that Faust's model of the estranged and marginalized intellectual explains him as well as any other. Yet it is not readily apparent how a sense of isolation, rejection, or special needs motivated Bledsoe to make a systematic defense of slavery or, for that matter, to write on any other subject. He is, take him all in all, something of an enigma.

Bledsoe's motives for defending the institution of slavery are admittedly not easy to read. Another explanation that seems just as probable and convincing as guilt, opportunism, situational ethics, and alienation is Bledsoe's sense of honor and duty. Bertram Wyatt-Brown has explored the language and symbolism that defined the southern idea of honor and duty, a moral code that regulated rhetoric and ethical behavior in the slaveholding South. That was true of issues other than slavery as well. But nowhere were the concepts of honor more intimately connected with self-perceptions than among slaveholders and their defenders. As Wyatt-Brown has observed, "If honor had meant nothing to men and women, if they had been able to separate it from slavery, there would have been no Civil War."[38] Honor and duty were conscious values with which Bledsoe was deeply concerned. His response to abolitionism in *Liberty and Slavery* was as much a defense of the ethics and character of slaveholders as anything else. He could no more separate the idea of honor from defending slavery than he later could from validating secession and the righteousness of the Lost Cause. The ethical principles and ideals of honor and duty were deeply ingrained in Bledsoe as a West Point cadet and were no less conspicuous in the precepts of his moral philosophy and theology. The self-declared duty to defend southern honor became a defining characteristic of Bledsoe's writings from 1856 onward and must be taken seriously.

Bledsoe's contribution to proslavery thought built upon the work of his predecessors and reflects many of the same concerns expressed in the writings of his contemporaries—most notably those of Holmes and Fitzhugh. Yet Bledsoe's defense of slavery differed from the arguments made by both writers in important ways. He showed no interest in attacking the alleged failure of northern society or indicting free labor as a means of deflecting criticism of slave labor. Eric L. McKitrick has argued that it was that aspect of the defense of slavery that had the least contemporary appeal for southerners and was the first to be forgotten after the Civil War and emancipation. Drew Gilpin Faust has similarly noted that historical interest in Fitzhugh, who has received the lion's share of attention, ironically appears to be largely due to "his very unrepresentativeness."[39] It is interesting to note, for example, that while a 187-page abridgment of Bledsoe's *Essay on Liberty and Slavery* appeared in E. N. Elliott's *Cotton Is King, and Pro-Slavery Arguments* (1860), neither Henry Hughes nor George Fitzhugh found a place.[40] Michael O'Brien has observed that the omission of Hughes and Fitzhugh from Elliott's anthology of proslavery thought is not a matter of surprise. "Both writers had been greeted with puzzlement, as eccentric and deviant, with no place in so safe a work as Elliott's *Cotton Is King.*"[41]

Bledsoe kept more to the mainstream of proslavery thought. He was content to defend the morality of slavery, advance the argument from the public good as to why the institution was necessary, and make a legalistic defense of the institution's constitutionality. He made no appeal to the argument from ethnology advanced in the respective writings of Dr. Josiah Clark Nott and Dr. Samuel A. Cartwright or to the sociology of Hughes and Fitzhugh. Yet his contribution to proslavery thought, if not as original as the arguments made by Hughes and Fitzhugh, had greater currency among his contemporaries. The views and opinions expressed in *Liberty and Slavery* are more representative of what most white southerners thought and spoke about the institution of slavery and its relationship to the deteriorating state of the Union. Even some of Fitzhugh's fellow apologists—notably Holmes, Dabney, and Ruffin—found his ideas strange and in many ways unacceptable. The question of representativeness raised by Drew Gilpin Faust looms large and suggests an inverse relationship between the significance of these individuals in their own day and the later assessments of historians.

But that does not mean that Bledsoe's defense of slavery was altogether conventional. His attempt to reconcile natural rights with slavery was unusual and a matter of complaint for Ruffin. While southerners had long argued that slavery was consistent with natural law, that was not the same as contending that it was compatible with natural rights. Defenders of slavery, Mitchell Snay has noted, developed a conservative interpretation of natural law as a means of repudiating the natural rights doctrine of the American Revolution. Indeed, it was a stronghold in the legal defense of slavery. James Philemon Holcombe (1820–73), the professor of equity jurisprudence at the University of Virginia, is a prime example. Holcombe argued that slavery was consistent with natural law in an address delivered before the Virginia State Agricultural Society in Petersburg on November 4, 1858, which appeared in the *Southern Literary Messenger* that same year. As Eugene D. Genovese has noted, however, Bledsoe's attempt to reconcile the defense of slavery with natural rights instead of natural law "looked increasingly idiosyncratic among proslavery theorists."[42]

Writers like Henry Hughes, George Fitzhugh, and Albert Taylor Bledsoe created a new vocabulary of proslavery argument—Bledsoe a conservative political theory of conditional liberty and Hughes and Fitzhugh a new sociology that affirmed the proclaimed virtues of southern society. Each in their own way gave southerners new grounds for defending slavery. The *Richmond Enquirer* in January 1857 characterized the changed attitude toward slavery in the South thusly: "It is within the memory of very young persons, when nobody in this country ventured to defend Slavery on principles of abstract justice and moral propriety. People of all classes and conditions united in stigmatizing it as a wrong and an iniquity." They now thought and spoke differently. "Slavery in the South no longer exists by sufferance of an insincere moral sentiment, but finds an impregnable stronghold in the affections, convictions, and interests of our people." Proslavery intellectuals had done their work. "We have, indeed, a proslavery literature."[43]

Yet for all the confident assertions made in defense of slavery, there was still an uneasiness or internal tension within proslavery thought. As the English traveler James Stirling remarked in *Letters from the Slave States* (1857), the slaveholders themselves seemed to have lingering doubts about the justice of the institution they so vigorously justified. After making a detailed comparison of Fitzhugh's *Sociology for the South* and Bledsoe's *Essay on Liberty and Slavery*, Stirling rendered the following verdict.

> With all his loud assertion, I do not believe that the slave-holder is thoroughly persuaded in his own mind of the truth of his doctrines. His creed, like many other creeds, is reiterated all the oftener and the more loudly from a lurking doubt of its perfect truth. The slave-holder

> defends his position ostensibly against the Abolitionist; but in reality against his inner self. Hence, too, his impatience of contradiction; his faith is all in all to him: therefore to doubt is to wrong him. Heresy is not only a blunder, it is a crime. And yet slave-owners cannot avoid the subject. They eternally introduce it. They are ill at ease, and must try to convince.[44]

Whether Bledsoe shared any of the misgivings that Stirling attributed to the defenders of slavery can only be surmised. Yet he was far too good a polemicist not to understand the burden of his own arguments.

Despite Bledsoe's self-assured criticisms of the abolitionists, however, he failed to answer several of their most fundamental complaints. His evasions are as numerous as they are telling. While he was unwilling to defend slave illiteracy as a matter of his own religious conscience—he explicitly affirmed that slaves should be encouraged to read the Bible—he was conspicuously silent about other insidious characteristics of the institution. He said nothing about disavowing the legitimacy and inviolability of slave marriages under the slave codes even though those laws contravened God's own instructions. And he largely dismissed concern about the existence of cruel and indifferent masters as figments of the abolitionists' imaginations. Nor did he respond to moral condemnations of slave auctions, which severed family and community ties by sending millions of men and women from the Upper South to the Lower. He likewise avoided the question of whether the state of "degradation" he arbitrarily assigned to the African race, which purportedly made them unfit for freedom, was an immutable or a remedial condition. Did blacks possess the same human nature and the same capacity for improvement as whites? Or was it, as the abolitionists maintained, the institution and laws of slavery that accounted for the disparities existing between southern whites and blacks? It was an inquiry he conveniently averted. Bledsoe was content to simply make the self-serving charge that the institution of slavery was the type of government best suited to the presumed capabilities of southern blacks. While those views and opinions resonated with like-minded southerners, they fell far short of adequately answering the objections of those who challenged the slave regime as uncivilized and morally reprehensible.

7

BROKEN FAITHS AND COVENANTS

Sectionalism, Secession, and War

THE EARLY PART OF 1860 FOUND Bledsoe comfortably entrenched at the University of Virginia, where he had been a faculty member for six years. At least for the moment, life at Charlottesville continued in its normal courses. Bledsoe was at the apogee of his academic career. He was widely known in southern intellectual circles as a scholar, teacher, and the controversial author of *A Theodicy* and *Liberty and Slavery*. Nor was his reputation confined solely to the South. In mid-February 1860 Bledsoe traveled to the nation's capital, where he lectured at the Smithsonian Institution on the topic "The Social Destiny of Man." The full text of those addresses is not known to have survived. Nor does it appear that they were ever published. But the *National Intelligencer* gave an account of the first lecture. It is a clear statement of Bledsoe's social and political views on the eve of secession and war.[1] The most important sign of the times, he said, was a tendency toward "excessive individualism." It was a phenomenon that bore directly on the social destiny of humankind, the laws of the state, and the presumed lessons of history. Bledsoe's critique of the extremes of individualism he attributed to American democracy is congruent with his earlier indictment of abolitionism in *Liberty and Slavery*. It also reflected convictions and concerns shared by George Frederick Holmes, George Fitzhugh, and many northern intellectuals as well.[2]

Whereas in the days of ancient Greece and Rome the state dwarfed the individual, Bledsoe affirmed, the individual now threatened to overwhelm the state. Individualism without restraint was "faith without principles," which was certain to devolve into fanaticism. Good intentions themselves were not proper limits or restraints upon individualism, since they were often accompanied by ignorance and vanity. The good intentions of individuals should always be regulated by the intentions and needs of society at large. "The consciences of individuals differ, and, for united and harmonious action, some guide should be selected that will apply equally to all." That conductor should be the final arbiter of differences in matters of conscience. The Constitution of the United States was one such mediator and the only one that should direct the affairs of the nation. If ever there was a political theorist who set his faith in a nation of laws and not of people, it was Albert Taylor Bledsoe.

Bledsoe chose his words carefully in explaining why the Constitution should be the final arbiter of political disputes instead of the "higher law" of individual conscience. The distinction is a clear reference to the well-known appeal to a "higher law" than the Constitution—the moral law of God and individual conscience—made by William Henry Seward on the floor of the U.S. Senate in March 1850, even though neither Seward nor his speech is mentioned by name. Bledsoe berated Seward's doctrine in *Liberty and Slavery*, where he argued that slavery was not incompatible with the law of God and indicted Seward as being an enemy of the Constitution. Yet he showed more restraint in his Smithsonian lectures as befitted the venue and occasion. The virtue of making the Constitution a law higher than individual conscience was that it aimed at promoting the greater good of all the constituent members of society. That could be done only if the Constitution had the authority to alleviate and negotiate differing and sometimes antithetical convictions. "It [the Constitution] is a conscience higher and broader than that of any individual." The restraints of constitutional law were designed not to prevent people from obeying their individual conscience—for that is their duty—but rather to prevent them "from encroaching upon and breaking into the consciences of others."

Individualism tended to run to excess and degenerate into self-indulgence and moral decadence. The history of Rome, said Bledsoe, was a case in point. "The Epicurean principles had seized upon the vitals of Rome long before she took to Epicurean philosophy. Evil lives cause error as truly as error causes evil lives; and the same fixed relation between fatality and error reigns everywhere." The excessive individualism that Bledsoe attributed to his own age struck him as being analogous to the corrupting influences of Epicureanism upon the greatness of Rome. He alluded to the observation made by Montesquieu in his *Thoughts on the Causes of the Greatness and Decline of the Romans* (1734) that Epicureanism corrupted the moral character of Roman society and was a cause of its gradual decline.[3] Epicureanism was an ancient form of licentiousness that in Bledsoe's view had its counterpart in the extreme individualism he attributed to his own day. Concern over the dangers arising to society from excesses of individualism, however, was far from unique to Bledsoe. His colleague George Frederick Holmes expressed similar sentiments three years earlier, attributing the enthusiasm for reform in the North to an exaggerated and misplaced idea of liberty and individualism. It was that erroneous concept of individualism, Holmes contended, that explained the various "isms" of the North, including the "multitudinous heresy of abolitionism." Mitchell Snay has observed on this very same point that "abolitionism was portrayed as part of a dangerous apotheosis of the individual."[4]

The Smithsonian lectures were well received. They earned Bledsoe an invitation from Joseph Henry, the secretary of the Smithsonian Institution, to repeat them at any such time as was convenient.[5] The *National Intelligencer* described Bledsoe as a man of great intellect. "He is evidently a great thinker, and his attainments are vast. As a metaphysician he has no superior in this country." It was further reported that an unnamed English authority had gone so far as to compare Bledsoe to the French philosopher and educator Victor Cousin (based on Bledsoe's *A Theodicy*), referring to Bledsoe as "the Cousin of America." As a lecturer, however, Bledsoe had his faults. "His manner is stiff, and perhaps awkward; his enunciation is indistinct, and his deliberation is more studied than natural."[6] Nonetheless, his lecture was reported to be interesting and to have closed with a beautiful appeal to his audience. He called upon them to avoid shallow intellectual systems that placed appeals to individual conscience above all other social considerations. There can be no doubt as to whom that comment was directed. The remark was yet another arraignment of abolitionism, albeit a muted one.

George Fitzhugh heartily approved of the views expressed in Bledsoe's Smithsonian lectures. Bledsoe's strictures against the baneful consequences of unrestricted individualism aligned with his own. Too much individualism led not to an ordered liberty but to the worst kind of disordered license. Bledsoe, said Fitzhugh, was the bearer of an unwelcome truth that had profound implications for society. Yet it was an idea whose time had apparently come. Those who defended the "social organism" of the South asserted that it was "the natural, rightful, and normal state of society." Southern members of Congress were even making so bold as to declare "that Southern society is *normal*, Northern society *exceptional* and *experimental*." Southerners eschewed social experimentation but embraced social preservation. "One of the last and best signs of the times," said Fitzhugh, "is that Professor Bledsoe is lecturing on this new idea at the National Metropolis. He justly argues that there is too much individuality in modern times. He hits the nail on the head."[7] Both Bledsoe and Fitzhugh were at war with the ascendant ideas and spirit of their age. Fitzhugh knew a kindred spirit when he saw one.

The secession crisis during the winter of 1860 and 1861 alarmed and baffled most Americans. Some had predicted its occurrence and enthusiastically welcomed the prospect of creating a southern nation, but most northerners and southerners were caught unawares. They held fast to the fading hope that sectional reconciliation might still be possible. Bledsoe attributed the fall of the American Union to many distinct causes, not the least of which was a blind allegiance to the spirit of political parties. Both the Republican and the Democratic parties in his estimation had essentially become sectional parties after 1856. The old Whig formula of amelioration and compromise on sectional issues had by then become a broken reed. Bledsoe held a low opinion of politicians generally and respected very few. Yet Senator Stephen A. Douglas was something of an exception—at least during the ordeal of the secession crisis. Bledsoe confided his views on the subject in a remarkably candid letter to Douglas in February 1861. Bledsoe knew him from his days as an attorney in Springfield, Illinois. Douglas at that time was successively secretary of the state of Illinois (1840–41), an associate justice on the Illinois Supreme Court (1841–43), a member of the U.S. Congress (1843–47), and a U.S. senator (1847).

Bledsoe fully shared Douglas's opinion that an unyielding allegiance to party platforms was sacrificing the Union upon an unholy altar of political ambition.[8] Douglas knew whereof he spoke. He felt the fire of political ambition course through his own veins as a presidential candidate in 1860 only to be disappointed. Southern Democrats deserted him as the standard-bearer of the Democratic Party at the fateful Democratic National Convention in Charleston, South Carolina. Douglas opposed secession during the 1860 campaign, despite his need for southern support, and wrecked his bid for the presidency by doing so. He made his final plea for the Union in a fervent speech given in the Senate on January 3, 1861. He could only hope that the incessant appeal to party would end and that cooler heads would prevail in bringing the secession crisis to an end. "Better that all platforms be scattered to the winds, better that every public man and politician in America be consigned to political martyrdom; better that all political organization be broken up, than that the Union be destroyed and the country plunged into civil war."[9] The spirit of compromise, and perhaps remorsefulness, exhibited in that appeal made a strong impression on Bledsoe. He does not appear to have been a supporter of Douglas or the Democratic Party at any time before the secession crisis or afterward. But he was nonetheless moved by Douglas's eleventh-hour entreaty on behalf of the Union.

Writing to Douglas on February 6, 1861—two days after the formation of the Provisional Government of the Confederate States of America in Montgomery, Alabama—Bledsoe paid him the highest compliment he had ever given a politician. "I am about to do an act which I have never done before in my life. That is, I am about to thank a distinguished man for his speech. I mean your last and great speech. It will do you more honor, in the eyes of posterity, than a thousand presidencies."[10] He rejoiced that Douglas had so thoroughly refuted the slanders heaped upon him by his political enemies. Those who confidently predicted that he would forsake the Democratic Party and join the ranks of the Republicans after the "black ingratitude" shown him at the Democratic National Convention were proven wrong. "For the sake of the country, I looked to [the] action of the Charleston Convention with an anxiety, which words can hardly express. No political event has ever caused me so bitter a pang as the failure of your nomination. Not even the election of Lincoln; for after the split in that Convention, I looked upon his election as certain." Douglas's final appeal for the Union, said Bledsoe, was "truly sublime," not only for its disinterested statesmanship but for the manner in which it captured the agonizing gasps of a purblind and dying nation. "Our Southern friends [in the Senate] could do nothing. And as I looked about the ranks of Northern members, it seemed to me that, for the most part, they stood shivering on the brink of the yawning abyss, consulting their own popularity, and not knowing what to do. I could see only one Curtius, one Leonidas, ready to willingly risk himself for the honor and safety of his country."

The fall of the American Union, Bledsoe continued, was certain to occupy the thoughts of historians for generations to come. He informed Douglas of his intention of writing a political history of the rise and fall of the American Republic. "*Is it not a grand theme?*" The projected work occupied much of Bledsoe's time and attention for many years to come. He never completed the project as initially conceived, but his inquiries into the subject eventually led to the production of *Is Davis a Traitor?* (1866) and several related articles on the origins of the American Civil War in the *Southern Review*. It was at the beginning of those historical investigations, moreover, that Bledsoe first read Douglas's speech on the Kansas-Nebraska Act of 1854. "It did me good to see how you left Senators spread on the floor around you. These were the blows of a giant." The controversy over passage of the Kansas-Nebraska Act and Douglas's sponsorship of the measure had been an unpleasant experience for the besieged Douglas. Numerous petitions to Congress protested the repeal of the

Missouri Compromise and its proscription of slavery north of 36°30′. Bledsoe lightheartedly asked Douglas if he remembered the congressional petition of New England clergy submitted against the passage of the Nebraska Bill. He knew full well, of course, that he did.[11] "You remember the petition of the 'three thousand preachers.' I have never forgiven them. One of that number [i.e., kind], the Rev. Charles Hodge, D. D. of Princeton, N. J. has recently come out with a pamphlet on the Missouri Compromise and its repeal. My friends have asked me to impale him, and I have done so."

Hodge was the editor of the *Princeton Review* and the most distinguished theologian in the Presbyterian Church. He responded to the secession of South Carolina in an article entitled "The State of the Country" that appeared in the *Princeton Review* for January 1861.[12] The opinions expressed in that article received wide circulation as a pamphlet and in the press and produced something of a firestorm in the South. Southerners had previously respected Hodge's conservative views. He held that slaveholding was not sinful per se and that denying church membership to slave owners was wrong. He further maintained that American citizens had a duty to abide by the Fugitive Slave Clause whatever the dictates of their own conscience. Bledsoe, indeed, made direct appeal in *Liberty and Slavery* to the *Princeton Review*'s denunciation of abolitionists for allegedly placing themselves above the word of God regarding the sinfulness of slavery. Hodge also denounced what many conservatives in both sections of the country regarded to be dangerous ideas pertaining to the rights of women. But when he charged southerners with bad faith regarding the repeal of the Missouri Compromise and denounced secession as an unlawful act, he was no longer a kindred spirit.

Bledsoe's impalement of Hodge appeared as a three-part reply in the conservative *New York Weekly Journal of Commerce* between February and April 1861.[13] Gerald Hallock—the editor and proprietor of the paper—was a proslavery Democrat. Hallock supported the rights of the South with regard to fugitive slaves and opposed the Free Soil and Republican parties. He defended the right of secession and opposed any attempt by the Lincoln administration to coerce the seceded states back into the Union.[14] Thus Bledsoe's reply to Hodge was assured a sympathetic reception among likeminded readers. Other southern voices responded to Hodge as well, but Bledsoe's rejoinder in the *Journal of Commerce* was arguably the most substantive.[15] Bledsoe stood before his northern readers as an admitted partisan. "I dare not profess to hold an even balance between the North and the South. I am, indeed, too sensible of the pressure of feeling not to fear that it may disturb the equilibrium of my mind, and warp the fairness of its determinations. Hence I shall make no professions of impartiality whatsoever." He considered all such professions, indeed, to be as worthless as the paper upon they were written. "Even when most sincere, they may only serve to prove (if proof were needed) that 'the heart is deceitful above all things.'"[16]

Bledsoe's declared purpose in answering Hodge was *"to vindicate the South against some of the foul aspersions cast on her honor."* He contended that Hodge's discussion of southern grievances was one sided, based upon manifold errors of historical fact, and it appeared to Bledsoe that he placed a disproportionate amount of blame for the nation's troubles on the South. "I hope to grind them to powder and scatter them to the winds." He asked his reader to judge the merits of their respective positions not by the clamor of a partisan press "but by the stern and inflexible standards of historic truth, by the unimpeachable archive and records of the country." Hodge and other detractors of the South, charged the self-assured Bledsoe, were in need of a history lesson relating to the Missouri Comprise—one that he was more than pleased to give them.

The argument from history was an important component of the sectional controversy. Salmon Portland Chase and Joshua Reed Giddings had partly based their *Appeal of the Independent Democrats* in January 1854—a manifesto against the repeal of the Missouri Comprise under the Kansas-Nebraska Act —upon presumably unassailable historical facts. The leaders of the new Republican Party impeached southerners in 1854 on the charge that they had entered into a solemn and sacred compact with the North regarding the issue of slavery in the territories under the 36°30' stipulation of the Missouri Compromise. The Republican press generally asserted that the North had observed this compact with the most scrupulous fidelity for thirty years, while the South had committed an act of bad faith in pursuit of a sectional advantage by supporting its repeal under the Kansas-Nebraska. But the evidence of the case, said Bledsoe, showed that southerners had done nothing for which they should offer apology. Not surprisingly, he laid most of the blame for the secession crisis at the feet of the Republican Party. Hodge had asked the central question: What were the political events of which the existing condition of the country is the natural consequence? The leaders of the Republican Party, for whom Bledsoe believed Hodge spoke, answered that the repeal of the Missouri Compromise, the effort to force the Lecompton Constitution upon the people of Kansas, and the refusal of southern politicians to unite in the nomination of a northern Democrat for the presidency were the causes of the present state of affairs.

Hodge explained northern outrage over the repeal of the compromise in stark terms. It mattered not whether the Missouri Compromise was constitutionally obligatory as law, for it was binding as a compact. Both sections of the Union voluntarily entered into the agreement, which "had been regarded as sacred for thirty years." Repealing the enactment was "a violation of honour and good faith" among the parties to the compact. Since much of the Kansas Territory lay north of the latitude of 36°30', Kansas would have been a free state but for the repeal of the compromise. "It was the conviction of the truth of these facts which called into existence the Republican Party. That party is not an antislavery party much less an abolition Party. It may suit politicians on either side so to represent it, but the mass of the people care little for politicians or for what they say." They cared even less for party platforms of which few took heed, but acted according to their own views and convictions. The repeal of the Missouri Compromise and the resultant civil strife in Kansas "offended the conscience of the people of the North," and it was in condemnation of those events that many northerners chose to vote for John Charles Fremont in 1856 and for Lincoln in 1860.[17]

By Bledsoe's reckoning, Hodge had devoted sixty lines to elucidating the position of the Republican Party regarding the repeal of the Missouri Compromise but only three lines to explaining the position of the South. Bledsoe provided the missing details as a means of countering Hodge's alleged sectional myopia. He denied the charge that the South acted in bad faith in the repeal of the Missouri Compromise and countered that it was the imposing attitude of the Republican Party regarding the issue of slavery in the territories that was largely responsible for the faltering condition of the Union. He attempted to neutralize Hodge's censure of the repeal of the Missouri Compromise by arguing that historically northern support of that measure had been just as conditional as southern support. The commonplace assertion made by Hodge and others that the entire North acquiesced in the Missouri Compromise of 1820 was contradicted by historical facts. It was a "fiction" promulgated by Republican newspapers and repeated by their "party preachers." The speeches made in Congress on both sides of the Missouri controversy between 1819 and 1821 revealed no such unanimity of opinion in the North. Bledsoe resurrected that discourse, analyzed the positions taken by the representatives of both sections of the nation, and tabulated the votes for and against the compromise.

Nothing could be further from the truth, Bledsoe protested, than the assertion that the whole North had accepted the Missouri Compromise. "So far is this from true, that within less than twelve months after that 'sacred compact,' as Republicans now delight to call it, was formed; *it was utterly disregarded by the North.*" Seward described the Missouri Compromise during debate on the Kansas-Nebraska Bill in 1854 as a measure that was not absolutely irrevocable in a legislative sense but that could not be repealed in a moral sense without violating honor, justice, and good faith. Senator Chase from Ohio incredulously asked: "And what does slavery ask for now? Why, sir, it demands that a time-honored and sacred compact shall be rescinded—a compact which has been universally regarded as inviolable, North and South—a compact the constitutionality of which few have doubted, and by which all have consented to abide." As Eric Foner has observed in *Free Soil, Free Labor, Free Men*, Chase did more than anyone to promote the free labor ideology of the Republican Party. He maintained that southern slaveholders were conspiring to control the federal government and make slavery the ruling interest of the Republic.[18]

Bledsoe readily conceded that the South at first looked upon the Missouri Compromise as both a binding agreement and a sectional victory. Charles Pinckney of South Carolina gave testimony to that effect in March 1820 in a brief letter to an unknown correspondent. "I hasten to inform you that this moment we have carried the question to admit Missouri and all Louisiana to the southward of 36°30' free of the restriction of slavery, and give the South, in a short time, an addition of six, and perhaps eight, members to the Senate of the United States. It is considered here by the slaveholding states as a great triumph." Edward Everett read that letter one the floor of the Senate during debate on the repeal of the Missouri Compromise in February 1854. He did so to show that the South had considered the Missouri Compromise a great triumph and that there was no need to repeal it as a means of redressing supposed southern grievances regarding the issue of slavery in the territories. The measure had promoted and not harmed southern interests.[19] Yet Bledsoe hastened to note that Pinckney's letter bore the date of March 2, 1820. It was written the evening of the very day on which the compromise became law (actually 3 o'clock in the morning, so technically the following day). Bledsoe did not deny that Pinckney's letter accurately reflected his sentiments on that occasion but pointed out that his opinion had dramatically changed at the very next session of Congress.

Pinckney sang a different song regarding the Missouri controversy in February 1821. It was clear by then that many of the northern members of Congress still opposed the admission of Missouri to the Union despite the compromise of the previous year. Pinckney fully concurred in the judgment rendered by Thomas Jefferson that the Missouri question was the most ominous issue to threaten the Union since the creation of the Republic. "This is the only one," said Pinckney, "that may, in its consequences, lead to the dissolution of that very Union, and prove the death-blow of all the political happiness and national importance once so rationally to be expected from it." It appeared that the compromise on Missouri that had been so laboriously and contentiously hammered out in the last Congress was in jeopardy of being unceremoniously discarded by the next. "I feel myself authorized to express this fear by the fact that the gentlemen in opposition have now thrown off the veil, and expressly declare their intention is to leave, if possible, this question to the next Congress." If that were to happen, the members of Congress would be at liberty to renew "the struggle for the imposition of the restriction on slavery in Missouri, which has, during the three last sessions, shaken the Union to its very foundations." Northern opponents of the admission of Missouri into the Union openly avowed that they did not consider themselves bound by the compromise of the preceding year that confined the restriction of slavery to the territory north of 36°30'. They now averred, said Pinckney, that "if they have strength enough to do so, their intention is to leave the next Congress free to decide it as they please."[20]

Pinckney's testimony supported Bledsoe's contention that the North had repudiated the compromise within less than a year of its adoption. Indeed, it was necessary to fashion a second Missouri Compromise in 1821, since the first one was no longer acceptable to most of the northern members of Congress. Pinckney's declaration, wrote Bledsoe, "throws a marvelous light on the history of the question now under consideration"—the representations made in the Republican press regarding the supposed sacredness of the Missouri Compromise and the assertion that the entire North had acquiesced to its adoption. Pinckney had been a member of the Constitutional Convention, where he represented the slaveholding interests of the South, and represented those same interests during the negotiation of the Missouri Compromise. His statements regarding the Missouri controversy clearly framed one of the issues that in time led to the collapse of the American Union: the determination of the South that the institution of slavery would not be restricted and the resolve of the North that it would be.

Slavery was not the only issue that blurred the boundaries of American federalism and dual sovereignty, but none did more so. And it was increasingly over the issue of slavery in the territories that northern and southern resentment became most vocal and divisive. Free-Soilers were determined to resist all efforts to introduce slavery into federal territories, while slaveholders were equally unwavering in their insistence that they could not be denied the right to take their constitutionally protected property into federal territories.[21] A national policy of restriction would politically emasculate the South by ensuring that no new slave states would be admitted into the Union. Bledsoe understood that political calculus and made that very point in his third and final reply to Hodge in April 1861. The Republican Party, said Bledsoe, did not intend to attack the institution of slavery directly but rather quarantine it within a "cordon" of free states. If no new slave states were admitted into the Union, the South could no longer maintain a balance of power in Senate. The political influence of the slave states would diminish as each new free state entered the Union. Such containment was death by numbers—a slow but certain suffocation.[22]

Bledsoe saw the Missouri controversy of 1819–21 as an omen of disunion. It held a pivotal place within his partisan yet discerning explanation of the nation's troubles. The compromise had simply deferred the day of reckoning on the issue of slavery in the territories to another day. He was not wrong. As Robert Pierce Forbes has observed, the two-year-long Missouri controversy was "in many ways a political dress rehearsal of the Civil War, which has been treated virtually as an epiphenomenon"—an occurrence of secondary or incidental importance that seemingly had little effect on subsequent developments in the sectional crisis. Forbes contends that "so basic a disagreement among historians about the meaning of such an important historical event is evidence, I would argue, of a fundamental discontinuity in the interpretation of American history—a crack in the master narrative, so to speak." He also corrects the flawed notion that authentic antislavery sentiment did not emerge until the Jacksonian period. "In a very real sense, the Missouri debates were the cradle of proslavery ideology."[23]

Hodge came before the nation in January 1861 bearing the olive branch of reconciliation in return for which he received a bush of southern thorns. He was a moderate who saw himself as a pacifier and eschewed extremism in both sections of the country. But he made it unequivocally clear that he regarded secession to be an act of rebellion and a self-defeating means of addressing southern anxieties and fears. Hodge acknowledged that southern grievances against northern opposition to the enforcement of the Fugitive Slave Law were warranted, but he argued that secession was not a legitimate means of addressing them. However, in defending the Republican Party against the wholesale indictment of being the party of abolition, his plea for appeasement in the South fell upon deaf ears. Hodge used the wrong language and made the wrong comparisons from the point of view of those, like Bledsoe, who were becoming more belligerent and less forgiving toward those who presumed to lecture or scold them, even when they did so with an open hand of friendship. By stating his views on the state of the country, Hodge only managed to exacerbate and not abate southern resentment—a result entirely at odds with his intentions. Hodge, indeed, was taken aback at the force and personal nature of the southern responses to his article and what it cost him in reputation and friendships in the South.[24]

Bledsoe began to lean in the direction of southern nationalism during the winter and spring of 1861, which is evident from the partisan warmth displayed in his response to Hodge. The creation of the Confederate States of America in February 1861 left little hope in his estimation that the Union would be peacefully restored. But neither that event nor his earlier defense of slavery necessarily made him a secessionist. Bledsoe was himself quite clear and emphatic in the matter. "We did not vote for Secession," Bledsoe observed in January 1870. "We voted for Bell and Everett; we coveted peace." That was the vote of a moderate and not a fire-eater. And again, during his controversy with Alexander Hamilton Stephens over the causes of the Civil War in July 1872, Bledsoe acknowledged that he had argued at length in his reply to Hodge that the refusal of the northern states to repeal their personal liberty laws was sufficient cause for the withdrawal or separation of the southern states from the Union. But he did not at that time call for the secession of Virginia or any other slaveholding state that yet remained in the Union. He simply maintained that the southern states that had already seceded had been justified in doing so. Referring to himself in the third person, he noted that when he made his reply to Hodge he had not yet become a secessionist. *But this was before he believed in or understood the right of Secession.*[25] Bledsoe's support of the Constitutional Union ticket of John Bell of Tennessee and Edward Everett of Massachusetts in the presidential election of 1860 indicates that he was still a conservative Whig at heart. It would be his final act of sectional moderation.

Unionists in the Upper South, be they slaveholders or not, were forced to take sides after passage of the secession ordinances of their respective states. It was then and not before that many Unionists became reluctant rebels.[26] Peter Wallenstein and Bertram Wyatt-Brown have noted that the secession crisis of 1860–61 compelled Unionists and southern nationalists in Virginia to "calculate their loyalties and priorities" very carefully and to "reconcile conflicting belief systems." Bledsoe is once again an instructive case in point. Only the most ideologically doctrinaire embraced secession in Virginia without reluctance, and that was not Bledsoe and many others prior to April 1861. His Unionism died a lingering death. There is every reason to believe the testimony given by Bledsoe's daughter Sophia that his decision to support the secession of Virginia was personally a very painful and bitter one.[27] It was so for many.

Yet historians have sometimes misread Bledsoe's original position on secession. Henry T. Shanks states that Bledsoe assisted Edmund Ruffin in his efforts to create sentiment in Virginia for a southern confederacy, but he offers no evidence in support of that contention. Likewise, J. W. Cooke depicted Bledsoe "as an ardent secessionist," as did John McCardell, who portrayed him as "a vociferous exponent of Southern nationalism in the classroom." Stephen E. Woodworth in his sketch of Bledsoe in *American National Biography* followed suit. Woodworth, apparently on Shanks's authority, states that Bledsoe used his faculty position at the University of Virginia to help Ruffin arouse secessionist sentiment in Virginia.[28] But the curious association of Bledsoe with Ruffin in the secession movement is misleading. It is too undifferentiated in point of time and miscasts Bledsoe in the role of a fire-eater like Ruffin. He belongs in no such company. Their attitudes and positions on secession initially were not the same. Both men shared a common destination as southern nationalists but arrived there along very different paths. Bledsoe at no time agitated for secession in association with Ruffin or in concert with anyone else, assertions to the contrary notwithstanding. Bledsoe *reacted* to the secession movement but at no time led it.

Shanks's statement linking Bledsoe and Ruffin in the secession movement appears to be a surmise based on Bledsoe's later defense of the right of secession in *Is Davis a Traitor?* and the testimony of Randolph Harrison McKim. A student at the University of Virginia during the secession crisis, McKim later described Bledsoe in *A Soldier's Recollections* (1910) as "an enthusiastic advocate of Secession, to such an extent that he would not infrequently interlard his demonstration of some difficult problem in differential or integral calculus . . . with some vigorous remarks in the doctrine of States' rights."[29] But Mc-

Kim's statement that Bledsoe was "an enthusiastic advocate of Secession" must be weighed carefully. It conflicts with Bledsoe's own testimony and that of his daughter that, despite his later views on the subject, he had been slow to warm to the idea of secession. Making "vigorous remarks" in support of states' rights doctrine, a set of ideas and principles to which Bledsoe clearly subscribed, did not make him ipso facto "an enthusiastic advocate of Secession" on the model of Ruffin. McKim may well have accurately reported Bledsoe's attitude toward secession as it existed in April 1861, but it is unwarranted to project that position any further back in time.

Bledsoe's embrace of southern nationalism, notwithstanding the views he expressed in his reply to Hodge between February and April 1861, remained tepid until it seemed clear that the Lincoln administration was willing to use force to keep the refractory Confederate states within the Union. When Lincoln called upon Virginia to provide its quota of troops, many conditional Unionists became secessionists seemingly overnight. Historians like Elizabeth Fox-Genovese and Eugene D. Genovese who have described Bledsoe as a southern moderate on sectional issues *before* the war have the correct view. Yet by 1861 even relatively restrained sectionalists like Bledsoe had come to see the congressional debates on the Missouri Compromise of 1820 and its repeal in 1854 as turning points in the defense of slavery and constitutional rights, which became increasing inseparable thereafter.[30] The election of Lincoln convinced him that further compromises on the issue of slavery in the territories were unlikely. He carefully weighed his conflicted loyalties and beliefs and cast his lot with the destiny of Virginia.

A further indication of Bledsoe's views on the eve of secession comes from Wayland Fuller Dunaway. The nineteen-year-old Dunaway arrived at the University of Virginia in the fall of 1860 with the intention of studying law under John Barbee Minor and James Philemon Holcombe. Those plans quickly changed, Dunaway later recalled, due to "the electric shock" of patriotic emotions that animated the students who rallied to the Confederate banner. "While I believed in the right of secession I deprecated the exercise of that right, because I loved the Union and the flag under which my ancestors had enjoyed the blessing of civil and religious liberty." He did not think that Lincoln's election was sufficient justification for secession. But when Lincoln issued his call for volunteers on April 15 and Virginia seceded two day later, Dunaway was forced to take sides. The heady days immediately following secession infused him with a martial spirit and instilled the conviction that he must join those who were preparing for the defense of Virginia. "I was influenced by speeches delivered by Governor Floyd, Professor Holcombe, and Dr. Bledsoe."[31] Dunaway shortly thereafter entered military service in the Fortieth Virginia Regiment of the Army of Northern Virginia. It should be noted, however, that Dunaway's statement is that Bledsoe's speech convinced him of the need to prepare for the defense of Virginia in the aftermath of secession. Bledsoe was not inciting secessionist sentiment in Virginia before the fact.

Virginia seceded from the Union on April 17, 1861, five days after the firing on Fort Sumter and two days after Lincoln's call for volunteers. Bledsoe's sympathies were now fully enlisted in the cause of southern independence. The threat of invasion revolutionized him as it did many Virginians. The University of Virginia rapidly became little more than a military academy. Students making up the Southern Guard and the Sons of Liberty, the first two student military companies established on campus, had already departed and were being integrated into provisional army units, while another student company formed by Bledsoe practiced drills on the lawn in front of the Rotunda. The *Richmond Enquirer* reported that the war spirit had so gripped the University of Virginia after passage of the secession ordinance that many students had left to join the military companies that were forming throughout the state and beyond. Those still on campus were also preparing for the coming conflict. A company of eighty students practiced military drills with Bledsoe as their captain, describing him as the "heart and hand for the cause." The unnamed student company formed by Bledsoe was the "Davis Guards," which he proudly described to Jefferson Davis as "the largest and finest looking company" of the three at the University of Virginia.[32]

Bledsoe was among the Virginians who encouraged President Jefferson Davis in May 1861 to move the capital of the Confederacy from Montgomery, Alabama, to Richmond, Virginia. Writing to Davis on May 10, he made a personal appeal to an old friend. "Your presence is desired in Richmond, nay, it is longed for, by every man, woman, and child in the State. Your appearance would take a mountain from her heart. I know this." Virginia needed more than anything else the authority of a single, trusted, and proven leader who could inspire confidence. "We have the highest opinion of Lee; but the Governor is [standing] in his way. . . . You are the man to whom all hearts turn. . . . You would be worth more than 50,000 men to us."[33] Bledsoe wrote Davis in so direct a manner, he said, not to flatter but because the good of the South implored him to speak as personally and urgently as he did.

Bledsoe conceded that Virginia had been exceedingly slow to embrace the cause of secession and had adopted an attitude that tried the patience of many of its citizens almost beyond endurance. But he assured Davis that the political situation in the state had greatly changed. It is clear that it had likewise changed with Bledsoe himself. "But this was because she [Virginia] lacked insight into the Yankee character, and could neither comprehend the perfidy of its designs, nor the malignity of its purposes." As soon as Virginians understood that the Lincoln administration intended to coerce the seceded states back into the Union, however, their "eyes were opened," and "the false promises" of Lincoln's emissaries "were given to the winds." Virginia withdrew from the Union it had long cherished but could no longer tolerate. "She nobly burst its rotten bonds asunder, & bared her breast to the gathering storm." It was in Virginia, said Bledsoe, that "the ferocity of Northern wrath" would be most certainly and fully directed. What he believed Virginia needed more than anything else at that particular moment, even more than men in the field, was leadership and arms.

Sober-minded Virginians like Robert E. Lee showed less enthusiasm for the looming prospect of war than did the more idealist and impetuous Bledsoe. Lee's apparent lack of zeal for the coming conflict appears to have annoyed Bledsoe. As he confided to Davis, "No one admires Genl. Lee more than I do. But I fear he is too despondent. His remarks are calculated to dispirit our people. I have heard such remarks myself, and energetically dissented from them. I have not repeated them because I thought they were calculated to do no good, even if true." Lee's life in the army had not directed his attention to "the great questions" of the sectional struggle with which Davis was presumably more familiar. "I am persuaded you would think he overrates the power of the North to attack, and underrates the means and power of the South to resist." Bledsoe considered this a great misfortune, both for Lee's position as a leader and for the whole South. "Noble and glorious as he is, I fear he does not know how good and how righteous our cause is, and consequently lacks one quality which the times demand. All eyes and all hearts turn to you."

The chaotic conditions exiting in Virginia in the aftermath of secession prompted Bledsoe to write Davis again the following day. "Our Governor [John Letcher] is a notorious drunkard; and, in every way, utterly unfit for the office he holds; *especially in times like these.* I can truly say this, in the names of thousands who voted for him." Decisive action was needed to prepare Virginians for the advent of Yankee retribution. "If Lee were not too modest, he would usurp authority; and every heart in Virginia would leap for joy. Your presence would supersede him [the governor], legally and quietly. There is no *one* head to the State; and this is working infinite mischief." A leader was needed to manage the unsettled and disquieting state of affairs at Richmond: *"We greatly need a deliverer, and we look to you."*[34] If Davis proved to be something less than a deliverer, Bledsoe was not wrong to look upon him as the symbol of Confederate nationalism—both its nascent aspirations and ultimate failure. Davis's leadership would come under a great amount of criticism from fellow Confederates both during the war and afterward, but his many friends remained personally loyal to him. None did more so than Bledsoe, who never failed to defend him.

Ratification of Virginia's secession ordinance in May 1861 prompted Bledsoe and many others to join provisional regiments of the Confederate army. Bledsoe's West Point education, two years of military service, and ardor for the defense of Virginia earned him the commission of colonel in the Thirty-sixth Regiment of Virginia, which he received on June 1, 1861, by order of Major General Robert E. Lee. As Philip Alexander Bruce quipped about Bledsoe's commission, "some humorous stroke of perverse destiny" found the professor of mathematics in the uniform of a colonel in the Confederate army.[35] Colonel Bledsoe never saw action but served the Confederacy in other ways. After the seat of the Confederate government moved from Montgomery to Richmond on May 24, 1861, Davis appointed Bledsoe as chief of the Bureau of War within the Confederate War Department. Unfortunately for Bledsoe, however, Davis made the appointment without the recommendation or the approval of Secretary of War Leroy Pope Walker. Bledsoe received a cool reception from a miffed Walker, who remained hostile toward him thereafter. The circumstances of Bledsoe's appointment stigmatized him as a special favorite of Davis. It was all that Walker could do to tolerate his presence as member of staff.

Bledsoe's tenure as a Confederate official was not a pleasant one. He worked in a crowded office in which there was literally no room for him and was given little of importance to do. Walker appointed one of Bledsoe's former students by the name of Shepherd as a clerk to assist him with correspondence and issuing passports, but that was all the support he ever received. Even more insulting was that a resentful Walker continued to shun Bledsoe whenever possible. The situation enraged him and made others in the War Department resent his seemingly superfluous presence. John Beauchamp Jones, an extremely able clerk who disliked Bledsoe, accurately observed of him that "he is like a fish out of water, and unfit for office." He was "drawing a fine salary and performing no services. Still, it is not without the sweat of his brow, and many groans." Bledsoe's disposition soured even further when Walker consistently reversed the intent of his correspondence, making the mercurial Bledsoe even moodier than usual. "The Colonel's temper is as variable as an April day—now all smiles and sunshine, but by-and-by a cloud takes all away! He becomes impatient with a long-winded story told by some business applicant—and storms whenever anyone asks him if the Secretary is in."[36]

Bledsoe's only bright moments came when Walker's continual state of ill health and trips to the field kept him out of the office. Bledsoe acted as secretary of war pro tem on those occasions and arrived at the office "in high spirits and full dress." Bledsoe's main contribution during his tenure in the War Department, claimed Jones, was merely to adapt the U.S. Army regulations to those of the Confederate army. "It is only to strike out U.S. and insert C.S., and yet the Colonel groans over it." Lacking any influence with Walker, a frustrated Bledsoe resigned his position on September 7, 1861—an action he had actually threatened to take soon after his arrival. But he was back at the Bureau of War within a matter of days, since Davis refused to accept his resignation. Jones's disapproving attitude toward Bledsoe clearly reflects that of Walker and must be weighed in the balance. Yet there is no reason to suppose that Jones's unflattering characterizations of Bledsoe do not accurately reflect his unfitness for the duties required of him. The daily rub of sensitive egos in the War Department bred turmoil and occasional moments of humor, as when Jones would amuse himself by watching Bledsoe briskly shuffle in pursuit of a refractory clerk with a matter of urgent business.

As chief of the Bureau of War, Bledsoe copied and transmitted battle reports, distributed passes to civilians for entering the field of operations, and attended to correspondence relating to appointments, reenlistments, furloughs, passports, and applications for commissions as surgeons. He also issued directives from his superiors concerning prisoners of war and the circumstances attending their capture and details regarding assignments of duty and the distribution of ordnance, and he handled the secretary of war's personal correspondence as directed. These were necessary but uninspiring duties. And given Bledsoe's aptitudes and propensities, the tedium of attending to such matters wore upon him heavily.[37] There were also those who called upon him for personal favors, like Episcopal bishop Stephen Elliott of Savannah, Georgia, who was endeavoring to obtain a commission in the Confederate army for his twenty-one-year-old son Robert. Elliot considered his son "entirely too good for Yankee bayonets or German gunpowder," yet like many ardent young men of the South "he pants to be in the field." Bledsoe had to attend to official correspondence, he informed Leonidas Polk, while he was surrounded by swarms of people "waiting to be waited on."[38] It was more than a serene man could bear and simply overwhelming for an impatient one like Bledsoe.

The situation for Bledsoe improved somewhat after Judah Philip Benjamin, a Davis loyalist like himself, succeeded Walker as secretary of war on September 17, 1861. Yet Bledsoe still complained of being ignored. When George Wythe Randolph replaced Benjamin as secretary of war on March 24, 1862, Bledsoe again resigned his position, on April 7 of that year. He does not appear to have had an issue with Randolph personally but rather with his perfunctory assignment of duties—an ongoing source of frustration and complaint. Davis that time accepted Bledsoe's resignation and rewarded his personal loyalty and service by promoting him as Robert Ould's successor as assistant secretary of war. The promotion prompted a resentful Jones to remark, "Now he is in his glory, and has forgotten me." Bledsoe had always said, according to Jones, that when he resigned he would ask that Jones replace him as chief of the Bureau of War. When Robert Garlic Hill Kean received the appointment instead of Jones, the clerk's dislike of Bledsoe grew even stronger.[39]

As the assistant secretary of war, Bledsoe issued dispatches on behalf of Secretary of War George Wythe Randolph to burn cotton and tobacco in order to keep them from falling into enemy hands. But he still lacked authority to originate any directives himself. Bledsoe used what little influence he had with his superiors to help friends. He predicted that Leonidas Polk, a Confederate general and the Episcopal bishop of the Diocese of Louisiana, would do glorious things for the Confederacy as a field officer. When Bledsoe learned that Polk entertained thoughts of resigning from the Confederate service and returning to his diocese, he beseeched him to reconsider. Bledsoe assured Polk that both he and Davis greatly valued his ardor for the cause and his abilities in the field. "But what is the opinion of man? What the opinion of presidents, or priests, or laymen, or bishops? You know, and you feel, that you have engaged in as great and as sacred a cause as ever enlisted the services of man; and, in this cause, you have just begun to act."[40] Bledsoe was certain that Polk still had valuable services to render the Confederacy. "I have said so from the first, and know it now more fully than before you were tried. Turn not back, I implore you, but hold right on in spite of all opposition of all kinds. Ten thousand hearts are with you, and look to you as one of our most efficient generals. We feel as if we could not spare you. I feel as if I were only uttering the sentiment of the people of the Confederacy when I say you must not resign."[41]

The Richmond correspondent of the *Charleston Mercury* reported on September 16, 1862, that it was rumored that Bledsoe would soon resign his position as assistant secretary of war.[42] He did so on September 24, 1862, with Davis's approval. Bledsoe continued his duties until October 1, 1862, when he happily took leave of Richmond and returned to the relative tranquility of Charlottesville. He was once again an academician, if only briefly. There is no evidence supporting the statement made by John Boyce Bennett that Bledsoe resigned his position as assistant secretary of war because he disagreed with a plan for defending Richmond. Bledsoe reportedly denounced as "a humbug" a proposal that members of the various departments of the Confederate government form themselves into a military organization or local guard for the defense of the capital and government archives. But his resignation owed little, if anything, to that attitude or difference of opinion.[43] Bledsoe stepped down as assistant secretary of war to undertake a new endeavor. He himself recognized that he was unsuited by interest and temperament for the position and could better serve the Confederate cause as a writer than as a miscast bureaucrat. That explanation of his resignation at least comports with what he actually did for the remainder of the war.

Davis's biographer Clement Eaton questioned the wisdom of Bledsoe's appointment as assistant secretary of war, citing it as an example of the weakness of Confederate leadership and lack of "business acumen" in government relative to that demonstrated by the Lincoln administration. Eaton referred to Bledsoe as "a man absolutely controlled by abstractions" and described his promotion to assistant secretary of war as "a ridiculous appointment."[44] It is a fair assessment. Bledsoe was an eccentric individualist who did not work well in harness with others. He was quick to take offense at perceived slights and sought a degree of deference and influence he never received beyond his ability to get Davis's ear. Davis wanted people in the Executive Department at Richmond who were personally loyal to him and was not disappointed in Bledsoe in that regard. But neither Bledsoe's talents nor disposition suited him for any position in the War Department or any other position in the Confederate government. It was far better to leave such a fiercely independent character as Bledsoe to his own devices in promoting the Confederate cause. Neither Bledsoe's personal loyalty to Davis nor his commitment to Confederate nationalism was ever in doubt. The only question was how he could best serve the cause.

Bledsoe was a thinker and a writer. He was emphatically a scholar in his habits and tastes. Those who knew him personally, or only from afar through his literary reputation, recognized that salient fact. It was clear to the blockaded British subject Catherine Cooper Hopley, who met Bledsoe several times in Richmond during his service in the War Department, that he was a man dedicated to the life of the mind. "He was a man of reflection, and apt to go off into a train of thought in the midst of a conversation; his face wearing a placid [,] satisfied expression, that informed you his meditations were not unpleasant."[45] Others acknowledged his scholarly demeanor and intellectual qualities too. "I hope that your duties in the War Office," wrote George Wythe Randolph in August 1861, "will not dry up your literary tastes. I was studying The Theodicy most carefully, with a view to swap a few lines about it, when this necessary but infernal war took me from my books, my home, and everything that I love, to swelter in the pestilent marshes of the Peninsula."[46] The war likewise removed Bledsoe from his books, his home, and the regularities of academic life and thrust him into his own personal hell in the War Department at Richmond. His duties did not dry up his literary talents but gave him precious little time to pursue them. That quickly changed following his resignation as assistant secretary of war and return to Charlottesville. Bledsoe took up his pen and committed himself heart and soul to justifying secession and the aspirations of southern nationalism. The scholar was once again in his element.

8

WRITING THE REVOLUTION
A Confederate Interpretation of the Civil War

BLEDSOE BEGAN HIS LITERARY mission for the Confederacy soon after his return to Charlottesville. When George Frederick Holmes dined at Bledsoe's home on the evening of November 13, 1862, Bledsoe read him the introduction to a manuscript entitled "The Fall of the American Union." Holmes observed in an entry to his diary that "he opens his subject with great vigor" but made no further comment.[1] A portion of Bledsoe's "Fall of the American Union" manuscript subsequently appeared as "Reflections on the War" in the *Army and Navy Messenger* on July 1, 1863. The *Army and Navy Messenger* was a semimonthly newspaper published in Petersburg, Virginia, by the Evangelical Tract Society.[2] The primary purpose of the *Messenger* was to promote the morale and spiritual well-being of Confederate soldiers and sailors in the face of disheartening realities. The role of religion in maintaining the motivation of Confederate fighting forces was most important. It was part of a self-conscious effort to promote the development of Confederate nationalism.[3] Home fires needed tending on both sides during the war, but creating and sustaining Confederate nationalism presented its own challenges.[4] Bledsoe's fugitive literary offerings on the war, first at home and then in the London press, represented one such effort.

"Reflections on the War" is the earliest known expression of Bledsoe's Confederate nationalism. It was a message he refined throughout the war and adamantly defended afterward.[5] When he first began to examine the deteriorating condition of the country, it was the slavery controversy that appeared to him to be the most profound cause of the nation's troubles. After further research and reflection, however, he concluded that slavery was a powerful yet "a very subordinate" cause of the difficulties that eventually led to secession and war. The history of the Republic, said Bledsoe, revealed an earlier struggle between the North and South than that which roiled the Republic over the slavery issue. It was a rivalry for political dominance within the new Union that figured prominently in the Constitutional Convention of 1787. Antagonism between the two rival sections ultimately centered on the issues of protective tariffs and the perpetuation of the institution of slavery, but the lineaments of distrust between the North and the South had been present at the very birth of the Republic itself. Bledsoe supposed at the time he began his historical investigations that he had gone to the bottom of his subject and had perceived the origins of "the present revolution" quite clearly. He now declared himself to have been gravely mistaken.

The true causes of the Confederate revolution, Bledsoe declared, ranged far beyond the slavery controversy. They were "as deep as the foundations of society itself, and as universal as the interests of humanity." Bledsoe saw the history of humankind as essentially a struggle of one portion of the species to subjugate and rule another, and the corresponding struggle of the oppressed portion of humanity to maintain its independence. The aptness of that thesis to the slavery controversy could not have escaped him. Yet in keeping with his contention that slavery was a powerful yet subordinate cause of the war, the remainder of his polemic discusses a different contest. Bledsoe uses the theme of struggle and oppression to explain the competition between the North and South for political dominance within the Union—the rivalry that ultimately led to armed conflict. Each of the adversaries in that struggle fell back upon opposite and hostile principles. "The North, in which there was nothing to limit or modify the democratic principle, fell back on the dogma of the most absolute equality of men, as the best means to weaken and humble the South, as well as to unite all her own citizens, whether native or foreign, in opposition and hatred of the smaller section." Northern politicians, he argued, adopted that course as a means of gaining permanent control of the national government, and in the contest for "power and plunder" they became more democratic than any other party ever known in history. "The democratic party [Democratic Party] itself was left far behind, and remained for a time, the great conservative element in the society of the North."

While the North descended into "the infinite [and] dark abyss of radicalism," the South chose a different course. Southern political theorists and leaders denied the absolute equality of all humankind—a principle that would immediately emancipate the slaves and confer upon them the same privileges and power enjoyed by whites. White southerners, Bledsoe affirmed with remarkable candor, sought a separate destiny. "Moved by the profoundest instinct of self-preservation, she [the South] retraced her steps and withdrew from the fearful brink of that abyss of democracy to which the infidel philosophy of the eighteenth century had conducted both sections of the Union." Southerners rejected egalitarian principles and, whether they were aware of it or not, Bledsoe asserted, adopted a view of society and politics that better accorded with the divine government and the teachings of the scriptures. "For God has made some difference among men as well as among the angels and the hierarchies of heaven; and sin has made much more." Human inequalities were a part of the natural order and ranged from "the lowest grade of barbarism to the highest type of civilization." Disparities in the human condition for Bledsoe represented "something more than the influence of human laws and institutions. . . . Hence we have not, unlike the infidel philosophers of France, any short and easy method for the 'regeneration of mankind.'" Such views were more in keeping with the discredited principles of federalism than anything else— its assumptions of aristocratic privilege and a restricted electoral franchise. Bledsoe's conservative social and political views were, indeed, neo-Federalist in many of their bearings. Nor would Bledsoe have objected too strenuously to the unapologetic sentiment once declared by John Randolph of Roanoke: "I am an aristocrat. I love liberty and hate equality."[6] It was precisely that same elitist sentiment that propelled his incessant attacks on egalitarianism.

The contest between the North and South, Bledsoe continued, gradually deepened into a struggle between "liberty and license, between freedom and fanaticism, between order and anarchy, between social happiness and social ruin, between the powers of light and the powers of darkness." The violent passions and bitterness occasioned by the sectional contest made the perpetuation of the once venerated Union a practical impossibility. "The decree of separation was written in heaven before it was enacted on earth. Two civilizations, so marked in their differences and so diverse in their tendencies, were not destined to remain under one and the same government." Each section acted in pursuit of its own self-interest and beliefs until they became estranged and hostile. One could eulogize the fall of the Union, said Bledsoe, without unduly criticizing the handiwork or the sagacity of the founders. At least as it was originally created, the American Republic was perhaps the best government that human wisdom had yet devised. It ran a short but brilliant course before ultimately perishing from unresolved problems present at its birth. Having answered its original purpose, the federal Union was "justly laid aside as a worn out garment" that no longer fit nor pleased those for whom it had been fashioned. "All the powers of earth could not have saved it. They might, perhaps, have saved its outer form, but not its inner life. For this had fled and left the Union."

The justness of the Confederate revolution was a fixed conviction with Bledsoe. Yet he entertained no illusions as to the enormous burden under which it labored. An attitude of seeming indifference and even hostility toward the Confederacy had dashed early hopes of receiving the approbation, recognition, and assistance of Great Britain, France, and other European nations that would have followed their example. "Misunderstood and despised by the civilized world, and cast forth from the sympathy of all nations, the South has alone, unaided and unfriended by man, girded up her loins for the great struggle she could not decline, and braved the tremendous perils of her position." All Christian nations had thus far ignored the existence of the Confederacy, excluding it from the unspeakable advantages enjoyed by its more powerful enemy in the North. "The South stands to-day, and she stands alone, in the Thermopylae of the universe, pleading as best she may the great cause of humanity and freedom. Meanwhile, the arts, the arms, and the commerce and the hungry hordes of Europe, all lend their aide to crush the Southern states into dust."

Bledsoe closed his flawed plea for the Confederacy with the oft-cited words written on the tomb of Leonidas, king of Sparta, who led the small band of warriors who resisted the Persian army of Xerxes I at the Battle of Thermopylae in 480 BC. "Go, tell the Spartans, we lie here in obedience to her laws." Just as the outnumbered Spartans had faced the Persian invader, the armies of the Confederacy were defending themselves against the invading armies of the northern Colossus. "Be this, then, the inscription on the monuments and tombs of Southern heroes, 'Go, tell the Christian world, we lie here in obedience to her principles and laws.' And this shall be our sublime revenge; this great record of her injuries and wrongs." While few Confederates questioned the justice of their cause, others outside the South recognized that Bledsoe's appeals to "the great cause of humanity and freedom" and to southern "injuries and wrongs" were one sided, incomplete, and altogether unacceptable to all but the most partisan of Confederate supporters. How could the freedom of one people be advanced at the expense of another in justification to Christian, democratic, and humanitarian principles? And were no injuries and wrongs committed against those held in bondage?

Bledsoe had determined, either on his own or in consultation with Jefferson Davis, that he could best make his case for the legitimacy of the Confederate revolution by joining other Confederate writers in London who were promoting the cause of southern independence in the English press. He did not go to London as a Confederate commissioner or agent in any formal sense. Bledsoe neither sought nor received a diplomatic appointment. He was no longer connected in any official capacity with the Confederate government, although he was still very much a partisan for the cause. He went to London as a private citizen of the Confederacy on a very personal undertaking. Confederate propagandists abroad, William C. Davis has noted, worked in different capacities: official, quasi official, "and far too many simply self-appointed."[7] Bledsoe's mission to London appears to have been largely, although perhaps not entirely, self-appointed. According to his daughter Sophia, it was Jefferson Davis who asked Bledsoe to conduct investigations into the constitutionality of secession as a means of vindicating the Confederate cause. It was further concluded that in order to most effectively undertake such a study Bledsoe would have to go to England. "All records of Congress and of the conventions which had formed the government, both federal and state, were inaccessible in the South, but were to be found in the British Museum."[8]

Bledsoe spent the next two years gathering the necessary materials for a historical and constitutional defense of the right of secession. He initially referred to the projected work as "The Grand Experiment," which was an inquiry into the rise and fall of the American Union. This was doubtless the same manuscript that Bledsoe earlier described to Stephen A. Douglas and read to George Frederick Holmes. He initially expected to find some sympathy and support for the work in England. Yet he sadly discovered soon after his arrival that he had been "greatly, egregiously mistaken."[9] Bledsoe's wife, Harriet, reportedly paid all or most of the expenses connected with his two-year residence in London from a limited family inheritance. Harriet supported the family during his absence and apparently paid the cost of publishing his defense of secession after his return—all presumably from that same family bequest.[10]

John Beauchamp Jones, one of the clerks in the Confederate War Department, chanced to encounter Bledsoe in August 1863 as he ambled his way toward the passport office in Richmond on the eve of his departure for England. Jones recorded what he knew about Bledsoe's trip, as well as his conjecture as to its probable purpose. "He said he was just about to start for London, where he intended publishing his book—on slavery, I believe. He had free passage on one of the government steamers, to sail from Wilmington." Bledsoe and Jones bid each other good-bye, and at parting Jones told him "I hoped he would not find us all hanged when he returned. I think it probable he has a mission from the President, as well as his book to publish."[11] Jones's statement that Bledsoe intended to publish a book on slavery in England, as he thought, is a mere surmise. Yet the supposition may have been at least partially true. Bledsoe went to London to publish a book on the constitutionality of secession and not slavery. But the two issues could not be conveniently separated in England, as he soon learned.

Bledsoe left New Inlet at Wilmington, North Carolina, on September 5, 1863, aboard the Confederate steamer and blockade-runner the *Cornubia*. He and his fellow passengers safely anchored at St. George's in Bermuda on the morning of September 9. He departed Bermuda aboard the steamship *Florida* on the morning of September 19 and after an unpleasant twenty-three-day passage arrived at Beamaris, Wales, on October 12. Bledsoe traveled by train from Beamaris directly to London. The London *Index*, published by the Confederate journalist and commercial agent Henry Hotze, briefly and unceremoniously announced Bledsoe's arrival on October 15, 1863: "Among recent arrivals from the Confederate States is Professor Bledsoe, of the University of Virginia, late Assistant-Secretary of War, and the author of several well-known works on the higher Mathematics, Political Ethics, and Logic." His purpose in London was not mentioned. But the foreign correspondent of the *Charleston Daily Courier* in Dieppe, France, was more specific. The *Courier* reported on August 12, 1864, that Bledsoe was in London promoting the Confederate cause. "His zeal for the cause of the South is so well known, and his abilities so unquestioned that we may hope much from the influence of his master mind in diffusing a correct knowledge of our institutions."[12]

Bledsoe brought with him to London several letters of introduction to members of the House of Lords and others who might be able to assist him in his literary enterprise. James Lyons—a prominent Richmond attorney, member of the first Confederate Congress, and a close friend of Jefferson Davis's—provided him with a letter of introduction to Lord Hartington (Spencer Compton Cavendish, Duke of Devonshire) in August 1863. When Lyons wrote Bledsoe's letter of introduction, Hartington was undersecretary of the British War Office. He introduced Bledsoe as the professor of mathematics at the University of Virginia and curiously made no mention of that fact that he was the former assistant secretary of war for the Confederate States of America. Lyons asked Hartington to introduce Bledsoe to his acquaintances. "You will find him a most estimable gentleman, a learned divine, and an accomplished scholar. He visits England for the purpose of bringing out several works of which he is the author [and] the means of publishing which properly are denied us in the Confederacy by this most infamous *war*."[13]

Another Virginian who wrote in support of Bledsoe's mission to England was Cornelia Grinnan of Fredericksburg. Grinnan wrote a letter of introduction for him in September 1863 to her relative the Duke of Argyll, George Douglas Campbell. Her letter speaks more directly to the purpose of Bledsoe's visit. Grinnan said of Bledsoe that he was "well known at home by the power of his argumentative pen, possessing great force of generalization, accompanied by a racy & lucid style. . . . He goes abroad to publish a work on our Revolution; as a thinker and active worker in this revolution and acquainted with our leading men, he is eminently fitted for the task."[14] Grinnan was sadly aware that Argyll was not a southern sympathizer but hoped he might yet be recruited to the cause. That was a forlorn wish, as Bledsoe discovered after his arrival in London. Argyll was a firm friend of the Union, Bledsoe noted, who used all his influence "to break down the South; and, consequently, I scorned to make his acquaintance." Neither did Bledsoe meet with Lord Hartington, Lord Ashburton, Lord Warncliffe, and others to whom he had letters of introduction. He did not do so, he grumbled, because "I went to England to work, and not to see Lords." He declined dozens of such invitations because of his "duty to the South as a writer."[15]

Bledsoe had enlisted the services of the Confederate sympathizer James Spence of Liverpool in furthering his literary labors even before his departure for London. Spence was a merchant, banker, stockbroker, shipper, Confederate financial agent, and author of *The American Union*, published in London in 1862. Spence's *American Union* appeared in four English editions and one American edition published in Richmond in 1863. The pamphlet significantly contains an inquiry into the constitutionality of secession and the causes of the war—expositions that Bledsoe greatly admired. Spence also wrote a pamphlet, *On the Recognition of the Southern Confederation*, published in London in 1862, that made the case for acknowledging the legitimacy of the Confederacy by the British government.[16] He was a contributor to the *Index* and to the London *Times*, an organizer of intervention rallies, and a founder of the Manchester Southern Independence Association. The Confederate commissioner James Murray Mason described Spence to Secretary of State Judah P. Benjamin in July 1862 as "the most intelligent counsel and active coadjutator" of southern interests in the British press.[17] Spence roundly approved of the purpose of Bledsoe's proposed trip and his projected work on secession: "I shall be glad to see your views in permanent shape—one that will command the attention of thinking men in this country." Spence continued to promote the cause of southern independence by contributing articles to the English press, where, as he told Bledsoe, he put "as good a face upon affairs" as he possibly could.[18]

The Confederate agent Edwin De Leon also offered Bledsoe his support. Writing Bledsoe from Paris, De Leon asked to be informed of his plan and specifically how he might assist him. Bledsoe had previously written De Leon asking if he had a copy of Cobb's work on slavery (Thomas Read Rootes Cobb), which De Leon said he would send if necessary to his mission.[19] It should not be inferred from that inquiry, however, that defending slavery was the *primary* purpose of his trip to England. His interest in obtaining a copy of Cobb suggests that he was prepared to make a legal and historical defense of slavery *if* warranted but nothing more. Bledsoe was well aware that the detestation of slavery garnered support for the Union in many parts of England, where Union and Emancipation Clubs were vocal in support of the Lincoln administration's prosecution of the war.

Even some of the warmest supporters of the Confederate cause in England made a clear distinction in their espousal of the right of secession and their loathing of the institution of slavery. James Spence—a warm supporter of southern independence and someone whose views on the right of secession Bledsoe greatly admired—nonetheless denounced slavery in his otherwise prosouthern *American Union* (1862). "It is a gross anachronism, a thing of two thousand years ago—the brute force of dark ages obtruding into the mist of the nineteenth century." No amount of legerdemain or sophistry could conceal the fact that slavery was wrong. "No reasoning—no statistics—no profit— no philosophy—can reconcile us to that which our instinct repels. After all the arguments have been poured into the ear—there is something in the heart that spurns them." Spence did not claim that all of humanity was born equal. But he did avow that an innate and irresistible conviction told the conscience "that a man was a man, and not a chattel." Slavery was "a foul blot" that offended all lovers of their own kind. Those views placed Spence at odds with Hotze and the Confederate government. Despite all he had done to garner support for diplomatic recognition of the Confederacy, Spence's unacceptable views on slavery resulted in his removal as the British financial agent of the Confederate government in 1864.[20] If making an aggressive defense of slavery was initially part of Bledsoe's literary mission to England, he wisely changed his mind.

Bledsoe's creed as a Confederate propagandist first appeared in a four-part series entitled "The Causes of the American War" in Henry Hotze's London *Index* between December 1863 and January 1864.[21] Those articles were followed by a nine-part series entitled "Secession" in the London *Evening Herald* between October 1864 and April 1865.[22] Bledsoe's writings in the *Index* and the *Evening Herald* provide the clearest evidence we have of the primary purpose of his residence in London. They are also the earliest expressions of ideas and arguments more fully elaborated in defense of the right of secession in *Is Davis a Traitor?* The articles on the causes of the American War in the *Index* are signed, while more in keeping with the customary practice of the British press, those on secession in the *Evening Herald* are unsigned. But there can be no question as to Bledsoe's authorship of the unsigned articles on secession in the *Evening Herald.* Many passages are word for word the same as those found in corresponding chapters of *Is Davis a Traitor?*, follow the same sequence of argument, are based upon the same sources, and are written in his signature style. It is quite likely that Bledsoe made contributions to other London papers, signed or otherwise, that have yet to be identified. He later said that the fine English wardrobe he acquired during his residence in London was due to the kindness of friends and "to our faithful goose quill," indicating that he was paid for his contributions to the press.[23]

Bledsoe's "Causes of the American War" in the London *Index* is a robust expression of Confederate nationalism. No one, he said, could witness "the great revolution" raging in America without wanting to understand its causes. A conflict of such immense proportions and atrociousness left thinking and caring people wanting to know "the dreadful secret" that could occasion such frightful miseries. "Hence every great revolution like the present has had it writers as well as its warriors." The English Civil War of 1641 had its Harrington, Hobbes, and Milton and the Glorious Revolution of 1688 a Sidney, Locke, Hoadley, Gorton, and a Plato Redivivus, all of whom discussed some of the great questions pertaining to the social condition and destiny of humanity. The French Revolution similarly gave rise to numerous speculations and theories regarding the origins of society, the foundations of government, and the causes of revolutions. It is as clear a statement of Bledsoe's literary and historical mission in London that has come down to us. He would explain the origin and meaning of "the American Revolution of 1861" for future ages. Writing the revolution would occupy a good deal of his time for many years to come.[24]

When the southern states seceded, some people said that it was because they refused to accept the election of a Republican president and no longer held power in the federal government. But Bledsoe countered that such facile explanations overlooked the long-term causes of disunion that had been gestating for many years. "We should not, however, be surprised at such an error. For it always happens, that a great revolution is ascribed, by those who do not like it or do not understand it, to some insignificant or unjustifiable cause, in order to render it contemptible in the eyes of mankind." The election of 1860 and the secession of the southern states were *occasions* of the war but not its true *causes*. Like all great revolutions, it was "the outburst of an age at war with itself. . . . It was, for at least twenty years, a war of races, and ideas, and interests, and passions, and words, before it became a war of deeds." It was but a "poor contemporary slander" to suggest that the southern states withdrew from the Union simply because they had rejected the legitimate result of a presidential election "or because they could no longer have all things in their own way."[25]

The real causes of secession and war, Bledsoe contended, sprang from numerous sources. "The truth is, if we weigh all the antecedents of any great revolution, if we consider all the influences which have brought it to pass, we shall find that the real causes are proportioned to the magnitude of the result." Just as Montesquieu said of the Roman Republic in his *Considérations sur les causes de la grandeur des Romains et de leur decadence* that it was necessary for the republic to perish due to its infirmities, "the only question was to know how and by whom it should fall." Nor had it been otherwise with the American Republic. "States do not fall for trifles. Trifles may be the occasion of their fall, but the *causes* lie deeper, and are more powerful in their operation." Those who would understand the true causes of the American war, Bledsoe affirmed, would do well to inquire into what characteristics it shared with other great revolutions. Neither the English Civil War, nor the American Revolution, nor the French Revolution, nor the American Civil War sprang from a single cause but from several converging causes of long duration.

Two of Bledsoe's converging causes of the war (he would later cite eight in *Is Davis a Traitor?*) were the slavery controversy and the tariff issue. Southern grievances over the tariff, however, receive a disproportionately larger amount of attention than slavery within Bledsoe's interpretive paradigm. It was a convenient way of minimizing the importance of the slavery issue as a cause of the war without ignoring it and of trying to place the Confederate cause upon higher moral ground. The tariff issue, argued Bledsoe, had on more than one occasion threatened to disrupt the Union. It was just as oppressive from a southern point of view as had been the taxation of the American colonies by Great Britain in the 1760s and 1770s. He further developed the analogy between the tariff as a cause of the American Civil War and taxation as a cause of the American Revolution by quoting Alexander Hamilton on the valuable lessons that Americans had learned from their British masters. The British had shown the American colonists quite clearly, said Hamilton, that "the power of legislating for us, *and of raising a revenue upon the articles of our commerce, would be* a sufficient degree of slavery." And such, said Bledsoe, was precisely the effect of the federal tariff upon the South. One portion of the South alone, or less than one-fourth of the entire nation, allegedly paid three-fourths of the taxes levied by the federal government. Senator Thomas Hart Benton, who Bledsoe said was by no means friendly to the South and was hostile toward the Calhoun school of politics, could still acknowledge on the floor of the U.S. Senate in 1828 that Virginia, the two Carolinas, and Georgia met three-fourths of the annual expenses of the federal government yet received little or no government expenditures in return.[26]

The injustices of the tariff were beyond dispute, Bledsoe declared; the only question was why the southern states had tolerated them for so long. The reason the South had patiently submitted to those inequities was a misplaced attachment to the Union—an understandable affection created through the mutual sacrifices of both sections of the nation. "She loved the Union, and, hollow though it was and heartless, she loved it far too well. That was one source of her patient and long-suffering submission to the proud dictation of the North." The South had been seduced into thinking that its prosperity depended upon the Union by that great tempter and compromiser Henry Clay. Clay had recommended to the South the great scheme of plunder known by the name of "the American system," so called because it was designed to protect American manufacturing from competition with British manufacturing and free trade through a protective tariff for the general revenue of the federal government. The domestic effect of that protective tariff, Bledsoe charged, robbed the South and enriched the North. He had once joined Abraham Lincoln and other Whigs in advocating the adoption of a tariff for revenues instead of direct taxation. He now counted himself among those who had been wrongly and regrettably duped into supporting the American system of Henry Clay.

The opinion that the protective tariff was the true cause of secession and war was in favor among those in the British government and press who were sympathetic to the Confederacy. But that view was not shared by those who supported the justice of the Union cause. Notable among them was the Manchester manufacturer, free trader, and member of Parliament Richard Cobden. Cobden was a noninterventionist who affirmed that it was slavery and not tariffs that had led to secession and war. "We are told in the House of Commons," said Cobden, "that this civil war was originated because the South wished to establish free-trade principles, and that the North would not allow it." The southern states did not secede over the issue of the tariff but as a means to protect slavery, and that was the true origin of the American conflict. "It is a war to establish a slave empire. This is the sole aim and object. The question of free trade and protection has nothing whatever to do with it. Slavery, Slavery, Slavery, that is all. It is this object and purpose with which the war was begun, and that in my opinion renders success to the Secessionists impossible." Cobden expressed those same sentiments in a speech given at Rochdale, which his supporters greeted with cheers and cries of "hear, hear."[27]

J. E. Cairnes, professor of jurisprudence and political economy at Queen's College in Galway, shared Cobden's opinion. Cairns forcefully took the position that slavery was the real cause of the American war in *The Slave Power: Its Character, Career, and Probable Designs* (1862). The argument or opinion that the main issue between the North and South was the tariff emerged in Great Britain early on in the conflict. But that contention received less support as it became evident that hostilities between the northern Union and the southern Confederacy would not be brief skirmishes. Cairnes acknowledged that several issues hung in the balance in the American conflict, the question of free trade being one of them. Yet as the principal cause of the war, the slavery controversy was of transcendent importance: "In spite of elaborate attempts at mystification, the real cause of the war and the real issue at stake are every day forcing themselves into prominence with a distinctness which cannot be much longer evaded." No facade could mask the fact "that it is slavery which is at the bottom of this quarrel, and that on its determination it depends whether the Power which derives its strength from slavery shall be set up with enlarged resources and increased prestige, or be now once and for all effectually broken. Cairnes hoped that "the greatest blot on modern civilization would be expunged from American soil."[28]

Bledsoe granted that the favorable reception given such views in many parts of Great Britain was damaging to the South. "We do not deny," wrote Bledsoe, "that the institution of slavery, or rather the violent and angry agitation of the slavery question, was one of the causes of the dissolution of the American Union. But how far this was a real cause, and how far it was only a hypocritical pretext to cover ulterior designs, is not the question now before us." There was ample evidence from both sections of the Union that the South regarded the tariff as "an incubus on her greatness and prosperity, from which secession and free trade would deliver her." Here, said Bledsoe, "opens the secret of the war." Northern greed for southern tariff revenues prompted the Lincoln administration to purposefully choose war over peace during the secession crisis. It was a sweeping assertion he later repeated in *Is Davis a Traitor?* Bledsoe bolstered his rebuttal of Cobden by citing statistics from Thomas Prentice Kettell's *Southern Wealth and Northern Profits,* published in 1860. Kettle, a New Yorker and the editor of the *Democratic Review,* was sympathetic to the southern position and wanted custom duties lowered as a means of addressing what he regarded to be legitimate grievances. Southern nationalists employed his statistics to justify secession precisely as Bledsoe did in his response to Cobden in the *Index.* Kettle estimated that by means of the tariff alone the South paid $40 million in customs annually to the North, while the estimate of some southern writers placed the amount as high $50 million. "No matter how great may be the production of wealth at the South," said Kettell, "it pours off into Northern coffers as rapidly as it is created, and, singularly enough, the Recipients of the Wealth are continually upbraiding the South with its production."[29]

The tariff was unquestionably a long-term cause of southern grievances and an impetus for the development of states' rights doctrine and the aspirations of southern nationalists. Its importance in that regard should not be diminished. But it was hardly a convincing argument that the tariff issue was just as important a cause of secession and war as the slavery controversy, especially when it was made by the author of *Liberty and Slavery.* It was a good contention for a Confederate publicist to make but not a persuasive one. Acknowledging the important fact that most of those who fought for the Confederacy were not slaveholders and did not fight for slavery in no way lessens its significance as the principal cause of secession and war.

William C. Davis has well said on this score that an important distinction needs to be made between the principal *cause* of the war and what motivated the majority of non-slaveholding southerners to *fight* after the commencement of hostilities: "for these are two entirely different things in myth and reality." As Davis reminds us, "Time after time, year after year, the states' rights argument always boiled down to the single issue of slavery, and not so much over the right to own slaves as over the right of a slaveholder to take such property into federal territories."[30] The southern states did not secede over the tariff issue, as intolerable as it was to those in the South who sought economic autonomy. Cobden and Cairnes had the better part of the argument over the principal cause of the American Civil War and not Bledsoe. Southern fire-eaters themselves during the secession crisis, moreover, explicitly named the defense of slavery and its attendant benefits as the cause of their clamor for disunion. Once the fighting began, however, the cause of southern nationalism shifted to allegedly loftier motives—states' rights, the defense of hearth and home, and libertarian ideals. The importance of the slavery controversy was not altogether denied as a cause of secession and war but most certainly demoted. Bledsoe's interpretation of the Civil War was instrumental in aiding that transformation. His goal as a Confederate journalist was to convince English readers of the legitimacy of secession and the Confederacy's right to exist as an independent and sovereign nation. It was easier to defend southern grievances against the tariff toward that end than to defend the institution of slavery.

A further expression of Bledsoe's Confederate nationalism is a nine-part series entitled "Secession" that appeared in the London *Evening Herald* between October 1864 and April 1865. The *Evening Herald* was decidedly sympathetic to the Confederate cause, although less overtly partisan than Hotze's *Index*. The opening line of Bledsoe's series on secession begins with a statement that later became the thesis of *Is Davis A Traitor?* "The final judgment of history, in relation to the war in America, will depend on its verdict with respect to the right of secession." If that right had not been denied by the North, there could have been no "pretext or plausible ground" for war. "Is it not wonderful, then, that a question of such magnitude and importance should have been so little considered or discussed before the war began? Perhaps no other great question of political philosophy or international law, pregnant with, and portending such awful calamities, has ever been so partially and so superficially examined as the one now under consideration." It was here that Bledsoe first criticized Daniel Webster, "the great expounder of the constitution," and Joseph Story, author of *Commentaries on the Constitution of the United States,* for the "eager partisan zeal" with which they endeavored "to obscure and refute the constitutional right of secession." And it was with an equal amount of partisan fervor that Bledsoe attempted to refute their nationalist constructions of the Constitution and the American Union in defending the right of secession.[31]

Ever since the Declaration of Independence, Bledsoe declared, there had been two political factions or parties in the United States. The opposing parties were known by different names throughout the nation's history, but the differences between them revolved around the same essential issue of consolidation *versus* state sovereignty. One party regarded the American people in all their diversities to be a single nation and labored to consolidate the power of the federal government. The other party took the name of the United States of America quite literally. It saw the Constitution as a compact between the states and the American Union as a confederacy of independent sovereignties. Adherents to the doctrine of states' rights zealously resisted attempts to consolidate the central authority of the national government from the ratification of the Constitution through the creation of the Confederacy. They insisted that the powers delegated by the states to the federal government under the Constitution could be reclaimed as reserved powers if their continuance in the Union became inimical to their rights and interests. Consolidationists, in contrast, sought a strong national government whose sovereignty transcended those of the states, at least within the bounds of its designated authority. The opposing factions or parties existed under the old Articles of Confederation even before the federal Constitution had been drafted and ratified, and afterward their opposing interests became more pronounced and entrenched.

Each party had its extreme wing. Ultraconsolidationists viewed the relationship of the state authorities to the national government as being analogous to that of so many counties within a state or individuals within a political community. Radical advocates of state sovereignty, in contrast, minimized the central authority of the federal government. They would have the states exercise their respective authorities and jurisdictions independently of each other much as they had done under the old confederation. The political difference between the parties of consolidation and states' rights, more important, soon took on a sectional character that overcame all other considerations. It was in the U.S. Senate in 1833, said Bledsoe, that the two antagonistic theories of the American Union were first drawn into bold relief in the debates of Daniel Webster and John C. Calhoun. "It was then predicted—and events have since verified the prediction—that the destinies of America would hinge and turn on the principles of that great debate. The war of words, then waged between the giants, is now a war of deeds and blood between the sections which they respectively represented. Now the question is, on which side is right, is truth, is justice?" Bledsoe's mission as a writer was to validate the Confederate revolution by arguing that secession was a constitutional right being denied the Confederate States of America by brute force. Secession was constitutional and the coercion of the Confederate states illegitimate.

When not occupied with writing, Bledsoe spent many hours fraternizing with Confederate sympathizers in London who sought to end the war. Prominent among his circle of acquaintances was the Reverend Francis William Tremlett (1821–1913), the Anglican minister and Vicar of St. Peter's in Belsize Park. Tremlett was an ardent Confederate sympathizer and chaplain aboard the Confederate sloop *Alabama,* commanded by Captain Raphael Semmes. He was the founder and secretary of the Society for Promoting the Cessation of Hostilities in America, which he led with the advice and assistance of the Confederate naval agent Matthew Fontaine Maury. Tremlett and Maury founded the society in London in the fall of 1863 and based its appeal to end the war in America upon humanitarian grounds. The slaughter of soldiers was pointless in a war in which neither side seemed able to gain a military advantage or lessen the will of the other to fight.[32] The society declared its purposes in the London *Standard* in February 1864, which Hotze reprinted in the *Index* on February 11, 1864. The American war was a stupendous calamity—a disaster not of a moment but of long and hard years, in which "a brave and dauntless people is being gradually exterminated by a process of slow torture." Indifference or aloofness to the conflict in England was an unworthy sentiment in the face of such unparalleled destruction, suffering, and loss of life.[33]

Bledsoe's association with Tremlett, Maury, Semmes, and the Society for Promoting the Cessation of Hostilities was more casual than formal, but he clearly moved within that circle. Tremlett, his mother, and his sister Louisa helped Bledsoe with house hunting and furnishings during his residence in London and instructed him in the subtleties of "Britishness."[34] He spent many pleasant hours in Tremlett's parsonage at Belsize Park—a place of hospitality, shelter, and good cheer for Confederates in London, and especially for Confederate and British naval officers.[35] Tremlett's sister Louisa A. Tremlett (1836–1912) was a twenty-eight-year-old charmer who was but a year older than Bledsoe's daughter Sophia. Louisa was the favorite of several Confederate agents in London. She often addressed Bledsoe in her letters to him as "My Dear Pater!" and he in his letters to her as "my child." He affectionately referred to Louisa, her mother, and her brother Francis as "our trio."[36] The Tremletts were Bledsoe's surrogate family during his residence in London, as they were, indeed, for several other Confederates as well. He dedicated an original poem entitled "The Beauty of the World" to Louisa in April 1865 as a token of his esteem.[37] He described the Reverend Francis William Tremlett to Jefferson Davis as "our best friend in this country, and *one who has done more work* for the Confederate cause than all other Englishmen put together."[38]

Bledsoe expressed a similar note of gratefulness for George McHenry—another of his acquaintances in London. Bledsoe and McHenry knew each other through their association with Hotze at the *Index*. All three were members of the Anthropological Society of London, although Hotze's activities within that organization were by far the most significant.[39] Bledsoe held a high opinion of McHenry. He was an expatriated Philadelphian, southern sympathizer, and author of the *Cotton Trade*, published in London in 1863.[40] The *Cotton Trade* was an influential work that advanced the claims of King Cotton and gave a sympathetic account of the system of black slave labor in the South. Bledsoe wrote McHenry a letter of introduction to Jefferson Davis for a proposed visit to the Confederate capital in the fall of 1864. He described McHenry as a friend and faithful servant of the cause who had firmly aligned his personal fortunes with "the despised and suffering South." The value of McHenry's service to the Confederacy, said Bledsoe, was the influence he exerted on public opinion in England as a writer for the *Index* and the author of the *Cotton Trade*. Tremlett was of the opinion that McHenry had done more for the cause of southern independence in England than anyone else. Bledsoe agreed. "He has, indeed, thought of nothing else, and labored for nothing else, since the commencement of the war."[41]

As the war continued through 1864, a great sorrow weighed upon Bledsoe's soul and darkened his mind. The destruction of property and the suffering of the southern people, to say nothing of that of his own family, were at times more than he could bear. Not even the pleasurable hours spent dining in the homes of English friends could brighten "the thickening gloom of the Confederacy" that hung like a pall over the dampened spirits of the Confederates in London. Greatly adding to his despondency was the unwelcome news that his longtime friend Leonidas Polk had been killed in action—an event of which Bledsoe learned in the London papers. The Episcopal bishop and Confederate general lost his life on the morning of June 14, 1864, when a federal battery shelled his position during a reconnaissance at Pine Mountain, Georgia.[42] Bledsoe had known Polk since their days together at the United States Military Academy. Polk's spiritual awakening at West Point led directly to Bledsoe's own. Chaplain Charles Pettit McIlvaine had received cadets Polk and Bledsoe into communion as members of the Protestant Episcopal Church in 1826. Polk had attempted to recruit Bledsoe as a faculty member at the University of the South in 1860, and during the war Bledsoe promoted Polk's claims to attention as an officer during his days as assistant secretary of war. He represented for Bledsoe all that was good and glorious about the cause of southern independence. After the war Polk became a veritable icon of the Lost Cause, however equivocal his legacy as a Confederate field commander.[43]

Bledsoe's disposition soured even further in August 1864 when he learned from the New York correspondent of the London *Herald* that Frederick Augustus Porter Barnard had been chosen as president of Columbia College in New York. Barnard was formerly the president of the University of Mississippi, Bledsoe's immediate successor as chair of mathematics and astronomy, and later the chair of chemistry. An enraged Bledsoe prepared an immediate response. He wrote a letter to the editor of the London *Evening Herald* on August 15, 1864, under the very pointed title "North or South?"[44] There he stated what he knew of the circumstances or, as Bledsoe insisted, the false pretenses attending Barnard's allegedly surreptitious departure from the Confederacy. He claimed to have firsthand knowledge in the matter, since Barnard's application for a passport was transacted through him in his former capacity as the assistant secretary of war. And the facts of the case were not, said Bledsoe, what they were purported to be in the letter of the New York correspondent to the *Evening Herald*. His attack on Barnard's character was merciless.

According to Bledsoe, the arrangement made was that Barnard would accompany his wife, Margaret McMurray Barnard, to Norfolk for the sole purpose of sending her across Confederate lines to friends and family in the North. It was known that she was unsympathetic to the Confederacy and wished to leave. But it was explicitly understood, Bledsoe insisted, that Barnard would return to Richmond after his wife's departure and assume a position in the Confederate service as chief of a new bureau of chemistry. "It is certain that he accepted, if he did not seek, the office tendered to him by President Davis." After Barnard arrived in Norfolk, however, he remained there instead of returning to Richmond. And when Norfolk fell into Union hands in May 1862, he left the Confederacy in the company of his wife and subsequently secured his position as president of Columbia College. Bledsoe indicted Barnard for not being a man of his word. "But these Yankees, even when they are doctors of divinity and Presidents of colleges, have very little of the virtue of the old heathen REGULUS." Bledsoe clearly felt used in the matter, and perhaps Davis did as well, and was determined to exact a measure of revenge against Barnard for his alleged breach of faith.[45]

Bledsoe and Barnard had a history. Just before the war Bledsoe received several letters from northerners and southerners in response to his reply—which appeared in the *New York Weekly Journal of Commerce* between February and April 1861—to Charles Hodge's article in the *Princeton Review* entitled "The State of the Country." Among those letters was one written by Barnard on May 14, 1861, in which he complimented Bledsoe for "the irresistible conclusiveness with which it demolished the position of your opponent, and vindicated the justice of the cause of the South." Bledsoe had rendered such a great service "to our common cause" that Barnard felt compelled to write a letter of thanks. Bledsoe's vindication was masterful and embodied "the most lucid, convincing and dispassionate investigation of the right and wrong involved in the controversy between the North and South which I have ever met with."[46] Yet as Bledsoe would have it, Barnard subsequently abandoned "our common cause" and went fishing for a better opportunity in the North, where his fellow Yankees rewarded him for deceit and deception by conferring upon him the presidency of Columbia College. Bledsoe struck hard at his distant foe by publishing Barnard's earlier letter to him in the *Herald*. He published the letter in full so that no suspicion might arise that omissions might contain expressions of sympathy for the Union, such as Barnard was known to have made after his departure from the South in May 1862.

Barnard made few new friends in the South, and most certainly estranged old ones, when he published his "Letter to the President of the United States, by a Refugee" in New York and Philadelphia in 1863. In it he vehemently attacked the Confederacy and endorsed Lincoln's prosecution of the war.[47] The letter was widely circulated and brought Barnard's name to the attention of the trustees of Columbia College, who were then in search of a new president. Barnard's biographer John Fulton has suggested that, since Barnard was a former slaveholder who once defended the soundness of his views on the institution before the trustees of the University of Mississippi, it would have been better had he left the condemnation of slavery to others. Instead, Barnard denounced slavery in his letter to Lincoln as "that relic of primeval barbarism, that loathsome monument of the brutalities of the ages of darkness, that monster injustice—cursed of Christian men and hated of God—domestic slavery."[48] Barnard's new view of slavery smacked of self-serving and unprincipled calculation in the South, especially in the partisan eyes of Bledsoe. It was another transgression for which he would have to pay a price.

Barnard defended himself against Bledsoe's strong accusations in a letter to the editor of the *New York Times*. Concerning his letter to Bledsoe in May 1861 Barnard said, "The thoughts and sentiments it expresses are those belonging to a period and state of things widely different from the present. In the protracted struggle between the North and South, which had agitated the country for years previously to the last Presidential election, my convictions and feelings had been with the section in which I lived." The article by Charles Hodge appearing in the *Princeton Review* in January 1861 stated "the Northern view of all the subjects in the [sectional] controversy." Bledsoe in responding to Hodge expressed the southern view of those issues in a "very forcible" and "convincing" manner, which was precisely the opinion that Barnard expressed in the private letter to Bledsoe that he had since seen fit to make public in the London *Herald*. "If, in the view I took of those questions at that time, I was wrong, I erred in common with many abler and better men, who have, nevertheless, cherished undyingly the love of the Union, and devoted all their energies to its maintenance."[49]

But it was of little importance in Barnard's estimation whether he had been right or wrong in expressing those views. "Secession and war have swallowed up all older issues; nor can these, in any contingency, be revived again. To secession I was ever opposed, as Mr. Bledsoe himself is aware, and my opinion on this subject was expressed in a letter of mine to a Southern friend, which was published in 1861."[50] Barnard ultimately found it impossible to reconcile his loyalty to the Union with his loyalty to the South, where he had lived since 1838 and for which he held great affection. He therefore ended his association with the University of Mississippi on October 1, 1861, with the determined purpose of immediately returning to the North—an intention he declared to the board of trustees at the time of his resignation. "And such was the manner of what Mr. Bledsoe calls my 'clandestine' escape from the Confederacy." Bledsoe's letter, whether fair to Barnard or not, served its purpose by making the rounds in the press and eliciting a response from the accused. Bledsoe placed a premium upon the values of honor, loyalty, and duty. He could be disparaging, even vindictive, toward those who he believed were lacking in those virtues. He considered Barnard, justly or otherwise, to be a turncoat who had been rewarded for his betrayal of the South.[51]

Bledsoe continued working on his justification of secession throughout his two-year residence in London. He wrote Jefferson Davis in September 1864 apprising him of his progress. "I have, at last, after much labor and trouble of mind, finished my two volumes on the so-called revolution in America." Much remained to be done, however, since "the mine in which I have worked seems scarcely to have been explored or examined by others. But though I have done little, I think I have brought many hidden things to light—many things not dreamed of by our friends—which will show the justice [of] our cause in new and convincing points of view." Although he had done little compared with what remained to be done, he was satisfied that he had made a good beginning and one that would stand. "After reading all the speeches in Congress, on both sides, I was profoundly ignorant of the transcendent merits of our cause; so little research had been done by our politicians. No cause, in my humble opinion, so great and so glorious, has ever been so feebly advocated by the pen, or so nobly by the sword."[52]

But Bledsoe never published his projected two volumes on the America Civil War during his residence in England, which one must suppose was his original intention. *Is Davis a Traitor?* was the only portion of that larger work he ever published. He had, in fact, received an offer to publish the manuscript as a series of articles in the *Church and State Review*—a periodical edited by the Anglican clergyman George Anthony Denison from 1862 to 1865. Denison offered to pay Bledsoe for his contribution, but he declined the offer because the series was to run over a two-year period. But whatever Bledsoe's original plans were regarding the publication of his manuscript, they immediately changed with Lee's surrender at Appomattox. The dramatic collapse of the Confederacy in April and May 1865 was not entirely a matter of surprise, since the news from home had been disheartening for some time. Yet the finality of it all bore its own crushing weight. "How these glorious States," Bledsoe observed, "shot forth, dazzling the Universe with the splendor of their career, and fell like stars from heaven."[53] He would spend the remainder of his life justifying the Lost Cause of southern independence and explaining the origins and meaning of the war from a Confederate perspective. The Confederate States of America was no more, but Bledsoe's self-declared mission of writing the revolution was just beginning.

Bledsoe's Civil War contained many personal ironies. None were more poignant, however, than his estrangement from Charles Pettit McIlvaine—his religious mentor and brother-in-law. The last time McIlvaine met Bledsoe before the war was as a guest of the Bledsoe family at the University of Virginia in the fall of 1859. They would not see each other again until a chance encounter occurred in a Baltimore street in October 1873.[54] One can assume that McIlvaine and Bledsoe parted from that accidental meeting as old friends, but it must have triggered both pleasant and painful memories: fond ones of their years together at West Point, Kenyon College, and of their families, and sorrowful ones regarding the war. The loyalties of Bledsoe and McIlvaine during that struggle could not have been more diametrically opposed. McIlvaine was a warm supporter of the Lincoln administration, which sent him on a diplomatic mission to England in 1861–62 to muster support for the Union cause and help ensure that Great Britain did not abandon its policy of neutrality.[55] He rejoiced at the news of Union victories in his correspondence with William Henry Seward, Salmon Portland Chase, and Lincoln, encouraging them to stay the course.[56] How strange it must have been for McIlvaine to know that Bledsoe was an apostle of Confederate nationalism, and how extraordinary for Bledsoe that McIlvaine was a staunch Unionist and the friend and warm supporter of Seward, Chase, and Lincoln.

No less ironic was an episode that occurred during Bledsoe's residence in London that once again connected the lives of the McIlvaine and Bledsoe families, if only briefly. McIlvaine wrote Lincoln in December 1864 requesting a pass through Union lines for his wife's sister Mrs. Harriet Coxe Bledsoe, wife of Albert Taylor Bledsoe. Harriet had earlier gone North by way of Harpers Ferry due to ill health and the desire to visit her daughter Sophia in New York and a sister in Philadelphia. She now wanted to return to her children in Charlottesville with a trunk containing clothes and a carpet bag. "She is a lady of such delicacy of conscience and honour," McIlvaine assured Lincoln, "as to be deserving of the most perfect confidence that a permit would in no sense or degree be used for purposes forbidden." Harriet gave McIlvaine her personal assurances that her husband no longer had any connection with the Confederate government. He was in London, where he was entirely occupied in the preparation and publication of "scientific and other books." Harriet's vague explanation of what her husband was doing in London must have given McIlvaine pause, since he knew his sympathies, but the matter at hand was reuniting his sister-in-law with her children in Charlottesville.[57]

McIlvaine asked Lincoln that if he was pleased to grant Harriet a pass to send it as soon as convenient to Salmon Portland Chase at Washington, who would know what to do with it. Harriet was someone Lincoln had known in a former life and McIlvaine a man whose word he trusted implicitly. He granted the pass on January 16, 1865: "Allow the bearer, Mrs. Harriet C. Bledsoe, to pass our lines with ordinary baggage and go South. A. Lincoln." According to a Bledsoe family tradition, McIlvaine originally made the application for Harriet's pass through Secretary of War Edwin M. Stanton, who is said to have refused it. It was presumably then that McIlvaine appealed the matter directly to Lincoln. Harriet's pass remained in the Bledsoe family as a memento of the war. And six years later, during a visit with the Bledsoe family, Jefferson Davis wrote a note across the back of the pass: "Jefferson Davis for his dear friend Miss Anna Bledsoe, May 15, 1871."[58] Bearing the signatures of both Lincoln and Davis, the pass became an even more coveted keepsake—a curious document that in its own way frames the paradoxes of Bledsoe's life as fully as any other.

9

THE JUDGMENT OF HISTORY

The Right of Secession and the Lost Cause

BLEDSOE RETURNED TO VIRGINIA in February 1866 and took an oath of loyalty to the Constitution and laws of the United States on June 27 of that year.[1] His demeanor on the occasion is not a matter of record, but one may suppose it was grave. Richmond and much else of the former Confederacy lay in ruins. His family's situation during the last two years of the war was precarious, though far from destitute. Bledsoe had been separated from his wife and daughters and absent from the University of Virginia for more than two years. The leave granted him from the university in the summer of 1863 had been for a year only. Having heard nothing from him regarding his intention of returning to the faculty over so prolonged a period, the board of visitors declared his position vacant on July 5, 1865. Nor apparently did Bledsoe seek reappointment at the university, "since the enemies of the South and my enemies [Republicans] were placed over that once noble institution."[2] Even more troubling was the fact that his longtime friend and former president Jefferson Davis was a state prisoner at Fortress Monroe. Federal authorities imprisoned Davis on May 22, 1865, as a suspect in the assassination of Lincoln and the attempted murder of Seward. A lack of creditable evidence failed to link Davis to either the death of Lincoln or the attempt on Seward's life. Yet Davis remained in federal custody since the U.S. Circuit Court in the District of Virginia indicted him for treason in June 1865. The U.S. Circuit Court in the District of Columbia issued a second indictment for treason later that same year.

Davis remained a state prisoner for two years awaiting a trial that was several times delayed and ultimately never happened. His defenders feared that if found guilty he would be executed. If that apprehension seems exaggerated in retrospect, it was a legitimate concern at the time. Bledsoe was among those alarmed about the state of Davis's health and doubtful future. He did not question that he was in imminent danger of being executed as a traitor. Bledsoe believed that the Yankees sought retribution for the war and that at the very least they would humiliate Davis as a means of further discrediting the Confederate cause. Those circumstances prompted him to recast the manuscript on the right of secession he brought with him from London and publish it as quickly as possible. *Is Davis a Traitor; Or Was Secession a Constitutional Right Previous to the War of 1861?* appeared in Baltimore in the fall of 1866. It was the only part of his two-volume manuscript on the Civil War he ever published, although he would continue to draw upon those materials for years to come as the editor of the *Southern Review.*

During the early part of August 1866—only a few months before the publication of *Is Davis a Traitor?*—Bledsoe visited Davis at Fortress Monroe. He did so to satisfy his own curiosity about the state of his health and how he was being treated.[3] Security measures had been greatly relaxed by that time. Davis was no longer a suspect in the Lincoln assassination and attempted execution of Seward. Andrew Johnson in April 1866 granted Davis's wife, Varina Howell Davis, permission to visit her husband after nearly a year's separation. Varina subsequently took up temporary quarters at Fortress Monroe. During that time, friends were allowed to visit her and prisoner Davis at the discretion of the commandant.[4] Bledsoe, much to his surprise, was one of those permitted to see them. He described his interview with Davis in a letter written to the Baltimore attorney David Maulden Perine on August 9, 1866, an account of which is given here for the first time.[5]

The authorities at Fortress Monroe permitted Bledsoe to spend the entire day with Davis in private. Not even the officer of the day monitored their conversation. Davis inquired about the progress of Bledsoe's manuscript on secession and intently listened as Bledsoe informed him of its contents. "He has always, indeed, taken the deepest interest in my writings and has said things about them which I neither forget nor repeat. He begged me, over and over again, to publish my little work on secession at once."[6] Bledsoe assured him that he had the work ready for the press and hoped to have it out by the first of September. He blissfully informed Davis that "an old-line Whig, and a celebrated politician, who used to swear by Mr. Webster, said, after reading this manuscript, 'You have just reduced Story and Webster to grease spots, wiped them out with the oil of vitriol!'" Bledsoe confidently declared that he had the better part of the argument—a boast he would subsequently repeat. "I know I have completely refuted all their [Joseph Story's and Daniel Webster's] sophisms, and vindicated the cause of the South. It is no great work, it only requires patience in labor, to vindicate a cause so noble and so just; and it has been with me 'a labor of love!'" Such self-congratulatory sentiments came all too easy to Bledsoe, but many of his admiring followers later accepted them at face value.

Bledsoe's promised vindication of secession made its appearance in Baltimore in either September or early October 1866. *Is Davis a Traitor; Or Was Secession a Constitutional Right Previous to the War of 1861?* concisely affirmed states' rights doctrine and the compact theory of Union and made an impassioned defense of the principles and good names of those who had embraced the Confederate cause. Bledsoe declared that it was not his purpose to reopen the subject of secession for the present or future but only in regard to the past. "The subjection of the Southern States, and their acceptance of the terms dictated by the North, may, if the reader please, be considered as having shifted the Federal Government from the basis of compact to that of conquest; and thereby extinguished every claim to the right of secession for the future." He examined the right of secession only in reference to the past in order to vindicate the names and memories of Jefferson Davis, Stonewall Jackson, Albert Sidney Johnston, Robert E. Lee, and all southerners who fought and suffered in "the great war of coercion." He intended to show that, however much the leaders of the Confederate cause might be assailed by "the ignorance, the prejudices, and the passions of the hour, they were nevertheless perfectly loyal to truth, justice, and the Constitution of 1787 as it came from the hands of the fathers."[7]

Bledsoe's defense of secession appeared during the early phase of Reconstruction. Ignominious defeat had placed the leaders of the Republican Party in control of a prostrate and humiliated South whose destiny was uncertain. But a defiant Bledsoe refused to allow the victors the last word regarding the motives and intentions of those who had seceded from the Union and fought for the Confederate States of America. The experience of defeat altered none of his views and only hardened his attitudes toward the victors. "The radicals themselves may, if they will only read the following pages, find sufficient reason to doubt their own infallibility, and to relent in their bitter persecutions of the South." He declared that the Confederate cause could yet be vindicated "and the final verdict of History determined in favor of a gallant, but downtrodden and oppressed, PEOPLE." That faith ensured that the Civil War would continue to be fought as a historical conflict by generations yet unborn. The clash of arms ended at Appomattox, but in Bledsoe's judgment the battle for posterity had only just begun. He was in the vanguard of those who pressed the claims of the Lost Cause before the bench and bar of history. Southern political principles, he confidently asserted, could yet be reclaimed and vindicated even in the new era of Republican rule.[8]

But why, asked Bledsoe, should these matters be reargued? Why the appeal to reason, history, and political philosophy in the name of secession? "Has not the war of secession been waged, and the South subjected? Can reason, however victorious, bind up the broken heart, or call the dead to life? Can reason cause the desolate, dark, waste places of the South to smile again, or the hearts of her downcast and dejected people to rejoice? Can reason strike the fetters from the limbs of the down-trodden white population of the South?" Reason could do none of those things yet still had "a high office and duty to perform." The South, for all its suffering and losses, still possessed something that was far more precious than either life or property. It still possessed the "moral wealth" of its Jacksons, Johnstons, Lees, and Davises and all those living and dead who had participated in the noble cause of southern independence. "These are her imperishable jewels; and, since little else is left to her, these shall be cherished with the greater love, with the more enthusiastic and undying devotion."[9] Bledsoe's homage to the Lost Cause, however defective from a Unionist perspective, struck a chord of appreciative affirmation among former Confederates.

Bledsoe's apologia centered on the premise that the federal Union established under the Constitution of the United States in 1787 was a compact of fully sovereign and independent states. It was *not* a sovereign nation created by the American people acting *independently* of the states. He reaffirmed old arguments when he declared that the states created the national government as their agent and not as their master. Yet slowly but surely the national government consolidated its powers and prerogatives at the expense of state sovereignty, confirming the worst fears of those who opposed the ratification of the federal Constitution in 1788 and 1789. Secession was a justified action based upon the reserved powers of the states under the federal Constitution, which became politically expedient when the slaveholding states of the South no longer believed they could maintain their rights and interests within the Union. Secession and the creation of a southern confederacy had been a constitutionally warranted action and in no way an act of treason or rebellion. These were arguments that Bledsoe first presented in his series on secession in the London *Evening Herald* between October 1864 and April 1865. He now elaborated and modified them relative to the outcome of the war and the pending trial of Jefferson Davis for treason.

States' rights advocates consistently maintained that the powers delegated by the states to the federal government under the Constitution could be reclaimed should they ever have just cause to do so. The states, argued Bledsoe, forfeited none of their sovereignty or independence by delegating certain powers to the federal government or through their individual acts of ratification. He flatly rejected the notion that if a state delegated a portion of its sovereign powers, or agreed not to exercise them, the state's sovereignty was thereby limited or abridged. The Swiss jurist and political theorist Emmerich de Vattel (1714–67) spoke directly to this point in his influential *Law of Nations or the Principles of Natural Law* (1758). Bledsoe brought Vattel's political theory to the attention of those who either ignored or minimized the sovereignty presumably possessed by the American states, since his views were well known to the architects of the American Union. Several sovereign and independent states, said Vattel, could form themselves into "a perpetual" confederacy without each of them ceasing to be sovereign and independent. By uniting in such a manner the states constituted a federal republic. But the joint deliberations of member states within a confederacy did not diminish their autonomy, even though they agreed to restrict the exercise of a portion of their powers. Here was a principle of natural law, Bledsoe affirmed, that had been recognized and embodied in the founding legislation of the American Republic. Secession under that view was a legitimate means of reclaiming state sovereignty and reserved rights.[10]

The doctrine of reserved rights could never be abandoned by those who justified secession as a constitutional right. The thirteenth article of the Articles of Confederation declared that the American Union "shall be perpetual," whereas the second article affirmed that "each state retains its sovereignty, freedom, and independence." The states under the Articles of Confederation voluntarily delegated a portion of their sovereignty to the general or national government, as they again did under the federal Constitution to an even greater degree. Yet Bledsoe maintained that those acts of delegation in no way weakened the individual sovereignties of the states that ratified the Constitution. Nor did the new federal government under the Constitution declare itself to be perpetual as had the old government under the Articles of Confederation. Neither did it assign any period for its duration. How much more clearly, Bledsoe asked, did the states "in the more perfect Union" retain their sovereignty unimpaired, since it never declared itself to be perpetual or set a time when it should expire or give way to a new scheme of confederation? He insisted that the longevity of the new Union was an open-ended proposition among the founders and that its duration would be decided by future events.

Bledsoe avowed that states' rights construction of the Constitution and American Union as vehemently as anyone.

One could not examine the proceedings of the Constitutional Convention and the ratification process, Bledsoe argued, without concluding that those who drafted and ratified the Constitution considered it a compact between the states. The delegates to the Philadelphia convention were elected by their respective states, deliberated and voted by state, and, when they had finished drafting the document, submitted it to state ratifying conventions for approval. The Constitution and "the more perfect Union" went into operation when eleven of the thirteen American states ratified it in September 1789 (ratification required only nine states), but it was not a binding arrangement for the two states that had not yet ratified it. North Carolina and Rhode Island remained aloof from the Union for several more months after the ratification of the Constitution. In November 1789 North Carolina entered the Union as the twelfth state, and in May 1790 Rhode Island entered as the thirteenth. Bledsoe maintained that they were under no compulsion to join the Union and theoretically could have stayed out it had they so chose. The vote of each state in ratifying the Constitution was an "absolutely free, sovereign, and independent act."[11]

The circumstances under which the authors of the Constitution drafted and submitted the document to the states for ratification clearly showed that "the allegiance of the citizen was originally and exclusively due to his State, and was extended to the Federal Government only by a sovereign act of his State, so by a like sovereign act, the State may reclaim his supreme allegiance." It was the intention of the founders "that the allegiance of the citizen should go with his affections; and cling to the sovereign will of the State in which he lives, whether that leads him into or out of the Union." The argument that a state could reclaim "the supreme allegiance" of its citizens, that their loyalty should rest upon their "affections," and that they should hold fast to the sovereign will of their respective states is essentially a static conception of citizenship and the American Union. The political understandings, compromises, and arrangements that met the needs of the Republic at its founding, however, were subject to change. The nature of Union itself was subject to change over time. Were the understandings and intentions of the founders always to decide the destinies of generations yet unborn? Were later generations of Americans not just as capable of formulating their own views regarding citizenship, allegiance, and the nature of the Union in relation to their own wants and needs? Bledsoe's position on the proper allegiance of citizens and the irrevocable nature of state sovereignty, however much special pleading is involved, directly speaks to the ambiguities and untidiness of American federalism before the claims of states rights' doctrine were reputed by the American Civil War.

Bledsoe directed the sharpest barbs of criticism at the constitutional constructions of Daniel Webster and Joseph Story. Webster denied in his great debate with John C. Calhoun in February 1833 that the Constitution was a compact. Story also argued against the idea of a compact in the third volume of his *Commentaries on the Constitution,* published that same year. According to Story, "the obvious deductions which may be, and, indeed, have been, drawn from considering the Constitution a compact between States, are that it operates as a mere treaty or convention between them, and has an obligatory force no longer than suits its pleasure or its consent continues." Here, said Bledsoe, was the central constitutional issue or point in controversy—the very one to be denied by nationalists and affirmed by secessionists. "Thus the great controversy is narrowed down to the single question—Is the Constitution a compact between the States? If so, then the right of secession is conceded, even by its most powerful and determined opponents; the great jurist, as well as by 'the great expounders' of the North."[12]

Those of the Webster-Story school denied that the Constitution was a compact. They argued that neither the states nor the people of the states created the Constitution but rather that it was the handiwork of the people of the United States in the aggregate acting in their collective and sovereign capacities as the citizens of one nation. Echoing the nationalist sentiments of Webster and Story, the American historian John Lothrop Motley affirmed in 1861 that "the States never acceded to the Constitution, and have no power to secede from it. It was 'ordained and established' over the States by a power superior to the States, by the people of the whole land in their aggregate capacity." The United States under that view was an indivisible nation-state. It was not a mere confederacy of fully autonomous states that could withdraw from the Union when it suited them and destroy the territorial integrity of the nation in the process. It was necessary for Motley and other nationalists to maintain that position because to assume any other would be to acknowledge, as Motley himself said, that "the same power which established the Constitution may justly destroy it."[13]

Bledsoe fully agreed with the logic of Motley's conclusion. The same power that created and ratified the Constitution—the states—could indeed destroy it, or at least a portion of it, by seceding from the Union. Yet when one examined the manner in which the founders actually wrote, debated, and ratified the Constitution, the declarations of Story, Webster, and Motley that the American people and not the states had created the American Union were exceedingly astonishing, if not altogether "inexplicable on the supposition that their authors were honest men." No reasonable reading of the historical record, Bledsoe insisted, could lead to any other conclusion than that the Constitution originated as a compact between fully sovereign states. "But who can measure the mysterious depths of party spirit, or the force of political passions in a democracy? I know something of that force; for, during the greater part of my life, I followed, with implicit confidence, those blind leaders of the blind, Mr. Justice Story and Daniel Webster. History will yet open the.eyes of the world to the strange audacity of their assertions."

What Bledsoe regarded as one of Webster's most audacious and untenable claims regarding the Constitution occurred in the U.S. Senate in February 1833. Webster protested against the language used by John C. Calhoun in a resolution on southern objections to the tariff. Calhoun resolved "that the people of the several States composing these United States are united as parties to a constitutional compact, to which the people of each State acceded as a separate sovereign community, each binding itself by its own particular ratification; and that the union, of which the said compact is the bond, is a union *between the States* ratifying the same." Webster supposed that, since the converse of accession was secession, Calhoun purposely introduced the word *accede* so it could be more plausibly argued that the states could secede from the Union. Yet Webster maintained that use of the term *accede* was out of place. The founders used no such form of expression in establishing the government of the United States, which rendered it "unconstitutional language."[14] But was this really a new word, asked Bledsoe? Was it really unconstitutional language? Bledsoe proceeded to demonstrate to good purpose that *accede* was far from being a new word or unconstitutional language—so much so that it was *the* very word that the founders themselves used to describe the act of ratifying the Constitution. He invalidated Webster's interpretation in no uncertain terms. By consulting the *Madison Papers, Elliott's Debates,* and the published papers of several of the delegates to the Constitutional Convention, Bledsoe showed that the use of the words *accede* and *accession* was as common and unexceptional to the framers of the Constitution as it was foreign and extraordinary to Webster. It was the strongest part of Bledsoe's historical exegesis into the origins of the federal Union and the understandings and intentions of the founders.[15]

Another important component in Bledsoe's defense of secession was his analysis of the language of the Constitution—specifically its preamble. "We, the people of the United States, in order to form a more perfect Union . . . do ordain and establish this Constitution for United States of America." It was upon the authority of that phrase that Story, Webster, and Motley argued that the Constitution was not a compact between the states and that the Constitution was not established or ratified as a federal act but as a national one. It was not ratified by the states but by a power superior to the states, the sovereign will of the entire American people acting collectively as one nation or political community. Bledsoe begged to differ. "The first clause of this preamble to the Constitution, wholly detached from its history and from every other portion of the same instrument, as well as from all the contemporary and subsequent expositions of its authors, is made the very corner-stone of the Northern theory of the general government of the United States. That tremendous theory, or scheme of power, has been erected on this naked, isolated, and, as we expect to show, grossly misrepresented clause." To arrive at the actual meaning of these words, it was unnecessary to use unconstitutional language or violate "any rule of interpretation."[16]

The meaning of the preamble to those who established the more perfect Union was quite different from that assigned it by Story, Webster, and Motley. "We, the people of the United States" unquestionably meant "We, the people of the States"—the authority by which the Constitution was created and ratified. No other explanation of the meaning of that phrase, Bledsoe affirmed, was even intelligible. The people of the states had ratified the Constitution for themselves alone and were not acting as an embryonic nation as a whole. Each state acted independently of the others. Bledsoe argued that "the Southern interpretation" of the preamble was the only "fair, legitimate, and reasonable" reading. John Taylor of Carolina, Abel P. Upshur of Virginia, and John C. Calhoun of South Carolina had all advanced the same view. And Bledsoe thought that those arguments had been especially well presented by James Spence of Liverpool in his *American Union* (1862), an "admirable work" he recommended to all who would understand the southern interpretation of the clause in question. "We have only said admirable; but, all things considered, Mr. Spence's work is truly a wonderful production." Spence's views on the constitutionality of secession and the American Union as a confederation of sovereign states were important influences on Bledsoe, which he freely acknowledged.

Bledsoe continued his campaign against Webster's interpretation of the

Constitution by making him confront himself in a chapter entitled "Mr. Webster versus Mr. Webster." Bledsoe ridiculed the contradictory speeches made by Webster in 1833, 1835, and 1851 as to whether the Constitution was a compact containing any stipulations made by the states. Webster asked in his reply to Calhoun in 1833: "If the States be parties [to the Constitution], as States, what are their rights, and what are their respective covenants and stipulations? And where are their rights, covenants, and stipulations expressed? The States engage for nothing, they promise nothing." Yet that opinion did not fully accord with the views propounded in Webster's speech at the Odeon in Boston on October 12, 1835, and on subsequent occasions. Webster noted in his address at the Odeon, where several thousand people gathered for the presentation of a commemorative vase honoring him as "the Defender of the Constitution," that stipulations by the states existed in the Constitution after all. Webster then stated that "the Constitution, again, is founded on compromise, and the most perfect and absolute good faith, in regard to every stipulation of this kind contained in it is indispensable to its preservation. Every attempt to accomplish even the best purpose, every attempt to grasp that which is regarded as an immediate good, in violation of these stipulations, is full of danger to the whole Constitution."[17]

Webster likewise noted on another occasion that "all the stipulations contained in the Constitution in favor of the slave States ought to be fulfilled. Slavery as it exists in the States, is beyond the reach of Congress. It is a concern of the States themselves; they have never submitted it to Congress, and Congress has no rightful power over it." And regarding the commerce clause of the Constitution Webster further acknowledged that states had delegated all their authority over imports to the general government, yet another right, covenant, and stipulation delegated by the states to the general government. The Daniel Webster of 1833, Bledsoe scoffed, denied that the Union was a compact and the Webster of 1835 and later years affirmed that it was. "But here, again, we may appeal from Philip drunk to Philip sober, from Webster intoxicated with the fumes of a false theory of [national] power to Webster under the influence of a simple view of truth." No man, charged Bledsoe, could have been more inconsistent in explaining his views on the Constitution than "the great expounder" himself. He was, by twists and turns, absolutely contradictory on the subject and uncertain of his own position. "It was, with him, either a compact between the States, or not a compact between the States, according to the exigencies of the occasion. He could be equally eloquent on both sides of the question."[18]

Bledsoe identified eight grounds or causes of secession in *Is Davis a Traitor?* that had justified the Confederates states in withdrawing from the Union: (1) the destruction of the balance of political power originally established between the North and South at the Constitutional Convention; (2) sectional legislation (the tariff) by which the original poverty of the North was exchanged for the wealth of the South; (3) the formation of a sectional faction (the Republican Party), or as Bledsoe was fond of calling it in the words of Wendell Phillips, "the party of the North pledged against the South"; (4) the subversion and disregard of all the checks in the Constitution designed for the protection of the minority against the majority, or "the lawless reign of the Northern Demos"; (5) "the unjust treatment of the slavery question" by which the northern states violated the constitutional protections of the institution while at the same time they insisted that the constitutional stipulations favoring their own interests be maintained; (6) "the sophistry and hypocrisy" by which the North justified the oppression of the South; (7) the abuse and slanders perpetrated against the South by the abolitionists through which southerners became a despised people; and (8) the denial of the right of secession and the threat of annihilation should the South ever attempt to exercise that right.[19] In the face of those alleged wrongs and grievances, Bledsoe asserted, secession had not been treason or rebellion but the legitimate exercise of a basic constitutional right. Those who were already persuaded of the righteousness of the southern cause needed little convincing of the correctness of his arguments and opinions. But those who had fought the war to repudiate the right of secession and restore the Union were little inclined to place much credence in them.

Bledsoe closed his defense of secession with a backward glance at the legislators of 1787. He portrayed them as political prophets, whom he divided into three classes: those who foresaw future difficulties between the North and the South in "the more perfect Union" and warned of their dangers, those who did not see those perils, and those who perceived them but minimized their likely import. Of those who possessed the gift of foresight, none in his estimation did more so than Charles Pinckney of South Carolina and George Mason and Patrick Henry of Virginia, all of whom expressed concern about the southern states being the minority section of the proposed Union. Pinckney worried that since the southern states would be in the minority and the regulation of trade would be the purview of the general government, the southern states would become little more than overseers for the interests of the northern states. Mason subscribed to the maxim that a majority would always oppress a minority when given the opportunity. The eight northern states held interests that were different from those of the five southern states and would likely command more votes in both branches of the legislature. The southern states thus had grounds for being suspicious of the new plan of government being offered them. Henry shared those fears and was certain that they would one day hurt the interests of the southern states. The prospect of allowing people who did not share the interests of Virginians to legislate for them deeply troubled him, for such an arrangement would place power in the hands of those whose advantage it would be to infringe them.

When Bledsoe's justification of secession made its appearance in the fall of 1866, Davis was still in prison awaiting trial for what Carl Schurz said would have been "the trial of the century" had it actually occurred.[20] Yet notwithstanding the topicality and timeliness of the work, it did not generate much notice in either the North or the South. The relative obscurity of *Is Davis a Traitor?* among Bledsoe's contemporaries, however, is not entirely a matter of surprise. Bledsoe had the work printed in Baltimore instead of placing it with a major publisher. And it was certainly asking too much for the northern literary establishment to pay much attention to a book that justified secession and repudiated the justice of the Union victory. Yet the work also received sparse notice in the South—a disheartening reality about which Bledsoe sometimes complained. Southern literary periodicals were in dire condition in the fall of 1866. They were only beginning to show the first signs of rebirth—a process of renewal in which Bledsoe himself would play a conspicuous part as the founder and editor of the *Southern Review*. The fact that southerners initially gave so little notice to *Is Davis a Traitor?* was a sign of the times. They were exhausted, impoverished, and eager to put the war behind them. So many young men had died, and there were so many uncertainties about the future. Southerners were little disposed to buy and read books in those difficult circumstances, even those that absolved them of dishonor in the aftermath of a humiliating defeat.

Yet southern newspapers did not entirely ignore Bledsoe's book. An anonymous reviewer in the *Baltimore Gazette* noted with a tinge of regret and sullenness in October 1866 that *might* had made *right* in returning a negative answer to the question of whether secession had been a legitimate expression of state sovereignty. "Education, interest, passion, prejudice, partisanship and brute force have done their full work upon it. That most irresistible form of human reason—the reason of the strongest—has settled it beyond appeal. The conquered may think what they please about it, but they are conquered, and what they think is of no practical importance." Even so, the reviewer found much to praise about Bledsoe's historical scholarship and rendered an insightful opinion as to how former Confederates would likely regard *Is Davis a Traitor?* "To the Southern people, whose convictions it maintains, with so much sympathy and vigor, it will be a text book and a record forever, though the doctrines which it maintains have gone down, with so many of their noblest lives, beneath the dust of battle and defeat."[21]

Is Davis a Traitor? is a classic of its genre. The work is thoroughly researched and well argued. But Bledsoe exaggerated the importance of the work beyond what was necessary or even credible. He made the improbable claim in the *Southern Review* for January 1876 that the arguments he made in defense of the right of secession prompted the federal government to drop legal proceedings against Davis on the charge of treason. The opinions and views expressed in *Is Davis a Traitor?*, crowed Bledsoe, were regarded as "absolutely conclusive, by all who have read it, whether friends or foes." Thaddeus Stevens reportedly confessed within the hearing of U.S. congressman Stevenson Archer, a resident of Baltimore, that he considered the work "unanswerable" and that Secretary of War Edwin M. Stanton was of the same opinion. "Hence, the leaders of the Republican Party entered a *nolli prosequi* in the case of Mr. Davis; because they believed it would be impossible to convict him, even within their own courts." Bledsoe restated that assertion in the *Southern Review* for July 1876: "Nay, it is a well-known fact, that the Republican leaders of Washington City, concluded to enter a *nolli prosequi* in the case of Jefferson Davis; *because it would be impossible to convict him either of treason or rebellion.* What a confession!"[22]

Bledsoe claimed much too much for himself in those statements, yet his bold assertion has often been repeated. His daughter Sophia restated it even more starkly: "Charles O'Connor [O'Conor], Mr. Davis's lawyer, said that he never could have saved Mr. Davis's life without the material collected together in this work."[23] Sophia sincerely believed that to have been the case, and for that matter, so did Bledsoe. Yet those in the South who regarded Bledsoe as a historical redeemer accepted his claim at face value. William Gordon McCabe, a former student at the University of Virginia, is a case in point. McCabe kept the tradition regarding Bledsoe's book alive in his memoirs published in 1925. *Is Davis a Traitor?*, said McCabe, "carried consternation in the ranks of Radical demagogues, who had been clamoring for President Davis's blood, and which by its inexorable logic and wealth of constitutional learning drove the reluctant law-officers of the government to advise the dismissal of the indictments against the Confederate Executive. Mr. Davis was never tried, because the Federal Government was afraid to try him."[24] It was a script that Bledsoe himself had written nearly fifty years earlier—in good faith but largely in self-delusion.

All historians who have examined Bledsoe's life in any detail encounter the bold and self-assured statement that the arguments made in *Is Davis a Traitor?* led to the government's decision not to bring Davis to trial for treason. Some have accepted it entirely, others in part, and some not at all. Edwin Mims stated in his sketch of Bledsoe in the *Dictionary of American Biography* that his book "proved to be a mine of materials for the lawyers who were defending Davis." David Rankin Barbee, a diligent and admiring student of Bledsoe's life, matter-of-factly stated that *Is Davis a Traitor?* was "a book that Stanton and Stevens said was unanswerable, a book that freed Jefferson Davis." Harry E. Pratt also repeated that assertion without further comment. Richard M. Weaver, like Mims, said that Davis's attorneys Robert Oulds and Charles' O'Conor "made use of the book in preparing their defense," but he stopped short of linking Bledsoe's defense of secession with the dismissal of the indictments of treason brought against Davis by the U.S. government. E. Merton Coulter less cautiously accepted the contention that the work was "a force in his [Davis's] ultimate release," citing Bledsoe's own assertion in the *Southern Review* that it had been so as supporting evidence.[25]

Other historians have been more skeptical. John Boyce Bennett observed that there is little evidence, apart from Bledsoe's own assertion, that his arguments spared Davis and the nation the ordeal of a trial for treason. Steven E. Woodworth also prudently noted in his notice of Bledsoe in *American National Biography* that the claim is "doubtful," while acknowledging that many of Bledsoe's contemporaries in the South sincerely believed that the book had prevented Davis from being indicted for treason.[26] That is most certainly true. The belief essentially established itself as a tradition within the ideology of the Lost Cause. One of Bledsoe's acquaintances, the Reverend Samuel Augustus Steel, gave powerful testimony to precisely that effect. Steel was at one time the chaplain of the University of Virginia and later the pastor of the Broad Street Church in Richmond. He was certainly in a position to know what people said and thought about Bledsoe's book within his sphere. "Many people think that Dr. Bledsoe's defense of Davis made his acquittal a foregone conclusion. No court could venture to condemn him in the face of such testimony without itself incurring condemnation before the bar of History."[27]

A review of the evidence for and against Bledsoe's claim is certainly warranted given the tradition's longevity. An entry in Bledsoe's memoranda concerning his correspondence refers to a letter received from William Bradford Reed of Philadelphia—one of Jefferson Davis's legal counsels who had written him in regard to the arguments presented in *Is Davis a Traitor?* Bledsoe said this was the only surviving letter of three from Reed that were once in his possession.[28] That Bledsoe and Reed corresponded regarding Bledsoe's book is certainly a tenable claim, notwithstanding the fact that the whereabouts of the letters mentioned in Bledsoe's memoranda are unknown and the letters are probably no longer extant. As one of Davis's defense counsels, Reed was no doubt familiar with *Is Davis a Traitor?* Two similar letters to Bledsoe from Davis's chief legal counsel, Charles O'Conor of New York, met the same fate due to Bledsoe's carelessness in preserving his correspondence. The letters are noted, however, in the memoranda on the correspondence that was still in Bledsoe's possession around 1868, when the memoranda were written. As in the case of Reed, it is in no way surprising that O'Conor had corresponded with Bledsoe during his preparation for Davis's defense.

Bledsoe further boasted, "When Davis begged me to publish the book, just before the time set for his trial, he said he knew that no one would analyze and discuss the subject [the right of secession] as I had done; and both Reed and O'Conner [O'Conor], the most eminent of his counsel, admitted that I opened and cleared up the great theme to their minds."[29] That claim is likely true. There is no reason for doubting that as members of Davis's counsel Reed and O'Conor, both of whom were prominent Peace Democrats during the war, would have been receptive to and even complimentary of the arguments made in Bledsoe's book on secession. This is actually among the more tenable of Bledsoe's claims. Given the purpose of Bledsoe's book, it would be truly surprising, extraordinary in fact, if he had not been in correspondence with Davis's defense counsel regarding its contents. But that in no way substantiates Bledsoe's assertion that his book was instrumental in the government's decision to drop its case against Davis. That is an entirely separate claim.

Evidence supporting Bledsoe's contention that *Is Davis a Traitor?* won Davis his freedom is entirely wanting. Those who believed and asserted that the book influenced the court's decision to forgo a trial receive no support from the records of the court. The legal proceedings in the case of the *United States vs. Jefferson Davis* make no mention of the right of secession whatsoever or of the arguments advanced in defense of it in *Is Davis a Traitor?* The decision not to bring Davis to trial was based upon a complex set of legal, constitutional, and political issues and maneuvers by the court and Davis's attorneys that had nothing to do with the contested right of secession. The technicalities of the case had everything to do with Davis's status as a state prisoner and the uncertain status of the former states of the Confederacy after passage of the congressional Reconstruction measures in 1867 and 1868.[30] The circumstances attending his incarceration and pending trial were unprecedented. The bale bond of $100,000 signed by Horace Greeley, Gerrit Smith, Cornelius Vanderbilt, and several Virginians had far more to do with effecting Davis's release from prison than anything written by Bledsoe. And what ultimately resulted in the dismissal of the government's charges against Davis again was not Bledsoe's book but the suggestion made by Chief Justice Salmon Portland Chase that Section 3 of the Fourteenth Amendment had already punished Davis once by banning him from ever again holding public office. Any further proceedings against him would be double jeopardy and therefore unconstitutional.

The pivotal points of law upon which the court's decision turned in the Davis case were not those that Bledsoe pleaded in defense of the right of secession. While it may well be true, as Edwin Mims and Paul Dennis Sporer have plausibly suggested, that Bledsoe's book provided Davis's attorneys with material for his defense, the fact is not reflected in the court record of *United States vs. Jefferson Davis*.[31] It is reasonable inference and nothing more. It was the opinion of Carl Schurz that by 1869 few in the government or in the North had a taste for the spectacle of a trial for treason.[32] The climate of opinion had been different at the time of Davis's arrest and incarceration. Attitudes toward Davis and Confederates in general were much harder in the immediate aftermath of Lincoln's assassination when the indictments for treason were handed down. They softened after Johnson's general pardon of Confederates on Christmas Day of 1868. Most Americans were willing by that time to put the war behind them and move on with their lives, even though the history of the conflict remained contested ground and the uncertainties and controversies of Reconstruction had yet to be resolved. Had the case of *United States v. Jefferson Davis* not been dismissed, Bledsoe's arguments would have had their day in court, but as it was, they were never heard in evidence.

Bledsoe bore the cost of printing *Is Davis a Traitor?*—or, more correctly, his wife did, according to their daughter Sophia. Bledsoe estimated that the cost was at least three hundred dollars. That sum was more than he received from its sale, to say nothing of what its production cost him in time and effort. "Is it any wonder, then, that we, who have done so much labor for the South for nothing, *and less than nothing,* should be poor?" He still had four hundred copies of *Is Davis a Traitor?* on hand in January 1876, having given away as many as he had sold. As he informed the readers of the *Southern Review:* "They are still for sale. See our advertisement." Bledsoe's disappointment that the book did not receive a wider circulation was directly proportional to amount of effort and conviction compressed into its closely argued pages. "The biography of our little work, 'Is Davis a Traitor; or was Secession a Constitutional Right?; ought to be written. It would teach several important lessons to the Southern people; especially to such of them as may dream of becoming authors."[33] If that note of self-pity is unbecoming, it is nonetheless understandable.

The reputation of *Is Davis a Traitor?* has grown rather than diminished since Bledsoe's own lifetime. Jefferson Davis acknowledged the importance of the work and *The Republic of Republics* by Bernard Janin Sage in the first of his two-volume *Rise and Fall of the Confederate Government* (1881).[34] He referred to Sage's book as "a learned, exhaustive, and admirable work, which contains a wealth of historical and political learning." Davis freely drew upon Sage's work in his own defense of the Lost Cause with the permission of the author. "A like liberty will be taken with the late Dr. Bledsoe's masterly treatise on the right of secession published in 1866, under the title, 'Is Davis a Traitor? Or, Was Secession a Constitutional Right?'" The credit of Bledsoe's work by Davis, which appeared in a note to his chapter on the drafting of the Constitution, was sparing but adequate. Writing to Harry F. Barrell in January 1887, Davis again expressed the opinion that Sage's *Republic of Republics* and Bledsoe's *Is Davis a Traitor?* were the most satisfactory expositions of the states' rights view on the origin of the Union that had been written by anyone other than the founders themselves. Sage's work was a "wonderful compendium" of the early political history of the country and Bledsoe's book "a work of few pages but of great erudition and powerful argument."[35]

It was not until the full flowering of the Lost Cause movement in the early twentieth century that Bledsoe's defense of the right of secession won a considerable audience. The United Confederate Veterans placed it on its recommended reading list. Mary Barksdale Newton reprinted *Is Davis a Traitor?* in memory of her husband, Virginius Newton, in Richmond in 1907, the year in which the United Confederate Veterans held a Confederate reunion in Richmond. It was on the last day of that celebration that the organization unveiled the Jefferson Davis Memorial on Monument Avenue, which depicts Davis lecturing from a history book. The Confederate reunion, the dedication of the Davis monument, and Barksdale's reissue of Bledsoe's work were not coincidental. Each of them was a way of reaffirming principles and refreshing memories regarding the war among former Confederates and their descendants.[36] Bledsoe's daughter Sophia Bledsoe Herrick made a similar offering of remembrance toward the end of her own life. Sophia and her brother-in-law William Dinwiddie published a revised edition of *Is Davis a Traitor?* in 1915 under the title *The War between the States.* More people may have read the 1915 edition of the work than the original, since the educational boards of several southern states reportedly endorsed *The War between the States* as a suitable reference book for high school libraries.[37] Several subsequent editions of *Is Davis a Traitor?* have appeared under its original or a modified title, most recently as *Is Secession Treason?* (2005).[38]

Historians, especially conservative ones, have remained respectful of the states' rights constitutionalism expounded in *Is Davis a Traitor?* without endorsing all of Bledsoe's assumptions and conclusions. The Southern Agrarian Richard M. Weaver, a keen student of Bledsoe's writings, described the work as "the masterpiece of the Southern apologias" and extolled its many merits as a statement of states' rights doctrine. "In the extensive body of Southern political writing there is no more brilliant specimen of polemic." Douglas Southall Freeman, the author of the four-volume *Life of Lee,* similarly referred to *Is Davis a Traitor?* as "that brief classic of American political argument." The work was "written at white heat," and its author was ever the "counsel for the defense" in constitutional matters relating the origin of the war.[39] Since the civil rights movement, however, scholars have taken a more critical approach in their assessments of the ideology of the Lost Cause, especially regarding the issue of slavery as a cause of the war and the legacy of racism. Yet they have continued to recognize the importance of Bledsoe's work. Foster M. Gaines has noted that even though Edward A. Pollard's *Lost Cause* is better known than Bledsoe's *Is Davis a Traitor?* the latter was the more significant in shaping the Confederate interpretation of the war. Charles Reagan Wilson has similarly acknowledged the work as "the most important constitutional defense of the South's right to secede."[40]

Bledsoe later reflected in the *Southern Review* on the motives that led him to publish *Is Davis a Traitor?* Although he always claimed to have taken an objective, detached view of the right of secession, such was hardly the case. His passion for the Confederate cause and his personal loyalties to its leaders were too firmly fixed to ever be impartial, although his convictions were as sincere as they were biased. "The object of our little book was a pious one. It was simply to do an act of justice to the dead." Bledsoe reargued the right of secession as a means of vindicating all those who had fought and suffered in the war, and most especially "to wipe off the charges of treason and rebellion from the names and memories of Jefferson Davis, Stonewall Jackson, Albert Sidney Johnston, and Robert E. Lee." Bledsoe praised Albert Sidney Johnston, who lost his life at Shiloh Church, Tennessee, in 1862, as "the simplest, bravest, grandest man we have ever known."[41] He had been intimately connected with the lives of those men for more than thirty years, with the exception of Jackson, whom he had only known for about twelve years. "We had, moreover, for the same period, been bound to them, one and all, by ties and associations as sacred, as endearing, and as disinterested, as for any men we have ever known."[42]

Those who fought the Civil War were anything but "disinterested." Yet they were most certainly bound to each other by ties and associations that were sacred and endearing. But those who fought for the Confederacy affirmed them all the more strongly because of the humiliation of defeat. "The Confederate experience," Charles Reagan Wilson has observed, "established a covenanted identity among Southerners, and it became the basis for the sense of Southern mission."[43] That shared identity and sense of mission largely defined Bledsoe during the last years of his life. The amount of aspiration and conviction invested in a cause, together with the sacrifices made in its name, will at some point determine how impartial one can ever be concerning that cause thereafter. That is true of those who fought on both sides of the Civil War, yet the burden of explanation weighed less heavily upon the victors than the vanquished. No one felt the weight of that burden more deeply than Bledsoe, and none better illustrate the difficulty of coming to terms with its legacy. But if there are healing benefits in making defeat seem honorable, valorous, and justifiable, Bledsoe fulfilled his partisan mission as the author of *Is Davis a Traitor?* He continued to defend the Lost Cause and all things southern, moreover, as the unremorseful and quarrelsome editor of the *Southern Review.*

10

RISING UP FROM THE ASHES

The Mission of the Southern Review

NO SOONER HAD BLEDSOE BROUGHT forward *Is Davis a Traitor?* than he established a southern literary and historical magazine called the *Southern Review.* The prospectus announced that the new quarterly would be edited and published in Baltimore and dedicated to "the despised, the disfranchised, and the down-trodden people of the South." Writing to Robert E. Lee in August 1866, Bledsoe informed him of his plans. Lee's response was supportive but characteristically measured. "I have not been unmindful of the subject of which it treats." He wished Bledsoe success in the venture but cautioned him to be temperate in the expression of his views. "I am glad to learn that you propose to devote yourself to the discussion of literature and history, and hope that through the . . . Southern Review, they will be presented to the American people in an agreeable and convincing manner. I feel assured that this end can be best accomplished by the exhibition of moderation, forbearance, and truth." Lee marked his man well. While Lee epitomized restraint and temperance, Bledsoe possessed few of those qualities himself. Unlike the voices of Lee and his friend Lucius Q. C. Lamar, Bledsoe's voice would not be one of sectional reconciliation.[1]

The Episcopal bishop Richard Hooker Wilmer of Mobile, Alabama—whom Bledsoe described as "an old, and intimate, and dearly loved friend"—wrote him in warm support of the proposed magazine in November 1866. Like many southern clergymen, Wilmer was an ardent southern nationalist during the war and a defender of the Lost Cause afterward. "With all my heart I greet you and with all my strength I will aid you." The principles for which they had struggled were "true and right." God would one day pass judgment in the matter of the Confederate cause however it should please him. Wilmer had no doubt, however, that both God and posterity would render a favorable verdict on its justness. "I believe in the resurrection of the dead." The memory of fallen compatriots should not be disgraced but remain "ever green and fresh." Those who died honorably in the cause of southern independence gave only their lives. Their ideals and deeds lived on in the recollections of the survivors of the war who would pay homage to their selfless sacrifices.[2] Bledsoe would echo Wilmer's sentiments many times over as the editor of the *Southern Review*. The views of Wilmer and Bledsoe are instructive of how the Lost Cause took on the trappings of a civil religion.[3]

The establishment of the *Southern Review* in Baltimore in January 1867 was a significant part of a larger literary movement. Efforts to resurrect southern literature in the aftermath of the war resulted in what Edwin Mims has called "a perfect avalanche of magazine writing."[4] By far the most significant of those efforts occurred in Baltimore, which emerged as a publishing center for books and periodicals aimed at a southern clientele. Baltimore was also a haven for expatriated Virginians. Bledsoe, his former colleague at the University of Virginia Basil Lanneau Gildersleeve, the attorney and former Confederate congressman Charles Wells Russell, and several of their mutual acquaintances—many of them former students at the University of Virginia— moved to Baltimore after the war. As Bledsoe noted in eulogizing his friend Russell, they left Virginia to escape "the awful scenes of a once glorious, but now ruined, country" and the worst of "the reign of injustice, and tyranny, and wrong" he attributed to Republican rule.[5] Baltimore, said Gildersleeve, was "the great hope and refuge" of former Confederates who sought a congenial place where they could begin life anew. "And it was to Baltimore that those of us who were trying to rebuild the waste places of the Old Dominion turned when the cherished project of creating a Southern literature was resumed."[6]

William Hand Browne (1828–1912) joined Bledsoe in that enterprise as coeditor and copublisher. Browne was educated at the University of Maryland as a physician. But after a brief period of medical practice he dedicated himself to literary and historical pursuits. At the time he joined Bledsoe at the *Southern Review* he was editing the short-lived *Statesman*, a weekly newspaper published in Baltimore by the Maryland Democratic Association. Bledsoe and Browne launched the *Review* in an attempt to give voice to southern authors, interests, and concerns. Literature, politics, history, education, art, science, philosophy, and other subjects of general interest were brought within its scope. "We desire this REVIEW to represent the South, not as a party, but as a people." The causes and consequences of the late war would be "temperately discussed; not with the view of awakening acrimonious or vindictive feeling, but of drawing profit from the experience of the past." The subject of education would also receive prominent attention. "The Southern people are awake to the fact that we can no longer trust the mental and moral training of our sons and daughters to teachers and books imported from abroad." The editors intended the periodical to be "the organ of Southern thought," and most of its content came from the pens of southern authors. Despite their decidedly sectional sentiments and proclivities, Bledsoe and Browne were not so prejudiced as to exclude contributions from northern authors—at least those sympathetic to southern interests and concerns.[7]

Browne edited and published the *Southern Review* with Bledsoe from January 1867 until October 1868. After ending his association with the *Review*, Browne established and edited the *New Eclectic Magazine* in Baltimore in late 1868, which he renamed the *Southern Magazine* in December 1870. Browne's *Southern Magazine* continued from 1871 to 1875. His literary abilities earned him an appointment as professor of English literature at the Johns Hopkins University in 1878. After Browne's departure from the *Southern Review*, two friends briefly assisted Bledsoe as associate editors. Richard M. Venable, a Baltimore attorney, lent a hand in 1869, and the Reverend Edward J. Sterns, a classical scholar and a "high-toned gentleman," helped in 1870. Stearns taught Latin and Greek at the Collegiate Institute for Young Ladies in Baltimore (formerly the Louisa School for Young Ladies), run by Bledsoe's daughter Sophia Bledsoe Herrick, and was also the associate principal and head of languages and philosophy at the Cambridge Military Academy in Cambridge, Maryland. Thereafter Bledsoe edited the *Southern Review* by himself until Sophia joined him as associate editor in January 1875.[8]

Nothing is known about the relationship between Bledsoe and Browne during their two-year association at the *Southern Review*. Judging from Browne's later attitudes toward Bledsoe, however, it was likely contentious. Writing to the Georgia poet, essayist, and former editor of *Russell's Magazine* Paul Hamilton Hayne in November 1870, Browne suggested that there was no love lost between him and Bledsoe. When Browne once reprinted an article from the *Southern Review* in the *New Eclectic*, he acknowledged the source of the contribution but apparently did not ask Bledsoe's permission to reprint it. Bledsoe became so indignant and insulting toward Browne in the matter that the latter party had nothing to do with Bledsoe or anything good to say about him thereafter. Bledsoe's characteristic brusqueness with those who either provoked or irritated him apparently alienated others too. Writing Hayne again in September 1871, Browne said that Bledsoe had fallen into disfavor within the literary circle of Baltimore. "He has outlived, or outworn his popularity here; made enemies and estranged friends." Browne and Bledsoe remained on bad terms.[9]

Contributions from Bledsoe's pen constituted a substantial amount of each issue of the *Southern Review*. All articles are anonymous, but internal evidence in most instances leaves little doubt as to which contributions are his. As James Wood Davidson observed in *The Living Writers of the South* (1869), "The *Review* is like its chief editor—fearless, able, bold, gloveless, scholarly, and distinctly Southern, though not belligerently sectional. The tone and manner are sometimes felt to be severe, and these features are hardly accidental."[10] One may agree with the first part of that assessment and demur from the second. Bledsoe was often "belligerently sectional," especially when reviewing northern histories of the war that he believed sanctified the Union cause by misrepresenting the origin and meaning of the war. The publication of the first volume of John William Draper's *History of the American Civil War* (1867), for instance, called forth his righteous indignation: "No carcase [carcass], perhaps, ever swarmed with living things more abundantly, than Dr. Draper's book with loathsome lies." And on another occasion, after scrutinizing eleven school histories of the United States, Bledsoe remarked that "the one grand moral of these books is, that the people of the North alone are fit to rule, while the people of the South deserve only to be ruled by them. They continually feed the mean pride of the North, and inspire its people with an abhorrence and contempt of the South."[11]

Nor was Bledsoe any gentler in his treatment of Davis's detractors among former Confederates. Bledsoe defended his old friend's character and leadership during the war in "Davis and Lee." The article is Bledsoe's response to the "unmitigated abuse" and "calumnies" set forth against Davis by James Dabney McCabe Jr. in his *Life and Campaigns of General Robert E. Lee* (1867).[12] He also assailed several of the opinions expressed in the first volume of Alexander H. Stephens's *A Constitutional View of the Late War between the States* (1868). The appearance of Stephens's work was something of a cause célèbre in the history of Confederate apologias. Its reception immersed the beleaguered author in several controversies in both the northern and southern presses. Bledsoe was one of his most prominent critics. His intemperate critique of the work appeared in the *Southern Review* for October 1868.[13] Richard Malcolm Johnston and William Hand Browne, Stephens's first biographers, have fairly said that Bledsoe wrote his review of *A Constitutional View* "with much asperity and personal feeling."[14] It is a fair statement. Bledsoe's appraisal initiated a heated controversy between him and Stephens on the origins of the war, which deserves more attention than it has received.

Bledsoe criticized Stephens for overemphasizing the constitutional issue of states' rights versus national consolidation as a cause of the war. He did not deny Stephens's contention that a contest between those opposing constitutional principles was a source of sectional discord. Yet he believed that Stephens "magnified" the importance of those doctrines as a cause of conflict at the expense of the slavery controversy and the tariff issue, especially the former. "The conflict in regard to slavery was, in our opinion, a more powerful cause of the war, than the one exclusively patronized by his [Stephens's] philosophy." The idea that northerners and southerners had waged war against each other over two conflicting interpretations of the Constitution was an absurdity. "A fight between two game-cocks would have done more to arouse their warlike passions, than a conflict between two political theories about which they knew little, and cared less." A divergence of opinion as to the nature of the federal Union existed from the foundation of the Republic to the commencement of hostilities in 1861, yet it caused neither war nor any sign of it until the issues of slavery and tariffs became the focus of sectional strife. "Is it not wonderful that, with all these facts before him, Mr. Stephens should have concluded that the conflict between the two theories of the Constitution alone and not the conflict about slavery produced the great war of 1861?"[15]

Bledsoe deemphasized the relative importance of the slavery issue as a cause of the war in his own writings both during the conflict and afterward (not a compelling argument by any means but a consistent one). He expressed the opinion in the *Southern Review* for April 1867, for example, that the most superficial observers of all were those who insisted that the institution of slavery *alone* was the cause of hostilities.[16] Yet Bledsoe never denied that the controversy over slavery was one of several converging causes of secession and war. It would, indeed, be difficult for the author of *Liberty and Slavery* to assume any other ground. He contended in his feud with Stephens that slavery was a more important cause of the war than rival theories of the Constitution, yet the fact that the slavery controversy was inseparable from states' right doctrine and quarrels about the Constitution is a historical reality that neither Bledsoe nor Stephens adequately addressed in their respective writings. Both polemicists were determined to represent the Confederate cause in the best possible light. But as a relative statement Bledsoe addressed the slavery issue as a cause of the war more candidly than did Stephens.

Bledsoe further arraigned Stephens for inconsistency in the sentiments he expressed on the subject of secession before and after the war. He cited Stephens's "Union Speech" delivered in the Georgia legislature on November 14, 1860, and later statements made in *A Constitutional View* as supporting evidence. Stephens opposed secession in his Union Speech, but in *A Constitutional View* Bledsoe believed he tacked a different course. Stephens now maintained that he had always supported the right of secession. Bledsoe quoted Stephens's Union Speech to show that the northern critics who accused him of having opposed secession before the war were not wrong. Bledsoe demonstrated the contradiction with solid evidence. Stephens opposed secession in his Union Speech, but in his postwar apology it appeared that he misrepresented and even denied his opposition to secession. In contrast, Bledsoe frankly acknowledged that he had changed his own opinion on the constitutionality of secession. He was "as profoundly ignorant" of the right of secession in 1860 as any old-line Whig, not excepting Stephens himself, but he had been "most grievously in error." Stephens, he insisted, should have adopted the same course he had taken. He appealed to the adage that while a wise man sometimes changes his mind a fool never does.[17]

Stephens first learned of Bledsoe's scathing review from a book notice appearing in the *Baltimore Leader* on October 3, 1868. Writing to his longtime acquaintance and future biographer Richard Malcolm Johnston, the enraged Stephens stated his intention of replying to Bledsoe's "tirade" against his work, "or rather his attack on me under the guise of reviewing the book." He was eager to have at Bledsoe but felt the need for restraint lest he write an equally ill-tempered response. "While the occasion and provocation might justify considerable passion, yet he shall see that I can and will show up his outrages on me with as much *cold-bloodedness* as that with which I have exhibited toward the enormous and infamous wrongs of those who wielded the Federal authority in the subjugation of the Southern States." Stephens's vindication of his views against Bledsoe's "assertions and misrepresentations," he assured Johnston, would be as full and as complete as his vindications of the southern cause of independence in *A Constitutional View*, and they would be "equally temperate in manner and expression." Stephens's retaliation fully rose to the occasion. He wrote his response to Bledsoe on October 22 as a letter to editors of the *Statesman*. There he vindicated himself against the allegations of his assailant.[18]

Stephens said that he had indeed opposed secession in his Union Speech as a *means* of redressing southern grievances—a fact he had never denied. But he made an important distinction. He opposed the *policy* of secession but not the *right* itself. As an alternative to the draconian measure of secession Stephens had called for a state convention in Georgia to draft a formal list of grievances. He wanted the declaration sent to the legislative, executive, and judicial branches of the northern states and directly to the northern people through the press. The remonstrance should explicitly state that refusal to comply with the Fugitive Slave Clause of the Constitution and nullification of the Fugitive Slave Law through the passage of personal liberty laws by northern legislatures repudiated their constitutional obligations. Stephens wanted the proposed convention to further stipulate that the repeal of those "obnoxious laws" was a necessary condition for Georgia to remain within the Union. If those protests were disregarded, the case for secession would only be strengthened. Yet he had never denied, or ever doubted, that the right of secession existed, Bledsoe's claim to the contrary notwithstanding.[19]

Bledsoe quickly retorted in the *Statesman*. He repeated his original charges and held Stephens's feet to fire regarding the alleged prevarications and rationalizations concerning his actual views on secession before the war. He essentially dismissed his explanation of his views on secession in 1860 as being a distinction without meaning. How, asked an incredulous Bledsoe, could one believe in the right of secession but not believe in exercising that right? Stephens's brother Linton Stephens sent him a copy of Bledsoe's rejoinder, along with another unidentified clipping regarding the Bledsoe-Stephens controversy that Linton believed bore the marks of someone who "either belongs or wishes to be considered as belonging to the Davis circle." Linton believed that his brother's advantage over Bledsoe would have been improved had he "carefully repressed all exhibition of passion or irritation," yet he admitted that Bledsoe's goading in the matter "was immense and the difficulty of calmness proportional." Stephens's friends, said Linton, gave him the nod for having displayed the more "*gentlemanly* tone and *temper*" in his controversy with Bledsoe. And the Baltimore attorney Severn Teackle Wallis reportedly found Bledsoe's performance in the controversy to be "juvenile, as that of professors often is—They write as if there was nobody in the *world* but boys of seventeen years old and *spankable*."[20]

The Bledsoe-Stephens controversy resurfaced four years later when Stephens published his *Reviewers Reviewed* (1872). Bledsoe was furious with Stephens because he did not reprint his critique of *A Constitutional View* but only Stephens's response to it. Nor did Stephens acknowledge Bledsoe's rejoinder in the *Statesman*. Bledsoe wanted the readers of the *Southern Review* to have a complete understanding of the differences between Stephens and him. He left the judgment to them as to who had the better part of the argument. Bledsoe also defended himself against Stephens's criticism of how the Confederate War Department had been run during his tenure as chief of the Bureau of War and assistant secretary of war. Stephens, indeed, was quite pointed and personal in his censure. "Had the Doctor, and those associated with him in the War Department at Richmond, during our late struggle, been governed more by calm good sense, and less by mere fierce and fiery passion and personal prejudices (such as he still exhibits), our present position might have been infinitely better than it is!" Bledsoe sardonically stated his regrets that Stephens's admonishment concerning passion and prejudice had not come in time to save the beleaguered Confederacy. He confessed that he had led "several indignation meetings—of *one*" in Richmond but had no idea that his personal "tempests in a tea-pot" had helped to shake the Confederacy to its very foundations until first learning of it from Stephens.[21]

There was, in truth, much needless pettiness, spitefulness, and posturing on the part of both belligerents in the Bledsoe-Stephens controversy. And it must be said in fairness to Stephens that Bledsoe drew first blood, which invited an equally sanguinary response. More common ground existed between the antagonists on the causes of the war than not, yet because of their personal animosity toward each other they chose to emphasize their differences. One must conclude that Bledsoe's animus toward Stephens largely stemmed from his failure to acknowledge Bledsoe's own constitutional defense of secession. The priority of Bledsoe's work on the subject did not receive a single mention by Stephens—a work of which he was doubtless familiar.[22] Bledsoe clearly believed, although he did *not* say, that Stephens merited hell at his hands. His hostility toward Stephens was further motivated by a desire to exact a measure of revenge against one of Davis's most consistent and prominent critics. Davis and Stephens were at cross-purposes throughout the war. Stephens disapproved of conscription, suspension of the writ of habeas corpus, impressments, and the Confederate government's financial policies, and he criticized Davis's military strategy. He delivered a speech before the Georgia legislature on March 16, 1864, in which he rebuked the administration for implementing those measures. He also supported a series of resolutions calling for a negotiated peace settlement. Afterward Davis loyalists had few good things to say about the former vice president.

Reconstruction for many former Confederates was a strange brew of irony and seeming vindictiveness—a forced contrition and painful repudiation of supposedly sacred truths regarding slavery and secession. It was not otherwise with Bledsoe. He regarded Reconstruction as nothing more than a mocking spectacle of the malice and despotism he attributed to the Radical Republicans. He seldom missed an opportunity to revile the Radicals as the vengeful despoilers of a world that no longer ran in its former courses. Even in the former slaveholding states that did not secede from the Union, life was different under Republican rule. Bledsoe occasionally traveled to St. Louis, Missouri, to visit family and attend to business connected with publishing the *Southern Review*. After one such trip in April 1870 he expressed astonishment to Jefferson Davis at the venal character he attributed to some of the local and federal office holders in St. Louis. "There are, no doubt, many better men in the penitentiaries than many of those who are now high in office. Has not the world been turned up-side down? I think so, and this is some consolation to me, who now find myself at the bottom of all things, and almost ground to powder. I do not complain. *The war has not ruined me. It has made me; and though I now die daily, I will live hereafter.*" As he observed on another occasion, the war was "a revolution that shook the foundations of the world, and turned all things else out of their courses."[23]

The beatification of Abraham Lincoln after the war was another bitter pill for many former Confederates.[24] Bledsoe was hardly an exception. His former association with Lincoln in Springfield, Illinois, was still a vivid memory when Ward Hill Lamon, an attorney and one of Lincoln's former law partners, published his *Life of Abraham Lincoln* in 1872.[25] Bledsoe reviewed the work in the *Southern Review* for April 1873. He rendered a judgment on Lincoln's life and character and how his biographers had treated their subject. Bledsoe's views are those of an embittered former Confederate. Yet notwithstanding that fact they are as remarkably even handed in certain particulars as they are unduly severe in others. "Some persons will think it a great honor, and some a great disgrace, that we have lived eight long years in the same region with Abraham Lincoln, and held almost daily intercourse with him at the Bar. We think it neither an honor nor a disgrace." He regarded it, quite to the contrary, as simply "a piece of good fortune." His years in Springfield provided him "the opportunity of seeing, scrutinizing, and forming an opinion of one of the most extraordinary human beings that has figured in history. The world will, perhaps, know him a little better because we have known him."[26]

Bledsoe confessed that Lincoln was "one of the most incomprehensible personages we have ever known." He was so little like other men that other men could not "penetrate the mystery of his peculiar make and mode of being." He denounced William Henry Herndon (Lincoln's third law partner and biographer) and other Illinois writers who donned the role of "great oracles" and presumed to instruct the world about "what manner of man Abraham Lincoln was." Those accounts, said Bledsoe, overemphasized Lincoln's faults and shortcomings while there was much about him "that reached beyond the range of their vision." Lincoln's life and character struck Bledsoe as being "a bundle of contradictions," and he frankly admitted he was "confounded by the mysteries of the single monad, 'Honest Old Abe.'" If he did not know Lincoln and his closest associates as well as Herndon, he believed he knew his essence better. Lincoln possessed many attributes and abilities that Bledsoe admired, not the least of which was an untrained but "powerful intellect" that made him extremely astute in arguing the law and effective at giving political speeches. Bledsoe ridiculed the rumor that Lincoln's speeches had been ghostwritten, especially those in which he opposed Stephen A. Douglas. "No other man in Illinois could have done that work for him. . . . He was a full match for Mr. Douglas, or for any other man of the day, on the stump or before the people."

Bledsoe's severest criticism of Lincoln concerned his character. What he most disliked about Lincoln was his alleged pride, hunger for distinction, and laziness that sometimes resulted in "dishonest measures" designed to achieve his ends. His overarching political ambition often led him to disguise his true disposition on an issue, a talent that Bledsoe believed was natural and spontaneous rather than calculated. "His most intimate friends and professed admirers admit that his apparent 'simplicity and candor' were put on for effect with the people." One of Lincoln's favorite political maxims, said Bledsoe, was that "'we must fight the devil with fire'; that is with his own weapons." He also lived by the precept that all was fair in politics. By the time Bledsoe wrote those lines, the years of sectional strife had clouded his judgment and fairness. Lincoln now appeared to him as the personification of the demagogues whose agitations were so fatal to the stability of republics. Bledsoe had once embraced that democracy himself and did so at Lincoln's side during the presidential campaigns of 1840 and 1844. But in later life he regarded those elections as an unfortunate time in the nation's political life when it seemed that the whole world had gone mad.[27]

Bledsoe watched Lincoln's rise to the presidency in utter amazement. He knew him, he said, when not even the poorest soul would show him reverence only to see his image in the storefronts of London. "How marvelous." Lincoln's remarkable ascension from humble and obscure origins to the pinnacle of power and fame had been "the wonder of all nations, and will, perhaps, be the wonder of all ages." Looking back on that extraordinary phenomenon, a jaundiced Bledsoe described Lincoln as the proverbial right man in the right place. "No man fitter than he, indeed, to represent the Northern Demos; or, as Wendell Phillips has it, the 'party of the North pledged against the party of the South.'" And who better to lead that party in its work of destruction than "the talented, but the low, ignorant and vulgar, rail-splitter of Illinois?"[28] Bledsoe never forgave Lincoln for the steeled determination with which he fought to preserve the Union and brought the exhausted and dispirited Confederacy to its knees.

Supporting the cause of southern literature and history for Bledsoe came with a hefty price. He persevered at the *Southern Review* in the face of many difficulties and discouragements that sometimes drove him to despair. The history of that enterprise, he complained, demonstrated two divergent and exasperating phenomena: that the intelligence and cultivation of southern authors were fully equal to the challenge of producing a first-class literary periodical and that those who were in a position to support southern literature were not disposed to do so. While the *Southern Review* was a literary success, it had financially languished from the start. "If, as we have often said to ourselves, we only had a machine to convert golden opinions into greenbacks, how splendid, in all respects, would be the success of the SOUTHERN REVIEW!" Even so great a literary figure as Dr. Samuel Johnson, Bledsoe scornfully remarked, would starve in Baltimore. He candidly confessed that a want of sufficient patronage and support for the *Review* had created considerable financial hardship: "Our life in Baltimore has been a terrible servitude." William Hand Browne observed to Paul Hamilton Hayne in August 1871 that, "as for Bledsoe, I am afraid it is a hopeless case." Browne had heard firsthand from a lawyer that "B. has no tangible assets and there were already a lot of judgments against him."[29]

A lack of support for the *Southern Review* made it impossible to pay contributors for their labors and caused no end of financial hardships for Bledsoe and his family. It was "more in sorrow than in anger" that he accused southerners of "a guilty indifference" to their own literature. "The proof of this melancholy fact, as exhibited in the history of Southern books, and Southern periodicals, is as absolutely overwhelming as it is disgraceful." Nor did Bledsoe accept the plea that the southern people were too impoverished to subscribe to literary reviews. The apology was "more specious than solid." Southerners were too poor to patronize southern periodicals but *not* northern ones. If as many copies of the *Southern Review* were sold in the city of Baltimore alone as were copies of *Harper's Monthly Magazine*, seethed Bledsoe, his pecuniary success would have been assured. Bledsoe's former partner William Hand Browne registered the same complaint. If southerners would only give southern periodicals as much support as they bestowed upon Harper's "vile" calumniations, southern editors and publishers could pay contributors as they wished to do. "They can help us and themselves through us if they choose: But they don't choose."[30] Equally fatal was the unremitting problem of nonpaying subscribers, which became so acute that in April 1876 Bledsoe and his coeditor, Sophia, struck more than a hundred names from the subscription list for nonpayment.

Financially Bledsoe and his family largely depended on the income that his daughters Sophia Bledsoe Herrick and Elizabeth McMurtrie Bledsoe earned from the Louisa School for Young Ladies. Bledsoe's daughter Sophia established the school in Baltimore in 1868 and initially ran it as the principal and later as vice principal until it closed in 1872. "These two women," an admiring father wrote, "by teaching a school for young ladies, have contributed far more largely than ourselves to the support of our family, while we, almost gratuitously, have labored in the great cause of the South."[31] The Louisa School was very much a family concern. Sophia taught arithmetic, algebra, geometry, and natural philosophy; her mother, Harriet Coxe Bledsoe, taught English grammar, geography, and history; and her sister Elizabeth taught Latin, French, and German. Another sister, Anna or "Annie," eventually taught there as well. Sophia's father reportedly taught moral philosophy, rhetoric, belles letters, English, and English composition and occasionally gave semimonthly evening lectures to invited audiences. Given the demands of editing the *Southern Review*, however, it is uncertain how much teaching and lecturing Bledsoe actually did. But he at least occasionally taught and also did some private tutoring.[32]

Bledsoe delighted in writing for the *Southern Review* and in editing the work of contributors. But the details regarding its management tried Bledsoe's patience and wearied his soul. Correcting proofs, dealing with the alleged dishonesty of literary agents, and getting tardy subscribers to pay up was an intolerable burden. He did all those things for many years but never well. Keeping account of subscriptions, donations, and printing expenses was as mind-numbing for Bledsoe as writing was agreeable. And there was also the contentious and sometimes embarrassing issue of not being able to pay those who made contributions to the *Southern Review*. Whether those authors were promised money by Bledsoe personally or merely expected it by custom is uncertain. Paul Hamilton Hayne did not receive payment for his poem "Daphles" and an article on Hugh Swinton Legaré that he contributed to the *Southern Review* for January 1870. Nor is it likely that he received any consideration for the sketch of his uncle Robert Young Hayne he contributed to the October 1870 number. Hayne did not have much good to say about Bledsoe thereafter. Writing to the Virginia poet Margaret Junkin Preston, whose work Bledsoe so greatly admired, Hayne credited Bledsoe with having "an excellent brain" but also called him "an *irreclaimable blackguard* and hypocrite." George Frederick Holmes never received the two hundred dollars he believed was due him for his own contributions to the *Southern Review*. When Bledsoe visited Holmes in August 1873, he was surprised and disappointed to learn that he would not be paid. The aggrieved Holmes quipped in his diary: "I should not have *Bled-soe*."[33]

Bledsoe sought relief from those vexations so he could devote himself exclusively to editing and working on his own manuscripts. He was convinced that he must either rid himself of the business department of the *Southern Review* or abandon the entire enterprise as being too much for him to manage. "But to abandon the *Southern Review* would be like the pang of death to me. It is the child of my affections." Making money had never been Bledsoe's purpose in founding the magazine, but even the most disinterested person could not live upon ideals alone. "I am willing to work for the South; nay, I am willing to be a slave for the South, but I am not willing to be worked to death in such servitude, without something like a reasonable compensation for my labor."[34] When Bledsoe learned in April 1870 that the General Conference of the Methodist Episcopal Church, South—which was about to be held in Memphis—would seriously consider the establishment of a quarterly magazine, he suggested that it adopt the *Southern Review* instead. He hoped by that means to rid himself of the business department and obtain a salary as the editor. He had been contemplating the introduction of theology into the *Review* for some time, and since his Arminian views more fully accorded with the doctrines of Methodism than with those of any other denomination, a publishing partnership seemed a natural alliance of mutual needs and interests. He broached the subject with the Reverend John Poisal, the publisher of the *Baltimore Episcopal*

Methodist, who was receptive to the idea. Poisal laid the proposed affiliation before the General Conference in Memphis in May 1870.

Bledsoe received advice and assistance in the matter from his old friend Lucius Q. C. Lamar, who was then practicing law in Memphis. Lamar and Bledsoe had not seen each other since October 1864, when they parted company in London. Lamar spoke of Bledsoe fondly. "I have never, since our separation in England, in feeling, thought, or outward deed swerved or wavered in the sentiment which a loyal friend always feels for his loyal friend." Lamar did his friend a good turn. He assisted Bledsoe in negotiating an arrangement with the General Conference by which he would be delivered from "the mechanical drudgery" and business details connected with publishing the *Southern Review* yet would continue to edit the journal at Baltimore.[35] The details regarding the printing and management of the *Southern Review* were ironed out between Bledsoe and his new publishing partner when the periodical began a new era in its existence. The Reverend John Poisal and the Reverend S. S. Roswell, who had previously published the *Review* in Baltimore, agreed to manage the periodical and pay Bledsoe a regular salary as editor. Beginning with the July 1871 number, the Southwestern Book and Publishing Company printed the *Southern Review* in St. Louis under the auspices of the Methodist Episcopal Church, South.

Bledsoe strengthened his new association with the Methodist Conference when he was admitted into the Methodist Church in 1870 after many years of being a communicant in the Protestant Episcopal Church. He furthered his commitment to Methodism when he became an ordained minister in either 1871 or 1872, which was the fulfillment of a long-standing goal. He noted in October 1870 that he had unsuccessfully sought entry into the ministry of the Methodist Episcopal Church "more than twenty five years ago," or about 1845.[36] The Reverend Bledsoe never had charge of a church but did occasionally deliver sermons by invitation.[37] Not everyone was pleased with the affiliation of the *Southern Review* with the Methodist Episcopal Church, South. Some subscribers canceled their subscriptions because they had no interest in receiving a Methodist publication. Yet Bledsoe had made his decision. He concluded that if he had to write for the *Southern Review* with little or no compensation he would write on those subjects that were the most agreeable to him. Thus Bledsoe earnestly and affectionately returned to writing on the subject of theology—his first love. He had come full circle.

William Hand Browne, although no longer connected with the *Review*, was dismayed at the new affiliation. Everything he and Bledsoe had accomplished at the *Southern Review* would now presumably be sacrificed to theology. The only literary productions that were apt to find a place would be those that did "not disagree with the Methodist digestion and palate." Browne was certain that the new arrangement would be "the death-blow to the Review." The quarterly in all likelihood would "dwindle to a purely theological paper, publishing the Rev. So-and-So's lucubrations on Original Sin: and the Rev. Somebody Else's Doctrine on Free Will."[38] Browne's gloomy prediction was premature. The *Southern Review* did not expire after its association with the Methodist Church, nor did it become an exclusively theological publication. It continued for another eight years even though religious subjects did become its primary focus after 1871 just as Browne predicted. Yet contributions to southern history, literature, science, and topics of general interest were never entirely absent from its pages. Bledsoe was sensitive about how his affiliation with the Methodist Conference might be perceived and was determined not to allow religious concerns to close out other subjects. He understood that some might think the affiliation of the *Southern Review* with Methodism was nothing more than a calculated means of enlarging his subscription list—that he had "turned Methodist" as a matter of expediency instead of conscience.

When some of his readers and critics complained that politics should be excluded from the pages of the *Southern Review* because of its affiliation with the Methodist Church, an unwavering Bledsoe addressed the issue directly. It had to be explicitly known and understood that even though the *Review* was edited by a Methodist and published under the auspices of Methodist Episcopal Church, South, it was still an *independent* journal. Those who believed it to be "a church periodical" labored under a false impression. It was a forum of opinion and not the pulpit or mouthpiece of a denomination. He did not believe that there ever had been what, properly speaking, could be called "party politics" in the pages of the *Southern Review.* He had disavowed allegiance to political parties and politicians years before. If the editor of the *Southern Review* was a supporter of any political party, Bledsoe affirmed, he was himself entirely unaware it. He would continue to devote his energies to discussions of the great moral, social, political, and religious questions of the past and present. While he understood that the fervor with which he stated his opinions on those subjects might offend some of his readers, he had no apology to offer and anticipated no change in the editorial policies of the *Southern Review.*

Bledsoe further refused to exclude discussion of the leading questions relating the causes and consequences of the late war—one of the principal objects for which the *Southern Review* had been established. While those issues were inherently political, they were far too sanctified to ever be discarded. Bledsoe had devoted more than ten years of close investigation to the causes and nature of the war, and his views on the subject were based upon "convictions which were, and still are, infinitely dearer to him than life itself." He could no more abandon discussion of the war than he could forsake himself. His identity and the issues of the war were inseparable: "His principles did not cave in with the Confederacy." And what was it, after all, that his critics were asking of him? Was he to deny himself and all he held sacred because some of his readers might not share his views? "Shall we, then, remain silent? Shall we look on, and listen, 'like the dumb dogs of Israel,' and say never a word in reply? Shall we bury, in the grave of the grandest cause that has ever perished on earth, all the little stories of history and philosophy which not an altogether idle life had enabled us to amass, and so leave the just cause, merely because it is fallen, to go without our humble advocacy? We would rather die."[39]

Bledsoe candidly confessed that the mission of the *Southern Review* regarding the origins and meaning of the war was a very personal one. It was a subject he could never disown with conscience or honor. "If there were no other reason (though there are many others), the last words of Robert E. Lee to us would render such a cowardly defection of principle, such a shameless disregard of the most sacred of duties utterly repugnant to the convictions and feelings of our very inmost soul." Bledsoe could never forget Lee's final words to him. "As he pressed our hand in his, for the last time, he said, with no little emotion: 'Doctor, you must take care of yourself; you have a great work to do; we all look to you for our vindication.'" Bledsoe resolved that they would not look in vain. "On the contrary, however humble our abilities, they shall all be exerted to repel and roll back the floods of vituperation and abuse with which a rampant North would fain cover the names and memories of our illustrious dead." Accordingly, articles on the war continued to find a place in the *Southern Review* even as late in Bledsoe's life as January 1876.[40] And he still clung to the faltering hope that he would live long enough to bring forward a history of the war. Such was not his good fortune. The inexorable demands of competing interests, obligations, priorities, and time ultimately took their toll on Bledsoe's unfinished history of the war.[41]

Bledsoe proudly announced to his readers in the January 1875 that his daughter Sophia Bledsoe Herrick would join him as the associate editor of the *Southern Review*. He was beginning to feel his years and told his wife, Harriet, he wanted to devote the remainder of his life to preparing his works for publication and his soul for eternity. Sophia assumed responsibility for most of the editing and all of the management of the *Southern Review*. She had already contributed several able articles during the previous eighteen months, which made up more than one-fifth of the journal's contents. She further assisted with the writing of book notices and attended to all correspondence and subscriptions. Bledsoe continued to contribute articles and made the final decision about the acceptance of manuscripts, while Sophia continued to write her own contributions to the *Review* and appears to have done nearly everything else. As the associate editor she made a notable contribution to keeping the *Southern Review* a going concern. Bledsoe had every confidence in her abilities and was certain that complaints about the mismanagement of the *Review* would soon end.[42]

There can be no question that Sophia greatly eased her father's burdens during the last years of his life. She was a strong and capable individual who overcame many hardships. Sophia married the Reverend James Burton Herrick in June 1860 and resided with him at his mission parish in New York. The couple separated in 1868, apparently owing to James's social views and growing interest in the Oneida Community. They never divorced, but Sophia assumed responsibility for raising their three children and reunited with her mother and father in Baltimore. In 1868 she established and became the principal of the Louisa School for Young Ladies in Baltimore, a position she held until 1872, intending that the school would be her livelihood and means of supporting her children. Sophia's biographer, Rebecca Starr, has likened her private life and secret relationship with Allen C. Redwood between 1870 and 1877, of whom Bledsoe did not approve, to a private civil war.[43]

Working for such an independent and irascible character as her father was not smooth sailing. Not the least of Sophia's frustrations was dealing with his habitual aversion to correspondence. She attended to the immense pile of unanswered letters that accumulated on his desk and made explanations to chagrined correspondents as best she could. "He hates writing letters," she wrote Paul Hamilton Hayne in July 1877, "and has indulged the dislike 'till it has become an unconquerable repugnance to him." He would fret and make himself utterly miserable over a mass of unanswered correspondence. Yet at the same time he made no attempt to remedy the situation. Bledsoe once confessed to Jefferson Davis, by way of apology, that writing letters was a nuisance and a distraction that often made him a poor correspondent. "But this weakness, this habit, has its roots partly in my strength, *which is a perfect absorption in the labors of the brain. . . .* I have often said, as well as felt to my sorrow, that it is easier for me to write a book than to write a letter. Especially is this true, if the subject of the book is one which has long occupied my mind, heart, and soul, as more than one subject has done."[44]

Bledsoe spent a good portion of his time after 1871 answering his critics and vindicating his religious views in the *Southern Review* just as Browne had predicted. He was no more orthodox as a Methodist than he had been as an Episcopalian. Bledsoe embroiled himself in doctrinal disputes regarding free will, divine sovereignty, and infant baptism with the Reverend Daniel D. Whedon, editor of the *Methodist Quarterly Review;* the Reverend Charles W. Miller of the Kentucky Conference of the Methodist Episcopal Church, South; and Robert Lewis Dabney, the conservative theologian of the Union Theological Seminary at Hampden-Sydney College.[45] Bledsoe had fewer problems with the Christian theology espoused by John Wesley than with that held by any other denomination. Yet he demurred from Wesley's idea of a "necessitated holiness in the first man, and a necessary sin in all of his descendents." If he accepted that notion, said Bledsoe, he would be a Calvinist, for both its premise and logic led back to Edwards, Calvin, and Saint Augustine and "the dark scheme of predestination"—a closed system of thought that imprisoned its devotees within the iron cell of their own logic.[46] His views on infant baptism were also unacceptable to some of his Methodist brethren. His stance on predestination, election, close communion, baptismal regeneration, perfection, falling from grace, and apostolic secession did not strictly accord with the doctrines of any church. He thought for himself and wrote for others who did likewise.

The besieged editor sometimes found himself being criticized not only by Calvinists but by Methodists who had no taste for his heterodoxy or Bledsoe-isms. As he observed in October 1875, "Behold us, then, a critic among critics, assailed on all sides! The cross fire is sharp, from Presbyterians on one side and from Methodists on the other: a multitude against one." Yet Bledsoe was often overly severe and unnecessarily personal in his treatment of his adversaries, which was occasionally a source of complaint against him. He was profoundly aware of that criticism and acknowledged that his "sins of temper" had been real as well as numerous. The Methodist theologian Wilbur F. Tillett, professor of systematic theology at Vanderbilt University, admired many aspects of Bledsoe's writings, his accomplishments across a broad spectrum of intellectual endeavor, and the fearlessness with which he advanced and defended his convictions. Yet Tillett fairly noted that Bledsoe had a tendency to make himself "a perfect martyr to truth, a hero, a 'Galileo,' whose persecutions were due to the ignorance and narrowness of his critics. . . . It would have been well for Dr. Bledsoe if he had never allowed himself to engage in exasperating controversies with many of his critics." The Reverend J. M. Hawley of Hamilton, Virginia—a Methodist and a Bledsoe admirer—also acknowledged that his caustic pen had earned him many enemies. "The man who feels the sting of the lash never loves the man who applies it. Dr. Bledsoe was feared but not esteemed, respected but not loved. His intensity in controversy angered his opponents and cooled the affection of his friends. He fought with the fury of Ajax, and his thrusts were so rapid and deep that many a plumed knight was laid in the dust. A Roman of this type may storm the citadel but few will volunteer to swell the paean of his praise."[47]

Bledsoe spent his final days among family and friends in Alexandria, Virginia, where he had been residing for several years. He was stricken with an attack of paralysis on November 9, 1877, his sixty-eighth birthday, while listening to an evangelist at Christ Church in Alexandra. Bledsoe was in his last days and knew it. His physical condition worsened over the next four weeks until he finally lost consciousness. He died quietly at his home in Alexandria at 11:00 on the evening of December 8, 1877, surrounded by his wife, children, and longtime friend Lucius Q. C. Lamar. A few days later the senior mathematics class at the University of Virginia bore him to his grave in the university cemetery. It was Bledsoe's request that he be buried on campus, where he was interred next to the grave of his old friend William Holmes McGuffey.[48] One of Bledsoe's former students at the University of Virginia anonymously paid him a fitting eulogy in a letter to the editor of the Richmond newspaper *The State*. The old Roman had finally come home after the close of a long campaign.

> As an old student's thoughts traveled back to the time when you, Mr. Editor, and I were working for mathematical honors under the spur of his rigorous teaching, there seemed a fitting sadness in thus bringing back the body of the strong, but weary old man, after so many vicissitudes of labor and life, after so many fierce struggles against fate, after so much of passionate excitement, and of combat, to rest here within the sound of his own familiar lecture bell, amid the quiet scenes where he had lived his happiest life, and had done, if not the most famous, at least the most useful and enduring part of his life's work.[49]

The *Southern Review* appeared in twenty-six volumes and fifty-one numbers over the eleven and a half years of its existence—a very respectable run in the evanescent world of nineteenth-century periodicals. And even though the magazine's circulation probably never exceeded three thousand copies, it most certainly reached more than a southern readership. Trubner and Company published the *Southern Review* in London from April 1870 until the appearance of its final issue in July 1879.[50] After Bledsoe's death Sophia continued to edit the periodical by herself, from January to October 1878, at which time she resigned her position. C. J. Griffith edited the final two numbers of the periodical in Richmond, Virginia, in January and July 1879, when it finally succumbed to indifference. Sophia subsequently became an accomplished editor and author in her own right. In 1879 she was an assistant editor at *Scribner's Monthly*, which later became *Century Magazine*. Sophia continued her editorial work at *Century* until her retirement in 1906. She died in 1919. All who knew Sophia (or "Sophie") were impressed with her learning, literary abilities, and strength of character. Bledsoe's old friend Lucius Q. C. Lamar said of her in March 1890: "Sophie has a rich and powerful nature, and my mind and character have never come in contact with her without imbibing a conscious enrichment and increase of moral strength." Robert Underwood Johnson, an editor at *Century Magazine*, described her in his memoirs as "one of the wisest and best women I ever knew." She was "an intellectual woman."[51]

Historians have often recognized the significance of Bledsoe's contributions as the editor of the *Southern Review,* especially as examples of how the Civil War shaped the thought of intractable conservatives like him. Edwin Mims considered Bledsoe as the most implacable of the champions of southern conservatism—a tireless vindicator of the Lost Cause and the ideals of education that prevailed in the South before the war. His articles were frequently "long and heavy, but to a student of the intellectual history of the Southern people they are absolutely indispensable." Bledsoe was an unyielding enemy of the changes afoot in the postwar South, which prompted Richard M. Weaver to describe him as "one of the most curious intransigents in American history. . . . Everything for which he battled was destined to be beaten."[52] The conservative Georgia historian E. Merton Coulter appreciatively noted that Bledsoe's *Southern Review* upheld a high standard of literary excellence. It was as learned and philosophical as any similar journal in the country, "though reverentially Southern." Bledsoe pontificated on the social, political, religious, scientific, educational, and philosophical issues that concerned him, including trademark discourses on the idea of liberty he first began to craft as the editor of the *Illinois Journal* two decades earlier.[53] William Henry Longton has aptly described Bledsoe's writings on his pet subjects as "long, angry, cynical, strident, and repetitious articles." The *Southern Review* was, indeed, a reflection of its editor's strengths and weakness, his reveries to the past and anxieties about the future. It was in every sense, Gaines M. Foster has observed, Bledsoe's "personal pulpit."[54]

Paul H. Buck has noted that southern intellectuals had difficult choices to make in the postwar period. Would they be truculent writers of "the Bledsoe school," or would they seek their own way without allowing the war to define them? Bledsoe was prominent among the literary figures of the postbellum South who continued to invoke the language and symbolism of the old order. "The most influential critic of materialism in the 1870s," notes Charles Reagan Wilson, "was Albert Taylor Bledsoe, one of the most anguished and embittered Lost Cause ministers." Francis Butler Simpkins has justifiably called Bledsoe and Robert Lewis Dabney "anti-Yankee extremists" who continued to advocate the proclaimed virtues of the Old South and criticize the corrupting influences of acquisitiveness they attributed to life under Republican rule. The American biographer, essayist, and Southern Agrarian John Donald Wade, not surprisingly, made a similar assessment. Wade described Bledsoe, Dabney, and Charles Colcock Jones as complex figures and veritable "prophets" whose regrets and fears for the present and future were "too intricate to be widely understood and valued." All three writers saw the Civil War as a titanic contest between a spiritual and a materialistic way of life. "They felt that more-and-more and not better-and-better was the inevitable motto of the new order, and they believed that such a premise was compatible only with the standardized and un-polite, the essentially un-human."[55] The problem with such an interpretation of agrarian ideals, however, is that antebellum southern planters and other men of means were just as avaricious as their northern counterparts, although they often claimed otherwise. King Cotton was a capitalist enterprise too and slavery even more exploitive than free labor, despite self-assuring arguments to the contrary.

Bledsoe devoted the last decade of his life to advancing the cause of southern literature, protecting the principles of the Lost Cause, defending his theology, and broadcasting his conservative views on a broad range of subjects. He decried attempts to remake the South in the image of the North and continued to disparage the egalitarian ideas of the Enlightenment that had unleashed the dogs of democracy against the social order of the South. He was decidedly hostile to the idea of equal political rights for women, and his views on that subject have aged no better than those on slavery and black suffrage.[56] Bledsoe reaffirmed his twin faiths in religion and science and continued to reproach the secularizing trends in science and society that took God out of the universe and scoffed at faith as superstition. What he considered to be modern atheism made no more of an impression on him than its earlier incarnations. Bledsoe clearly perceived the challenges that the secularizing tendencies of his age presented to his natural theology and to revelation. The Darwinian revolution was particularly threatening, since it explained the origin and development of creation outside a theistic framework.[57]

The legacy of the civil war for many white southerners was a disconcerting and resentful one. There was little, if anything, about the new order that Bledsoe liked and much that he feared. The emerging imperatives of the New South had no room for a man so wedded to the ideals and values of the past. He found himself living amid greatly altered political and social conditions that questioned earlier verities and gave him little encouragement for the future. As he attested in January 1873, "Our hopes have fled, and we sit in darkness. The lights which once seemed to guide us safely, and to cheer us on our way, have gone out; and the ground, once apparently so firm under our feet, is still unsettled and heaving from the mighty volcanic throes of the late revolution." Uncertainty about the present and future produced a general sense of "distrust, anxiety, and discontent." Doubt, along with disappointment, "sits and broods, like an awful incubus, on the minds, hearts, and imagination of all thinking men." Yet even so obdurate and disgruntled a figure as Bledsoe understood that southerners faced hard decisions regarding the future. "Shall we, then, take 'our ancestral faiths' along with us into the new era? We should neither take all, nor leave all." Instead, southerners should carefully examine those faiths and determine which were true and which false. And in considering such matters they should above all adopt the motto of the *Southern Review:* "Prove all things, and hold fast the good."[58]

As the learned and cantankerous editor of the *Southern Review,* Bledsoe held fast to the ancestral faiths he believed were good. He continued to seek the old paths. Yet not everyone in the postwar South cleaved to the earlier beliefs with same steadfastness as he, nor did they share all his hopes, fears, and prejudices. Southerners began to reorient themselves quite naturally to new imperatives, exigencies, and aspirations after the war. Bledsoe's requiems to the past appealed to a diminishing number of readers, even though the causes he championed were far too sanctified to ever be entirely abandoned. White southerners on the whole did not so much reject Bledsoe's version of the past as they did his time-worn and tattered prescriptions for the present and future— an important distinction. The voice of Albert Taylor Bledsoe remained quintessentially that of the Old South throughout Reconstruction until the end of his days—events that ironically and fittingly coincided. He lived to see the military occupation of the South end, the withdrawal of troops taking place in the last year of his life. When reading Bledsoe's exonerations of discredited causes, one is reminded of Don Quixote tipping his lance at windmills or the legendary Saint George wielding his trenchant blade in combat with the Dragon. Few matched him as a centurion of the Old South. Bledsoe died a man decidedly out of season, whose disconsolate writings in the *Southern Review* hold a conspicuous place within the tradition of southern conservatism.

WRITING A LIFE

A Note on Sources

WRITING A BIOGRAPHY OF BLEDSOE is a challenging endeavor because so few of his personal papers have survived. Only fragments of his life appear in the extant correspondence. Writing letters was a confessed burden for Bledsoe, and he occasionally apologized for being a poor correspondent. The meagerness of his surviving letters, however, owes far more to his negligence in preserving them than to his admitted aversion to correspondence. The small number of letters that passed into the hands of Bledsoe's children after his death in 1877 was but the remnant of a larger correspondence. As he ruefully noted, "I have lost, or destroyed, hundreds of similar papers." Most of Bledsoe's correspondence dating from before 1860, including testimonials concerning some of his writings, did not survive the war. Bledsoe was himself uncertain as to the fate of those letters. He said only that he placed them in the archives of the University of Virginia, where they were either stolen or destroyed by "some unfriendly hand."[1] Nor does it appear that the manuscripts relating to Bledsoe's various theological, historical, and scientific interests—including his unfinished history of the American Civil War—remain in existence. Clearly much has been lost.

An equally unkind fate befell most of Bledsoe's correspondence from after the war. The entries in his Memorandum Book refer to letters still in his possession around 1868, when he wrote the memoranda, and to others that had already been lost or destroyed. What happened to most of the letters that were still extant when he wrote the memoranda is largely a matter of conjecture. But they possibly perished in a fire at the Bayonne, New Jersey, residence of Bledsoe's eldest daughter, Sophia Bledsoe Herrick, at some point after his death. What little we know of that fire is based on a statement made by Elizabeth McMurtrie Bledsoe Wayland (1846–1933)—the last of Bledsoe's surviving children. Elizabeth stated in a letter written to Langbourne M. Williams in January 1931—during her eighty-fifth year—that her sister Sophia, being the eldest child, had all the family papers. "She lived in Bayonne and had a bad fire. Some of her papers were burned, but which ones I do not know."[2] It is only a surmise that most of Bledsoe's postwar letters were destroyed in that fire, albeit a plausible one.

What remains of Bledsoe's correspondence has come down to us from his daughters Sophia Bledsoe Herrick (1837–1919) and Emily Albertine Bledsoe Dinwiddie (1840–1913) and his son-in-law William Dinwiddie. Sophia passed on the family papers in her possession to her daughter Virginia Herrick Fox and Emily Bledsoe to her daughter Emily Wayland Dinwiddie. Virginia lent the items in her possession to David Rankin Barbee, who made photostatic copies in the late 1920s or early 1930s.[3] The materials once in the possession of Sophia Bledsoe Herrick and her daughter Virginia today form the Bledsoe-Herrick Family Papers in the Arthur and Elizabeth Schlesinger Library at the Radcliffe Institute for Advanced Study at Harvard University. The Bledsoe-Herrick Family Papers consists of letters to and from Bledsoe's fiancée, Harriet Coxe, whom he married in 1836, and biographical and genealogical information about Bledsoe compiled by his eldest child, Sophia. Most of the correspondence and manuscript material in the Bledsoe-Herrick Family Papers, however, relate to Sophia, including her unpublished memoirs, a long series of letters to her daughter Louise Herrick Wall, and notes on family history and genealogy. There are also photographs of Sophia and her family, including two of her father, Albert Taylor Bledsoe.

The Emily Wayland Dinwiddie Materials at the Virginia Historical Society date from 1931 to 1948 and consist of some three hundred items. Emily compiled these notes for a biography of her grandfather she planned to write with her cousin Louise Herrick Wall. The work was never completed beyond what is contained in Emily's unpublished "Tales of a Grandfather: Albert Taylor Bledsoe, His Life and Times." The manuscript is undated and unpaginated but was completed around 1948 near the end of Emily's life and numbers 198 pages. Emily's account of her grandfather, however, is all genealogy and no "life and times." It is peripheral to Bledsoe's own life and thought. Nonetheless, the manuscript contains valuable information based on wills and the property, tax, and marriage records that Emily unearthed in Virginia and Kentucky. Those records establish, for example, that Bledsoe's father and mother at one time owned slaves, as did their respective families going back several generations. No collection of Bledsoe papers exists at the Virginia Historical Society, but there are Bledsoe letters in eighteen of the society's manuscript collections.

The Bledsoe materials in the Albert and Shirley Small Special Collections Library at the University of Virginia are the more significant in terms of Bledsoe's life and thought. The Dinwiddie Family Papers (1846–1937) consists of some fifty items, which include thirty-nine letters of William Dinwiddie dating from 1846 to 1878 and a scrapbook of press clippings and obituaries relating to Bledsoe's writings and activities compiled toward the end of his life.[4] The Bledsoe Family Papers at the University of Virginia include a letter written by Bledsoe to his wife, Harriet, in May 1837 concerning a religious convention in Danville, Kentucky, and informs her of a review he had written and intended to publish. It also includes a letter from Louise Herrick Wall, Bledsoe's granddaughter, regarding critical comments about Bledsoe made by Philip Alexander Bruce in his *History of the University of Virginia* and by Edwin Mims in his sketch of Bledsoe in the *Dictionary of American Biography*. The Bledsoe papers still in the possession of Emily Wayland Dinwiddie in April 1932 were lent to David Rankin Barbee for transcription and microfilming at the University of Virginia.

Those sources are available as the David Rankin Barbee Microfilm Collection of Albert Taylor Bledsoe Materials—microfilm 517, document series 3311—at the Albert and Shirley Small Special Collections Library of the University of Virginia. The letters and press clippings contained in the collection number approximately one hundred items and are available for loan. Barbee collected those materials between about 1928 and 1932 for a projected biography of Bledsoe. A typescript of Bledsoe's Memorandum Book, left by Sophia Bledsoe Herrick to her daughter Virginia Herrick Fox, is also a part of the Barbee Microfilm Collection. The Bledsoe materials on microfilm 517 appear numerically as document series 3311 (the last series on the roll). The other documents on the roll do not relate to Bledsoe. The Barbee Microfilm Collection contains the same correspondence found in the Letters of Albert Taylor Bledsoe, 1858 to 1875, MS 3461, in the Albert and Shirley Small Special Collections Library at the University of Virginia, as well as additional Bledsoe materials available in microfilm only.

All students of Bledsoe's life owe a debt of gratitude to David Rankin Barbee (1874–1958) for his diligent efforts in compiling many of the fugitive sources of Bledsoe's life. Barbee, a feature writer for the *Washington Post* from 1928 until his retirement in 1942, started his journalistic career with the *Nashville Banner* in 1896. He continued to do yeoman's work at several newspapers in Memphis, Chattanooga, Montgomery, Mobile, New Orleans, and Ashville. Barbee nurtured a serious interest in Abraham Lincoln, the Civil War, and Albert Taylor Bledsoe. He was a diligent researcher who corresponded widely with archivists in the late 1920s and early 1930s. He compiled copies of some one hundred pages of Bledsoe letters, memoranda, articles, and press notices with the idea of writing a biography. Barbee never completed that work but had the forethought to make copies of those materials and deposit them in the Library of Congress, the University of Virginia, and Georgetown University. Barbee drew upon some of that research in *An Excursion in Southern History* and a brief manuscript entitled "Lincoln's Lost Friends," which is as far as he ever got with his anticipated biography of Bledsoe.[5]

While Barbee's compilation of fugitive Bledsoe letters and press clippings is invaluable, care must be taken in using his notes, correspondence, and writings on Bledsoe. Barbee occasionally conflates his facts regarding the details of Bledsoe's life, indulges in hearsay evidence, and makes sweeping generalizations. He was an uncritical admirer of Bledsoe and prone to overstatement. Barbee wrote in the tradition of the unreconstructed southerner, and his pronounced southern loyalties often clouded his judgment. He echoes Bledsoe in many of his views and was just as adamant that northern historians distorted southern history, especially concerning the origin and meaning of the Civil War. Barbee was determined to expose "suppressed history" regarding Lincoln, the war, and historical treatments of Jefferson Davis, which he amply demonstrated in his articles on the capture of Jefferson Davis and his life in prison.[6] Barbee had a journalist's nose for a good story, wrote well, and compiled valuable source materials, but he was still fighting the Civil War— self-consciously and fearlessly. He was a keen student of Bledsoe in many senses of the word.

Apart from Bledsoe's books, most of the printed sources of his life are found in the yellowing pages of the *Southern Review*. The *Review* featured articles on biography, history, politics, literature, education, natural history, science, astronomy, mathematics, philosophy, theology, ecclesiology, and the Civil War. The articles are all unsigned, but Bledsoe contributed several hundred printed pages of his own writings to most, if not all, of those volumes until his death in December 1877. One authority places the number of articles contributed to the *Southern Review* by Bledsoe at 135.[7] Toward the end of life he sometimes reprinted articles in the *Review* that had originally appeared decades earlier. Those writings are cited in the endnotes with a note regarding their subsequent reappearance in the *Southern Review*. Yet several articles in the *Southern Review* that are often attributed to Bledsoe in the secondary literature are not ascribed to him here. Internal or collateral evidence suggests in those instances that they were probably written by anonymous contributors to the *Southern Review*. Since establishing authorship for several of these writings is a hazardous undertaking, I have placed prudence ahead of intuition in assigning authorship to Bledsoe. Problems of attribution for specific articles appearing in the *Southern Review* are discussed in the endnotes to Chapter 10. One may reasonably infer, however, that they would not have found a place in the *Southern Review* if Bledsoe did not, for the most part, agree with the author's views and opinions.

Nor should it be supposed that all of Bledsoe's contributions to newspapers and to periodicals besides the *Southern Review* have yet been determined. He began writing literary criticism at least as early as 1837 and often anonymously. He informed his wife, Harriet, in May of that year that he had nearly finished a review of Lord Henry Brougham's *Discourse of Natural Theology* (1835) he was writing for Caleb Sprague Henry's *New-York Review*. "I have several other pieces on the stocks, and shall furnish at least one article for each succeeding no." Bledsoe's unsigned review of "Lord Brougham's Natural Theology" appeared in the *New-York Review* for October 1837 and is his earliest known writing.[8] His letter to Harriet suggests that he probably made other anonymous contributions to the *New-York Review* as well. It is likely that he contributed unsigned reviews to other journals also. He stated in an autobiographical sketch submitted to George W. Cullum at West Point in May 1850—still relatively early in his literary career—that he was a contributor to the principal literary, scientific, and theological reviews of the country, although he did not specify which ones or what he contributed.[9] Since his known contributions to theological journals in the 1840s, his editorials in the *Illinois Journal* in 1847 and 1848, and at least some of his contributions to the English press from 1863 to 1865 were all unsigned, it is quite likely that not all of Bledsoe's writings have yet been identified.

The writings of Albert Taylor Bledsoe examined in the narrative include several of his more significant minor writings, some of which are explored here for the first time. Even so, the works cited make no claim to completeness regarding Bledsoe's numerous contributions as the editor of the *Southern Review*. Several of his known contributions to the periodical are, indeed, noticeably absent. The chapter endnotes include only the articles discussed in the text. As substantial as these writings are, however, they are but a portion of a much larger body of work. While an inclusive list of all of Bledsoe's known writings in the *Southern Review* would be valuable as an exercise in bibliotheca, it serves no particular purpose here. Such a list would include writings on extraneous subjects not discussed in the narrative or mentioned only incidentally. I have cited only the contributions to the *Southern Review* that in my estimation more fully frame Bledsoe's historical significance.[10]

The secondary literature relating to various aspects of Bledsoe's multifarious interests and experiences is extensive. These writings contextualize his life and thought in important ways, even though he has received relatively little attention as a subject of historical inquiry in his own right. The more important monographic and journal literature relating to the subject matter upon which Bledsoe wrote is discussed in the text and cited in the chapter endnotes but is not repeated in a separate bibliography.

NOTES

ABBREVIATIONS

ALPL   Abraham Lincoln Presidential Library, Springfield, Illinois

BLMC   Eleanor S. Brockenbrough Library, The Museum of the Confederacy, Richmond, Virginia

MDLC   Manuscript Division, Library of Congress, Washington, D.C.

MUA   Miami University Archives, Oxford, Ohio

SCLDU   Rare Book, Manuscript, and Special Collections Library, Duke University Libraries, Durham, North Carolina

SCLMU   Walter Havinghurst Special Collections Library, Miami University, Oxford, Ohio

SCLUV   Albert and Shirley Small Special Collections Library, University of Virginia, Charlottesville

SLHU   The Arthur and Elizabeth Schlesinger Library on the History of Women in America, Radcliffe Institute for Advanced Study, Harvard University, Cambridge, Massachusetts

VHS   Virginia Historical Society, Richmond

INTRODUCTION

1. Samuel Augustus Steel, "Albert Taylor Bledsoe: Sometime Editor of This Review," *Methodist Quarterly Review* 64 (April 1915): 211. Morris R. Cohen similarly commented on Bledsoe's "versatility" in *The Cambridge History of American Literature*, vol. 3, ed. William Peterfield Trent, John Erskine, Stuart P. Sherman, and Carl Van Doren (New York: G. P. Putnam's Sons; Cambridge: Cambridge University Press, 1921), 255n1.

2. John Wilson Townsend, *Kentucky in American Letters, 1784–1912*, vol. 1 (Cedar Rapids, IA: Torch Press, 1913), 171.

3. Albert Taylor Bledsoe, Memorandum Book, ca. 1868, entry 58, in the Notebooks of Albert Taylor Bledsoe, MS 104-a, SCLUV (cited hereafter as Bledsoe, Memorandum Book). A typescript of the memoranda is also available in the David Rankin Barbee Microfilm Collection of Albert Taylor Bledsoe Materials, microfilm 517, 3311, SCLUV.

4. Eugene D. Genovese, *The Slaveholders' Dilemma: Freedom and Progress in Southern Conservative Thought, 1820–1860* (Columbia: University of South Carolina Press, 1992), 2; Joseph L. Blau, *Men and Movements in American Philosophy* (New York: Prentice Hall, 1952), 78; Douglas Ambrose, "Southern Intellectual Life," in *Encyclopedia of American Cultural and Intellectual History*, vol. 1, ed. Mary Kupiec Cayton and Peter W. Williams (New York: Charles Scribner's Sons, 2001), 480.

5. John McCardell, *The Idea of a Southern Nation: Southern Nationalists and Southern Nationalism, 1830–1860* (New York: W. W. Norton and Co., 1979), 9.

6. David W. Blight, *Race and Reunion: The Civil War in American Memory* (Cambridge: Harvard University Press, Belknap Press, 2001), 261; Charles Reagan Wilson, *Baptized in Blood: The Religion of the Lost Cause, 1865–1920* (Athens: University of Georgia Press, 1980), 141; Douglas Southall Freeman, *The South to Posterity: An Introduction to the Writing of Confederate History* (New York: Charles Scribner's Sons, 1939), 33.

7. Peter Knupfer, "Aging Statesmen and the Statesmanship of an Earlier Age: The Generational Roots of the Constitutional Union Party," in *Union and Emancipation: Essays on Politics and Race in the Civil War Era*, ed. David W. Blight and Brooks D. Simpson (Kent, OH: Kent State University Press, 1997), 65.

8. Robert Penn Warren, *The Legacy of the Civil War: Meditations on the Centennial, 1961–1965* (New York: Random House, 1961), 3, 64, 49–50, 99; David R. Goldfield, *Still Fighting the Civil War: The American South and Southern History* (Baton Rouge: Louisiana State University Press, 2002), 1, 12. See also C. Van Woodward, *Thinking Back: The Perils of Writing History* (Baton Rouge: Louisiana State University Press, 1986), 108.

9. Genovese, *Slaveholders' Dilemma*, 3; Bertram Wyatt-Brown, *Southern Honor: Ethics and Behavior in the Old South* (New York: Oxford University Press, 1982), viii; Drew Gilpin Faust, "A Southern Stewardship: The Intellectual and the Proslavery Argument," *American Quarterly* 31 (Spring 1979): 63.

10. Samuel Elliott Morison, *The Oxford History of the United States*, vol. 2 (New York: Oxford University Press, 1927), 15.

11. See Michael O'Brien, *Conjectures of Order: Intellectual Life and the American South, 1810–1860*, 2 vols. (Chapel Hill: University of North Carolina Press, 2004); Michael O'Brien, *All Clever Men, Who Make Their Way: Critical Discourse in the Old South* (Athens: University of Georgia Press, 1992); and Eugene D. Genovese, *The Southern Tradition: The Achievements and Limitations of an American Conservatism* (Cambridge: Harvard University Press, 1994), 22.

12. See James C. Cobb, *Away Down South: A History of Southern Identity* (New York: Oxford University Press, 2005). Drew Gilpin Faust has observed that southerners have been so preoccupied with explaining themselves and their region for so long that exploring regional identity "is like looking at a reflection of a reflection. Attempts at self-interpretation have become one of the region's most characteristic cultural products." Faust, *The Sacred Circle: The Dilemma of the Intellectual in the Old South, 1840–1860* (Baltimore: Johns Hopkins University Press, 1977), ix. See also Fred C. Hobson, *Tell about the South: The Southern Rage to Explain* (Baton Rouge: Louisiana State University Press, 1983).

13. David Moltke-Hansen, "Intellectual and Cultural History of the Old South," in *A Companion to the American South*, Blackwell Companions to American History, no. 3 (Malden, MA: Blackwell Publishing, 2004), 212–26; John B. Boles and Evelyn Thomas Nolen, *Interpreting Southern History: Historiographical Essays in Honor of Sanford W. Higginbotham* (Baton Rouge: Louisiana State University Press, 1987), viii; C. Vann Woodward, "The Elusive Mind of the South," in *American Counterpoint: Slavery and Racism in the North-South Dialogue* (Boston: Little, Brown, 1971; New York: Oxford University Press, 1983).

14. There was no absence of discord on these issues in the South either before or during the war. See Lacy K. Ford, *Deliver Us from Evil: The Slavery Question in the Old South* (Oxford: Oxford University Press, 2009); Carl N. Degler, *The Other South: Southern Dissenters in the Nineteenth Century*, Southern Dissent Series, with a new preface and foreword by Stanley Harrold and Randall M. Miller, series eds. (Gainesville: University Press of Florida, 2000); David J. Eicher, *Dixie Betrayed:*

How the South Really Lost the Civil War (New York: Little, Brown, 2006; Lincoln: University of Nebraska Press, 2007); William W. Freehling, *The South vs. the South: How Anti-Confederate Southerners Shaped the Course of the Civil War* (Oxford: Oxford University Press, 2001); and George C. Rable, *The Confederate Republic: A Revolution against Politics* (Chapel Hill: University of North Carolina, 1994).

CHAPTER ONE

1. Willard Rouse Jillson, *The Newspapers and Periodicals of Frankfort, Kentucky, 1795–1945* (Frankfort: Kentucky State Historical Society, 1945), 6, 8; Ludie J. Kinkead, ed., in association with Thomas D. Clark, *Checklist of Kentucky Newspapers Contained in Kentucky Libraries* (Lexington: Kentucky Library Association, 1935), 6–7. The *Argus of Western America* identified itself an "Independent Republican" paper in 1808 and as a "Democratic" concern in 1823. John Hay Farnham joined Moses Bledsoe as copublisher of the *Commentator* in 1818, but in January of the following year Moses was again the sole publisher. He continued to edit and publish the *Commentator* until May 1819, when he sold his interest in the paper to Jacob H. Holeman and William B. Holeman.

2. Sophia Bledsoe Herrick, "Coxe Family," 73, MS 2820, SCLUV (cited hereafter as Herrick, "Coxe Family"); Emily Wayland Dinwiddie, "Tales of a Grandfather: Albert Taylor Bledsoe, His Life and Times," [5, 8], Emily Wayland Dinwiddie Materials, MS 5:9 D6195:1, VHS (cited hereafter as Dinwiddie, "Tales of a Grandfather"). Tax records for Franklin County show that Moses Bledsoe was taxed in 1809 for the ownership of three slaves, two of whom were above the age of sixteen. He was again taxed on those or other slaves in 1817.

3. Note from the Record of Marriages, Franklin County, Kentucky, 1794–1851, Emily Wayland Dinwiddie Materials, VHS; Dinwiddie, "Tales of a Grandfather," [34].

4. Sophia Bledsoe Herrick, "Personal Recollections of My Father and Mr. Lincoln and Mr. Davis," *Methodist Quarterly Review* 64 (October 1915): 665; Herrick, "Coxe Family," 72–73. Nothing further is known regarding the slaves once owned by Moses and Sophia Bledsoe or whether the slaves once owned by Moses were the same as those inherited by Sophia. Both Sophia's father, Samuel Taylor, and uncle Creed Taylor were planters and slaveholders, so it is likely that her reported inheritance of slaves came from the Taylor family or a related family in Virginia or Kentucky. Creed Taylor Jr., Bledsoe's cousin on his mother's side of the family, remained a slave owner through the Civil War. Slaveholding in the Taylor family of Virginia is discussed in the Papers of Creed Taylor, 1791–1873, accession #1232, SCLUV.

5. The only mention by Bledsoe regarding his early education is that Nicholas Pike's *New and Complete System of Arithmetic* grounded him in the fundamentals and was his entrée into the sublime logic of mathematical problems. Pike's *Arithmetic* was all he needed to advance from the bottom to the top of the mathematical ladder. Albert Taylor Bledsoe, "Notices of Books," *Southern Review* 5 (January 1869): 243. Richard M. Weaver incorrectly says that Bledsoe attended Transylvania University in Lexington, where his uncle Jesse Bledsoe taught law. Richard M. Weaver, "Albert Taylor Bledsoe," *Sewanee Review* 52 (January–March 1944): 34. The error has occasionally been repeated in the secondary literature relating to Bledsoe's life. Jesse Bledsoe, Albert's great-uncle, was a tutor at Transylvania University from 1795 to 1797 and a law professor from 1822 to 1825. Student records, however, do not show that Albert Taylor Bledsoe ever attended the school.

6. *Official Register of the Officers and Cadets of the U.S. Military Academy, West Point, New York, 1818–1899*, printed document, United States Military Academy Printing Office, June 1826, 5, 12–

15; George W. Cullum, *Biographical Register of the Officers and Graduates of the U.S. Military Academy, West Point, New York,* 3rd ed. rev., vol. 1 (Boston: Houghton Mifflin and Co., 1891), 456; Sophia Bledsoe Herrick, "Albert Taylor Bledsoe," *Alumni Bulletin of the University of Virginia* 6 (May 1899): 2; Herrick, "Coxe Family," 75.

7. *Official Register of the Officers and Cadets of the U.S. Military Academy, 1818–1899,* June 1827, 13; June 1828, 11; and June 1829, 8; Cullum, *Biographical Register of the Officers and Graduates of the U.S. Military Academy,* 1:456; *Official Register of the Officers and Cadets of the U.S. Military Academy, 1818–1899,* June 1830, 6; Robert E. Lee to the Board of Visitors of the University of Virginia, June 23, 1854, Letterbook of Robert E. Lee, 1842–60, VHS, which further attests to Bledsoe's standing as second in his class in mathematics; Bledsoe to William Holmes McGuffey, June 24, 1854, McGuffey Papers, SCLMU (cited hereafter as McGuffey Papers).

8. Sidney Forman, *West Point: A History of the United States Military Academy* (New York: Columbia University Press, 1950), 59. Bledsoe later challenged Paley's notion of civil liberty in *Liberty and Slavery.* Albert Taylor Bledsoe, *An Essay on Liberty and Slavery* (Philadelphia: J. B. Lippincott and Co., 1856), 13, 20.

9. Bledsoe relates the story of his solution of Archimedes' geometry problem in Albert Taylor Bledsoe, "Christian Theology," *Southern Review* 20 (October 1876): 299–300. His diagram and answer to the problem appear in Albert Taylor Bledsoe, "Article XI.—Miscellany," *Southern Review* 21 (January 1877): 247–48.

10. Albert Taylor Bledsoe, "Education of the Intellect," *Southern Review* 2 (October 1867): 317.

11. Bledsoe, Memorandum Book, entry 10.

12. *Official Register of the Officers and Cadets of the U.S. Military Academy, 1818–1899,* June 1826, 3; June 1827, 3; William Carus, ed., *Memorials of the Rt. Rev. Charles Pettit McIlvaine, D.D., D.C.L.* (New York: Whittaker, 1882), 10; Alfred Lee, *In Memoriam: Charles Pettit McIlvaine, Late Bishop of the Diocese of Ohio. A Sermon* (Cleveland: Leader Printing Co., 1873), 9. McIlvaine appropriately preached the sermon at Polk's consecration ceremony held at Christ Church in Cincinnati on December 9, 1838. See Charles P. McIlvaine, *The Apostolical Commission: The Sermon Preached at the Consecration of the Rt. Rev. Leonidas Polk, D.D., Missionary Bishop for Arkansas; in Christ Church, Cincinnati, December 9, 1838* (Gambier, OH: G. W. Myers, 1838). McIlvaine relates the story of Polk's conversion at West Point and its effects on other cadets on pages 36–39. See also McIlvaine to the Rt. Rev. C. T. Quintard, Cincinnati, December 31, 1868, Polk Collection, Archives and Special Collections, Jessie Ball duPont Library, University of the South, Sewanee, Tennessee (cited hereafter as Polk Collection).

13. Charles Pettit McIlvaine to My Dear Friend and Brother, Cincinnati, April 26, 1872, in Albert Taylor Bledsoe, "How and Why I Became a Methodist," *Southern Review* 14 (January 1874): 110; John N. Waddel, *Memorials of Academic Life* (Richmond: Presbyterian Committee of Publication, 1891), 280.

14. James Milnor to McIlvaine, New York, June 17, 1826, in Rev. John S. Stone, D.D., *A Memoir of the Life of James Milnor, D.D. Late Rector of St. George's Church, New York* (New York: American Tract Society, 1848), 268; Albert Taylor Bledsoe, "Terms of Communion," *Southern Review* 21 (January 1877): 171.

15. Bledsoe to George W. Cullum, University of Mississippi, May 15, 1850, Register of Graduates, No. 602, George W. Cullum Files, United States Military Academy Archives, West Point, New York.

16. See Jesse Bledsoe, *An Introductory Lecture on the Study of Law. Delivered in the Chapel of Transylvania University, on Monday November 4, 1822* (Lexington, KY: Joseph Ficklin, 1822). Jesse at various times served within both houses of the Kentucky legislature and sat for one term in the U.S. Senate during the War of 1812. He later served as the secretary of state of Kentucky and a circuit judge before teaching law at the University of Transylvania. One of Jesse's law students at Transylvania was the young Mississippian Jefferson Davis. Jesse Bledsoe left Kentucky for Mississippi in 1833 but soon moved to Texas, where he died in 1836 while collecting material for a history of the new republic of Texas.

17. See William Hamilton Bryson, *Essays on Legal Education in Nineteenth Century Virginia* (Buffalo, NY: W. W. Hein, 1998), which is a compilation of law lectures by Creed Taylor, St. George Tucker, his sons Nathaniel Beverly Tucker and Henry St. George Tucker, John Barbee Minor, and many others.

18. *Kenyon Catalogue, 1833–1834*, 7; *Kenyon Catalogue, 1834–1835*, 5, 16–17. Bledsoe and fellow seminarian Joshua T. Eaton are identified as tutors in *Laws of Kenyon College and Theological Seminary* (Gambier, OH: Acland Press, 1833), 2. Bledsoe's statement that he was adjunct professor of mathematics and a teacher of French at Kenyon for the academic year 1833–34 appears in Bledsoe to George W. Cullum, University of Mississippi, May 15, 1850, Register of Graduates, No. 602, George W. Cullum Files, United States Military Academy Archives, West Point, New York.

19. Albert Taylor Bledsoe, "The Late William Sparrow, D.D.," *Southern Review* 20 (July 1876): 22; Herrick, "Albert Taylor Bledsoe," *Alumni Bulletin of the University of Virginia*, 2–3; Samuel Willard, "Personal Reminiscences of Life in Illinois, 1830 to 1850," *Transactions of the Illinois State Historical Society*, no. 11 (Annual 1906): 81. The quote from Bledsoe regarding his motive for entering the theological seminary at Kenyon is from Bledsoe, "Late William Sparrow," 22–23.

20. George Franklin Smythe, *Kenyon College: Its First Century* (New Haven: Yale University Press, 1924), 157.

21. Bledsoe, "Late William Sparrow," 19–26, 30, 32; J. Barrett Miller, "The Theology of William Sparrow," *Historical Magazine of the Protestant Episcopal Church* 43 (1977): 443–54. Miller's account explains the principles of Sparrow's Arminian theology and his understanding of the doctrine of justification by faith. His assessment is based upon an analysis of Sparrow's surviving sermons. See William Sparrow, *Sermons, by William Sparrow* (New York: Thomas Whittaker, 1877).

22. Bledsoe-Herrick Family Papers, MC 290, "Children of Albert Taylor and Harriet (Coxe) Bledsoe," typescript, p. 5, SLHU; Mary McIlvaine to Charles Pettit McIlvaine, April 5, 1835, McIlvaine Papers, Kenyon College, Gambier, Ohio; Emily Wayland Dinwiddie, "Notes," in Emily Wayland Dinwiddie Materials, VHS; "Albert Taylor Bledsoe," *National Cyclopaedia of American Biography*, vol. 8 (New York: James T. White and Co., 1924), 273; Herrick, "Personal Recollections of My Father," 679; Emily Wayland Dinwiddie, a biographical note regarding Sophia McIlvaine Bledsoe in Emily Wayland Dinwiddie Materials, VHS; Sophia Bledsoe Herrick, "Bledsoe Family History," typescript, microfilm 517, 3311, SCLUV. The surviving children of Albert and Harriet Bledsoe were Sophia McIlvaine Bledsoe Herrick (1837–1919), Emily Albertine Bledsoe Dinwiddie (1840–1913), Elizabeth McMurtrie "Lillie" Bledsoe (1846–1933), and Anna Bledsoe (1851–1923). Sophia, the eldest daughter, was born at Bishop McIlvaine's home in Gambier, Ohio, on March 26, 1837. Harriet Coxe Bledsoe's recollection of the death of her daughter Louise M. Bledsoe, who died in 1857, is contained in the Bledsoe-Herrick Family Papers, MC 290, ser. 3, Sophia Bledsoe Herrick: Writings and Correspondence, sections 4 and 5, SLHU.

23. *Journal of the Protestant Episcopal Church, Ohio, 1835,* 1, 22; *Journal of the Protestant Episcopal Church, Ohio, 1836,* 11; *Catalogue. Theological Seminary. Kenyon College. Kenyon Preparatory School, 1835–1836* (Gambier, OH: Western Protestant Episcopal Press, 1836), 22; *Journal of the Protestant Episcopal Church, Ohio, 1837,* 11.

24. "Board of Trustees Journal, 1809–1852," 332, 339, 367, 374; Bledsoe to Joel Collins, October 9, 1835, MUA. Albert Taylor Bledsoe, "Report from Professor Bledsoe," March 28, 1836, "Journal of the President and Trustees of Miami University, 1809–1852," 348, MUA; Bledsoe to McGuffey, Sandusky City, January 17, 1837, McGuffey Papers; *Journal of the Protestant Episcopal Church, Ohio, 1836,* 24.

25. Bledsoe to McGuffey, Sandusky City, January 17, 1837, McGuffey Papers; *Journal of the Protestant Episcopal Church, Ohio, 1836,* 24.

26. James H. Rodabaugh, *Robert Hamilton Bishop,* vol. 4 of *Ohio Historical Collections* (Columbus: Ohio State Archaeological and Historical Society, 1935), 86; Charles Pettit McIlvaine to McGuffey, Gambier, Ohio, January 11, 1836, McGuffey Papers.

27. "Statement of John Witherspoon Scott to the Board of Trustees of Miami University with Regard to the Difficulties Connected with McGuffey," September 1, 1836, John Witherspoon Scott Collection, box 1, folder 14, MUA. Box 1, folder 14 of the Scott Collection contains a transcript and a photocopy of Scott's statement to the board of trustees, the original of which is in the vault of the Walter Havighurst Special Collections Library.

28. Bledsoe stated his grievances against Miami in Bledsoe to William Holmes McGuffey, Sandusky City, September 23, 1836, and Bledsoe to McGuffey, Sandusky City, January 17, 1837, McGuffey Papers.

29. "Journal of the President and Trustees of Miami University, 1809–1852," September 26, 1836, 365–66, MUA; Scott, "Statement of John Witherspoon Scott to the Board of Trustees," September 1, 1836, MUA.

30. Bledsoe to Harriet Coxe, Gambier, Ohio, February 23, 1835, MC 290, Bledsoe-Herrick Family Papers, SLHU.

31. The unfounded speculation that President Bishop's antislavery sentiments might have been another reason for Bledsoe's opposition to his administration appears in Rodabaugh, *Robert Hamilton Bishop,* 109–115, and John Boyce Bennett, "Albert Taylor Bledsoe: Social and Religious Controversialist of the Old South" (Ph.D. diss., Duke University, 1942), 15.

32. Bledsoe to William Holmes McGuffey, Sandusky City, September 23, 1836, and January 17, 1837, McGuffey Papers; copy of a letter from McIlvaine to the Wardens and Vestry of Grace Church, Sandusky, Ohio, Gambier, January 31, 1837, Harry E. Pratt Research Collection containing materials regarding Albert Taylor Bledsoe, ALPL.

33. *Journal of the Protestant Episcopal Church, Ohio, 1837,* 3, 20; Herrick, "Personal Recollections of My Father," 666.

34. Bledsoe to Harriet Coxe Bledsoe, Lexington, Kentucky, April 14, 1837, Bledsoe-Herrick Family Papers, SLHU; Bledsoe to Harriet Coxe Bledsoe, Lexington, [Kentucky], May 8, 1837, Papers of the Bledsoe Family, MS 3461-a, SCLUV; *Journal of the Protestant Episcopal Church, Ohio, 1838,* 44–46.

35. A. T. Bledsoe to Dr. John Poisal, April 30, 1870, in Albert Taylor Bledsoe, "The First Eight Volumes of the Southern Review. From January 1867 to January 1871," *Southern Review* 8 (October 1870): 424–27; Albert Taylor Bledsoe, "The Suffering and Salvation of Infants," *Southern Review* 16 (January 1875): 78; Bledsoe, "How and Why I Became a Methodist," 107–8, 111–13.

36. Bledsoe, "First Eight Volumes of the Southern Review," 426, where he says he had sought admission into the Methodist ministry "more than twenty five years ago," or around 1845; Herrick, "Personal Recollections of My Father," 667.

CHAPTER TWO

1. An earlier account of Bledsoe's Springfield years is Terry A. Barnhart, "Albert Taylor Bledsoe: The Political Creed of an Illinois Whig, 1840–1848," *Journal of Illinois History* 3 (Spring 2000): 3–30.

2. Samuel Willard, "Personal Reminiscences of Life in Illinois, 1830 to 1850," *Transactions of the Illinois State Historical Society,* no. 11 (Annual 1906): 73; William Stephen Hamilton, Moses O. Bledsoe, and Bowling Green, "Courier Extra. Springfield, Monday Morning, July 26, 1830," campaign circular, broadside B-28, ALPL.

3. *National Cyclopaedia of American Biography* vol. 8 (New York: James T. White and Co., 1924), 272. Samuel Willard, who knew Moses during his own residence at Carrollton, described him as "an old lawyer." Willard, "Personal Reminiscences," 84–85. Wilber F. Tillett also stated in his sketch of Bledsoe's life that his father, Moses, was "a lawyer of more than ordinary ability." Wilbur F. Tillett, "Albert Taylor Bledsoe," *Quarterly Review of the Methodist Episcopal Church, South,* n.s. 14 (July 1893): 222.

4. Untitled notice, *Sangamo Journal,* July 19, 1839, no pagination. The members of the bar practicing law in Carrollton listed in this notice were D. M. Woodson, R. L. Doyle, and A. T. Bledsoe. The date of March 15, 1839, for Bledsoe's admission to the Illinois bar is from Adam F. Block [clerk of the Supreme Court of the State of Illinois] to Harry E. Pratt, Springfield, January 8, 1934, Harry E. Pratt Papers, box 1, folder 2, ALPL.

5. "Law Notice," *Sangamo Journal,* December 27, 1839, no pagination. The notice is dated December 25, 1839; "Professional Cards," *Sangamo Journal,* February 21, 1840. The card of Thomas and Bledsoe is dated February 15, 1840. Jesse Burgess Thomas Jr. was the nephew of Jesse Burgess Thomas, author of the Missouri Compromise. In 1843, following the resignation of Stephen Arnold Douglas, the Illinois General Assembly appointed the younger Thomas to the Illinois Supreme Court, where he served until 1848. J. F. Snyder, "Forgotten Statesmen of Illinois," *Transactions of the Illinois State Historical Society* (Annual 1904): 523–24.

6. The announcement that Thomas and Bledsoe had dissolved their legal partnership by "mutual consent" is dated August 15, 1840, and appears in the *Sangamo Journal,* August 21, 1840. The notice that Baker and Bledsoe were partners-in-law appears in ibid., May 14, 1841.

7. "Springfield Junto," *Illinois State Register,* November 23, 1839; Charles Manfred Thompson, *The Illinois Whigs before 1846* (Urbana: Graduate School, University of Illinois, 1915), 67n, 76.

8. An account of Baker's life and relationship with Lincoln is Harry C. Blair and Rebecca Tarshis, *The Life of Colonel Edward D. Baker: Lincoln's Constant Ally* (Portland: Oregon Historical Society, 1960).

9. Daniel W. Stowell, ed., *The Papers of Abraham Lincoln: Legal Documents and Cases,* vol. 1 (Charlottesville: University of Virginia Press, 2008), 133, 177, 184; Harry E. Pratt, "Albert Taylor Bledsoe: Critic of Lincoln," *Transactions of the Illinois State Historical Society,* no. 41 (Annual 1934): 159; James Joyce Bennett, "Albert Taylor Bledsoe: Social and Religious Controversialist of the Old South" (Ph.D. diss., Duke University, 1942), 23; Sophia Bledsoe Herrick, "Albert Taylor Bledsoe,"

Alumni Bulletin of the University of Virginia 6 (May 1899): 3; Sophia Bledsoe Herrick, "Albert Taylor Bledsoe, 1809–1877," in *Library of Southern Literature*, vol. 1, ed. Edwin Anderson Alderman and Charles Alphonso Smith (Atlanta: Martin and Hoyt Co., 1929), 395–96. Records relating to Bledsoe's legal cases before the Illinois Supreme Court appear in J. Young Scammon, *Reports of Cases Argued and Determined in the Supreme Court of the State of Illinois*, vol. 5 (Chicago: Callaghan and Co., 1886), 170–609. An account of the appeals cases in which Bledsoe faced Lincoln is found in Dan W. Bannister, *Lincoln and the Illinois Supreme Court*, ed. Barbara Hughett (Springfield: Dan W. Bannister, 1994), 36, 49, 66, 114, 134, 158.

10. Samuel Willard (1821–1913) and his father, Julius A. Willard (1793–1884), were both abolitionists. They were indicted in February 1843 for aiding a fugitive slave. Willard relates his experiences with assisting fugitive slaves in Illinois in two narratives: "My First Adventure with a Fugitive Slave" and "My Second Adventure with a Fugitive Slave." Both accounts are in the Samuel Willard Family Papers, ALPL.

11. Willard, "Personal Reminiscences," 86–87. The quote attributed to John Todd Stuart is from *History of Sangamo County, Illinois* (Chicago: Interstate Publishing Co., 1881), 92–93.

12. See Daniel Walker Howe, "The Whigs and Their Age," in *What Hath God Wrought: The Transformation of America, 1815–1848* (New York: Oxford University Press, 2007), 570–612; Daniel Walker Howe, *The Political Culture of the American Whigs* (Chicago: University of Chicago Press, 1979); Michael F. Holt, *The Rise and Fall of the American Whig Party: Jacksonian Politics and the Onset of the Civil War* (New York: Oxford University Press, 1999); Michael F. Holt, *Political Parties and American Political Development: From the Age of Jackson to the Age of Lincoln* (Baton Rouge: Louisiana State University Press, 1992); Lawrence Frederick Kohl, *The Politics of Individualism: Parties and the American Character in the Jacksonian Era* (New York: Oxford University Press, 1989); and Thomas Brown, *Politics and Statesmanship: Essays on the American Whig Party* (New York: Columbia University, 1985). For Illinois Whigs, see Kirk R. Salmela, "Illinois Whiggery, Politics, and Statesmanship: A Study of Destiny, Dissent, and Bitterness in the Era of Southwestern Expansion, 1844–1848" (Ph.D. diss., Illinois State University, 1989), and James Carroll Ferguson, "The Whig Party in Illinois and Indiana, 1844–1854" (M.A. thesis, Illinois State University, 1963).

13. Isabel Jamison, "The Young Men's Convention and Old Soldiers' Meeting at Springfield, June 3–4, 1840," *Transactions of the Illinois State Historical Society* (1914): 162 and 166–170. Jamison's account is based on the report of the Whig Convention appearing in the *Sangamo Journal*, June 5, 1840.

14. Albert Taylor Bledsoe, "Alexander Hamilton," *Southern Review* 6 (July 1869): 19.

15. "Proceedings in Reference to the Death of the President," *Sangamo Journal*, May 7, 1841; Albert T. Bledsoe, "Eulogy, on the Life and Character of William Henry Harrison," *Sangamo Journal*, May 14, 1841. All quotes appearing in the following account are from Bledsoe's "Eulogy" as printed in the *Sangamo Journal*.

16. "Whig Meeting in Springfield Precinct," *Sangamo Journal*, July 22, 1842; "Clay Club," *Sangamo Journal* (August 12, 1842); A. G. Henry, C. Birchall, J. M. Cabaniss, P. A. Saunders, J. N. Francis, A. T. Bledsoe, A. Lincoln, Robert Irwin, and J. M. Allen "To Henry Clay," Springfield, Illinois, August 29, 1842, "Correspondence," *Sangamo Journal*, September 23, 1842; "Resolutions at a Whig Meeting," March 1, 1843, in *Collected Works of Abraham Lincoln*, ed. Roy P. Basler, vol. 1 (New Brunswick, NJ: Rutgers University Press, 1953), 307–8, which is reprinted from the *Quincy Whig*, March 15, 1843. The invitation of the Springfield Clay Club to Henry Clay also appears in Basler, *Collected Works of Abraham Lincoln*, 1:297.

17. A. Lincoln, S. T. Logan, and A. T. Bledsoe, "Address to the People of Illinois," campaign circular, March 4, 1843, in Basler, *Collected Works of Abraham Lincoln*, 1:309–18. The "Address" originally appeared in Whig papers across the state. The original source of the document was probably the *Extra Journal*—a Whig campaign paper printed for the 1843 elections by Simeon Francis at the office of the *Sangamo Journal*. The address appeared in the first issue of the *Extra*. See Mark E. Neely Jr., *The Extra Journal: Rallying the Whigs of Illinois* ([Fort Wayne, IN]: Louis A. Warren Lincoln Library and Museum, 1982).

18. "Illinois: Mass Convention at Vandalia, July 17th, 1844," *Sangamo Journal*, August 8, 1844; "The Delegates from Sangamo County," *Sangamo Journal*, July 25, 1844.

19. Robert Todd Lincoln was born at the Globe Tavern on August 1, 1843. Harriet Bledsoe and her six-year-old daughter Sophia apparently helped care for both mother and child. We are told by Sophia, who vividly remembered those childhood days, that her mother did not care for Mrs. Lincoln's personality but was still very attentive to her at the time of Robert's birth. Herrick, "Coxe Family," 75; Herrick, "Personal Recollections of My Father and Mr. Lincoln and Mr. Davis," *Methodist Quarterly Review* 64 (October 1915): 667–68.

20. Lincoln's "Rebecca" letter is reproduced in Basler, *Collected Works of Abraham Lincoln*, 1:291–97. Todd and Jayne wrote a third caricature of Shields as a poem by "Cathleen."

21. E. H. Merryman, "Memorandum of Instructions to E. H. Merryman, Lincoln's Second, September 18, 1842," in *Complete Works of Abraham Lincoln*, ed. John G. Nicolay and John Hay, new and enlarged ed., vol. 1 (New York: Francis D. Tandy Co., 1905), 236–38.

22. E. H. Merryman, William Butler, and A. T. Bledsoe, Missouri, September 22, 1842, in William H. Herndon and Jesse W. Weik, *Herndon's Life of Lincoln: The History and Personal Recollections of Abraham Lincoln* (New York: Albert and Charles Boni, 1930), 202. Bledsoe's role in the Lincoln-Shields affair also receives notice in Albert J. Beveridge, *Abraham Lincoln, 1809–1858*, vol. 1 (Boston: Houghton Mifflin Co., 1928), 352, and Harry E. Pratt, *Lincoln: 1840–1846: Being the Day-by-Day Activities of Abraham Lincoln from January 1, 1840 to December 31, 1846* (Springfield, IL: Abraham Lincoln Association, 1939), 143.

23. Herrick, "Coxe Family," 76; Sophia Bledsoe Herrick, "Bledsoe Family History," typescript, microfilm 517, 3311, SCLUV; Herrick, "Personal Recollections of My Father," 669–70, 679n; A. T. Bledsoe, "Mr. Martin's Examination of Prof. Tappan's Review of Edwards on the Will, Reviewed," *Biblical Repository and Classical Review* 2 (January 1846): 138, which identifies Bledsoe as a resident of Philadelphia. The three cases in which Bledsoe and Coxe represented plaintiffs together before the U.S. Supreme Court between January 1845 and the winter of 1845–46 were *Stockton v. Bishop*, 4 Howard, 155; *Crookendarfer v. Preston*, 4 Howard, 317; and *Alexander Canal Company v. Swann*, 5 Howard, 83.

24. S. Francis and Co., "Prospectus of the Illinois Journal," *Illinois Journal*, September 2, 1847. Bledsoe took his place in the editor's chair on September 9, 1847. S. Francis and A. T. Bledsoe, eds., untitled editorial statement, ibid., September 9, 1847.

25. "The State Register," *Illinois Journal*, September 16, 1847.

26. Anson G. Henry to Lincoln, Pekin, Illinois, December 29, 1847, Abraham Lincoln Papers, MDLC (cited hereafter as the Lincoln Papers).

27. "The Locofoco Press," *Illinois Journal*, November 18, 1847; "He Said, 'If He Were a Mexican,'" ibid., November 18, 1847. Corwin wrote the letter to Bledsoe from Lebanon, Ohio, on October 26, 1847.

28. "Mr. Secretary Buchanan and the Wilmot Proviso," *Illinois Journal*, October 7, 1847.

29. Albert Taylor Bledsoe, "Republicanism," *Illinois Journal*, October 28, 1847.

30. "John C. Calhoun," *Illinois Journal*, November 4, 1847. Bledsoe's authorship of the unsigned editorial on Calhoun is established by an autobiographical aside. The author mentions that he once found a book on mathematics at the library at West Point that discussed "the properties of a curve described by the tail of a dog following his master." Bledsoe thought it a fitting metaphor for the way in which the people of South Carolina had obediently followed Calhoun through the twists and turns of his long and distinguished political career, first as a nationalist and later as an originator of states' rights doctrine.

31. Willard Murrell Hays, "Polemics and Philosophy: A Biography of Albert Taylor Bledsoe" (Ph.D. diss., University of Tennessee, 1971), 536.

32. "Mr. Clay and His Opponents," *Illinois Journal*, December 9, 1847; "Henry Clay," ibid., December 16, 1847.

33. Albert Taylor Bledsoe, "Liberty," *Illinois Journal*, September 9, 1847.

34. Albert Taylor Bledsoe, "The Spirit of Liberty," *Illinois Journal*, March 30, 1848.

35. Albert Taylor Bledsoe, "The Nature of Civil Liberty, No. I," *Illinois Journal*, April 6, 1848; "The Nature of Civil Liberty, No. II," ibid., April 13, 1848; and "The Nature of Civil Liberty, No. III," ibid., April 20, 1848.

36. Bledsoe, "Nature of Civil Liberty, No. II."

37. Bledsoe, "Nature of Civil Liberty, No. II" and "Nature of Civil Liberty, No. III."

38. Bledsoe, "Republicanism." He restated the axiom regarding public order and private liberty in "The Nature of Civil Liberty, No. III" and reaffirmed it in *An Essay on Liberty and Slavery* (Philadelphia: J. B. Lippincott and Co., 1856), 40–41.

CHAPTER THREE

1. Bledsoe, Memorandum Book, entry 7; John N. Waddel, *Memorials of Academic Life: Being an Historical Sketch of the Waddel Family* (Richmond, VA: Presbyterian Committee of Publication, 1891), 249–50, 252, 254.

2. Albert Taylor Bledsoe, *Three Lectures on Rational Mechanics; Or, The Theory of Motion* (Philadelphia: T. K. and P. G. Collins, Printers, 1854) and *A Brief Sketch of the Rise and Progress of Astronomy, in Three Lectures* (Philadelphia: King and Baird, Printers, 1854). Bledsoe's contributions to the teaching and theory of mathematics and his related interest in astronomy are recognized in Florian Cajori, *The Teaching and History of Mathematics in the United States, Bureau of Education Circular of Information No. 3* (Washington, DC: Government Printing Office, 1890), 198, 229, and Samuel Marx Barton, "The South's Contribution to Mathematics and Astronomy," in *The South in the Building of the Nation*, vol. 7, ed. John Bell Henneman (Richmond, VA: Southern Historical Publication Society, 1909), 205.

3. Michael O'Brien discusses the experience of southerners who went North for their education in the first chapter of his *Conjectures of Order: Intellectual Life and the American South, 1810–1860*, vol. 1 (Chapel Hill: University of North Carolina Press, 2004).

4. Neal C. Gillespie, *The Collapse of Orthodoxy: The Intellectual Ordeal of George Frederick Holmes* (Charlottesville: University of Virginia Press, 1972), 31.

5. Jacob Thompson, *Address, Delivered on Occasion of the Opening of the University of the State of Mississippi, in Behalf of the Board of Trustees, November 6, 1848* (Memphis, TN: Franklin Book and

Job Office, 1849), 5–6; George Frederick Holmes, *Inaugural Address, Delivered on Occasion of the Opening of the University of the State of Mississippi, November 6, 1848* (Memphis, TN: Franklin Book and Job Office, 1849), 12.

6. Alexander M. Clayton, *Address Delivered at the First Annual Commencement of the University of Mississippi, July 12, 1849* (Oxford: Printed at the "Organizer" Office, 1849), 16.

7. Holmes, *Inaugural Address,* 12; George Frederick Holmes, "Professor John Millington, M.D.," *William and Mary Quarterly* 3, 2nd ser. (January 1923): 32; Waddel, *Memorials of Academic Life,* 252. Frederick Augustus Porter Barnard, who succeeded Bledsoe as professor of mathematics at the University of Mississippi, surmised that Millington received his faculty appointment because he offered the use of his scientific apparatus to the university. Sanford Charles Gladden, "A History of the Department of Physics and Astronomy at the University of Mississippi, 1848–1932," typescript, University of Mississippi, 4.

8. Florence E. Campbell, "Journal of the Minutes of the Board of Trustees of the University of Mississippi, 1845–1860" (M.A. thesis, University of Mississippi, 1939), 109; Albert Taylor Bledsoe, *Address Delivered at the First Annual Commencement of the University of Mississippi* (Oxford, MS: Printed at the "Organizer" Office, 1849), 26 (cited hereafter as Bledsoe, *Address at the University of Mississippi*); Waddel, *Memorials of Academic Life,* 267.

9. Waddel, *Memorials of Academic Life,* 270–71; Gillespie, *Collapse of Orthodoxy,* 34–36; Bledsoe, *Address at the University of Mississippi,* 27.

10. Bledsoe, *Address at the University of Mississippi,* 28.

11. Holmes, *Inaugural Address,* 18.

12. This quote and the following ones are from Bledsoe, *Address at the University of Mississippi,* 36–37, 39–41.

13. Reuben Davis, *Recollections of Mississippi and Mississippians* (Boston: Houghton Mifflin and Co., 1889), 317.

14. Wirt Armistead Cate, *Lucius Q. C. Lamar: Secession and Reunion* (Chapel Hill: University of North Carolina Press, 1935), 37–40; Edward C. Mayes, *Lucius Q. C. Lamar: His Life, Times, and Speeches, 1825–1893* (Nashville, TN: Publishing House of the Methodists Episcopal Church, South, 1896), 57.

15. Mayes, *Lucius Q. C. Lamar,* 51–54. See also the *Democratic Flag,* May 5, 1852, which contains a letter from Lamar declaring his continued devotion to states' rights and the right of secession, and James B. Murphy, *L. Q. C. Lamar: Pragmatic Patriot* (Baton Rouge: Louisiana State University Press, 1973), 16–18.

16. The following quotes are from Davis's address to the Phi Sigma and Hermean societies: Jefferson Davis, "Speech at Oxford" [July 15, 1852], in *The Papers of Jefferson Davis,* ed. Lynda Lasswell Crist et al., vol. 4, *1849–1852* (Baton Rouge: Louisiana State University Press, 1983), 275–80, 282.

17. *Democratic Flag,* July 21, 1852, press clipping, David Rankin Barbee Microfilm Collection of Albert Taylor Bledsoe Materials, microfilm 517, 3311, SCLV.

18. Sophia Bledsoe Herrick, "Personal Recollections of My Father and Mr. Lincoln and Mr. Davis," *Methodist Quarterly Review* 64 (October 1915): 671, and "Explanatory Preface," in Albert Taylor Bledsoe, *The War between the States, or Was Secession a Constitutional Right Previous to the War of 1861–1865* (Lynchburg, VA: J. P. Bell Co., 1915), 8; Davis to Joseph Henry, undated [1849–52], in Crist et al., *Papers of Jefferson Davis,* 4:401.

19. Campbell, "Minutes of the Board of Trustees," 204.

20. Bledsoe to the Board of Trustees of the University of Mississippi, July 12, 1854, "Minutes of

the Board of Trustees of the University of Mississippi," vol. 1, Wednesday, July 12, 1854, 219, and Friday, July 14, 1854, 226; Campbell, "Minutes of the Board of Trustees," 210, 212, 214; Albert Taylor Bledsoe, "How and Why I Became a Methodist," *Southern Review* 14 (January 1874): 108; *Catalogue of Kenyon College, and of the Theological Seminary of the Diocese of Ohio, 1825–1872* (Gambier, OH: Edmunds and Hunt, 1873), 59.

21. Bledsoe to William Holmes McGuffey, Washington, June 24, 1854, McGuffey Papers; Susan Pendleton Lee, *Memoirs of William Nelson Pendleton, D.D.* (Philadelphia: J. B. Lippincott and Co., 1893), 105, "communicated to the author by Harriet Bledsoe."

22. Robert E. Lee to the Board of Visitors of the University of Virginia, U.S. Military Academy, West Point, New York, June 23, 1854, Robert Edward Lee Letter Book, 1842–60, 320, Lee Family Papers, VHS; R. E. Lee to the Board of Visitors of the University of Virginia, U.S. Military Academy, West Point, January 26, 1854, in Lenoir Chambers, *Stonewall Jackson*, vol. 1 (New York: William Marrow and Co., 1959), 255; Bledsoe to William Holmes McGuffey, Washington, [Mississippi?], June 24, 1854, McGuffey Papers; Bledsoe, Memorandum Book, entries 2, 7.

23. "University of Virginia R & V Minutes," 3:634–35, 650; J. A. Harrison, "The Pavilions and Their Early Occupants," *Alumni Bulletin of the University of Virginia* 3 (May 1896): 1; T. Vernon Rankin to Harry E. Pratt, University of Virginia, March 1, 1934, Pratt Papers, box 1, folder 3, ALPL; Bledsoe to George Frederick Holmes, University of Virginia, May 13, 1856, Holmes Papers, SCLDU (cited hereafter as Holmes Papers).

24. George Frederick Holmes, "Diary, Agricultural and War, 1856 to 1864," entry for January 27, [1857], Holmes Papers. The Bledsoe letter referred to by Holmes no longer appears to be extant, but Holmes acknowledges receipt of the letter and describes its contents in the January 27 entry in his diary.

25. Bledsoe to George Frederick Holmes, University of Virginia, February 14, 1857, Holmes Papers.

26. Bledsoe to George Frederick Holmes, University of Virginia, February 14, 1857, Holmes Papers; Philip Alexander Bruce, *History of the University of Virginia, 1819–1919*, vol. 3 (New York: Macmillan Co.), 1921), 141–42.

27. James Lawrence Cabell, *The Testimony of Modern Science to the Unity of Mankind; Being a Summary of the Conclusions Announced by the Highest Authorities in the Several Departments of Physiology, Zoology, and Comparative Philology in Favor of the Specific Unity and Common Origin of All the Varieties of Man. With an Introductory Notice by James W. Alexander, D.D.* (New York: Robert Carter and Brothers, 1859).

28. William Pleasant Thurman, "Notebook, 1857–1858," MS 3932, SCLDU; Lancelot Minor Blackford, "Intermediate and Senior Mathematics Exercises, 1855–1856," MS 12013, SCLUV; Cajori, *Teaching and History of Mathematics*, 121, 198.

29. William Dinwiddie to Louise [Herrick Wall], January 31, 1934, Dinwiddie Family Papers, 1846–1937, MS 2808, SCLUV.

30. Cajori, *Teaching and History of Mathematics*, 197; Bledsoe to Polk, University of Virginia, October 8, 1860, Polk Collection. The extract from Smith's letter to Cajori regarding Bledsoe is undated, but it was probably written in the late 1880s just before the publication of Cajori's work in 1890.

31. John McCardell, *The Idea of a Southern Nation: Southern Nationalists and Southern Nationalism, 1830–1860* (New York: W. W. Norton and Co., 1979), chap. 5, "Northern Domination in Our

Schools and Pulpits," especially pp. 203–26. See also John S. Ezell, "A Southern Education for Southrons," *Journal of Southern History* 17 (August 1951): 303–27.

32. Delegates to the southern commercial conventions in both the antebellum and postwar South addressed themselves to a wide range of economic, political, social, and cultural concerns. See Vicki Vaughn Johnson, *The Men and the Vision of the Southern Commercial Conventions, 1845–1871* (Columbia: University of Missouri Press, 1992).

33. "Southern Convention at Savannah," *De Bow's Review* 22 (January 1857): 100.

34. Charles Henry Ambler, *Sectionalism in Virginia from 1776 to 1861* (Chicago: University of Chicago Press, 1910), 279–81.

35. Leonidas Polk, *A Letter to the Right Reverend Bishops of Tennessee, Georgia, Alabama, Arkansas, Texas, Mississippi, Florida, South Carolina and North Carolina from the Bishop of Louisiana* (New Orleans: B. M. Norman, 1856); Leonidas Polk to Stephen Elliot, New Orleans, July 23, 1856, and Polk to Elliot, New Orleans, August 20, 1856, Polk Collection; Polk, *Address of the Commissioners for Raising the Endowment of the University of the South* (New Orleans: B. M. Norman, 1859).

36. Richard H. Wilmer, *In Memoriam. A Sermon in Commemoration of the Life and Labors of the Rt. Rev. Stephen Elliot, D.D. (Late Bishop of Georgia)*, Delivered in Christ Church, Savannah, Ga., on Sunday, January 27, 1867 (Mobile: Farrow and Dennett, 1867), 13–14; Glenn Robins, *The Bishop of the Old South: The Ministry and Civil War Legacy of Leonidas Polk* (Macon, GA: Mercer University Press, 2006), 218; McCardell, *Idea of a Southern Nation*, 166, 176.

37. Bledsoe to Polk, Richmond, September 11, 1860, and Cabell to Polk, University of Virginia, April 18, 1860, Polk Collection; Joseph H. Parks, *General Leonidas Polk, C.S.A.: The Fighting Bishop* (Baton Rouge: Louisiana State University Press, 1962), 148. Similarities in the replies of Cabell and Bledsoe suggest that they consulted with each other at some point before submitting their respective recommendations to Polk. Parks, *General Leonidas Polk*, 147.

38. Bledsoe to Polk, University of Virginia, October 8, 1860, Polk Collection; Robins, *Bishop of the Old South*, 137. Bledsoe later published the manuscript on the philosophy of calculus as *The Philosophy of Mathematics, with Special Reference to the Elements of Geometry and the Infinitesimal Method* (Philadelphia: J. B. Lippincott and Co., 1868). He variously referred to the manuscript on moral philosophy as "The Spiritual System of the Universe" and the "Moral Cosmos, or Unity, Order, Harmony, and Beauty of the Universe," which he conceived as a sequel to *A Theodicy*. He never completed the work as planned, but his daughter Sophia posthumously published portions of it in four parts in the *Southern Review*. See Albert Taylor Bledsoe, "The Christian Cosmos; or, System of the Spiritual Universe," *Southern Review* 23 (January 1878): 103–44; 23 (April 1878): 253–312; 24 (July 1878): 5–48; 24 (October 1878): 253–91.

39. Jonas Viles, *The University of Missouri: A Centennial History* (Columbia: University of Missouri, 1939), 89–90.

CHAPTER FOUR

1. See Albert Taylor Bledsoe, "Arminian Inconsistencies and Errors," *Southern Review* 22 (October 1877): 464–94.

2. Elizabeth Fox-Genovese and Eugene D. Genovese, *The Mind of the Master Class: History and Faith in the Southern Slaveholders' Worldview* (Cambridge: Cambridge University Press, 2005), 537.

The authors' description of Bledsoe as "an unchurched theologian" is made in reference to his views on the compatibility of religion and science (595).

3. Thomas A. Langford, *Practical Divinity: Theology in the Wesleyan Tradition*, vol. 1 (Nashville, TN: Abingdon Press, 1998), 90–91, 113, 183, 227, 251.

4. Albert Taylor Bledsoe, "Capital Punishment," *Methodist Quarterly Review* 6 (July 1846): 462–75; "Bacon's Philosophy," *Methodist Quarterly Review* 7 (January 1847): 22–52; "The Divine Government," *Quarterly Review of the Methodist Episcopal Church, South* 1 (April 1852): 280–301; and "M'Cosh on the Divine Government," *Methodist Quarterly Review* 4 (July 1852): 458–75.

5. John N. Waddel, *Memoirs of Academic Life: Being an Historical Sketch of the Waddel Family* (Richmond, VA: Presbyterian Committee of Publication, 1891), 280; Sophia Bledsoe Herrick, "Albert Taylor Bledsoe," *Alumni Bulletin of the University of Virginia* 6 (May 1899): 3; H. C. [Harriet Coxe] to Albert Taylor Bledsoe, Bristol College, February 25, [1836], Bledsoe-Herrick Family Papers, SLHU.

6. Albert Taylor Bledsoe, "The Late William Sparrow, D.D.," *Southern Review* 20 (July 1876): 26–28.

7. E. Brooks Holifield, *Theology in America: Christian Thought from the Age of the Puritans to the Civil War* (New Haven: Yale University Press, 2003), 174; Bruce Kuklick, *A History of Philosophy in America, 1720–2000* (Oxford: Clarendon Press, 2001), 62; Mark A. Noll, *America's God: From Jonathan Edwards to Abraham Lincoln* (Oxford: Oxford University Press, 2005), 234–36, 248–49; Theodore Dwight Bozeman, *Protestants in an Age of Science: The Baconian Ideal and Antebellum American Religious Thought* (Chapel Hill: University of North Carolina Press, 1977), 144–59.

8. See Bledsoe, "Bacon's Philosophy," 22–52. Twenty-eight years later Bledsoe reprinted the article in the *Southern Review*. See Albert Taylor Bledsoe, "Bacon's Philosophy," *Southern Review* 18 (October 1875): 301–36.

9. Albert Taylor Bledsoe, *An Examination of President Edwards' Inquiry into the Freedom of the Will* (Philadelphia: H. Hooker, 1845), 35. Edward's stature as a theologian earned him the presidency of the College of New Jersey (later Princeton University) in 1757. Thereafter he was often referred to as President Edwards.

10. Kuklick, *History of Philosophy in America*, 73.

11. The teaching of moral philosophy, which occupied a conspicuous place in the collegiate curriculum in the early and mid-nineteenth century, is examined in Donald H. Meyer, *The Instructed Conscience: The Shaping of the American National Ethic* (Philadelphia: University of Pennsylvania Press, 1972), and Wilson Smith, *Professors and Public Ethics: Studies of Northern Moral Philosophers before the Civil War* (Ithaca, NY: Published for the American Historical Association by Cornell University Press, 1956).

12. Bledsoe, *Examination of President Edwards' Inquiry*, 39–40.

13. Bledsoe, *Examination of President Edwards' Inquiry*, 233.

14. "An Examination by Albert T. Bledsoe," *Methodist Quarterly Review* 5 (October 1845): 640; "Examination of Edwards on the Will," *Methodist Quarterly Review* 6 (October 1846): 598, 600; Albert Taylor Bledsoe, "Examination of Edwards on the Will," *Southern Review* 21 (April 1877): 432; Holifield, *Theology in America*, 265.

15. "Short Notices," *Princeton Review* 17 (October 1845): 636–39.

16. "Short Notices," 637–38.

17. "Short Notices," 638.

18. [Benjamin N. Martin], "Bledsoe's Examination of Edwards's Inquiry," *New Englander and Yale Review* 5 (July 1847): 337–47. Bledsoe identifies Martin as his anonymous reviewer in Albert Taylor Bledsoe, "Vindication of Our Philosophy," *Southern Review* 21 (January 1877): 136.

19. Rev. Benjamin N. Martin, "Examination of Professor Tappan's Review of Edwards on the Will," *American Biblical Repository*, 2nd ser., 9 (January 1843): 33–59; A. T. Bledsoe, "Mr. Martin's Examination of Prof. Tappan's Review of Edwards on the Will, Reviewed," *Biblical Repository and Classical Review* 2 (January 1846): 138–60. Bledsoe reprinted his critique of Martin's review thirty years later as "Martin versus Tappan," *Southern Review* 20 (July 1876): 43–63.

20. Bledsoe, "Vindication of Our Philosophy," 136.

21. [Martin], "Bledsoe's Examination of Edwards's Inquiry," 337–38, 342, 344, 346–47.

22. Bledsoe, "Late William Sparrow," 27–28; Bledsoe, "Vindication of Our Philosophy," 150.

23. Bledsoe, "Late William Sparrow," 28. Bledsoe first stated the premise that "a necessitated virtue, or holiness, is a contradiction in terms" and that a rational God could not work a contraction in Albert Taylor Bledsoe, "The Divine Government," *Quarterly Review of the Methodist Episcopal Church, South* 1 (April 1852): 293, 298.

24. Elizabeth Flower and Murray G. Murphey, *A History of Philosophy in America*, vol. 2 (New York: G. P. Putnam's Sons, 1977), 536.

25. Albert Taylor Bledsoe, *A Theodicy; Or, Vindication of the Divine Glory, As Manifested in the Constitution and Government of the Moral World* (New York: Carlton and Phillips, 1853), 132–34.

26. An account of Caleb Sprague Henry's contributions to American philosophy is Ronald Vale Wells, *Three Christian Transcendentalists: James Marsh, Caleb Sprague Henry, Frederic Henry Hedge* (New York: Columbia University Press, 1943).

27. Victor Cousin, *Elements of Psychology, including a Critical Examination of Locke's Essay on the Human Understanding, by Victor Cousin . . . Translated from the French, with an Introduction, Notes, and Additions, by C. S. Henry* (Hartford, CT: Cook and Co., 1834). The quote regarding "positive cognition" is from Holifield, *Theology in America*, 438.

28. Albert Taylor Bledsoe, "A Distinction in Mental Science," *Southern Review* 20 (July 1876): 197–98, 209; Bledsoe, "Vindication of Our Philosophy," 145. See also Albert Taylor Bledsoe, "The Relation of the Will to the Feelings," *Southern Review* 17 (April 1875): 435–49. An early but still useful account of the influence of Cousin's eclecticism on American philosophy is Woodbridge Riley, *American Thought: From Puritanism to Pragmatism and Beyond* (New York: H. Holt and Co., 1915), 389–97.

29. Quotes in this paragraph and the next are from Bledsoe, *Theodicy*, 197–98. A similar statement appears in Bledsoe, "The Divine Government," *The Quarterly Review of the Methodist Episcopal Church, South* 1 (April 1852): 298. "A constrained virtue, a necessitated holiness, a caused good" is thus a contradiction. God was no more capable of creating such a negation of principles in the moral world than he could make "two and two equal five, or the properties of the circle the same as those a triangle" in the physical universe.

30. Noll, *America's God*, 293; Irving H. Bartlett, *The American Mind in the Mid-Nineteenth Century* (New York: Y. Crowell Co., 1967), 7; Donald Meyer, "The Dissolution of Calvinism," in *Paths of American Thought*, ed. Arthur M. Schlesinger Jr. and Morton White (Boston: Houghton Mifflin Co., 1963), 71–85. See also H. Shelton Smith, *Changing Conceptions of Original Sin: American Theology since 1750* (New York: Charles Scribner's Sons, 1955).

31. "A Theodicy," *Quarterly Review of the Methodist Episcopal Church, South* 8 (April 1854): 265–97; 8 (July 1854): 427–49; 9 (January 1855): 98–111.

32. "Theodicy," *Quarterly Review of the Methodist Episcopal Church, South* 8 (April 1854): 280, on Bledsoe's blustering immodesty, and ibid. 9 (January 1855), 107, for the quote "Who will dare to say that it might not?"

33. "A Theodicy," *Methodist Quarterly Review* (January 1854): 132.

34. "Reviewer Reviewed," *Methodist Quarter Review* 9 (July 1855): 402.

35. E. Brooks Holifield, *The Gentleman Theologians: American Theology in Southern Culture, 1795–1860* (Durham, NC: Duke University Press, 1978), 201; Robert Eugene Chiles, *Theological Transition in American Methodism: 1790–1935* (New York: Abingdon Press, 1965), 52; John Boyce Bennett, "Albert Taylor Bledsoe: Social and Religious Controversialist of the Old South" (Ph.D. diss., Duke University, 1942), xii.

36. [Thomas E. Peck], "'A Theodicy; or, Vindication of the Divine Glory, As Manifested in the Constitution and Government of the Moral World,' by Albert Taylor Bledsoe," *Presbyterial Critic and Monthly Review* 1 (January 1855): 13–20. Thomas Ephraim Peck was one of the editors of the *Presbyterial Critic and Monthly Review.* Authorship of the anonymous review is attributed to Peck in Morton H. Smith, *Studies in Southern Presbyterian Theology* (Phillipsburg, NJ: Presbyterian and Reformed Publishing Co., 1987), 352.

37. Quotes in this paragraph and the next are from [Peck], "Theodicy," 13–15, 17–20.

38. [John Holmes Bocock], "Bledsoe's Theodicy," *Southern Presbyterian Review* 8 (April 1855): 516–45 and "Modern Theology—Taylor and Bledsoe," *Southern Presbyterian Review* 9 (April 1856): 492–512.

39. [Bocock], "Bledsoe's Theodicy," 517, 531.

40. [Bocock], "Modern Theology—Taylor and Bledsoe," 492–512.

41. On New School Presbyterianism and Taylor, see George M. Marsden, *The Evangelical Mind and the New School Presbyterian Experience: A Case Study in Thought and Theology in Nineteenth-Century America* (New Haven: Yale University Press, 1970), and Sidney E. Mead, *Nathaniel William Taylor, 1786–1858: A Connecticut Liberal* (Chicago: University of Chicago Press, 1942).

42. Bledsoe, Memorandum Book, entry 7; William Henry Harrison to Bledsoe, Wigwam, Virginia, September 25, 1854, accession #6440, SCLUV.

43. Herrick, "Albert Taylor Bledsoe," *Alumni Bulletin of the University of Virginia,* 5; Wilbur F. Tillett, "Albert Taylor Bledsoe," *Quarterly Review of the Methodist Episcopal Church, South,* n.s., 14 (July 1893): 230. Bledsoe in one place says *A Theodicy* appeared in eleven editions and in another some fifteen or sixteen. Bledsoe, Memorandum Book, entry 4, where he says "eleven editions," and Bledsoe, "Late William Sparrow," 29, where he says "some fifteen or sixteen editions." Assuming that Bledsoe's accounting is correct, one can extrapolate from those different numbers that *A Theodicy* had appeared in eleven editions when Bledsoe wrote his memoranda around 1868 and fifteen or sixteen when he wrote his account of Sparrow in July 1876. *A Theodicy* also received the flattering attention of the Oxford theologian and philosopher Henry Longueville Mansel (1820–71). Mansel was professor of moral and metaphysical philosophy at Magdalen College before being elected professor and fellow at St. John's College in 1864. It was a consequence of Mansel's high opinion of *A Theodicy* that Saunders, Otley, and Company published an English edition of the work in London in 1864 at the behest and recommendation of Mansel. Bledsoe, Memorandum Book, entry 2.

44. "Editorial Reviews," *Methodist Review* 9 (September 1893): 829; Samuel Augustus Steel, "Albert Taylor Bledsoe: Sometime Editor of this Review," *Methodist Quarterly Review* 64 (April 1915): 211, 222; Samuel Augustus Steel, *Eminent Men I Met along the Sunny Road* (Nashville, TN: Cokesbury Press, 1925), 30; Rev. J. M. Hawley, "An Intellectual Giant," *Christian Advocate* 76 (May 7, 1915): 9.

CHAPTER FIVE

1. Albert Taylor Bledsoe, "Capital Punishment," *Methodist Quarterly Review* 6 (July 1846): 462–75; reprinted in the *Southern Review* 20 (October 1876): 395–411. The article on capital punishment in the *Methodist Quarterly Review* was the basis of a shorter editorial on the same subject in the *Illinois Journal*, where Bledsoe again referred to the social contract theory as "a splendid fiction." See Albert Taylor Bledsoe, "Capital Punishment," *Illinois Journal*, March 9, 1848, no pagination.

2. Herbert W. Schneider, *A History of American Philosophy* (New York: Columbia University Press, 1946), 217.

3. Albert Taylor Bledsoe, *An Essay on Liberty and Slavery* (Philadelphia: J. B. Lippincott and Co., 1856), 5–6, 47, 269. Bledsoe indicted Theodore Parker as the worst type of political preacher. Just as cobblers should stick to their lasts, he affirmed, all such preachers as Parker should stick to their pulpits and leave the cause of abolitionism to others (262–63n).

4. Elizabeth Fox-Genovese and Eugene D. Genovese, *The Mind of the Master Class: History and Faith in the Southern Slaveholders' Worldview* (Cambridge: Cambridge University Press, 2005), 492.

5. Bledsoe, *Liberty and Slavery*, 6.

6. Bledsoe, *Liberty and Slavery*, 8.

7. Bledsoe, *Liberty and Slavery*, 10, 12. Bledsoe's depiction of abolitionists as lawless despots was an important theme in the justification of southern slavery. Fellow Virginian George Fitzhugh, for example, made the same characterization. See Robert J. Loewenberg, *Freedom's Despots: The Critique of Abolition* (Durham, NC: Carolina Academic Press, 1986).

8. Bledsoe, *Liberty and Slavery*, 18, 21, 22, 27, 35, 39, 41–42.

9. Francis Wayland, *Elements of Moral Science* (Boston: Gould, Kendall and London, 1835), 221; Joseph L. Blau, ed., *Elements of Moral Science*, by Francis Wayland (Cambridge: Harvard University Press, Belknap Press, 1963), xiv. A discussion of Wayland's moderate antislavery views is Deborah Bingham Van Broekhoven, "Suffering with Slaveholders: The Limits of Frances Wayland's Antislavery Witness," in *Religion and the Antebellum Debate over Slavery*, ed. John R. McKivigan and Mitchell Snay (Athens: University of Georgia Press, 1998), 196–220.

10. Richard Fuller and Francis Wayland, *Domestic Slavery Considered as a Scriptural Institution: In a Correspondence between the Rev. Richard Fuller of Beaufort, S. C, and the Rev. Francis Wayland, of Providence, R.I. Revised and Corrected by the Authors* (New York: Lewis Colby; Boston: Gould, Kendall, and Lincoln, 1845), 50, 89, 92, 113, 119, 120; Bledsoe, *Liberty and Slavery*, 63–80, for his criticisms of Wayland; J. H. Cuthbert, *Life of Richard Fuller* (New York: Sheldon and Co., 1879), 105, 157; Thomas Armitage, *A History of the Baptists*, vol. 2 (New York: Bryan, Taylor and Co., 1890), 760.

11. "Masters, give unto servants that which is just and equal; knowing that ye also have a Master in heaven" (Colossians 4:1). A similar injunction appears in Ephesians. "And, ye masters, do the same things unto them [your servants], forbearing threatening: knowing that your Master also is in heaven; neither is there respect of persons with him" (Ephesians 6:9). See William T. Hamilton, *The Duties of Masters and Slaves Respectively: Or, Domestic Servitude as Sanctioned by the Bible: A Discourse Delivered in the Government-Street Church, Mobile, Alabama* (Mobile: F. A. Brooks, 1845); James Henley Thornwell, *The Rights and Duties of Masters. A Sermon Preached at the Dedication of a Church, Erected in Charleston, S. C., for the Benefit and Instruction of the Coloured Population* (Charleston: Steam Power Press of Walker and James, 1850); and William A. Smith, *Lectures on the Philosophy and Practice of Slavery, As Exhibited in the Institution of Domestic Slavery in the United States: With Duties of Masters to Slaves*, ed. Thomas O. Summers (Nashville: TN: Stevenson and

Evans, 1856). The duties of masters to slaves as a defense of slavery is examined in Mitchell Snay, *Gospel of Disunion: Religion and Separatism in the Antebellum South* (New York: Cambridge University Press, 1993), chap. 3, "Slavery Sanctified: The Slaveholding Ethic and the Religious Mission to the Slaves," 78–112.

12. See Clifford Stephen Griffin, *Their Brothers' Keepers: Moral Stewardship in the United States, 1800–1865* (New Brunswick, N J: Rutgers University Press, 1960), especially 152–76 and 177–97.

13. Bledsoe, *Liberty and Slavery*, 54–55.

14. Bledsoe, *Liberty and Slavery*, 56.

15. Bledsoe, *Liberty and Slavery*, 59–61.

16. Bledsoe, *Liberty and Slavery*, 61–62. Bledsoe first made the Apollo Belvidere analogy in "Republicanism," *Illinois Journal*, October 28, 1847, no pagination. He did so as a criticism of President Polk's determination to extend the blessings of free institutions to Mexico by the sword and for having the impudence to assure the Mexicans that the mission of the U.S. Army in their country was to liberate them from tyranny. According to Bledsoe, Polk had shown himself to be "disgracefully ignorant of the very first elements of political philosophy," for he had not considered whether Mexican society was suited to a republican form of government. Bledsoe maintained that it was not.

17. Bledsoe, *Liberty and Slavery*, 49, 127–29. Eugene D. Genovese has noted that Bledsoe's antiegalitarian assumptions are essentially the same as those expressed by the Virginia jurist and legal scholar Henry St. George Tucker, the son of St. George Tucker, in his *Lectures on Government* (1844). Eugene D. Genovese, *The Southern Tradition: The Achievements and Limitations of an American Conservatism* (Cambridge: Harvard University Press, 1994), 50. See Henry St. George Tucker, *Lectures on Government* (Charlottesville, VA: James Alexander, 1844), 31, 34, 51–52.

18. Josiah Clark Nott, "Unity of the Human Race," *Southern Quarterly Review* 9 (1846): 1–56; *Two Lectures on the Connection between the Biblical and Physical History of Man* (New York: Bartlett and Welford, 1849); and "Ancient and Scripture Chronology," *Southern Quarterly Review*, n.s., 2 (November 1850): 385–426. See also Samuel A. Cartwright, "Slavery in the Light of Ethnology," in E. N. Elliott, ed., *Cotton Is King, and Pro-Slavery Arguments: Comprising the Writings of Hammond, Harper, Christy, Stringfellow, Hodge, Bledsoe, and Cartwright on this Important Subject* (Augusta, GA: Pritchard, Abbott, and Loomis, 1860), 691–728.

19. Josiah Clark Nott and George Robins Gliddon, *Types of Mankind* (Philadelphia: Lippincott, Grambo, and Co., 1854).

20. Albert Taylor Bledsoe, "Philosophy versus Darwinism," *Southern Review* 13 (October 1873): 254. It was that same threat to scriptural authority and the assumptions of Bledsoe's moral philosophy that later prompted him to attack Darwinism.

21. See James Lawrence Cabell, *The Testimony of Modern Science to the Unity of Mankind; Being a Summary of the Conclusions Announced by the Highest Authorities in the Several Departments of Physiology, Zoology, and Comparative Philology in Favor of the Specific Unity and Common Origin of All the Varieties of Man. With an Introductory Notice by James W. Alexander, D.D.* (New York: Robert Carter and Brothers, 1859).

22. Concerning the nineteenth-century debate about human origins and racial distinctiveness, see William R. Stanton, *The Leopard's Spots: Scientific Attitudes toward Race in America, 1815–1859* (Chicago: University of Chicago Press, 1960), and Reginald Horsman, *Josiah Nott of Mobile: Southerner, Physician, and Racial Theorist* (Baton Rouge: Louisiana State University Press, 1987). An account of Nott's intellectual relationship with fellow ethnologist Ephraim George Squier is Terry A.

Barnhart, *Ephraim George Squier and the Development of American Anthropology* (Lincoln: University of Nebraska Press, 2005), especially chap. 11, "The Science of Men and Nations: Ephraim George Squier and the American School of Ethnology," 281–316. There are forty-two letters from Nott to Squier dating from 1848 to 1872 in the Ephraim George Squier Papers at the Library of Congress, Washington, D.C. See also Thomas E. Will, "The American School of Ethnology: Science and Scripture in the Proslavery Argument," *Southern Historian* 19 (Annual 1998): 14–34.

23. See Larry E. Tise, *The American Counterrevolution: A Retreat from Liberty, 1783–1800* (Mechanicsburg, PA: Stackpile Books, 1998), and Joseph L. Blau, *Men and Movements in American Philosophy* (New York: Prentice Hall, 1952), 73, 76, 78.

24. See Andrew Burstein, "The Continuing Debate: Jefferson and Slavery," in *Jefferson's Secrets: Death and Dying at Monticello* (New York: Basic Books, 2005), 113–50; Andrew Burstein, "Jefferson's Rationalizations," *William and Mary Quarterly*, 3rd ser., 57 (January 2000): 183–97; Paul Finkelman, *Slavery and the Founders: Race and Liberty in the Age of Jefferson*, 2nd ed. (Armonk, NY: M. E. Sharpe, 2001); and Robert McColley, *Slavery in Jeffersonian Virginia* (Urbana: University of Illinois Press, 1964).

25. Bledsoe, *Liberty and Slavery*, 81–82.

26. Thomas Jefferson, *Notes on the State of Virginia* (Boston: Wells and Lilly, 1829), 169–70; Thomas R. Dew, *Review of the Debate in the Virginia Legislature of 1831 and 1832* (Richmond, VA: T. W. White, 1832), 108–9.

27. Quotes in this paragraph and the next are from Bledsoe, *Liberty and Slavery*, 109–11.

28. Bledsoe, *Liberty and Slavery*, 122–23.

29. Bledsoe, *Liberty and Slavery*, 124.

30. Janet Duistman Cornelius, *"When I Can Read My Title Clear": Literacy, Slavery, and Religion in the Antebellum South* (Columbia: University of South Carolina Press, 1991), 35.

31. Bledsoe, *Liberty and Slavery*, 125–26.

32. See William A. Link, *Roots of Secession: Slavery and Politics in Antebellum Virginia* (Chapel Hill: University of North Carolina Press, 2003), chap. 7, "To Light the Torch of Servile Insurrection: The Secession Crisis," 213–44.

33. Albert Barnes, *An Inquiry into the Scriptural Views of Slavery* (Philadelphia: Perkins and Purves; Boston: B. Perkins and Co., 1846), 383. The controversy concerning slavery and the Bible has received a significant amount of attention. See Mark A. Noll, *God and Race in American Politics: A Short History* (Princeton, NJ: Princeton University Press, 2008), chap. 1, "The Bible, Slavery, and the 'Irrepressible Conflict,'" 13–46; *The Civil War as a Theological Crisis* (Chapel Hill: University of North Carolina Press, 2006), 31–50, 51–74; "The Bible and Slavery," in *America's God: From Jonathan Edwards to Abraham Lincoln* (Oxford: Oxford University Press, 2005), 386–401; and "The Bible and Slavery," in *Religion and the American Civil War*, ed. Randall N. Miller, Harry S. Stout, and Charles Reagan Wilson (New York: Oxford University Press, 1998), 43–73; and Snay, *Gospel of Disunion*, 53–77.

34. Petition of the Citizens of Albany, New York, *Journal of the Senate*, vol. 41, March 25, 1850, in the *Congressional Globe* (Washington, DC: Blair and Rives, 1850), 232; Bledsoe, *Liberty and Slavery*, 153. Deuteronomy 23:15–16 also formed the basis of an earlier petition from the citizens of Pennsylvania submitted to Senator James Buchanan in March 1844 and a later petition submitted to Representative Joshua Giddings of Ohio in April 1850. *Journal of the Senate*, vol. 35, March 8, 1844, in the *Congressional Globe* (Washington, DC: Blair and Rives, 1844), 155; *Journal of the House*, vol. 45, April 10, 1850, in the *Congressional Globe* (Washington, DC: Blair and Rives, 1850), 769.

35. On Moses Stuart, see Laura L. Mitchell, "'Matters of Justice between Man and Man': Northern Divines, the Bible, and the Fugitive Slave Act of 1850," in McKivigan and Snay, *Religion and the Antebellum Debate over Slavery*, 139–44, 148–49, 152, 164.

36. Moses Stuart, *Conscience and the Constitution: With Remarks on the Recent Speech of the Hon. Daniel Webster in the Senate of the United States on the Subject of Slavery* (Boston: Crocker and Brewster, 1850), 30–32; Bledsoe, *Liberty and Slavery*, 155–57.

37. Sarah Wentworth Apthorp Morton as quoted in Charles Sumner, "The Fugitive Slave Law—Mr. Sumner," August 26, 1852, *Congressional Globe*, Senate, 32nd Cong., 1st sess., appendix to the *Congressional Globe*, 1105. On Morton, see Kathryn Gin, "Three Anti-Slavery Women Writers," in *Early American Abolitionists: A Collection of Anti-Slavery Writings, 1760–1820*, James G. Basker, general ed., and Justine Ahlstrom et al., associate eds. (New York: Gilder Lehrman Institute of America History, 2005), 185–89. "The African Chief" originally appeared in the *Columbian Centinel* in 1792. Morton later reprinted the poem in *My Mind and Its Thoughts, in Sketches, Fragments, and Essays* (Boston: Wells and Lilly, 1823).

38. Bledsoe, *Liberty and Slavery*, 171.

39. Charles Sumner, *The Anti-Slavery Enterprise: Its Necessity, Practicability, and Dignity, with Glimpses of the Special Duties of the North. An Address before the People of New York, at the Metropolitan Theatre, May 9, 1855* (Boston: Ticknor and Fields, 1855), 12–13.

40. Sumner, *Anti-Slavery Enterprise*, 14; Bledsoe, *Liberty and Slavery*, 177–82.

41. Barnes, *Inquiry into the Scriptural Views of Slavery*, 340.

42. Albert Barnes, *Notes, Explanatory and Practical on the Epistles of Paul to the Thessalonians, to Timothy, to Titus, and to Philemon* (New York: Harper and Brothers, 1845), 344–46, 352–55. See also Barnes's discussion of the case of Onesimus in *An Inquiry into the Scriptural Views of Slavery*, 318–40. An opposing opinion in justification of slavery is Augustus Baldwin Longstreet, *Letters on the Epistle of Paul to Philemon, or the Connection of Apostolical Christianity with Slavery* (Charleston, SC: B. Jenkins, 1845).

43. Bledsoe, *Liberty and Slavery*, 183–96, 198–99; McKivigan and Snay, *Religion and the Antebellum Debate over Slavery*; McKivigan, *The War against Proslavery Religion: Abolitionism and the Northern Churches, 1830–1865* (Ithaca, NY: Cornell University Press, 1984), especially chap. 1, "No Christian Fellowship with Slaveholders," 18–35.

44. Fox-Genovese and Genovese, *Mind of the Master Class*, 526; Eric L. McKitrick, "The Defense of Slavery," in *Slavery Defended: The Views of the Old South*, ed. Eric L. McKitrick (Englewood Cliffs, NJ: Prentice Hall, 1963), 2.

45. "Uncle Tom's Cabin: Present State and Prospects of American Slavery," *Prospective Review* 8 (November 1852): 506.

46. Stephen R. Haynes, *Noah's Curse: The Biblical Justification of American Slavery* (Oxford: Oxford University Press, 2002), 11–14, 126.

47. [Charles Hodge], "West India Emancipation," *Princeton Review* 10 (October 1838): 603. The article is unsigned but was probably written by the editor Charles Hodge.

48. McKivigan, *War against Proslavery Religion*, 7, 15, 17.

49. Bledsoe, *Liberty and Slavery*, 227–28.

50. Bledsoe, *Liberty and Slavery*, 229.

51. See Seymour Drescher, *The Mighty Experiment: Free Labor versus Slavery in British Emancipation* (New York: Oxford University Press, 2002); Thomas C. Holt, *The Problem of Freedom: Race,*

Labor, and Politics in Jamaica and Britain, 1832–1938 (Baltimore: Johns Hopkins University Press, 1992); and Thomas C. Holt, "An Empire over the Mind: Emancipation, Race, and Ideology in the British West Indies and the American South," in *Region, Race, and Reconstruction: Essays in Honor of C. Vann Woodward*, ed. J. Morgan Kousser and James M. McPherson (New York: Oxford University Press, 1982), 283–313.

52. Gurney earlier stated his antislavery views in Joseph John Gurney, *Speech on the Abolition of Negro Slavery, Delivered at a Public Meeting Held in the Guild-Hall, in the City of Norwich on Wednesday, 28th January, 1824* (Liverpool: Ruston and Melling, 1824).

53. Bledsoe, *Liberty and Slavery,* 237. Bledsoe is rebutting the encouraging prospects that reportedly existed in the West Indies based on Gurney's firsthand observations. See Joseph Bevan Braithwaite, ed., *Memoirs of Joseph John Gurney, with Selections from His Journal and Correspondence,* vol. 2 (Philadelphia: Lippincott, Grambo, 1854), 213–14.

54. Bledsoe, *Liberty and Slavery,* 290–91; George M. Fredrickson, *The Black Image in the White Mind: The Debate on Afro-American Character and Destiny, 1817–1914* (New York: Harper and Row, 1971), 61–64; Paul Goodman, *Of One Blood: Abolitionism and the Origins of Racial Equality* (Berkeley: University of California Press, 1998), 20.

55. H. Shelton Smith, *In His Image, but . . . Racism in Southern Religion, 1780–1910* (Durham, NC: Duke University Press, 1972), 143.

56. "Slavery in the United States," *Edinburgh Review* 101 (April 1855): 297, 300, 312, 316, 329; Bledsoe, *Liberty and Slavery,* 293–96.

57. Bledsoe, *Liberty and Slavery,* 299; Fuller and Wayland, *Domestic Slavery Considered as a Scriptural Institution,* 131. Bledsoe's description of slavery as a "school of correction" is reminiscent of Ulrich Bonnell Phillips's representation of the institution as a "school for civilizing Africans" in his *American Negro Slavery: A Survey of the Supply, Employment, and Control of Negro Labor* (New York: D. Appleton and Co., 1918; Baton Rouge: Louisiana State University Press, 1966), 118. Gaines M. Foster has described Phillips's interpretation of slavery as a benign and uplifting institution as "proslavery historiography," which largely went unchallenged by professional historians until the 1950s. Gaines M. Foster, "Guilt over Slavery: A Historiographical Analysis," *Journal of Southern History* 56 (November 1990): 666, 670.

58. See the discussion of the evangelical paternalism movement in the Lower South—those who promoted it and those who opposed it—in Lacy K. Ford, *Deliver Us from Evil: The Slavery Question in the Old South* (Oxford: Oxford University Press, 2009).

59. Bledsoe, *Liberty and Slavery,* 298–99.

60. William Henry Seward, *The Works of William H. Seward,* new ed., vol. 3, ed. George E. Baker (Boston: Houghton, Mifflin, and Co., 1887), 301; Bledsoe, *Liberty and Slavery,* 306. Bledsoe's quote of Seward's Cleveland, Ohio, address reads "household gods" instead of "paternal gods."

61. Charles Sumner, *Freedom National; Slavery Sectional. Speech of Hon. Charles Sumner, of Massachusetts, on His Motion to Repeal the Fugitive Slave Bill, in the Senate of the United States, August 26, 1852* (Washington, DC: Buell and Blanchard, 1852).

62. Charles Sumner, *The Demands of Freedom. Speech of Hon. Charles Sumner, in the Senate of the United States, on His Motion to Repeal the Fugitive Slave Bill, February 23, 1855* (Washington, DC: Buell and Blanchard, 1855), 7; Bledsoe, *Liberty and Slavery,* 314.

63. Sumner, *Freedom National; Slavery Sectional,* 6–7; Bledsoe, *Liberty and Slavery,* 314–16.

64. Bledsoe, *Liberty and Slavery,* 322–23n; Franklin Pierce, "Third Annual Message to Congress,

Washington, D.C., December 31, 1855," in *A Compilation of the Messages and Papers of the Presidents, 1789–1897*, ed. James D. Richardson, vol. 5 (Washington, DC: Published by Authority of Congress, 1901), 349.

65. On northern reaction to *Prigg v. Pennsylvania*, a very complicated case in which seven justices wrote separate opinions, see Paul Finkelman, "*Prigg v. Pennsylvania* and Northern State Courts: Anti-Slavery Use of a Pro-Slavery Decision," *Civil War History* 25 (January 1979): 5–35, and Robert M. Cover, *Justice Accused: Antislavery and the Judicial Process* (New Haven: Yale University Press, 1975), 166–74. See also Thomas D. Morris, *Free Men All: The Personal Liberty Laws of the North, 1780–1861* (Baltimore: Johns Hopkins University Press, 1974), and Norman L. Rosenberg, "Personal Liberty Laws and the Sectional Crises: 1850–1861," *Civil War History* 17 (January 1971): 5–35.

66. Bledsoe, *Liberty and Slavery*, 382–83.

CHAPTER SIX

1. Joseph Sabin, ed., *Bibliotheca Americana: A Dictionary of Books Relating to America, from Its Discovery to the Present Time*, vol. 2 (New York, 1869; repr., Amsterdam: N. Israel, 1961), entry C. 5892, p. 224. Several libraries have copies of *Liberty and Slavery* showing 1857 as the date of publication, although there appear to be more extant copies of the original 1856 printing. J. B. Lippincott and Company possibly printed fewer copies of the 1857 edition.

2. R., "Liberty and Slavery—Professor Bledsoe," *Southern Planter* 16 (May 1856): 149–53; *Southern Literary Messenger* 22 (May 1856): 382–88; Frank G. Ruffin, "Professor Bledsoe's Book," *Southern Planter* 16 (May 1856): 148–49. All subsequent citations of R.'s review are from the *Southerner Literary Messenger*.

3. R., "Liberty and Slavery," 382.

4. R., "Liberty and Slavery," 384–85, 386, 387–88.

5. Bledsoe's response to R., like R.'s review itself, appeared simultaneously in the *Southern Planter* and the *Southern Literary Messenger*. Bledsoe, "Communication. To the Editor of the Southern Planter," *Southern Planter* 16 (July 1856): 193–97, and "Mr. Bledsoe's Review of His Reviewer," *Southern Literary Messenger* 23 (July 1856): 20–25.

6. Bledsoe, "Mr. Bledsoe's Review of His Reviewer," 20–22, 25.

7. William Kauffman Scarborough, ed., *The Diary of Edmund Ruffin*, vol. 1, *Toward Independence, October, 1856–April, 1861* (Baton Rouge: Louisiana State University Press, 1972), 90, 140.

8. Avery Craven, *Edmund Ruffin Southerner: A Study in Secession* (Hamden, CT: Archon Books, 1964), 127.

9. [George Fitzhugh], "Bledsoe on Liberty and Slavery," *Daily Richmond Enquirer* (July 24, 1856): no pagination. All quotes in this paragraph and the next are from this review.

10. Dabney carried some of those arguments forward in his later defense of the Lost Cause. See Robert Lewis Dabney, "Autobiography," MS, 1895, p. 46, Robert Lewis Dabney Papers, box 4, accession #38–219, SCLUV; Robert Lewis Dabney, *A Defense of Virginia (and through Her of the South), in Recent and Pending Contests against the Sectional Party* (New York: E. J. Hale and Son, 1867), 21; and Thomas Cary Johnson, *Life and Letters of Robert Lewis Dabney* (Richmond, VA: Presbyterian Committee of Publication, 1903), 128–30, 273.

11. [Robert Lewis Dabney], "An Essay on Liberty and Slavery: By Albert Taylor Bledsoe," *Presbyterial Critic and Bi-Monthly Review* 2 (May 1856): 152–58. The Dabney quotes appearing in the

following paragraphs are from pages 152, 153, 153–54, 156–57, and 158. The review is reprinted in *Discussions by Robert L. Dabney, D.D., L.L.D.*, vol. 3, *Philosophical*, ed. C. R. Vaughan, D.D. (Harrisonburg, VA: Sprinkle Publications, 1996), 61–69.

12. [George Frederick Holmes], "Bledsoe on Liberty and Slavery," *De Bow's Review* 21 (August 1856): 132–47. The quotes from Holmes's analysis of *Liberty and Slavery* appear on pages 132–33, 134–36, 139–42, and 145.

13. See Harvey Wish, "George Frederick Holmes and the Genesis of American Sociology," *American Journal of Sociology* 46 (March 1941): 698–707.

14. James Stirling, *Letters from the Slave States* (London: John W. Parker and Son, 1857), 120.

15. A Citizen of the South [Charles B. Shaw], *Is Slavery a Blessing? A Reply to Prof. Bledsoe's An Essay on Liberty and Slavery; with Remarks on Slavery as It Is* (Boston: John P. Jewett and Co. and C. Rand and Avery, 1857). American bibliographer Joseph Sabin (1821–88) appears to be the first authority to attribute authorship of this anonymous work to Shaw. Sabin, *Bibliotheca Americana*, vol. 19 (New York, 1891; repr., Amsterdam: N. Israel, 1962), entry H. 79900, pp. 376–77. The Papers of Charles Brion Shaw in the Special Collections Library at the University of Virginia, however, make no reference to a reply to Bledsoe or to any mention of Shaw's views on slavery. While the attribution of authorship to Shaw is far from conclusive, there is no compelling reason to contest it. It is more likely that Shaw was the "Citizen of the South" who responded to Bledsoe than not. He was at the right place, at the right time, and had the right interests and background.

16. Antislavery sentiment in the South is examined in Carl N. Degler, *The Other South: Southern Dissenters in the Nineteenth Century* (New York: Harper and Row, 1974; Gainesville: University Press of Florida, 2000). See also Kenneth M. Stamp, "The Southern Refutation of the Proslavery Argument," *North Carolina Historical Review* 21 (January 1944): 35–45. The standard account of the suppression of free thought and speech in response to abolitionism is Clement Eaton, *Freedom of Thought in the Old South* (Durham, NC: Duke University Press, 1940), where he notes that the general acceptance of proslavery thought in the South demonstrates the "imperialism that an idea can wield over a section" (247). See also Clement Eaton, *The Mind of the Old South* (Baton Rouge: Louisiana State University Press, 1964).

17. Citizen of the South, *Is Slavery a Blessing?* 4.

18. Citizen of the South, *Is Slavery a Blessing?* 6–7.

19. Douglas Ambrose, *Henry Hughes and Proslavery Thought in the Old South* (Baton Rouge: Louisiana State University Press, 1996), 5, 180, 187, and "Statism in the Old South: A Reconsideration," in *Slavery, Secession, and Southern History*, ed. Robert Louis Paquette and Louis A. Ferleger (Charlottesville: University of Virginia Press, 2000), 101–25. See also Bertram Wyatt-Brown, "Modernizing Southern Slavery: The Proslavery Argument Reinterpreted," in *Region, Race, and Reconstruction: Essays in Honor of C. Vann Woodward*, ed. J. Morgan Kousser and James M. McPherson (New York, 1982), 27–49; modified and reprinted as chap. 5, "From Piety to Fantasy: Proslavery's Troubled Evolution," in Bertram Wyatt-Brown, *Yankee Saints and Southern Sinners* (Baton Rouge: Louisiana State University Press, 1985), 155–82.

20. See, for example, J. D. B. De Bow, "The Non-Slaveholders of the South," in *The Interest in Slavery of the Southern Non-Slaveholder*, by J. D. B. De Bow et al. (Charleston, SC: Evans and Cogswell, 1860).

. 21. Citizen of the South, *Is Slavery a Blessing?* 98.

22. The quotes appearing in this paragraph and the next are from Citizen of the South, *Is Slavery a Blessing?* 119–20.

23. "Liberty and Slavery," *Putnam's Monthly Magazine* 7 (May 1856): 550.

24. "A Bunch of Books," *Leader*, May 3, 1856, 426–27.

25. William S. Jenkins, *Pro-Slavery Thought in the Old South* (Chapel Hill: University of North Carolina Press, 1935), 89; Ralph E. Morrow, "The Proslavery Argument Revisited," *Mississippi Valley Historical Review* 48 (June 1961): 79–80.

26. David Donald, "The Proslavery Argument Reconsidered," *Journal of Southern History* 37 (February 1971): 5–6.

27. See Thomas H. O'Connor, *Lords of the Loom: The Cotton Whigs and the Coming of the War* (New York: Scribner, 1968); Philip Sheldon Foner, *Business and Slavery: The New York Merchants and the Irrepressible Conflict* (Chapel Hill: University of North Carolina Press, 1941); and the relevant chapters of Allan Nevins, *The Emergence of Lincoln*, vol. 2 (New York: Scribner, 1978).

28. Jean H. Baker, *Affairs of Party: The Political Culture of Northern Democrats in the Mid-Nineteenth Century* (Ithaca, NY: Cornell University Press, 1983), 319; Wyatt-Brown, *Yankee Saints and Southern Sinners*, 193.

29. [Charles Hodge], "West India Emancipation," *Princeton Review* 10 (October 1838): 603.

30. George Fitzhugh, "The Conservative Principle; Or, Social Evils and their Remedies," *De Bow's Review* 22 (1857): 427.

31. William Harper, "Slavery in the Light of Social Ethics," in *Cotton Is King, and Pro-Slavery Arguments: Comprising the Writings of Hammond, Harper, Christy, Stringfellow, Hodge, Bledsoe, and Cartwright on this Important Subject*, ed. E. N. Elliott (Augusta, GA: Pritchard, Abbott, and Loomis, 1860), 550–51; Harvey Wish, *George Fitzhugh, Propagandist of the Old South* (Baton Rouge: Louisiana State University Press, 1943), 122. Wish gives a fascinating account of the Fitzhugh-Phillips debate in New Haven on 128–42.

32. [George Frederick Holmes], "On Slavery and Christianity," *Southern Quarterly Review* 3 (January 1843): 252–53.

33. Samuel Cartwright as quoted in "Editorial and Literary Department. 8.—Studies on Slavery, by John Fletcher, A. M., of Louisiana," *De Bow's Review* 12 (April 1852): 461. See John Fletcher, *Studies on Slavery, in Easy Lessons. Compiled into Eight Studies, and Subdivided into Short Lessons for the Convenience of Readers* (Natchez, MS: Jackson Warner; Philadelphia: T. Cowperthwait and Co., 1852).

34. Bertram Wyatt-Brown, "Proslavery and Antislavery Intellectuals: Class Concepts and Polemical Struggle," in *Antislavery Reconsidered: New Perspectives on the Abolitionists*, ed. Lewis Perry and Michael Fellman (Baton Rouge: Louisiana State University Press, 1979), 311, 316, 317, 333; Larry E. Tise, "The Interregional Appeal of Proslavery Thought: An Ideological Profile of the Antebellum Clergy," *Plantation Society in the Americas* 1 (February 1979): 58–72.

35. Bledsoe to Jefferson Davis, University of Virginia, November 12, 1859, in Dunbar Rowland, ed., *Jefferson Davis, Constitutionalist: His Letters, Papers, and Speeches*, vol. 4 (Jackson: Mississippi Department of Archives and History, 1923), 94–95; *The Papers of Jefferson Davis*, vol. 6, *1856–1860*, ed. Lynda Lasswell Crist et al. (Baton Rouge: Louisiana State University, 1989), 618.

36. On the interpretation of proslavery intellectuals as unhappy and maladjusted individuals who hungered for recognition, see David Donald, "The Proslavery Argument Reconsidered," *Journal of Southern History* 37 (February 1971): 3–18. Ralph E. Morrow also raised the question of the personal benefits (i.e., reputation) that accrued to southern intellectuals who defended slavery as a likely motive for doing so. See Morrow, "Proslavery Argument Revisited," 79–94.

37. Drew Gilpin Faust, "Introduction: The Proslavery Argument in History," in *The Ideology*

of Slavery: Proslavery Thought in the Antebellum South, 1830–1860, ed. Drew Gilpin Faust (Baton Rouge: Louisiana State University Press, 1981), 1–20; "A Southern Stewardship: The Intellectual and the Proslavery Argument," *American Quarterly* 31 (Spring 1979): 63–80; and *A Sacred Circle: The Dilemma of the Intellectual in the Old South, 1840–1860* (Baltimore: Johns Hopkins University Press, 1977). The "guiltomania" quote regarding the interpretations of Wilber J. Cash and Charles G. Sellers Jr. is from Faust, *Ideology of Slavery,* 7. The most thorough analysis of the southern guilt thesis is Gaines M. Foster, "Guilt over Slavery: A Historiographical Analysis," *Journal of Southern History* 56 (November 1990): 665–94. Foster examines the social and intellectual contexts in which the hypothesis emerged among historians, its underlying assumptions, and the paucity of supporting evidence.

38. Bertram Wyatt-Brown, *Southern Honor: Ethics and Behavior in the Old South* (New York: Oxford University Press, 1982), xii, xviii. See also Bertram Wyatt-Brown, *The Shaping of Southern Culture: Honor, Grace, and War, 1760s–1890s* (Chapel Hill: University of North Carolina Press, 2001).

39. Eric L. McKitrick, "The Defense of Slavery," in *Slavery Defended: The Views of the Old South,* ed. Eric L. McKitrick (Englewood Cliffs, NJ: Prentice Hall, 1963), 4–5; Faust, "Introduction: The Proslavery Argument in History," 18.

40. A. T. Bledsoe, "Liberty and Slavery: Or, Slavery in the Light of Moral and Political Philosophy," in Elliott, *Cotton Is King,* 271–458.

41. Michael O'Brien, *Conjectures of Order: Intellectual Life and the American South, 1810–1860,* vol. 2 (Chapel Hill: University of North Carolina Press, 2004), 966.

42. Mitchell Snay, *Gospel of Disunion: Religion and Separatism in the Antebellum South* (New York: University of Cambridge Press, 1993), 67, 69; James P. Holcombe, "Is Slavery Consistent with Natural Law?" *Southern Literary Messenger* 27 (December 1858): 401–21, published separately as *An Address Delivered before the Seventh Annual Meeting of the Virginia State Agricultural Society, November 4th, 1858* (Richmond, VA: Macfarlane and Fergusson, 1858); Eugene D. Genovese, *The Slaveholders' Dilemma: Freedom and Progress in Southern Conservative Thought, 1820–1860* (Columbia: University of South Carolina Press, 1992), 51. Robert M. Cover discusses the application of natural law to the defense of slavery and the decisions of courts in *Justice Accused: Antislavery and the Judicial Process* (New Haven: Yale University Press, 1975), 8–25, 33, 35, 93–99. See also Benjamin F. White Jr., *American Interpretations of Natural Law: A Study in the History of Political Thought* (Cambridge: Harvard University Press, 1931), 210–42.

43. "Pro-Slavery Literature—'Cannibals All!'" *Richmond Enquirer,* January 23, 1857, as reprinted in "The Pro-Slavery Press of the South," *National Era,* February 26, 1857, 36.

44. Stirling, *Letters from the Slave States,* 123.

CHAPTER SEVEN

1. The following quotes are from "Smithsonian Lecture," *Daily National Intelligencer,* February 15, 1860, no pagination.

2. The repudiation of individualism in the North is examined in George M. Fredrickson, *The Inner Civil War: Northern Intellectuals and the Crisis of Union* (New York: Harper and Row, 1965; Urbana: University of Illinois Press, 1993), with a new preface.

3. Bledsoe makes precisely that same observation, for example, in Albert Taylor Bledsoe, "J. J. Rousseau," *Southern Review* 3 (January 1868): 118.

4. George Frederick Holmes, "Theory of Political Individualism," *De Bow's Review* 22 (February 1857): 133–49; Mitchell Snay, *Gospel of Disunion: Religion and Separatism in the Antebellum South* (New York: Cambridge University, 1993), 62.

5. Joseph Henry to Bledsoe, Smithsonian Institution, February 29, 1860, Letters of Albert Taylor Bledsoe, MS 3461, SCLUV.

6. "Smithsonian Lecture," no pagination.

7. George Fitzhugh, "Oliver Goldsmith and Doctor Johnson," *De Bow's Review* 28 (November 1860): 505–6, 513.

8. Douglas's opinion that the spirit of party was sacrificing the Union for the selfish ends of both parties is compatible with the thesis presented in Michael F. Holt's *The Fate of Their Country: Politicians, Slavery Extension, and the Coming of the Civil War* (New York: Hill and Wang, 2004). Holt argues that partisan politics, even more than economic differences between the North and South and the moral issue of slavery, was the principal cause of secession and war. Short-sighted politicians worsened the sectional crisis by demagoguing the issue of slavery in the territories and placing their own reelections ahead of the need for sectional comity.

9. Stephen A. Douglas, "State of the Union." Speech of Hon. S. A. Douglas, of Illinois, in the Senate, January 3, 1861, 36th Cong., 2nd sess., *Congressional Globe* (Washington, DC: Congressional Globe Office, 1861), app., 42. The impact of Douglas's speech upon Bledsoe was profound, the entire text of which appears on pages 35 to 45 of the appendix to the *Congressional Globe*. Douglas's discourse is worth reading in relation to the views that Bledsoe himself expressed on the repeal of the Missouri Compromise, the policy of nonintervention with slavery in the territories, and the secession crisis in his reply to Charles Hodge, which appeared in the *New York Weekly Journal of Commerce* between and February and April 1861.

10. This quote and the following ones are from Bledsoe to Stephen A. Douglas, University of Virginia, February 6, 1861, Stephen A. Douglas Papers, Special Collections Research Center, University of Chicago Library. Douglas made the notation on this letter that he answered Bledsoe on February 7, but his reply does not appear to have survived.

11. The congressional petition of 3,050 New England clergymen to which Bledsoe refers is dated March 1, 1854, Boston. The appeal and extracts from the ensuing Senate debate, including the response of Stephen A. Douglas, are reprinted in David Christy, *Pulpit Politics; Or, Ecclesiastical Legislation on Slavery, in Its Disturbing Influences on the American Union* (Cincinnati: Farran and McLean, 1862), 598–604. Christy, like Douglas and Bledsoe, regarded the petition as an egregious example of "political preaching." The Reverend Charles Hodge was *not* a New Englander. He does not appear to have been a signer of the congressional petition of three thousand clergymen. Bledsoe, although vague in the matter, does not appear to suggest that Hodge himself was one of the three thousand petitioners but rather implies that *like* those clergymen he was also a political preacher and a presumed mouthpiece of the Republican Party.

12. Rev. Charles Hodge, "The State of the Country," *Biblical Repertory and Princeton Review* 33 (January 1861): 1–36. The *Biblical Repertory and Princeton Review* was often cited merely as the *Princeton Review.*

13. [Albert Taylor Bledsoe], "Reply to the Rev. Charles Hodge, D.D. 'On the State of the Country,'" *New York Weekly Journal of Commerce*, February 14, 1861, March 7, 1861, and April 4, 1861, no pagination. The articles are unsigned, but the editors of the *Journal* identify Bledsoe as the author in introducing the first of the series, as did Bledsoe himself in the *Southern Review* for July 1872. The first installment of Bledsoe's reply to Hodge in the *New York Weekly Journal of Commerce*—that

for February 14, 1861—also appeared anonymously in the *Virginia University Magazine* in March 1861. Bledsoe later revised and reprinted the article in the *Southern Review* for April 1868 as "The Missouri Compromise." [Gerald Hallock et al., eds.], "'The State of the Country.' Review of Prof. Hodge's Article on This Subject in the Princeton Review," *New York Weekly Journal of Commerce*, February 14, 1861; [Albert Taylor Bledsoe], "Reply to the Rev. Charles Hodge," *Virginia University Magazine* 5 (March 1861): 265–95; "The Missouri Compromise of 1820," *Southern Review* 3 (April 1868): 346–77; and "Hon. A. H. Stephens on the Late War," *Southern Review* 11 (July 1872): 133–34, where Bledsoe identifies himself as the author of the three-part reply to Hodge in the *New York Weekly Journal of Commerce*.

14. Frank Luther Mott, *American Journalism: A History of Newspapers in the United States through 250 Years, 1690–1940*, vol. 1 (New York: Macmillan, 1941; London: Routledge/Thoemmes, 2000), 182, 352.

15. William John Grayson of South Carolina made his own reply to Hodge, as did the *Southern Presbyterian Review*. See [William John Grayson], *Reply to Professor Hodge, on the "State of the Country"* (Charleston, SC: Steam-Power Presses of Evans and Cogswell, 1861) and "The Princeton Review on the State of the Country," *Southern Presbyterian Review* 14 (1861): 1–44. The *Constitutionalist*—published in Augusta, Georgia—likewise gave answer. See "The State of the Country," *Constitutionalist*, March 22–24, 1861, 1. The editors of the *Constitutionalist* denounced the once respected Hodge and exclaimed disbelief at his sentiments on secession: "et tu Brute!"

16. These quotes and those appearing in the following paragraphs are from [Bledsoe], "Reply to the Rev. Charles Hodge, D.D., 'On the State of the County,'" *New York Weekly Journal of Commerce*, February 14, 1861, no pagination.

17. Hodge, "State of the Country," 5.

18. William Henry Seward, "Freedom and Public Faith. Speech of Hon. W. H. Seward, of New York, in the Senate, February 17, 1854," *Congressional Globe*, Senate, 33rd Cong., 1st sess., appendix, 151; Salmon Portland Chase, "Maintain Plighted Faith. Speech of Hon. S. P. Chase, of Ohio, in the Senate, February 3, 1854," *Congressional Globe*, Senate, 33rd Cong., 1st sess., appendix, 134; Eric Foner, *Free Soil, Free Labor, Free Men: The Ideology of the Republican Party before the Civil War* (New York: Oxford University Press, 1970), 73.

19. "Nebraska and Kansas Bill. Speech of Hon. E. Everett of Massachusetts, in the Senate, February 8, 1854," *Congressional Globe*, Senate, 33rd Cong., 1st sess., appendix, 162–63.

20. Charles Pinckney, "Admission of Missouri," *Annals of Congress*, House of Representatives, 16th Cong., 2nd sess., February 1821, 1129–30.

21. See Holt, *Fate of Their Country*, and Michael A. Morrison, *Slavery and the American West: The Eclipse of Manifest Destiny and the Coming of the Civil War* (Chapel Hill: University of North Carolina Press, 1997). See also Frederick J. Blue, *The Free Soilers: Third Party Politics, 1848–54* (Urbana: University of Illinois Press, 1973); Joseph G. Rayback, *Free Soil: The Election of 1848* (Lexington: University of Kentucky Press, 1971); and Foner, *Free Soil, Free Labor, Free Men*.

22. [Bledsoe], "Reply to the Rev. Charles Hodge, D.D., 'On the State of the County,'" *New York Weekly Journal of Commerce*, April 4, 1861, no pagination.

23. Robert Pierce Forbes, *The Missouri Compromise and Its Aftermath: Slavery and the Meaning of America* (Chapel Hill: University of North Carolina Press, 2007), 3, 6.

24. Richard J. Carwardine, "The Politics of Charles Hodge," in *Charles Hodge Revisited: A Critical Appraisal of His Life and Work*, ed. John W. Stewart and James H. Moorehead (Grand Rapids, MI: William B. Eerdmans Publishing, 2002), 282.

25. Albert Taylor Bledsoe, "Notices of Books," *Southern Review* 7 (January 1870): 242; [Bledsoe], "Hon. A. H. Stephens on the Late War," 134.

26. Charles F. Irons, "Reluctant Protestant Confederates: The Religious Roots of Conditional Unionism," in *Virginia's Civil War*, ed. Peter Wallenstein and Bertram Wyatt-Brown (Charlottesville: University of Virginia Press, 2005). Irons's conclusion is that "white Virginians considered slavery and secession distinct and divergent moral issues," even though most historians have "continually conflated the two" (73). See also Daniel W. Crofts, *Reluctant Confederates: Upper South Unionists in the Secession Crisis* (Chapel Hill: University of North Carolina Press, 1989).

27. Wallenstein and Wyatt-Brown, *Virginia's Civil War*, 6; Sophia Bledsoe Herrick, "Personal Recollections of My Father and Mr. Lincoln and Mr. Davis," *Methodist Quarterly Review* 64 (October 1915): 673.

28. Henry T. Shanks, *The Secession Movement in Virginia, 1847–1861* (Richmond, VA: Garrett and Massie, 1934), 71, 232n38; J. W. Cooke, "Albert Taylor Bledsoe: An American Philosopher and Theologian of Liberty," *Southern Humanities Review* 8 (Spring 1974): 217; John McCardell, *The Idea of a Southern Nation: Southern Nationalists and Southern Nationalism, 1830 to 1860* (New York: W. W. North and Co., 1979), 215; Stephen E. Woodworth, "Albert Taylor Bledsoe," in *American National Biography*, vol. 3, ed. John A. Garraty and Mark C. Carnes (New York: Oxford University Press, 1999), 11.

29. Randolph H. McKim, *A Soldier's Recollections: Leaves from the Diary of a Young Confederate with an Oration on the Motives and Aims of the Soldiers of the South* (New York: Longmans, Green, and Co., 1910), 3.

30. Elizabeth Fox-Genovese and Eugene D. Genovese, *The Mind of the Master Class: History and Faith in the Southern Slaveholders' Worldview* (Cambridge: Cambridge University Press, 2005), 86.

31. Wayland Fuller Dunaway, *Reminiscences of a Rebel* (New York: Neale Publishing Co., 1913), 8–10.

32. Walter C[reigh] Preston to John N. Preston Sr., University of Virginia, April 29, 1861, Virginiana, #11143, SCLUV; "The War Spirit at the University," *Richmond Enquirer*, May 8, 1861, no pagination; Bledsoe to Jefferson Davis, University of Virginia, May 10, 1861, Jefferson Davis Papers, SCLDU; W. H. Crenshaw to [Edward Crenshaw], University of Virginia, May 28, 1861, SCLDU.

33. This quote and the following ones are from Bledsoe to Jefferson Davis, University of Virginia, May 10, 1861, Jefferson Davis Papers, SCLDU. Another manuscript copy of this letter, missing the last page, is in the Samuel W. Richey Confederate Collection, vol. 1, SCLMU. The letter is printed in full in *The Papers of Jefferson Davis*, vol. 7, *1861*, ed. Lynda Lasswell Crist, coed. Mary Sexton Dix (Baton Rouge: Louisiana State University Press, 1992), 159–61.

34. Bledsoe to Jefferson Davis, University of Virginia, May 11, 1861, Frederick M. Dearborn Collection, bMS Am 1649.24 (56), Houghton Library, Harvard University, Cambridge, Massachusetts.

35. R. S. Garnett, Adjutant-General, Headquarters, Richmond, Virginia, June 1, 1861, General Orders, No. 24, by order of Major General Robert E. Lee, in *The War of the Rebellion: A Compilation of the Official Records of the Union and Confederate Armies*, ser. 1, vol. 51, pt. 2 (Washington, DC: Government Printing Office, 1897), 123; Philip Alexander Bruce, *History of the University of Virginia, 1819–1919*, vol. 3 (New York: Macmillan Co., 1921), 81.

36. The quotes in this paragraph and the next are from John Beauchamp Jones, *A Rebel War Clerk's Diary at the Confederate States Capital*, vol. 1, new and enlarged ed., ed. Howard Swiggett (New York: Old Hickory Bookshop, 1935), 49, 50, 51, 52, 58–59, 61, 62, 70, 73.

37. Six letters written by Bledsoe in 1861 and 1862 as chief of the Confederate Bureau of War relating to these matters are in the Huntington Library, San Marino, California. See also Bledsoe

to G. T. Beauregard, Confederate States of America, War Department, Richmond, Va., October 8, 1861, unbound "Beauregard" file, Samuel W. Richey Confederate Collection, SCLMU.

38. Stephen Elliott to Bledsoe, Savannah, August 19, 1861, Letters of Albert Taylor Bledsoe, MS 3461, SCLUV; Bledsoe to General Leonidas Polk, Richmond, December 26, 1861, War Division, National Archives, Washington, D.C. A typescript of Bledsoe's letter to Polk is in the David Rankin Barbee Microfilm Collection of Albert Taylor Bledsoe Materials, microfilm 517, 3311, SCLUV.

39. Hermes, "Richmond News and Gossip," *Charleston Mercury*, April 5, 1862, no pagination; Edward Younger, ed., *Inside the Confederate Government: The Diary of Robert Garlick Hill Kean* (New York: Oxford University Press, 1957), xxiv, 27; Jones, *Rebel War Clerk's Diary*, 1:55, 78, 119.

40. A. T. Bledsoe, Assistant Secretary of War, to Major-General M. Lovell, Richmond, May 2, 1862, signed G. W. Randolph, Secretary of War, in "Cotton Burning," *New York Times*, May 31, 1862, 2, and Bledsoe to General Leonidas Polk, Richmond, December 26, 1861, War Division, National Archives, Washington, D.C., in David Rankin Barbee Microfilm Collection of Albert Taylor Bledsoe Materials, microfilm 517, 3311, SCLUV.

41. Bledsoe to Polk, February 3, 1862, Confederate States of America, War Department, Richmond, in William M. Polk, *Leonidas Polk: Bishop and General*, vol. 1, 2nd and rev. ed. (New York: Longmans, Green, and Co., 1915), 383. Bledsoe also recommended Polk to Jefferson Davis in November 1862 as the successor of George Wythe Randolph as secretary of war. "His talent is Executive; and he would be a great worker. I know no man better fitted for the place." Bledsoe to Jefferson Davis, the University of Virginia, November 19, 1862, Jefferson Davis Papers, SCLDU. On Polk's contributions to the Confederate service, see Glenn Robins, *The Bishop of the Old South: The Ministry and Civil War Legacy of Leonidas Polk* (Macon, GA: Mercer University Press, 2006); Joseph H. Parks, *General Leonidas Polk, C.S.A: The Fighting Bishop* (Baton Rouge: Louisiana State University Press, 1992); and the two volumes of Polk, *Leonidas Polk*. Longmans and Green published the original two-volume edition in 1893.

42. Hermes, "The News from Richmond," *Charleston Mercury*, September 20, 1862, no pagination. The report of "Hermes," the Richmond correspondent for the *Mercury*, bears the date September 16, 1862.

43. John B. Bennett, "Albert Taylor Bledsoe: Transitional Philosopher of the Old South," *Methodist History* 11 (January 1972): 8–9; Jones, *Rebel War Clerk's Diary*, 1:136.

44. Clement Eaton, *Jefferson Davis* (New York: Free Press, 1977), 196–97, and "The Confederacy" in *Interpreting American History: Conversations with Historians*, vol. 1, ed. John A. Garraty (New York: Macmillan, 1970), 328.

45. [Catherine Cooper Hopley], *Life in the South from the Commencement of the War, by a Blockaded British Subject*, vol. 2, "S. L. J." [Sarah L. Jones, pseudonym] (London: Chapman and Hall, 1863), 73–74.

46. G. W. Randolph to Bledsoe, Richmond, August 26, 1861, in *The War of Rebellion: A Compilation of the Official Records of the Union and Confederate Armies*, ser. 1, vol. 51, pt. 2, Supplement (Washington, DC: Government Printing Office, 1897), 251.

CHAPTER EIGHT

1. George Frederick Holmes, "Diary, Agricultural and War, 1856 to 1864," November 13, 1862, SCLDU.

2. The Reverend Philip Slaughter edited the *Army and Navy Messenger* from May 1863 to April 1864. Slaughter (1808–90) was an Episcopal clergyman, rector of Cavalry Church in Culpeper County, chaplain of the Nineteenth Regiment of Virginia Volunteers, and one of Bledsoe's most respected acquaintances. Bledsoe wrote the introduction to Slaughter's *Man and Woman; or, The Law of Honor Applied to the Solution of the Problem, Why Are So Many More Women Than Men Christians? With an Introduction by A. T. Bledsoe, L.L.D. of the University of Virginia.* (Philadelphia: J. B. Lippincott and Co., 1860).

3. See Jason Phillips, "Religious Belief and Troop Motivation: For the Smiles of My Blessed Saviour," in *Virginia's Civil War,* ed. Peter Wallenstein and Bertram Wyatt-Brown (Charlottesville: University of Virginia Press, 2005), 101–13, and Kurt O. Berends, "'Wholesome Reading Purifies and Elevates the Man': The Religious Military Press in the Confederacy," in *Religion and the American Civil War,* ed. Randall M. Miller, Harry S. Stout, and Charles Reagan Wilson (New York: Oxford University Press, 1998), 131–66.

4. See Drew Gilpin Faust, *The Creation of Confederate Nationalism: Ideology and Identity in the Civil War South* (Baton Rouge: Louisiana State University Press, 1981); Ian Bennington, "'They Have Made A Nation': Confederates and the Creation of Confederate Nationalism" (Ph.D. diss., University of Illinois at Urbana-Champaign, 2004); and Ian Bennington, "Promoting the Confederate Nation: The Southern Illustrated News and the Civil War" in Wallenstein and Wyatt-Brown, *Virginia's Civil War,* 114–22. See also Michael Thomas Bernath, "Confederate Minds: The Struggle for Intellectual Independence in the Civil War South" (Ph.D. diss., Harvard University, 2005).

5. All quotes are from A. T. Bledsoe, "Reflections on the War. No. 1.," *Army and Navy Messenger,* July 1, 1863, no pagination. Bledsoe intended his "Reflections on the War. No. 1" to be the first of a series of articles in the *Messenger,* but it was the only number ever published. His departure for London appears to the reason that no more numbers appeared. Copies of the *Army and Navy Messenger* are rare and complete files even more so. A whole file is in the holdings of the BLMC. I wish to thank Dr. John M. Coski, historian and library director at the Museum of the Confederacy, for providing me with a copy of Bledsoe's "Reflections of the War" article taken from that file.

6. As quoted in Russell Kirk, *John Randolph of Roanoke: A Study in American Politics,* 3rd ed. (Indianapolis: Liberty Fund, 1978), 46.

7. William C. Davis, ed., *Secret History of Confederate Diplomacy Abroad* (Lawrence: University of Kansas Press, 2005), xxx.

8. Sophia Bledsoe Herrick, "Albert Taylor Bledsoe," *Alumni Bulletin of the University of Virginia* 6 (May 1899): 5. Similar statements appear in Sophia Bledsoe Herrick, "Personal Recollections of My Father and Mr. Lincoln and Mr. Davis," *Methodist Quarterly Review* 64 (October 1915): 673; "Explanatory Preface" in Bledsoe, *The War between the States, or Was Secession a Constitutional Right Previous to the War of 1861–65* (Lynchburg, VA: J. P. Bell Co., 1915, [8]; and "Albert Taylor Bledsoe, 1809–1877," in *Library of Southern Literature,* vol. 1, ed. Edwin Anderson Alderman and Charles Alphonso Smith (Atlanta: Martin and Hoyt Co., 1929), 396. In Herrick's accounts appearing in the *Methodist Quarterly Review* and the *Library of Southern Literature,* however, she says that both Davis and Robert E. Lee asked her father to undertake a vindication of secession as a constitutional right. It seems more likely, however, that Davis would make such a request rather than Lee.

9. Albert Taylor Bledsoe, "The Legislation of 1787," *Southern Review* 11 (April 1872): 252.

10. Herrick, "Personal Recollections of My Father," 673, and "Explanatory Preface," in Bledsoe, *War between the States,* [8].

11. John Beauchamp Jones, *A Rebel War Clerk's Diary at the Confederate States Capital*, vol. 2, new and enlarged ed., ed with an introduction and historical notes by Howard Swiggett (New York: Old Hickory Bookshop, 1935), 21.

12. *Official Records of the Union and Confederate Navies in the War of Rebellion*, ser. 2, vol. 2 (Washington, DC: Government Printing Office, 1921), 813; untitled notice, *Index*, October 15, 1863, 391; untitled press clipping, *Charleston Daily Courier*, October 12, 1863, David Rankin Barbee Microfilm Collection of Albert Taylor Bledsoe Materials, microfilm 517, 3311, SCLUV.

13. James Lyon to Lord Hartington, Laburnum near Richmond, August 21, 1863, MS 6440, SCLUV. The lack of adequate publishing facilities in the South was itself an impediment, although not a fatal one, to the development of Confederation nationalism. Southerners expressed their national identity and ideology in newspapers, periodicals, and song, but the lack of printing paper, ink, and new type was a common lament. As the war dragged on, it became increasing difficult to even print newspapers. Faust, *Creation of Confederate Nationalism*, 17–18, 91–92n31 and n32.

14. Cornelia Grinnan to the Duke of Argyll (George Douglas Campbell), near Fredericksburg, Virginia, September 12, 1863, Letters of Albert Taylor Bledsoe, MS 3461, SCLUV.

15. Bledsoe, Memorandum Book, entry 18.

16. James Spence, *The American Union: Its Effect on National Character and Policy, with an Inquiry into Secession as a Constitutional Right, and the Causes of the Disruption*, 4th and rev. ed. (London: R. Bentley, 1862). West and Johnston published the first American edition in Richmond in 1863, which is based on the fourth and revised English edition. See also James Spence, *On the Recognition of the Southern Confederacy* (London: R. Bentley, 1862).

17. Charles P. Cullop, *Confederate Propaganda in Europe, 1861–1865* (Coral Cables, FL: University of Miami Press, 1969), 45; Jay Monaghan, *Diplomat in Carpet Slippers: Abraham Lincoln Deals with Foreign Affairs* (Indianapolis: Bobbs-Merrill Co., 1945), 159; James Murray Mason to Judah P. Benjamin, London, July 31, 1862 in *Messages and Papers of Jefferson Davis and the Confederacy, Including Diplomatic Correspondence, 1861–1865*, ed. James D. Richardson, vol. 2 (New York: Chelsea House-Robert Hector Publishers, in association with R. R. Bowker, 1966), 293.

18. James Spence to Bledsoe, Liverpool, January 7, 1863, Letters of Albert Taylor Bledsoe, MS 3461, SCLUV.

19. Edwin De Leon to Bledsoe, Paris, November 27, 1863, Letters of Albert Taylor Bledsoe, MS 3461, SCLUV. See Thomas Read Rootes Cobb, *An Inquiry into the Law of Negro Slavery. To Which Is Prefixed an Historical Sketch of Slavery* (Philadelphia: T. and J. W. Johnson; Savannah: W. Thorne Williams, 1858). See also the introduction by Paul Finkelman to the reprint of the work in *An Inquiry into the Law of Negro Slavery in the United States of America, by Thomas R. R. Cobb, Studies in the Legal History of the South* (Athens: University of Georgia Press, 1999).

20. Spence, *American Union* (1862 ed.), 131–32; D. P. Crook, *Diplomacy during the American Civil War* (New York: John Wiley and Sons, 1975), 69; Cullop, *Confederate Propaganda in Europe*, 46–47.

21. Albert Taylor Bledsoe, "The Causes of the American War," *Index*, December 10, 1863, 518–19; December 17, 1863, 539; December 31, 1863, 571–72; January 7, 1864, 11.

22. Albert Taylor Bledsoe, "Secession," nos. 1–9, *Evening Herald*: no. 1, October 25, 1864, 6–7; no. 2, December 19, 1864, 3; no. 3, December 26, 1864, 2; no. 4, January 2, 1865, 2; no. 5, January 6, 1865, 7; no. 6, January 12, 1865, 2; no. 7, January 26, 1865, 2; no. 8, January 31, 1865, 7; and no. 9, April 15, 1865, 3.

23. Albert Taylor Bledsoe, "D. D. Whedon, D.D.," *Southern Review* 12 (July 1872): 228.

24. Bledsoe, "Causes of the American War," December 10, 1863, 518. Bledsoe later restated that historical mission thusly: "Every great revolution has had its writers as well as its warriors." Albert Taylor Bledsoe, "The Origin of the Late War," *Southern Review* 1 (April 1867): 257.

25. The quotes in this and the next paragraph are from Bledsoe, "Causes of the American War," December 10, 1863, 519.

26. Thomas Hart Benton, *Thirty Years' View; Or, A History of the Working of the American Government for Thirty Years, from 1820–1850*, vol. 1 (New York: D. Appleton and Co., 1854), 98–99.

27. Cobden as cited in Bledsoe, "Causes of the American War," December 10, 1863, 519, and "The Confederate Cause in Lancashire," *Index*, December 10, 1863, 518.

28. J. E. Cairnes, *The Slave Power: Its Character, Career, and Probable Designs* (London: Parker, Son, and Bourn, 1862), ix, 304.

29. Bledsoe, "Causes of the American War," December 31, 1863, 571; Albert Taylor Bledsoe, *Is Davis a Traitor; Or Was Secession a Constitutional Right Previous to the War of 1861?* (Baltimore: Printed for the Author, by Innes and Co., 1866), 143–44; Thomas Prentice Kettell, *Southern Wealth and Northern Profits, As Exhibited in Statistical Facts and Official Figures: Showing the Necessity of Union to the Future Prosperity and Welfare of the Republic* (New York: G. W. and J. A. Woods, 1860), 127.

30. William C. Davis, *The Cause Lost: Myths and Realities of the Confederacy* (Lawrence: University of Kansas, 1996), 180–81.

31. The quotes appearing in this and the following paragraphs are from Bledsoe, "Secession," *Evening Herald*, October 25, 1864, 6.

32. The correspondence of the Reverend Francis William Tremlett and his sister Louisa A. Tremlett with Raphael Semmes is in the Semmes Papers, MS 1 Se353a, VHS, and correspondence from Francis William Tremlett to Matthew Fontaine Maury regarding Maury's service as a Confederate agent in England is in the Matthew Fontaine Maury Papers, MDLC.

33. "The Society for Promoting the Cessation of Hostilities in America," *Index*, February 11, 1864, 87. A printed appeal of the Society for Promoting the Cessation of Hostilities in America dated July 4, 1864, is in the Matthew Fontaine Maury Papers, vol. 20, MDLC.

34. F. W. Tremlett to Bledsoe, [Belsize Park, London], n.d. [ca. October 1863], Letters of Albert Taylor Bledsoe, MS 3461, SCLUV.

35. The Confederate naval officer John McIntosh Kell (1823–1900) noted in his memoirs that the Tremlett home was a favorite gathering place for Confederate and British naval officers. "The friendship for Mr. Tremlett and his family here formed has been earnest and lifelong." John McIntosh Kell, *Recollections of A Naval Life, Including the Cruises of the Confederate States Steamers, "Sumter" and "Alabama"* (Washington, DC: Neale Co., 1900), 179.

36. Bledsoe, Memorandum Book, entry 27.

37. Bledsoe's "The Beauty of the World" is a fifty-one-page manuscript poem dedicated by him to Louisa A. Tremlett, which he completed in London on April 21, 1865. The poem is a theological excursus reflecting upon themes expounded in his *Theodicy* and has nothing to do with the war. The manuscript is in a bound volume of the Raphael Semmes Papers, MS 1 Se535a 166, section 8, VHS. Bledsoe later published the poem, unsigned and with a slightly altered title, in the *Southern Review* for January 1871, which appears without the earlier dedication to Louisa. See Albert Taylor Bledsoe, "The Beauty of the Universe. A Poem," *Southern Review* 9 (January 1871): 205–24.

38. Bledsoe to Jefferson Davis, London, September 21, 1864, in *The Papers of Jefferson Davis*, vol. 11, ed. Lynda Lasswell Crist (Baton Rouge: Louisiana University Press, 2003), 57. The original letter is in the Jefferson Davis Papers, War Records Office, National Archives, Washington, D.C., Record

Group 109. Bledsoe expressed that same sense of gratitude after the war, noting that Tremlett "did more for Confederates in London, and for the Confederate cause itself, as well as made greater sacrifices of time and money, than any other man in England, or in Europe. The South and the friends of the South owed him and his household a debt of gratitude that the wealth of worlds could not adequately discharge." Albert Taylor Bledsoe, "The Sumter and Alabama—Admiral Semmes," *Southern Review* 5 (January 1869): 229. Bledsoe also referred to Francis William Tremlett and his sister Louisa A. Tremlett in his Memorandum Book as "the best friends of the Confederates in London." Bledsoe, Memorandum Book, entry 27.

39. The names of Bledsoe and McHenry appear as new members under the date of December 1, 1863, in *Journal of Anthropological Society of London* 2 (1864): xxiii. A cozy relationship existed between Hotze and the president of the society, James Hunt. Anthropology and racism made common cause in Hunt's paper "On the Negro's Place in Nature," which he read before the Anthropological Society of London on November 17, 1863. The most complete discussions of Hotze's views on slavery and race are Lonnie A. Burnett, ed., *Henry Hotze, Confederate Propagandist: Selected Writings on Revolution, Recognition, and Race* (Tuscaloosa: University of Alabama Press, 2008), and Robert E. Bonner, "Slavery, Confederate Diplomacy, and the Racialist Mission of Henry Hotze," *Civil War History* 51 (September 2005): 288–316.

40. George McHenry, *The Cotton Trade: Its Bearing upon the Prosperity of Great Britain and Commerce of the American Republics, Considered in Connection with the System of Negro Slavery in the Confederate States* (London: Saunders, Otley and Co., 1863). See also McHenry, *The African Race in America, North and South: Being Correspondence between Two Pennsylvanians* (London: Bradbury and Evans, 1861).

41. Bledsoe to Jefferson Davis, London, September 21, 1864, in Crist, *Papers of Jefferson Davis,* 11:57. There are letters from McHenry to Hotze in the Henry Hotze Papers, MS 26534, MDLC.

42. Bledsoe, Memorandum Book, entries 38, 40; "News in Brief—Bishop Polk," London *Times,* July 8, 1864, 12; "Death of Lieutenant-General Polk," London *Times,* July 30, 1864, 5. An account of the circumstances in which Polk accepted his military commission appeared in "The Late Bishop Polk," *Index,* September 15, 1864, 581.

43. Reverend Stephen Elliott, *Funeral Services at the Burial of the Right Rev. Leonidas Polk, D.D. Together with the Sermon Delivered in St. Paul's Church, Augusta, Ga., on June 29, 1864: Being the Feast of St. Peter the Apostle* (Columbia, SC: Printed by Evans and Cogswell, 1864), 26. Stephen Elliot was the Episcopal bishop of the Diocese of Georgia and senior bishop of the Episcopal Church in the Confederate States of America. Bledsoe regarded Elliott's tribute to their mutual friend to be one of the most moving and beautiful things ever written in the English language. And Bledsoe said of Elliott that a "nobler" or "purer spirit" had seldom, if ever, lived. Bledsoe, Memorandum Book, entries 9, 10. An excellent account of Polk's significance as a religious leader and his place within collective memory about the war is Glenn Robins, *The Bishop of the Old South: The Ministry and Civil War Legacy of Leonidas Polk* (Macon, GA: Mercer University Press, 2006).

44. Bledsoe to the editor, August 13, 1864, "North or South?" *Evening Herald,* August 15, 1864, 7; reprinted as [Albert Taylor Bledsoe], "President Barnard, of Columbia College. A Curious Statement by the Rebel Ex-Secretary of War," *New York Times,* August 30, 1864, 2, col. 2.

45. [Bledsoe], "President Barnard, of Columbia College," 2, col. 2. Marcus Atilius Regulus was a Roman general and consul during the First Punic War (264–241 BC). After a series of successes he was defeated at the Battle of Tunis and taken prisoner by the Carthaginians. According to tradition, his captors released him and sent him to Rome as a special envoy to negotiate either a peace

settlement or an exchange of prisoners. After his arrival, however, Regulus urged the Roman Senate to reject both proposals and continue the war. Against the advice of his friends, he honored his promise to return to Carthage as a prisoner of war, whereupon he was summarily executed. Romans esteemed Regulus as a man of honor and patriotism. Bledsoe's allusion to Regulus was to suggest that Barnard was entirely lacking in those virtues.

46. P. A. T. Barnard to Bledsoe, University of Mississippi, May 14, 1861, as printed in [Bledsoe], "President Barnard, of Columbia College," 2, col. 2.

47. See Frederick A. P. Barnard, *Letter to the President of the United States, by a Refugee* (New York: C. S. Westcott; Philadelphia: J. B. Lippincott and Co., 1863).

48. John Fulton, *Memoirs of Frederick A. P. Barnard . . . , Tenth President of Columbia College in the City of New York* (New York: Published for Columbia University Press by Macmillan and Co., 1896), 292, 298; William J. Chute, *Damn Yankee! The First Career of Frederick A. P. Barnard, Educator, Scientist, and Idealist* (Port Washington, NY: Kennikat Press, National University Publications, 1978), 188.

49. F. A. P. Barnard to the editor of the *New York Times*, New York, August 31, 1864, as printed in "President Barnard—His Position and Opinions," *New York Times*, September 1, 1864, 5.

50. "President Barnard—His Position and Opinions," 5. It should be further noted that Barnard had stated his opposition to secession even earlier in an address delivered in Tuscaloosa, Alabama, on July 4, 1851, in which he argued that southern objections to the admission of California into the Union as a free state were no cause for disunion. See Frederick A. P. Barnard, *No Just Cause for a Dissolution of the Union in Any Thing Which Has Hitherto Happened, but the Union the Only Security for Southern Rights* (Tuscaloosa, AL: Printed by J. W. and J. F. Warren, "Observer Office," 1851).

51. "President Barnard—His Position and Opinions," 5. Bledsoe later renewed his assault on Barnard's character in the *Southern Review*. See Albert Taylor Bledsoe, "Letter from President Barnard, of Columbia College, Regarding the Great [Telescopic] Instrument at the Douglas University," *Southern Review* (July 1869): 233–37. When Barnard published a letter on February 20, 1869, in which he took credit for the invention of the telescopic instrument then in use at Douglas University in Chicago, Bledsoe lashed out at him again. Barnard did not dwell on the fact that he initially had the microscope made for the University of Mississippi during his tenure there as a faculty member and chancellor. Nor did he volunteer the fact that the "Great Instrument," and the great man who made it, had traveled north together when he left the South during the early part of the war.

52. Bledsoe to Jefferson Davis, London, September 21, 1864, Crist, *Papers of Jefferson Davis*, 11:57.

53. Bledsoe, Memorandum Book, entries 38, 41.

54. McIlvaine to "My Dear Friend and Brother," Cincinnati, April 26, 1872, in Albert Taylor Bledsoe, "How and Why I Became a Methodist," *Southern Review* 14 (January 1874): 111.

55. See Kara M. McClurken, "For Love of God and Country: McIlvaine's Mission," *Anglican and Episcopal History* 69 (Annual 2000): 315–47.

56. See McIlvaine to William H. Seward, London, February 21, 1862, Lincoln Papers, ser. 1, General Correspondence, 1833–1916, and in the same series of correspondence McIlvaine to Salmon P. Chase, Cincinnati, July 6, 1863, and McIlvaine to Abraham Lincoln, Cincinnati, July 27, 1863. See also McIlvaine to Salmon P. Chase, Cincinnati, December 21, 1864, Salmon Portland Chase Papers, vol. 94, Historical Society of Pennsylvania, Philadelphia.

57. McIlvaine to Abraham Lincoln, Cincinnati, December 21, 1864, Lincoln Papers, ser. 1, General Correspondence, 1833–1916. The *Jersey City Journal*, February 8, 1930, reported that Harriet "ran the blockade" so she could get clothing material for her children in the North. But it is more

likely that she obtained a pass from Confederate authorities to go north via Harpers Ferry, as indicated in McIlvaine's letter to Lincoln, or with assistance managed to slip through Union lines surreptitiously. There is no evidence that she went north by running the blockade.

58. A. Lincoln, "Pass for Mrs. Harriet C. Bledsoe," January 16, 1865, in *The Collected Works of Abraham Lincoln*, ed. Roy P. Basler, vol. 8 (New Brunswick, NJ: Rutgers University Press, 1953), 218. The printed version of the pass in Basler shows Lincoln's signature *only*. The original pass bearing the signature of Lincoln and Jefferson Davis's signed and dated note to Anna Bledsoe on the verso are in the Letters of Albert Taylor Bledsoe, MS 3461, SCLUV.

CHAPTER NINE

1. Bledsoe's daughter Sophia Bledsoe Herrick says he returned to the United States in January 1866 in "Albert Taylor Bledsoe," *Alumni Bulletin of the University of Virginia* 6 (May 1899): 5, but later says February 1866 in her "Personal Recollections of My Father and Mr. Lincoln and Mr. Davis," *Methodist Quarterly Review* 64 (October 1915): 673, and again in "Albert Taylor Bledsoe, 1809–1877," in *Library of Southern Literature*, vol. 1, ed. Edwin Anderson Alderman and Charles Alphonso Smith (Atlanta: Martin and Hoyt Co., 1929), 396. Sophia appears to have corrected herself in the two later accounts, which both agree that February was the month of her father's return. The list of passenger arrivals in the *New York Times* for February 10, 1866, confirms it. The list shows that a "T. Bledsoe" arrived in New York from Liverpool on the steamship *Australasian* on February 9, 1866. "Passengers Arrived," *New York Times*, February 10, 1866, 8. Bledsoe's granddaughter Louise Herrick Wall gives the date of his loyalty oath as June 27, 1866, in Wall to [Emily] Wayland Dinwiddie, February 27, 1934, Dinwiddie Family Papers, 1846–1937, MS 2808, SCLUV.

2. Bledsoe, "Memorandum Book," entries 7, 58.

3. The state of Davis's health was one of the issues connected with his continuing imprisonment. See Harris D. Riley Jr., "Jefferson Davis and His Health. Part II: January, 1861–December, 1889," *Journal of Mississippi History* 49 (1987): 261–87.

4. The granting of those privileges is acknowledged in the legal proceedings against Davis known as the *United States v. Jefferson Davis*, Case No. 3,621a, Circuit Court, District of Virginia, 7 F., Case 63.

5. Bledsoe to David Maulden Perine, Greenwood Depot, Albemarle County, Virginia, August 9, 1866, the Perine Family Papers, MS 645, Maryland Historical Society, Baltimore. The letter is unsigned but written in Bledsoe's unmistakable hand and style. The envelope in which Perine received the letter, moreover, bears his own notation: "From Dr. Bledsoe." Internal evidence further confirms that Bledsoe was the author of the unsigned letter. It was written at Greenwood Depot in Albemarle County, Virginia, where Bledsoe and his family were then living, and discusses the work on secession he intended to publish in Baltimore that fall. What previous relationship existed between Perine and Bledsoe is uncertain, but he was clearly someone whom Bledsoe trusted. All quotes in the next paragraph are from this letter.

6. Bledsoe again said that Davis pleaded with him to publish the book the soonest possible in Bledsoe, Memorandum Book, entry 44, and Albert Taylor Bledsoe, "Miscellany: The Biography of a Book," *Southern Review* 19 (January 1876): 252.

7. Albert Taylor Bledsoe, *Is Davis a Traitor; Or Was Secession a Constitutional Right Previous to the War of 1861?* (Baltimore: Printed for the Author, by Innes and Co., 1866). Bookstores in Baltimore

sold the work at a $1.50 a copy. Copies were also available through J. B. Lippincott and Company in Philadelphia and A. D. Appleton in New York. Advertisement, *Southern Review* 1 (January 1867): x.

8. Bledsoe, *Is Davis a Traitor?* v–vi. See David R. Goldfield, *Still Fighting the Civil War: The American South and Southern History* (Baton Rouge: Louisiana State University Press, 2002).

9. Bledsoe, *Is Davis a Traitor?* 4–5. Bledsoe's description of Jackson, Johnston, Lee, and Davis as the "imperishable jewels" of the South is a reference to the famed statement attributed to the Roman matron Cornelia Scipionis Africana (ca. 190–100 BC). When Cornelia, the mother of Tiberius and Gaius Gracchus, was once asked about her wealth and jewels, she is reputed to have pointed to her two sons and said: "These are my jewels." It was a classical allusion that resonated with veterans of both the Confederate and the Union armies.

10. Emmerich de Vattel, *Law of Nations or the Principles of Natural Law*, 3, as cited in Bledsoe, *Is Davis a Traitor?* 131. Vattel's *Law of Nations* appeared in many American editions, which makes it difficult to know which one Bledsoe cited. It was possibly *The Law of Nations; or, Principles of the Law of Nature, Applied to the Conduct and Affairs of Nations and Sovereigns*, with additional notes and reference, by Edward D. Ingraham, Esq. (Philadelphia: T & J. W. Johnson, 1852). Other editions by Ingraham appeared in 1853, 1855, and 1859. St. George Tucker also cited Vattel in note D of the appendix to the first volume of his *Blackstone's Commentaries: With Notes of Reference* (Philadelphia: William Young Birch and Abraham Small, 1803). Vattel was Tucker's authority for his discussion of the nature of the U.S. Constitution and the manner of its adoption.

11. The quotes appearing in this paragraph and the next are from Davis, *Is Davis a Traitor?* 122, 170–71.

12. Joseph Story, *Commentaries on the Constitution of the United States*, vol. 3 (Boston: Hilliard, Gray, and Co.; Cambridge, MA: Brown, Shattuck, and Co., 1833), 287; Bledsoe, *Is Davis a Traitor?* 6.

13. The quotes in this paragraph and the next are from John Lothrop Motley in *The Rebellion Record: A Diary of American Events, with Documents, Narratives, Illustrative Incidents, Poetry, etc.*, vol. 1, ed. Frank Moore (New York: G. P. Putnam, 1861), 211, 214; Bledsoe, *Is Davis a Traitor?* 6–7.

14. Daniel Webster, *Speech of Mr. Webster, in the Senate, in Reply to Mr. Calhoun's Speech, on the Bill "Further to Provide for the Collection of Duties on Imports," Delivered on the 16th of February, 1833* (Washington, DC: Gales and Seaton, 1833), 3, 6–10; Bledsoe, *Is Davis a Traitor?* 11.

15. Bledsoe, *Is Davis a Traitor?* 12–14.

16. Bledsoe's analysis of the meaning of the preamble in this paragraph and the next is from Bledsoe, *Is Davis a Traitor?* 59, 59n; Albert Taylor Bledsoe, "Secession," *Evening Herald*, January 26, 1865, 2, 2n.

17. Webster, *Speech of Mr. Webster, in the Senate, in Reply to Mr. Calhoun's Speech*, 21; Daniel Webster, "Presentation of a Vase," in *The Works of Daniel Webster*, vol. 1 (Boston: C. C. Little and J. Brown, 1851), 331; Bledsoe, *Is Davis A Traitor?* 94.

18. Webster, *Works*, 2:318, 5:347; Bledsoe, *Is Davis A Traitor?* 95–97, 102.

19. Bledsoe, *Is Davis a Traitor?* 256–57. Bledsoe later reduced the grounds of secession or causes of the war from eight to six. See Albert Taylor Bledsoe, "Alexander H. Stephens on the War," *Southern Review* 4 (October 1868): 264–65.

20. Carl Schurz, *The Reminiscences of Carl Schurz*, vol. 3 (Garden City, NY: Doubleday, Page, and Co., 1917), 144.

21. "Is Davis a Traitor; Or Was Secession a Constitutional Right Previous to 1861?" *Baltimore Gazette*, October 23, 1866, no pagination.

22. Bledsoe, "Miscellany: The Biography of a Book," 252; Albert Taylor Bledsoe, "Notices of Books," *Southern Review* 20 (July 1876): 222.

23. Herrick, "Albert Taylor Bledsoe," *Alumni Bulletin of the University of Virginia*, 5. Similar statements appear in Herrick, "Personal Recollections of My Father," 673, and "Albert Taylor Bledsoe, 1809–1877," 396.

24. Armistead Churchill Gordon, *Memoirs and Memorials of William Gordon McCabe*, vol. 1 (Richmond, VA: Old Dominion Press, 1925), 70.

25. Edwin Mims, "Albert Taylor Bledsoe," in *Dictionary of American Biography*, vol. 2, ed. Allen Johnston (New York: Charles Scribner's Sons, 1929), 364; David Rankin Barbee, "Bishop Charles Pettit McIlvaine," *Southern Churchman*, September 10, 1932, 13; Harry E. Pratt, "Albert Taylor Bledsoe: Critic of Lincoln," *Transactions of the Illinois State Historical Society*, no. 41 (1934): 167; Richard M. Weaver, "Albert Taylor Bledsoe," *Sewanee Review* 52 (January–March 1944): 40; E. Merton Coulter, *The South during Reconstruction, 1865–1877*, vol. 8 of *A History of the South*, ed. Wendell Holmes Stephenson and E. Merton Coulter (Baton Rouge: Louisiana State University Press and the Littlefield Fund for Southern History of the University of Texas, 1947), 176.

26. John Boyce Bennett, "Albert Taylor Bledsoe: Social and Religious Controversialist of the Old South" (Ph.D. diss., Duke University, 1942), 45; Steven E. Woodworth, "Albert Taylor Bledsoe," in *American National Biography*, vol. 3, ed. John A. Garraty and Mark C. Carnes (New York: Oxford University Press, 1999), 12.

27. Samuel Augustus Steel, "Albert Taylor Bledsoe: Sometime Editor of this Review," *Methodist Quarterly Review* 64 (April 1915): 215–16, and *Eminent Men I Met along the Sunny Road* (Nashville, TN: Cokesbury Press, 1925), 30, 31, 37. A statement of Steel's own views on the causes of secession and war is his brief but pithy *The South Was Right* (Columbia, SC: R. L. Bryan Co., 1914), which he wrote primarily for students in schools and colleges. The work is written within the Confederate tradition of the war and the Bledsoean mold. "Northern writers have never understood our side, and even when disposed to be friendly, are incapable of interpreting our motives" ([3]).

28. Bledsoe, Memorandum Book, entry 44.

29. Bledsoe, Memorandum Book, entry 44.

30. The political, constitutional, and legal issues involved in the case are examined in Eberhard P. Deutsch, "United States v. Jefferson Davis: Constitutional Issues in the Trial for Treason," *American Bar Association Journal* 52 (February 1966): 139–45, and 52 (March 1966), 263–68; Roy Franklin Nichols, "United States vs. Jefferson Davis, 1865–1869," *American Historical Review* 31 (January 1926): 266–84; David K. Watson, "The Trial of Jefferson Davis: An Interesting Constitutional Question," *Yale Law Journal* 24 (June 1915): 669–76; and Charles M. Blackford, *The Trial and Trials of Jefferson Davis* (Lynchburg, VA: J. P. Bell Co., 1901), a paper read before the twelfth annual meeting of the Virginia State Bar Association in July 1900. Blackford's paper is reprinted under the same title in *Southern Historical Papers* 29 (January–December 1901): 45–81. The court record of the case is reprinted in Dunbar Rowland, ed., *Jefferson Davis Constitutionalist: His Letters, Papers, and Speeches*, vol. 7 (Jackson: Mississippi Department of Archives and History, 1923), 138–227. Davis's year-and-a-half imprisonment and the government's legal proceedings against him are also discussed in Varina Davis, *Jefferson Davis: Ex-President of the Confederate States of America. A Memoir by His Wife*, vol. 2 (New York: Belford Co., 1890), 631–735, 800–802.

31. Albert [Taylor] Bledsoe, *Is Secession Treason?* ed. Paul Dennis Sporer (Chester, NY: Anza Publishing, Quanterness Press, 2005), I.

32. Schurz, *Reminiscences*, 3:144.

33. Bledsoe, "Miscellany: The Biography of a Book," 252.

34. [Bernard J. Sage], *The Republic of Republics: Or, American Federal Liberty, by P. C. Centz, Barrister*, 4th ed. (Boston: Little, Brown, and Co., 1881). Sage's pseudonym in the title, "P. C. Centz, Barrister," was a pun on "Public Common Sense."

35. Jefferson Davis, *Rise and Fall of the Confederate Government*, vol. 1 (New York: D. Appleton and Co., 1881), 97n; Jefferson Davis to Harry F. Barrell, Beauvoir, Mississippi, January 31, 1887, Jefferson Davis Papers, SCLDU.

36. Gaines M. Foster, *Ghosts of the Confederacy: Defeat, the Lost Cause, and the Emerging South, 1865 to 1913* (New York: Oxford University Press, 1987), 117, 158; Albert Taylor Bledsoe, *Is Davis a Traitor; Or Was Secession a Constitutional Right Previous to the War of 1861?* (Richmond, VA: Hermitage Press, 1907).

37. Albert Taylor Bledsoe, *The War between the States, or Was Secession a Constitutional Right Previous to the War of 1861–1865* (Lynchburg, VA: J. P. Bell Co., 1915). The edition bears the copyright of the Danville Chapter of the United Daughters of the Confederacy. *The War between the States* has an "Explanatory Preface" by Sophia and different pagination and omits a few sections of the original edition published in 1866. The assistance she received from her brother-in-law William Dinwiddie in preparing the 1915 edition of the work is acknowledged in Herrick, "Personal Recollections of My Father," 674n, although Dinwiddie's help is not credited in the volume itself. The statement that *The War between the States* was being endorsed as a recommended reference book for high school libraries also appears in Sophia's "Personal Recollections of My Father," 674n.

38. Bledsoe, *Is Secession Treason?* Sporer's unabridged edition modifies Bledsoe's chapter titles and pagination, converts his footnotes to endnotes (with corrections), and includes an index absent in the original edition.

39. Richard M. Weaver, "Albert Taylor Bledsoe," *Sewanee Review* 52 (January–March 1944): 38–39; Douglas Southall Freeman, *The South to Posterity: An Introduction to the Writing of Confederate History* (New York: Charles Scribner's Sons, 1951), 33, 34, 49. Willard Murrell Hays seconded Weaver's opinion, noting that *Is Davis a Traitor?* is based on more thorough scholarship and legal knowledge than that exhibited in the better-known works of Stephens and Davis. Willard Murrell Hays, "Polemics and Philosophy: A Biography of Albert Taylor Bledsoe" (Ph.D. diss., University of Tennessee, 1971), 478.

40. Foster, *Ghosts of the Confederacy*, 49; Charles Reagan Wilson, *Baptized in Blood: The Religion of the Lost Cause, 1865–1920* (Athens: University of Georgia Press, 1980), 141. On Pollard, see Jack P. Maddex Jr., *The Reconstruction of Edward A. Pollard: A Rebel's Conversion to Postbellum Unionism* (Chapel Hill: University of North Carolina Press, 1974).

41. Albert Taylor Bledsoe, "Davis and Lee," *Southern Review* 2 (July 1867): 242, and "General Albert Sidney Johnston," *Southern Review* 11 (January 1872): 78.

42. Albert Taylor Bledsoe, "Notices of Books," *Southern Review* 20 (July 1876): 222–23.

43. Wilson, *Baptized in Blood*, 80.

CHAPTER TEN

1. Robert E. Lee to Bledsoe, Lexington, Virginia, October 8, 1866, Robert E. Lee Papers, accession #3461, box 2, Special Collections, University of Virginia Libraries. Lee was responding to

a letter received from Bledsoe on August 27, 1866. A copy of Lee's letter is in the Letters of Albert Taylor Bledsoe, MS 3461, SCLUV. The prospectus for the *Southern Review* appeared in "Literariana. American," *Roundtable*, December 8, 1866, 312 and elsewhere.

2. Bledsoe, Memorandum Book, entry 8; R. H. Wilmer to Bledsoe, Mobile, Alabama, November 13, 1866, Letters of Albert Taylor Bledsoe, MS 3461, SCLUV.

3. See Gaines M. Foster, "The Legacy of Confederate Defeat," in *A Companion to the Civil War and Reconstruction*, ed. Lacy K. Ford (Malden, MA: Blackwell Publishing, 2005), 423–46; Gaines M. Foster, *Ghosts of the Confederacy: Defeat, the Lost Cause, and the Emerging South, 1865 to 1913* (New York: Oxford University Press, 1987); Charles Reagan Wilson, *Baptized in Blood: The Religion of the Lost Cause, 1865–1920* (Athens: University of Georgia Press, 1980); and Rollin G. Osterweis, *The Myth of the Lost Cause, 1865–1900* (Hamden, CT: Archon Books, 1973). The reactions of southern white Christians to the Confederate defeat are also examined in Daniel W. Stowell, *Rebuilding Zion: The Religious Reconstruction, 1863–1877* (New York: Oxford University Press, 2001), and Eugene D. Genovese, *A Consuming Fire: The Fall of the Confederacy in the Mind of the White Christian South* (Athens: University of Georgia Press, 1998).

4. Edwin Mims, "Southern Magazines," in *The South in the Building of the Nation*, vol. 7, *History of the Literary and Intellectual Life of the South*, ed. John Bell Henneman (Richmond, VA: Southern Historical Publication Society, 1909), 457.

5. Albert Taylor Bledsoe, "Biographical Notice," in Charles Wells Russell, *Roebuck; A Novel, by the Late Hon. Charles Wells Russell, with A Biographical Notice of the Author, by Prof. A. T. Bledsoe* (Baltimore: Henry Taylor and Co., 1868), iii. Russell, whose law office was on St. Paul Street in Baltimore, was an anonymous contributor to the *Southern Review* before his death on November 22, 1867. Bledsoe stated his intention of preparing an account of Russell's life and writings but never completed the project. He did, however, express his admiration of Russell's character in an obituary that appeared in the *Baltimore Gazette*, November 30, 1867, 1, which he reprinted in the *Southern Review*. See Albert Taylor Bledsoe, "Book Notices. Roebuck," *Southern Review* 3 (April 1868): 507–8.

6. Basil Gildersleeve in James Wilson Bright, "In Memoriam. William Hand Browne, 1828–1912," *Johns Hopkins University Circular*, no. 2, n.s. (February 1913): 19.

7. Albert Taylor Bledsoe and William Hand Browne, Baltimore, January 1, 1867, "The Southern Review," *Southern Review* 1 (January 1867): [258], back cover. The editors expressed their "cordial thanks" to northern friends who assisted them by contributing valuable articles in Albert Taylor Bledsoe and William Hand Browne, January 1, 1868, "The Southern Review," ibid. 3 (January 1868): [250], back cover.

8. Bright, "In Memoriam. William Hand Browne," 6, 6n4, 9; William F. Messner, "Southern Magazine, 1868–1875," in *The Conservative Press in Eighteenth- and Nineteenth-Century America*, ed. Ronald Lora and William Henry Longton (Westport, CT: Greenwood Press, 1999), 268; Albert Taylor Bledsoe, "Notices of Books," *Southern Review* 6 (July 1869): 247n; "Collegiate Institute for Young Ladies," advertisement, *Southern Review* 6 (July 1869): x; "Cambridge Military Academy," advertisement, *Southern Review* 2 (October 1867): xviii; Albert Taylor Bledsoe, "The First Eight Volumes of the Southern Review. From January 1867 to January 1871," *Southern Review* 8 (October 1870): 419.

9. Browne to Paul Hamilton Hayne, Baltimore, November 4, 1870, September 11, 1871, Hayne Papers, SCLDU. It should not be supposed in light of Browne's statement that Bledsoe was altogether friendless despite his irascible nature. The Baltimore schoolteacher Thomas Eldridge Ayres,

Sr (1847–74) counted himself among Bledsoe's friends. Ayres was a former student at the University of Virginia. He enlisted in Colonel Henry C. Cabell's Artillery Battalion of the Army of Northern Virginia in June 1863, serving as a private in the First Richmond Howitzers. After the war he moved to Baltimore, where he taught at George Gibson Carey's School for Boys and became an ordained Methodist minister in July 1872. Ayres wrote about his friendship with Bledsoe and members of his family in the entries of his diary. See Thomas Eldridge Ayres, Diary, 1870–71, MS 2581, mimeographed typescript, Special Collections, Maryland Historical Society Library, Baltimore. John Ayres Greenlee of Fairfax Station, Virginia, made the typescript of the diary in 1982. The original Ayres diary for 1870–71—and the originals of two additional volumes for January 1872–August 1874—are in the possession of Paul Richard White Sr. of Nashville, Tennessee. I am indebted to John Ayres Greenlee for information about the Ayres diary and his friendship with Bledsoe.

10. James Wood Davidson, *The Living Writers of the South* (New York: George W. Carleton; London: S. Low, Son, and Co., 1869), 52.

11. Albert Taylor Bledsoe, "Draper's History of the War," *Southern Review* 3 (January 1868): 41, and "School Histories of the United States," ibid. 3 (January 1868): 155. See also Albert Taylor Bledsoe, "The New America of Mr. Dixon," ibid. 1 (April 1867): 462–93.

12. Albert Taylor Bledsoe, "Davis and Lee," *Southern Review* 2 (July 1867): 231–42.

13. Albert Taylor Bledsoe, "Alexander H. Stephens on the War," *Southern Review* 4 (October 1868): 249–300.

14. Richard Malcolm Johnston and William Hand Browne, *Life of Alexander H. Stephens* (Philadelphia: J. B. Lippincott and Co., 1878), 495.

15. Bledsoe, "Alexander H. Stephens on the War," 260.

16. Albert Taylor Bledsoe, "The Origin of the Late War," *Southern Review* 1 (April 1867): 259.

17. Bledsoe, "Alexander H. Stephens on the War," 270.

18. Stephens to Johnston, n.p., n.d. [October 1868], as cited in Johnston and Browne, *Life of Alexander H. Stephens*, 495–96.

19. Alexander H. Stephens, *The Reviewers Reviewed; A Supplement to the "War between the States," etc., with an Appendix in Review of "Reconstruction," So Called* (New York: D. Appleton and Co., 1872). 12–17. Stephens's publisher printed his reply to Bledsoe as a pamphlet after it originally appeared in the *Baltimore Leader*. See Alexander H. Stephens, *The Reviewer Reviewed. Reply of Hon. Alexander H. Stephens to the Baltimore Leader's Notice of the "Review" of the "War Between the States, etc." by Albert Taylor Bledsoe, LL.D.* (Philadelphia: National Publishing Co., 1868).

20. Linton Stephens to Alexander H. Stephens, Sparta, Georgia, December 18, 1868, and Mrs. Slater to Alexander H. Stephens, n.p., n.d. [June, 1870], Alexander H. Stephens Papers, Brady Memorial Library, Manhattanville College, Purchase, New York. The letter from Mrs. Slater quoting the opinion of Severn Teackle Wallis is enclosed in a letter from Linton Stephens to Alexander H. Stephens written in Sparta, Georgia, and is dated June 10, 1870.

21. Stephens, *Reviewers Reviewed* (1872), 22; A. T. Bledsoe to the Editors of the Statesman, "Dr. Bledsoe's Reply to Mr. Stephens," as reprinted in "Hon. A. H. Stephens on the Late War," *Southern Review* 11 (July 1872): 148.

22. Bledsoe's name appears in an appendix to volume 2 of Stephen's work as the assistant secretary of war for the Confederacy in 1862, but his constitutional defense of the right of secession is passed over in silence. Alexander H. Stephens, *A Constitutional View of the Late War between the States; It Causes, Character, Conduct, and Results*, vol. 2 (Philadelphia: National Publishing Co., 1870), 760.

23. Bledsoe to Jefferson Davis, Baltimore, April 26, 1870, Jefferson Davis Family Collection, box 4, BLMC; Bledsoe, "Biographical Notice," in Russell, *Roebuck*, x. Scathing indictments of Republican rule appear in "The Legal Status of the Southern States," *Southern Review* 1 (January 1867): 70–95, and "Imprisonment of Davis," in the same issue, 233–55. Authorship of these unsigned articles is sometimes ascribed to Bledsoe. Internal and external evidence, however, does not entirely warrant the attribution, even though he most certainly agreed with the views expressed by the respective contributors. The writer of the "Imprisonment of Davis," if not Bledsoe, was possibly the Baltimore attorney Severn Teackle Wallis. That, at least, was the opinion of William B. Reed of Philadelphia, one of Davis's defense attorneys and himself an anonymous contributor to the first number of the *Southern Review*. As Reed said of the article and its unknown author, "It is very spirited. From certain earmarks, I think tho' I do not know, it is by S. T. Wallis." William B. Reed to Burton N. Harrison, Philadelphia, January 6, 1867, in Dunbar Rowland, ed., *Jefferson Davis, Constitutionalist: His Letters, Papers, and Speeches*, vol. 7 (Jackson: Mississippi Department of Archives and History, 1923), 86.

24. See Michael Davis, *The Image of Lincoln in the South* (Knoxville: University of Tennessee Press, 1971), especially chap. 4, "Lincoln and the Lost Cause," 105–34.

25. Ward H. Lamon, *The Life of Abraham Lincoln, from His Birth to His Inauguration as President* (Boston: James R. Osgood and Co., 1872); Albert Taylor Bledsoe, "Lamon's Life of Lincoln," *Southern Review* 12 (April 1873): 328–68. Lamon's *Life of Abraham Lincoln* was ghostwritten by Chauncey F. Black.

26. The quotes in this paragraph and the next are from Bledsoe, "Lamon's Life of Lincoln," 328. Critical appraisals of the sources of information on Lincoln's early life are Douglas L. Wilson and Rodney O. Davis, eds., with the assistance of Terry Wilson, *Herndon's Informants: Letters, Interviews, and Statements about Lincoln* (Urbana: University of Illinois Press, 1998), and Douglas L. Wilson and Rodney O. Davis, eds., *Herndon's Lincoln* (Galesburg, IL: Knox College Lincoln Studies Center; Urbana: University of Illinois, 2006). See also Douglas L. Wilson, *Honor's Voice: The Transformation of Abraham Lincoln* (New York: Alfred A. Knopf, 1998), which separates fact from fiction during the period of Lincoln's life from 1831 to 1842.

27. Bledsoe, "Lamon's Life of Lincoln," 360–61.

28. Bledsoe, "Lamon's Life of Lincoln," 364.

29. Bledsoe, "First Eight Volumes of the Southern Review," 420, 440; Browne to Paul Hamilton Hayne, Baltimore, August 18, 1871, Hayne Papers, SCLDU.

30. Bledsoe, "First Eight Volumes of the Southern Review," 442; Albert Taylor Bledsoe, "Miscellany, Business Notices," *Southern Review* 18 (April 1876): 494, and "Miscellany. One More Appeal," *Southern Review* 20 (October 1876): 495; William Hand Browne to Paul Hayne, Baltimore, July 11, 1870, Hayne Papers, SCLDU.

31. Bledsoe, "First Eight Volumes of the Southern Review," 441.

32. "Louisa School for Young Ladies," advertisement, *Southern Review* 4 (October 1868): x; ibid. 5 (April 1869): v; "Biographical Notes and Memos," Emily Wayland Dinwiddie Materials, MS 5:9 D6195:1, VHS. The Louisa School changed its name to the Collegiate Institute for Young Ladies sometime between April and July 1869. The following year the name changed again to Bledsoe's Collegiate Institute for Young Ladies, with Bledsoe as the principal and Sophia as the vice principal. "Collegiate Institute for Young Ladies," advertisement, *Southern Review* 6 (July 1869): x; "Bledsoe's Collegiate Institute for Young Ladies," advertisement, *Southern Review* 7 (January 1870): i; 8 (July 1870): i; 9 (April 1871): ii. I am indebted to Rebecca Starr at the University of Gloucester,

who is currently writing a biography of Sophia Bledsoe Herrick, for information about the Louisa School for Young Ladies in Baltimore. Personal communication, e-mail, Rebecca Starr to author, January 7, 2007.

33. Paul Hamilton Hayne to Margaret Junkin Preston, January 16, 1873, Hayne Papers, SCLDU; George Frederick Holmes, "Diary, 1873," entry for August 23, 1873, Holmes Papers.

34. Bledsoe, "First Eight Volumes of the Southern Review," 421, 422.

35. Lamar to Bledsoe, Memphis, May 29 and 30, 1870, Letters of Albert Taylor Bledsoe, MS 3461, SCLUV. A photostatic copy of this letter is in the Papers of James Dodson Barbee and David Rankin Barbee, box 9, MDLC.

36. Bledsoe, "First Eight Volumes of the Southern Review," 426; "Religious News and Gossip," *New York Times,* December 25, 1870, 5; Sophia Bledsoe Herrick, "Personal Recollections of My Father and Mr. Lincoln and Mr. Davis," *Methodist Quarterly Review* 64 (October 1915): 667.

37. A surviving specimen of Bledsoe's orations at the pulpit is Albert Taylor Bledsoe, "The Sun of Righteousness: A Sermon," *Southern Review* 19 (January 1876): 164–81. "But unto you that fear my name, shall the Sun of Righteousness arise with healing in his wings" (Malachi 4:2).

38. Bledsoe, "First Eight Volumes of the Southern Review," 422, 430–31; Browne to Paul Hamilton Hayne, Baltimore, July 11, 1870, Hayne Papers, SCLDU.

39. The quotes in this paragraph and the next are from Bledsoe, "Notices of Books," *Southern Review* 12 (April 1873): 497–98, 502. The quote regarding Lee's last words to Bledsoe appears on p. 502. Bledsoe made the same declaration regarding Lee's charge to him in Bledsoe to William Wilson Corcoran, Baltimore, December 3, 1872, Corcoran Papers, vol. 19, MDLC.

40. Albert Taylor Bledsoe, "History of the Late War," *Southern Review* 19 (January 1876): 1–47. See also his earlier writings on the subject in the *Southern Review:* "Origin of the Late War," 257–73; "The North and the South," 2 (July 1867): 122–46; "The North and the South in the Convention of 1787," 2 (October 1867), 358–87; and "The Legislation of 1787," 11 (April 1872): 249–72. Of related interest is "De Tocqueville and the Sovereignty of the People," 1 (April 1867): 302–52, and "New England and Secession," 9 (January 1871): 95–123.

41. There are many unanswered questions regarding Bledsoe's projected two-volume "History of the Late War" and why he never completed it. What appears to be the best explanation is that time simply ran out on him. See Bledsoe to Jefferson Davis, Baltimore, April 14, 1872, Jefferson Davis Family Collection, box 4, BLMC; Bledsoe to William Wilson Corcoran, Baltimore, December 3, 1872, Corcoran Papers, vol. 19, MDLC; "A Few Words to Our Readers," *Southern Review* 18 (October 1875): 493; and Sophia Bledsoe Herrick, "Albert Taylor Bledsoe, 1809–1877," in *Library of Southern Literature,* vol. 1, ed. Edwin Anderson Alderman and Charles Alphonso Smith (Atlanta: Martin and Hoyt Co., 1929), 397–98.

42. A. T. Bledsoe, "Notice," *Southern Review* 16 (January 1875): 243–44; Bledsoe to Harriet Coxe Bledsoe, Alexandria, Virginia, September 24, [1875], Bledsoe-Herrick Family Papers, MC 290, SLHU; Albert Taylor Bledsoe and Sophia Bledsoe Herrick, "A Word to Our Readers," *Southern Review* 17 (April 1875): 491–92.

43. Bledsoe-Herrick Family Papers, MC 290, "Children of Albert Taylor and Harriet (Coxe) Bledsoe," typescript, page 5, SLHU; Rebecca Starr, "'What the Heart Arranged': The Civil War of Sophie Bledsoe Herrick, 1870–1877," in *Ways of Remembering: Revisiting North American Sources and Documents, Canada and the United States,* ed. Roberto Marccarini (Milan: Silene Edizioni, 2006), 65–81. See also Stephen Davis and Robert Pollard III, "Allen C. Redwood and Sophia Bledsoe Herrick: The Discovery of a Secret, Significant Relationship," *Maryland Historical Magazine* 85 (Fall

1990): 256–63. Allen C. Redwood was a former Confederate officer and illustrator of the popular "Battles and Leaders of the Civil War" series that appeared in *Century Magazine* between 1884 and 1887.

44. Sophia Bledsoe Herrick to Paul Hamilton Hayne, Greenwood Depot, Albemarle County, Virginia, July 9, [1877], Hayne Papers, SCLDU: Bledsoe to Jefferson Davis, Baltimore, April 26, 1870, Jefferson Davis Family Collection, box 4, BLMC. Many of Bledsoe's problems at the *Southern Review* were directly attributable to his chronic neglect of correspondence and business concerns, for which he sometimes found it necessary to apologize. See, for instance, Bledsoe to William W. Corcoran, Baltimore, February 23, 1867, Corcoran Papers, vol. 16, MDLC.

45. See Albert Taylor Bledsoe, "Whedon on the Will," *Southern Review* 9 (April 1871): 347–81; "The Reviewers Reviewed" 9 (January 1871): 166–205, and 9 (April 1871), 437–60; and "D. D. Whedon D.D.," 12 (July 1872): 219–24; Rev. C. W. Miller, *The Southern Review and Infant Baptism: Or, Methodist Literature Vindicated against the Attacks of Dr. A. T. Bledsoe* (Nashville, TN: Southern Methodist Publishing House, 1874) and Bledsoe's response in *Infant Baptism: Or, Review of Mr. Miller's "Methodist Literature Vindicated against the Attacks of Dr. A. T. Bledsoe"* (St. Louis: Southwestern Book and Publishing Co., 1875), reprinted from the *Southern Review* for January 1875; "Our Critics," *Southern Review* 18 (October 1875): 444–84; the following articles by Albert Taylor Bledsoe in the *Southern Review:* "An Extraordinary Scene," 22 (July 1877): 219–42; "A Word to Young Believers," 22 (October 1877); 496–97; "Vindication of Our Philosophy," 21 (January 1877): 106–59; and "Plymouth Brethrenism," 21 (April 1877), 254–332; and Sophia Bledsoe Herrick, "Dr. Dabney and Dr. Bledsoe," *Southern Review* 23 (April 1878): 461–78.

46. Albert Taylor Bledsoe, "Christian Theology," *Southern Review* 20 (October 1876): 288–89.

47. Bledsoe, "First Eight Volumes of the Southern Review," 437; Wilbur F. Tillett, "Albert Taylor Bledsoe," *Methodist Quarterly Review,* n.s., 14 (July 1893): 233; Rev. J. M. Hawley, "An Intellectual Giant," *Christian Advocate,* May 7, 1915, 9.

48. John N. Waddel, *Memorials of Academic Life: Being an Historical Sketch of the Waddel Family* (Richmond, VA: Presbyterian Committee of Publication, 1891), 282; Wilbur F. Tillett, "Albert Taylor Bledsoe," *Quarterly Review of the Methodist Episcopal Church, South,* n.s., 14 (July 1893): 241–42; Sophia Bledsoe Herrick, "Personal Recollections of My Father," 679; Bessie W. Dinwiddie to Louise Herrick Wall, February 14, 1934, Dinwiddie Family Papers, 1846–1937, MS 2808, SCLUV; T. V. R. [T. Vernon Rankin] to Harry E. Pratt, University of Virginia, March 6, 1934, Pratt Papers, box 1, folder 4, ALPL.

49. "The Late Dr. Bledsoe," *The State,* Richmond, Virginia, undated press clipping [December 1877], in the A. B. Dinwiddie Scrapbook, Dinwiddie Family Papers, 1846–1937, MS 2808, SCLUV. A copy of the clipping is in the David Rankin Barbee Collection, microfilm 517, 3311, SCLUV.

50. The estimated circulation of three thousand copies is from Sophia Bledsoe Herrick, "Albert Taylor Bledsoe," *Alumni Bulletin of the University of Virginia* 6 (May 1899): 6.

51. L. Q. C. Lamar to Anna Bledsoe, Washington, D.C., March 24, 1890, photostatic copy, Albert Taylor Bledsoe Correspondence in the James D. and David R. Barbee Papers, box 9, MDLC; Robert Underwood Johnson, *Remembered Yesterdays* (Boston: Little, Brown and Co., 1923), 121, 126.

52. Mims, "Southern Magazines," 463–65; Richard M. Weaver, "Albert Taylor Bledsoe," *Sewanee Review* 52 (January–March 1944): 34 and 44. Weaver further commented in the *Southern Tradition at Bay* that Bledsoe was perhaps "the most brilliant of all the Southern apologists. . . . A doctrinaire and perhaps the most perfect intransigent of his age, Bledsoe seemed to thrive on frustration. Opposition and failure only inflamed his curious temper." Richard M. Weaver, *The Southern Tradition*

at Bay: A History of Postbellum Thought, ed. George Core and M. E. Bradford (New Rochelle, NY: Arlington House, 1968), 115.

53. E. Merton Coulter, *The South during Reconstruction, 1865–1877*, vol. 8 of *A History of the South*, ed. Wendell Holmes Stephenson and E. Merton Coulter (Baton Rouge: Louisiana State University Press, 1947), 284–85. For Bledsoe's discourses on the idea of liberty, see Albert Taylor Bledsoe, "John Stuart Mill and Dr. Lieber on Liberty," *Southern Review* 2 (July 1867): 52–86; "The Nature of Civil Liberty," ibid. 3 (January 1868): 251–77; and "What Is Liberty?" ibid. 5 (April 1869): 249–275. See also "The State of Nature," ibid. 4 (July 1868): 125–49.

54. William Henry Longton, "Southern Review, 1867–1879," in *The Conservative Press in Eighteenth- and Nineteenth-Century America*, ed. Ronald Lora and William Longton (Westport, CT: Greenwood Press, 1999), 256; Foster, *Ghosts of the Confederacy*, 49.

55. Paul H. Buck, *The Road to Reunion, 1865–1900* (Boston: Little, Brown and Co., 1937), 55, 200, 222; Wilson, *Baptized in Blood*, 84; Francis Butler Simkins, *The South Old and New: A History, 1820–1947* (New York: Alfred A. Knopf, 1947), 7, 328–29; Francis Butler Simkins, "The Everlasting South," *Journal of Southern History* 13 (August 1947): 313; John Donald Wade, *Selected Essays and Other Writings of John David Wade*, ed. Donald Davidson (Athens: University of Georgia Press, 1966), 83, 152.

56. Albert Taylor Bledsoe, "The Great Error of the Eighteenth Century," *Southern Review* 5 (January 1869): 1–18 and "The Mission of Woman," *Southern Review* 10 (October 1871): 923–42. Bledsoe originally delivered "The Mission of Woman" essay as an annual address before the Lee and Jackson Literary Society of the Wesleyan Female College at Staunton, Virginia, on June 14, 1871. Senator Benjamin R. Tillman of South Carolina reprinted Bledsoe's "The Mission of Woman" article in July 1913 during his opposition to the women's suffrage movement. When several senators objected that the views expressed in Bledsoe's article were insulting to women, they were expunged from the *Congressional Record*. See "Recent Attack on Women," *New York Times*, July 30, 1913, 1, and *The Mission of Women, an Article*, 63rd Cong., 1st sess., 1913, S. Doc. 174 (Washington, DC: Government Printing Office, 1913). See also Albert Taylor Bledsoe, "The Education and Influence of Woman," *Southern Review* 8 (October 1870): 406–19.

57. Albert Taylor Bledsoe, "The Correlation of Reason and Faith," *Southern Review* 11 (January 1872): 1–13; "Modern Atheism," ibid., 120–58; "Philosophy versus Darwinism," ibid. 13 (October 1873): 253–73; and "The Conflict between Religion and Science," ibid. 18 (July 1875): 122–52.

58. Albert Taylor Bledsoe, "The Present Crisis," *Southern Review* 13 (January 1873): 1–2, 12, 39. Bledsoe adopted as the motto of the *Southern Review* the command of Saint Paul given in 1 Thessalonians 5:21 to "Prove all things, and hold fast the good." The maxim appeared on the cover in the original Greek for first time in April 1870.

A NOTE ON SOURCES

1. Bledsoe, Memorandum Book, entry 58. Apart from the letters that Bledsoe either lost or destroyed himself, he is rather vague regarding the fate of others. He said that all the testimonials regarding his *Theodicy*, for example, were either lost or destroyed, "since the enemies of the South and my enemies were placed over that once noble institution [the University of Virginia] by Pierpont [Governor Francis Harrison Pierpont]. "Thank God! They cannot destroy what I have myself written, and what I intend to write." Bledsoe, Memorandum Book, entry 7.

2. Mrs. L. M. Wayland to L. M. Williams, Bayonne, New Jersey, January 9, 1931, the David Rankin Barbee Microfilm Collection of Albert Taylor Bledsoe Materials, microfilm 517, 3311, SCLUV. A transcript of this letter is in box 1, folder 4 of the Harry E. Pratt Papers, ALPL. Mrs. L. M. Wayland was Elizabeth McMurtrie Bledsoe (1846–1933), who went by the name of "Lilly." She married Jeremiah Fink Wayland in Baltimore on July 1, 1870. Lilly's correspondent concerning the whereabouts of her father's papers was Langbourne M. Williams of Richmond, Virginia—a banker, editor of the *Southern Churchman,* publisher of southern history, and an acquaintance of David Rankin Barbee's.

3. Barbee to Harry E. Pratt, Washington, D.C., December 9, 1933, Pratt Papers, box 1, folder 2, ALPL.

4. William Dinwiddie, Dinwiddie Family Papers, 1846–1937, MS 2808, SCLUV.

5. David Rankin Barbee, *An Excursion in Southern History* (Richmond, VA: Langbourne M. Williams, 1928), which originally appeared in the *Asheville (NC) Sunday Citizen* in May 1927. See also Barbee's thirty-three-page "Lincoln's Lost Friends" manuscript [1933], a typescript of which is in box 1, folder 21, of the Harry E. Pratt Papers, ALPL.

6. Examples of Barbee's unreconstructed views are present in David Rankin Barbee, "The Capture of Jefferson Davis," *Tyler's Quarterly Historical and Genealogical Magazine* 29 (July 1947): 6–42; "Dr. Craven's 'Prison Life of Jefferson Davis'—An Exposé," ibid. 32 (April 1951): 282–95; and *An Excursion in Southern History.*

7. Wilbur F. Tillett, "Albert Taylor Bledsoe," *Quarterly Review of the Methodist Episcopal Church, South,* n.s., 14 (July 1893): 231. Tillett doubtless derived his information from Bledsoe's daughter and former coeditor Sophia Bledsoe Herrick.

8. Bledsoe to Harriet Coxe Bledsoe, Lexington, [Kentucky], May 8, 1837, Bledsoe Family Papers, MS 3461-a, SCLUV; [Albert Taylor Bledsoe], "Lord Brougham's Natural Theology," *New-York Review* 1 (October 1837): 298–336; reprinted in *Southern Review* 19 (April 1876): 363–406. Bledsoe's review is of Lord Henry Brougham, *A Discourse of Natural Theology, Showing the Nature of the Evidence and the Advantages of the Study* (Philadelphia: Carey, Lea and Blanchard, 1835).

9. Bledsoe to George W. Cullum, University of Mississippi, May 15, 1850, Register of Graduates, No. 602, George W. Cullum Files, United States Military Academy Archives, West Point, New York.

10. A more complete listing of Bledsoe's contributions to the *Southern Review* is found in the bibliography of John Boyce Bennett, "Albert Taylor Bledsoe: Social and Religious Controversialist of the Old South" (Ph.D. diss., Duke University, 1942). Yet in some instances Bennett attributes authorship of articles to Bledsoe in the *Southern Review* upon what seems to me to be insufficient grounds.

INDEX

Abbott, M. P., 120

abolitionism: ATB's attempt to discredit the egalitarian principles of, 3, 75, 76, 84, 110, 117, 125, 127; ATB's depiction of the cause of immediate abolitionism as "a despotic and lawless power," 77, 233n7; ATB possibly open to the idea of, 80; dread of immediate abolition, 77, 79–80, 93–94; gradual abolition, Henry Clay's proposal for in Kentucky, 34

Acts 17:26, 83

Address Delivered at the University of Mississippi (1849) by ATB, 42, 43–45

Address to the People of Illinois (1843) by A. Lincoln, S. T. Logan, and A. T. Bledsoe, 22, 28

"African Chief, The" (1792), 89

African colonization, 96, 116

African race: alleged inferiority of, 82–83, 107; degraded condition of justified by ATB, 79, 124; racial theories regarding, 82, 111; social constructions of the, 81, 82

Alabama, Confederate sloop, 161

Ambrose, Douglas, 5

American Antislavery Society, 76

American Civil War: ATB on the causes of, 146–47, 155–59; ATB's unfinished history of, 211; early histories of, 191; legacy of for white southerners, 209; place of within collective memory, 6, 7, 171

American federalism: ambiguities of regarding slavery, 98–99, 135; antagonistic theories of, 5, 47, 48–49, 160; divergence of opinions regarding the origin and nature of the American Union, 175, 192

American Revolution, 26–27

"American System," 28, 156

American Whig Party, 11, 22, 24–25; and the slavery issue, 32–34

Anthropology Society of London, 162

antiegalitarianism, 80–82, 83, 84, 147–48, 208

Apollo Belvidere analogy, 81, 234n16

Archimedes, geometry problem of, 12–13, 220n9

Argus of Western America, The, 10, 219n1

Argyll, Duke of (George Douglas Campbell), 151

Aristotle, 68, 82, 105

Arminian theology, 17, 57–59, 63–64, 68, 71–72, 74, 200, 221n21

Arminius, Jacobus, 17, 57

Army and Navy Messenger, 146, 246n5

Ayres, Thomas Eldridge Sr., diary of, x, 255n9

Bacon, Francis, 59–60

Baconian empiricism in American theology, 59–60

Baird, Robert, 95

Baker, Edward Dickinson, 23, 24, 25, 27, 31

Baltimore, Maryland, 167, 171, 189

Barbee, David Rankin, 182, 212, 213–14

Barnard, Frederick Augustus Porter: ATB's attack on the character of, 163–65, 227n7

Barnes, Albert, 87, 91, 110

Barrett, Richard F., 25

Beattie, James, 64

Bell, John, 136

Benjamin, Judah P., 143, 152

Bennett, John Boyce, 71, 80, 144, 182, 261n10

Benton, Thomas Hart, 156

Berkeley, Bishop George, 52, 64

Bigelow, John, 95

Bishop, Robert Hamilton, 18–19, 222n31

Blackstone, William, 15, 36

Blau, Joseph L., 5, 83

Bledsoe, Albert Taylor (hereafter ATB): apologist for the Lost Cause, 1, 4–5, 6, 121, 166, 172–71, 186, 187, 188–89, 207, 208; assessments of, 6, 186, 207–10; assistant secretary of war, 4, 143–45; chief of the Confederate bureau of war, 4, 141–43, 195; children of, 221n22; as co-editor of the *Illinois Journal*, 22, 30–38; death of, 206; early life and education, 10, 219n5; editor and proprietor of the *Southern Review*, 191, 198–99, 199–200, 204, 214; Episcopal clergyman, 17, 19–21; the epitome of the unreconstructed and unrepentant southerner, 7, 171–72, 186–87, 207–10; historian and Confederate publicist, 1, 129, 131–35, 146–49, 150, 154–61, 166; Illinois Whig, 24–28, 30–38; at Kenyon theological seminary, 15–17; loyal friend and defender of Jefferson Davis, 191, 195; memorandum book of, 73, 211, 213, 217n3; Methodist clergyman, 5, 201, 258n37; old-line Whig, 6, 136, 170, 193; personal papers of, 211–12; personality and character of, 1–2, 19, 65–66, 141–42, 145, 205–6, 232n32; political theorist, 22, 26, 35, 38, 126; professor of mathematics and astronomy, 17–18,

Bledsoe, Albert Taylor (*continued*)
  51–53, 226n2; southern educator, 53–56; southern intellectual, 2, 8–9; Springfield, Illinois, attorney, 23–24, 30, 38; studies law at Richmond, Virginia, 10, 11, 15; theistic worldview of, 37, 44, 74; theologian, 58–74; unfinished history of the Civil War, 150, 166, 170, 203, 211, 258n41; at West Point, 10, 11–14
Bledsoe, Anna or "Annie" (daughter of ATB), 168, 199, 221n22
Bledsoe, Elizabeth McMurtrie Wayland (daughter of ATB), aka "Lillie," 211, 199, 211, 221n22
Bledsoe, Emily Albertine (daughter of ATB), 212, 221n22
Bledsoe, Harriet Coxe (wife of ATB), 17, 19, 28, 29, 150, 167–68, 184, 199, 213, 215, 225n19; surviving children of, 221n22
Bledsoe, Jesse, 15, 219n5, 221n16
Bledsoe, Louise M., 221n22
Bledsoe, Moses Owsley (father of ATB), 10–11, 15, 22–23, 219n1, n2, and n4; 223n3
Bledsoe, Sophia Childress Taylor (mother of ATB), 10, 11, 219n4
Bledsoe, Sophia McIlvaine (daughter of ATB). *See* Herrick, Sophia McIlvaine Bledsoe
Bledsoe, William (brother of ATB): death of, 16
Blight, David W., 4
Bocock, John Holmes, 72–73
Bozeman, Theodore Dwight, 60
Brief Sketch of the Rise and Progress of Astronomy, In Three Lectures, A (1854), 40
British West Indies: alleged failure of emancipation in, 94–95, 105
Brooke, Reverend John T., 20
Brougham, Lord Henry, 215
Browne, William Hand, 5, 189–90, 191, 198, 199, 201
Bruce, Philip Alexander, 141, 213
Buchanan, James, 32; Buchanan wing of the Democratic Party, 117
Buck, Paul H., 208
Burke, Edmund, 27, 43
Butler, William, 29

Cabell, James Lawrence, 51, 55, 83, 229n37
Cairnes, J. E., 157
Cajori, Florian, 228n30
Calhoun, John C., 33–34, 160, 175, 176, 177, 226n30
California, controversy over its admission to the Union, 45, 46
Calvin, John, 58
Calvinist theology, 58, 59, 64
capital punishment, 75, 233n1
Carey, Henry Charles, 95

Carrollton, Illinois, 16, 21, 22
Cartwright, Samuel A.: on ethnology and slavery, 82; recommends Fletcher's *Studies on Slavery*, 118–19
causality, 13, 59, 61–62, 67. *See also* free will-determinism debate; moral necessity
"Causes of the American War, The" (1863–64) by ATB, 154–58
Chamberlaine, Jeremiah, 48
Channing, William Ellery, 76, 109, 111
Chase, Samuel Portland, 76, 98, 100, 131, 133, 167, 184
Chiles, Robert Eugene, 71
"Christian Cosmos" by ATB, 229n38
Christianity, 44, 96
Christy, David on pulpit politics, 242n11
civil liberty and natural liberty: ATB's criticism of received opinion regarding, 35, 36–38
civil rights movement: effect on interpretations of the Lost Cause, 186
Clay Club (Springfield, Illinois), 22, 27–28
Clay, Henry, 27–28, 31, 34
Clayton, Alexander M., 41
close communion, 58, 205
Cobb, Thomas Read Rootes, 153
Cobden, Richard, 157
coercion: Confederate appellation for the Civil War as a war of, 161, 171
Cohen, Morris R., 217n1
Coke, Edward, 15
Colossians 4:1, 233n11
Columbia College, New York, 163, 164
Commentator (Frankfort, Kentucky), 10–11, 219n1
common sense realism (Scottish realists): as an influence on ATB's philosophy of the will, 64, 66, 67
compact theory of Union, 171, 172, 174–76
Compromise Measures of 1850, 45
Comte, Auguste, 52
Confederate nationalism, 7, 141, 145, 146–49, 154–60, 247n13
Confederate publicist in London, 4, 149, 158
Confederate War Department at Richmond: ATB as the assistant secretary of war, 4, 143–45, 195; ATB as chief of the war bureau, 4, 141–43, 195
consolidation v. state sovereignty, 48, 160, 172, 192
Constitutional Union Party, 4
Constitutionalist, The (Augusta, Georgia), 243n15
"converging causes" of secession and war, 155, 192
Cooke, J. W., 141, 137
Cornelia, "These are my jewels," 252n9
Cornubia, Confederate steamship and blockade-runner, 151
Corwin, Thomas, 31–32, 96
Coulter, E. Merton, 182, 207

Courtenay, Edward H., 49, 51
Cousin, Victor, 67–68, 127
Cover, Robert M., 241n42
Coxe, Harriet. *See* Bledsoe, Harriet Coxe
Coxe, Margaret, 30
Coxe, Richard Smith, 30
Cullum, George W., 215

Dabney, Robert Lewis, 105–7, 205, 208, 238n10
Darwinism, 209, 234n20
Davidson, James Wood, 191
Davies, Charles, 12, 13, 52
"Davis Guards," 139
Davis, Jefferson, 5, 13, 45, 46, 48, 50, 53, 139–41, 150,
    162, 166, 168, 169, 180, 185, 204, 221n16
Davis, Reuben, 45–46
Davis, Varina Howell, 170, 253n30
Davis, William C., 150, 158
De Bow's Review, 107, 119,
Declaration of Independence: the antislavery argu-
    ment from, 85
De Leon, Edward, 153
Democratic Party, 4, 116, 117, 128, 129, 147
Democratic Party National Convention of 1860
    (Charleston, South Carolina), 129
Denison, George Anthony, 166
Determinism. *See* causality; free will-determinism
    debate; moral necessity.
Deuteronomy 23:15–16, 88–89, 98, 235n34
Dew, Thomas Roderick, 84
Dinwiddie, Emily Albertine Bledsoe (daughter of
    ATB), 212, 221n22
Dinwiddie, Emily Wayland (granddaughter of ATB),
    212
Dinwiddie, William, 52, 186, 212, 213
divine foreknowledge, 64
divine government, 71, 148
divine sovereignty, 59, 205
divinity, attributes of, 57
doctor of laws degrees (honorary): conferred on ATB
    by the University of Mississippi and by Kenyon
    College, 49
Donald, David, 116, 120
Douglas, Stephen A., 128–30, 197, 242n8, 243n9
Dunaway, Wayland Fuller, 138–39

Eaton, Clement, 144
Edinburgh Review, 96, 97
Edwards, Jonathan, 58, 59, 60
egalitarianism, 80–82, 83, 148, 208
Elliott, E. N., 120, 122,
Elliott, Reverend Stephen, 55, 142–43, 249n43

Enlightenment, 27, 208
Ephesians 6:9, 233n11
Epicureanism, 126
Epistle of Saint Paul to Philemon, 90–91
Essay on Liberty and Slavery, An (1856), 2–3, 33, 36, 75,
    101, 220n8, 226n36; reviews of, 101–16
evangelical paternalism movement and the religious
    instruction of slaves, 96–97, 237n58
Evening Herald (London): ATB's articles on "Secession"
    in, 154, 159–61, 172; ATB attacks the character Fred-
    erick Augustus Porter Barnard in, 163–65
Everett, Edward, 133, 136
Evil: the problem of in Christian theology, 17, 57, 69
*Examination of President Edwards' Inquiry into the Free-
    dom of the Will, An* (1845), 1, 30, 39, 57, 58–59, 60–3;
    reviews of, 63–66

faculty psychology, 66
Faust, Drew Gilpin, 8, 120–21, 122, 218n12
Fitzhugh, George, 3, 75, 101, 104–5, 117, 118, 121, 122,
    123, 125, 127, 233n7
Fletcher, John, 118–19
Florida (Confederate steamship), 151
Foner, Eric, 133
Foote, Henry Stuart, 45, 46
Forbes, Robert Pierce, 135
Fort Gibson (Indian Territory), 14
Fortress, Monroe (Hampton, Virginia), 169, 170
Foster, Gaines M., 186, 208, 237n57, 240n37
Fox, Virginia McIlvaine Herrick (granddaughter of
    ATB), 212
Fox-Genovese, Elizabeth, 58, 76, 92, 138
Francis, Simeon, 25, 30–31
Fredrickson, George M., 96
free blacks, 82, 86, 96, 100, 119
free labor, 3, 94, 104, 105, 107, 112, 122, 133, 208
free will-determinism debate, 57, 59, 62, 205. *See also*
    causality; moral necessity
Freeman, Douglas Southall, 4, 186
Fremont, John Charles, 132
French Revolution, 26–27, 35
Fugitive Slave Clause of the Constitution, 98, 100,
    130, 194
Fugitive Slave Law of 1793, 98, 100, 136
Fugitive Slave Law of 1850, 45, 46, 48, 88–89, 97–100,
    194
Fuller, Richard, 78, 96

Garrison, William Lloyd, 76
Genovese, Eugene D., 7–8, 9, 58, 76, 92, 123, 138,
    234n17
Gerard, Willard, 10

Giddings, Joshua Reed, 131, 235n34

Gildersleeve, Basil Lanneau, 189

Globe Tavern, 28, 225n19

Goldfield, David R., 7

Grayson, William J., 243n15

Greeley, Horace, 184

Griffith, C. J., 207

Grinnan, Cornelia, 152

Gurney, Joseph John, 94, 237n52

Hallock, Gerald, 130

Hamilton, Sir William Sterling, 66, 68

Harper, William Joseph, 118

Harper's Monthly Magazine, 199

Harrison, William Henry: eulogy on by ATB, 22, 26–27

Harrison, William Henry (of Wigwam, Virginia), 73

Hartington, Lord (Spencer Compton Cavendish), 151

Hawley, Reverend J. M., 74, 206

Hayne, Paul Hamilton, 190, 198, 200, 204

Haynes, Stephen R., 92

Hays, Willard Murrell, 33, 254n39

Henry, Anson G., 25, 31

Henry, Caleb Sprague, 67, 215, 231n26

Henry, Joseph, 48, 127

Henry, Patrick, 179, 180

Herndon, William H., 197

Herrenvolk democracy, 96

Herrick, Reverend James Burton, 204

Herrick, Sophia McIlvaine Bledsoe (daughter of ATB), 20, 28, 29, 186, 199, 212, 221n22, 225n19; associate editor of *Southern Review,* 5, 190, 203–5

"higher law" of individual conscience, 48, 97, 126

Hobbes, Thomas, 36–38

Hodge, Charles Reverend, 92, 130; ATB's reply to regarding the secession crisis, 130-36, 164, 165, 242n11, 242n13, 243n15

Holcombe, James Philemon, 123, 138

Holifield, E. Brooks, 60, 64, 71

Holmes, George Frederick, 40, 41, 42, 43, 50–51, 53, 101; reviews *Liberty and Slavery,* 107–10, 118, 125, 126–27, 146, 200

Holt, Michael F., 242n8

Holt, Thomas C., 94

honor and duty: ATB as self-professed vindicator of southern honor, 131, 171–72, 203; a premium placed on the values of honor, loyalty, and duty by ATB, 165; as southern values and code of behavior, 121

Hopley, Catherine Cooper, 145

Hotze, Henry, 151, 153, 154, 161, 162

Hughes, Henry, 3, 75, 105, 113, 119, 122, 123

human consciousness and volitions, 59, 60–61, 63, 66

human nature, 26, 36, 37–38, 43–45, 57, 61–62

human origins, the debate concerning, 82–83, 234n22

Illinois Journal (Springfield, Illinois), 22, 25, 30, 43, 75, 208

Illinois State Register (Springfield, Illinois), 30–31, 32, 34

imprisonment of Jefferson Davis, 169, 251n3, 253n30, 257n23

inalienable rights: ATB's definition of in relation to slavery, 85, 103–4

Index, The (London), 151, 154, 161

Individualism: concern over "excessive individualism," 105, 125–27

infant damnation: doctrine concerning the suffering and salvation of infants, 20, 58, 70; infant baptism, 205

Irons, Charles F., 244n26

Is Davis a Traitor; Or Was Secession a Constitutional Right Previous to the War of 1861? (1866), 154, 159, 166, 170, 171–80, 185; subsequent opinion on, 185–86

Jackson, Thomas Jonathan ("Stonewall"), 49

Jamaica, 95

Jayne, Julia M., 29

Jefferson, Thomas, 83–84, 134

Jenkins, William Sumner, 116

Johnson, Andrew: general pardon for former Confederates, 184

Johnson, Robert Underwood, 207

Johnson, Samuel, 64, 198

Johnston, Albert Sidney, 13

Johnston, Joseph Eggleston, 13

Johnston, Richard Malcolm, 191

Jones, Charles Colcock, 97, 208

Jones, John Beauchamp, 141–42, 143, 150

Kansas-Nebraska controversy, 48, 129–30

Kant, Immanuel, 68

Kell, John McIntosh, 248n35

Kent, Chancellor James, 15

Kenyon College: ATB attends Episcopal theological seminary at, 15–17; 221n19

Kettell, Thomas Prentice, 158

Knupfer, Peter, 6

Kuklick, Bruce, 60, 62

Lamar, Lucius Quintus Cincinnatus, 46, 201, 206, 207, 227n15

Lamon, Ward Hill, 196

"Lamon's Life of Lincoln" (1873) by ATB, 196–98

Lanphier, Charles Henry, 31

Leader, The (London), 115

Lecompton Constitution, 131

Lee, Robert E., 13, 50, 139, 140, 141, 171, 187, 188, 203, 246n8, 254n1

Leibnitz, Gottfried Wilhelm, 52, 71

Letcher, John, 140

Letcher, Robert Perkins, 11

Lincoln, Abraham, 22, 24, 25, 27, 28, 29, 156, 167–68, 196–98

Lincoln, Mary Todd, 28, 29, 225n19

Lincoln, Robert Todd, 28, 225n19

Lincoln-Shields affair, 28–29

Linder, Usher F., 28

Lippincott, J. B. and Company (Philadelphia), 101, 115, 119; Lippincott, Grambo, and Company, 119

Locke, John, 36, 68, 104, 105

Logan, Stephen Trigg, 22, 27, 28

Longstreet, August Baldwin, 46, 236n42

Longton, William Henry, 208

"Lost Cause" of southern independence: ATB as a vindicator of, 1, 4–6, 121, 187; Lost Cause Movement, 185–86

Louisa School for Young Ladies (Baltimore, Maryland), 199, 204

Lyons, James, 151

Macaulay, Thomas Babington, 81

Malachi 4:2, 258n37

Mansel, Henry Longueville, 232n43

Martin, Benjamin Nicholas, 65–66

Mason, George, 179, 180

Mason, James Murray, 152

master-slave relationships: representations of 85, 96

Maury, Matthew Fontaine, 161, 248n32

McCabe, James Dabney, Jr., 191

McCabe, William Gordon, 181

McCardell, John, 3, 53, 137

McGuffey, William Holmes, 12, 18, 50, 53, 206

McHenry, George, 162, 249n39 and 249n41

McIlvaine, Reverend Charles Pettit, 13–14, 15–16, 17, 19–20, 49, 162, 166–68, 220n12

McKim, Randolph Hamilton, 137–38

McKitrick, Eric L., 92, 122

McKivigan, John R., 93

Merryman, Elias H., 12

Metaphysics, 58, 63, 74

Methodism, 21, 57, 58, 71, 200, 201, 202

Methodist Episcopal Church, South, 5, 200, 201, 202

Methodist Quarterly Review, 63, 71, 75

Methodist Review, 74

Mexican-American War: Whig opposition to, 22, 31–32, 234n16

Miami University (Oxford, Ohio), 17–19

Miller, Rev. Charles W., 205

Millington, John, 41, 227n7

Milnor, James, 14

Mims, Edwin, 182, 184, 89, 207, 213

Minor, John Barbee, 138, 221n17

minority rights of the southern states within the American Union, 48, 179–80

Mississippi gubernatorial election of 1851, 45–47

Missouri Compromise: history of, 131–35; repeal of 3, 48, 130

monogenesis-polygenesis controversy regarding human origins, 51, 83

Montesquieu, Charles Louis de Secondat, 35, 126, 155

moral accountability and free will, 57, 58, 61

moral necessity: ATB argues against the existence of, 61, 66, 69; ATB considers to be contradictions in terms, 66, 205, 231n23 and 231n29. *See also* causality; free-will determinism debate

moral philosophy, 37, 57, 62, 229n38, 230n11

Morison, Samuel Elliot, 8

Morrow, Ralf E., 116

Morton, Sarah Wentworth Apthorp, 89, 236n37

Motley, John Lothrop: repudiates the right of secession, 175

Mott, Lucretia, 76

National Intelligencer (Washington, D.C.), 125, 127

nationalist construction of the U. S. Constitution and American Union, 159

natural law, 7, 16, 37, 122–23, 173, 122–23, 241n42

natural rights, 3, 7, 36, 37, 74, 75, 85–86, 95, 103, 104, 122–23

Needham Law School (Virginia), 11

New Englander and Yale Review, 65

Newton, Mary Barksdale: re-issues *Is Davis a Traitor?* at Richmond in 1907, 185

Newton, Sir Isaac, 13, 52

New-York Review, 215

New York Times, 165

New York Weekly Journal of Commerce, 130, 164. 242n13

Noll, Mark A., 60, 70

North American Review, 112

North and South: rivalry between for dominance as the principal cause of war, 146–47

"North or South?" (1864) by ATB, 163

northern conservatism, 116–17, 147

northern "radicalism": southern fear of, 40–41, 117, 147

Notes on the State of Virginia (1782), 84

Nott, Josiah Clark: ATB on Nott and Gliddon, 83; Nott and Gliddon's *Types of Mankind*, 83; racial theory of, 82

INDEX

Oakland College, 48
O'Brien, Michael, 9, 40, 122, 226n3
O'Conor, Charles, 181, 182, 183
Old Solider (Springfield, Illinois), 25
Onesimus, 90–91
ordered liberty, 85, 127
original sin, 20, 57, 58, 59, 69, 70
Otey, James Hervey, 97

Paley, William, 12, 220n8
Parker, Theodore, 76, 233n3
Peck, Thomas Ephraim, 71–72, 232n36
Pekin (Illinois) Whig, 31
Pendleton, William Nelson, 12, 13, 49–50
Perine, David Maulden, 170, 251n5
personal liberty laws, 46, 48, 99–100, 194
petition of the three thousand and fifty clergymen to
    Congress (1854), 130
Phi Sigma and Hermean literary societies (University
    of Mississippi), 46
Philadelphia, Pennsylvania, 29, 30
Philemon, Epistle of Saint Paul to, 90
Phillips, Ulrich Bonnell, 237n57
Phillips, Wendell, 118; on the Republican Party as a
    "sectional party," 179, 198
Philosophy of Mathematics, The (1868), 52–53
Pierce, Franklin, on the issue of slavery in the ter-
    ritories, 99
Pierpont, Francis Harrison, 260
Pike, Nicholas, 219n5
Pinckney, Charles, 133–34, 179
Poisal, Reverend John, 200–1
political preaching against slavery: ATB's loathing of,
    76, 233n3, 242n11
Polk, James K., 22, 32, 234n16
Polk, Leonidas, 13, 14, 52, 54–56, 96, 143, 162–63,
    220n12, 245n41, 249n43
Pollard, Edward A., 186, 254n40
Pratt, Harry E., 182
predestination and election, 20, 58, 59, 64, 69, 205
Presbyterial Critic and Bi-Monthly Review, 105
Presbyterial Critic and Monthly Review, 71
Preston, Margaret Junkin, 200
Prigg v. Pennsylvania (1842), 46, 100, 238n65
Princeton Review, 64, 92, 117, 130
Pritchard, Abbot, and Loomis (Augusta, Georgia), 120
proslavery literature, 7–8, 101, 123; intersectional
    dimension of the slavery debate, 101, 106, 119; mo-
    tives of proslavery authors and intended audiences,
    101, 116–21; "proslavery historiography," 237n57;
    proslavery religion, 93, 113–14
Prospective Review, The (London), 92

public order and private liberty, 7, 38, 77, 226n38
Putnam's Monthly Magazine, 115

*Quarterly Review of the Methodist Episcopal Church,
    South*, 71
Quitman, John Anthony, 45

"R.," reviewer of *Liberty and Slavery*, 102–4
racism: and the defense of slavery, 7, 8, 82, 94, 107; the
    legacy of, 186
Radical Republicans, 171, 181, 196
Randolph, George Wythe, 143, 145
Randolph, John of Roanoke, 148
Rawle, William, 15
Rebecca Letters, 29
Reconstruction, 171, 195–96
Redwood, Allen C., 204. 258n43
Reed, William Bradford, 183
"Reflections on the War" (1863) by ATB, 146–49,
    246n5
Reformers: ATB's disdain for, 35, 42
Regulus, 163, 249n45
Reid, Thomas, 64, 67
religion and science: compatibility of in ATB's world-
    view, 40, 209, 229n2
"Reply to the Rev. Charles Hodge, D. D." (1861) by
    ATB, 130- 36, 164, 165, 242n11, 242n13
Republican Party, 4, 53, 131, 132, 133, 135, 136, 171,
    179, 181
"Republicanism" (1847) by ATB, 32–33, 234n16
reserved powers of the states: as justification for seces-
    sion, 172–73
Richmond, Virginia, 4, 10, 11, 15, 21, 139, 141, 144,
    145,169, 185, 206, 207
Robins, Glenn, 55
Roswell, Reverend S.S., 201
Ruffin, Edmund, 104, 122, 137
Ruffin, Frank G., 102
Russell, Charles Well, 189, 225n5

Sage, Bernard Janin, 185
St. George's Island (Bermuda), 151
Sangamo Journal (Springfield, Illinois), 25, 29, 30,
    225n17; superseded as the *Illinois Journal*, 30
Schneider, Herbert Wallace, 76
Schurz, Carl, 180, 184
Scott, John Witherspoon, 18–19
"Secession" (1864–1865) by ATB, 154, 159–61, 172
secession crises: ATB's eight grounds or causes of se-
    cession, 179; ATB's response to, 128–30
sectionalism, 2, 55, 114
Semmes, Rafael, 161

Seward, William H., 76, 88, 97–98, 126, 133, 167

Shanks, Henry T., 137

Shaw, Charles B.: replies anonymously to ATB's *Liberty and Slavery*, 110–15, 239n15

Shields, James, 28. *See* Lincoln-Shields affair.

Simpkins, Francis Butler, 208

sin: as a problem in Christian theology, 68–69

Slaughter, Reverend Philip, 246n2

slave codes, 82, 86, 124

slave trade: domestic, 8, 90, 96, 124

slaveholders: representations of, 97; rights and duties of, 78–79

slavery (as a domestic institution of the South): argument from the public good, 75, 80, 85, 93–94, 96, 103, 104; 122; argument from the scriptures, 87–93, 235n33; and Christian stewardship, 79, 86; and the Constitution, 97–100; defense of as a "beneficent" institution, 78–79, 84, 97; and guilt thesis, 120, 237n57, 240n37; as a "positive good," 84, 114; as a "school of correction," 96, 97, 237n57

slavery controversy: as a cause of war, 146, 156, 157–59, 192

slaves: denied the right to read, 86; evangelical movement to promote religion among, 96–97; religious instruction of, 86; representations of, 97; slave literacy, fear of, 86–87, 96, 124

Smith, Francis Henry, 52, 228n30

Smith, Gerrit, 184

Smith, Reverend Benjamin B., 20

Smith, H. Shelton, 96

Smithsonian Institution, 48, 125, 126, 127

Snay, Mitchell, 123, 127

social contract theory, 36–38, 74, 75, 102, 105, 233n1

"Social Destiny of Man," a lecture by ATB (1860), 125

Society for Promoting the Cessation of Hostilities in America, 161

southern clergy, 83, 96–97, 113–14, 188

southern commercial conventions: resolutions concerning education, 53–54, 229n32

southern conservatism: ATB's place within the tradition of, 9, 117, 207–9, 210

southern discord and dissent, 218n14

southern identity, 9, 39, 108; and the Civil War, 187, 203, 218n12

Southern Independence Association (Manchester, England), 152

southern intellectual history: ATB's place in, 2, 8–9

southern intellectuals: concerns and assumptions of, 2, 7–9

southern literature: efforts to revive after the war, 180, 189, 198

southern nationalism and education, 39, 40–41, 47, 53–55, 136, 138

southern orthodoxy regarding slavery and states' rights, 2–3, 39, 40, 53, 54, 114, 116, 120, 121

Southern Review (1867–1879): affiliation of with the Methodist Episcopal Church, South, 200–2; articles on the causes and consequences of the Civil War in, 202–3; ATB's contributions to, 191, 214; ATB defends his religious views in, 205; content of, 214; ATB's financial difficulties as editor and proprietor, 198–99; management of, 199–200, 204; mission of, 5, 188–90, 203; Sophia McIlvaine Bledsoe Herrick (daughter of ATB) joins him as associate editor, 203–5; the subject of theology in, 200, 201–2

Southwestern Book and Publishing Company, St. Louis, Missouri, 201

Sparrow, William, 16–17, 58–59, 66, 221n21

Speed, Joshua Fry, 25

Spence, James: his *American Union* (1862) an influence on ATB's views on secession and the causes of the war, 152–53, 177; slavery "a foul blot" on humanity, 153

"Spirit of Liberty, The" (1848) by ATB, 43, 226n34

Sporer, Paul Dennis, 184

Squier, Ephraim George: his correspondence on ethnology with Josiah Clark Nott, 234n22

Starr, Rebecca, x, 204, 257n32

state of nature, 36, 37, 38, 102, 104

State Rights Party (Mississippi), 45–46

states' rights construction of the U. S. Constitution and American Union, 174, 186

Steel, Samuel Augustus, 74, 182

Stephens, Alexander Hamilton: controversy with ATB on the causes of the Civil War, 136, 191–94

Stephens, Linton, 194

Sterns, Reverend Edward J., 190

Stewart, Dugald, 64

Stirling, James, 110, 123–24

Story, Joseph, 159, 100, 170, 175, 176

Stuart, John Todd, 24

Stuart, Moses, 88–89

Sumner, Charles, 76, 89, 90, 98–99

Synod of Dort, 58

Tappan, Philip Henry, 65

tariff issue: as a cause of war, 155–59, 192

Taylor, Chancellor Creed, 11, 219n4, 221n17

Taylor, Creed, Jr., 219n4

Taylor, John of Carolina, 177

Taylor, Nathaniel William, the "new theology" of, 73

Taylor, Samuel, 11, 219n4

Taylor, Samuel, Jr., 11, 15

Taylor, Zachary, 22

Testimony of Modern Science to the Unity of Mankind (1859), 51

Theodicy; Or, Vindication of the Divine Glory As Manifested in the Constitution and Government of the Moral World, A (1853), 1, 57, 66–70; reviews of, 70–74

Theology: ATB's "new theology," 73; ATB's study of, 15–17, 58, 66

Thomas, Jesse Burgess, Jr. (law partner with ATB), 23, 223n5

Thompson, Jacob, 40–41, 53

Thompson, John Reuben, 102

Thornwell, James Henley, 71, 97

Three Lectures on Rational Mechanics; Or, The Theory of Motion (1854), 40

Tillett, Wilber F., 205–6, 223n3

Tillman, Benjamin R., 260n56

Tise, Larry E., 83, 119

Townsend, John Wilson, 1

Tremlett, Louisa A., 161–62, 248n32, 248n37, 249n38

Tremlett, Reverend Francis William, 161–62, 248n32, 249n38

Trubner and Company (London), 115, 207

Tucker, Henry St. George, 221n17, 234n17

Tucker, Nathaniel Beverley, 221n17

Tucker, St. George, 15, 221n17, 252n10

Tyler, John, 27

Types of Mankind (1854), 83

Uncle Tom's Cabin, 48; ATB's reference to the characters of George Harris, Eliza, and Uncle Tom, 97

Union Party (Mississippi), 45–46

United Confederate Veterans, 185

United Daughters of the Confederacy (Danville, Virginia Chapter), 254n37

United States Constitution: southern interpretation of the meaning of the preamble to, 177; states "accede" to the ratification of, 176

United States Military Academy, ATB as cadet at, 10, 11–14

United States v. Jefferson Davis, 169, 183–84; ATB's unsubstantiated claims regarding the influence of *Is Davis a Traitor?* in the federal government's *nolli prosequi* (unwilling to prosecute) declaration in the case of, 181–84

University of Mississippi, 2, 39–49; ATB acting president of, 40, 42; commencement address as, 42–45

University of Missouri: ATB's candidacy as president of, 56

University of the South, 54–56

University of Transylvania, 15, 219n5, 221n16

University of Virginia, 2, 39, 49–53, 139, 167, 169; senior mathematics class of, 206

Upshur, Abel P., 177

Vanderbilt, Cornelius, 184

Vattel, Emmerich de, 173, 252n10

Venable, Richard M., 190

Wade, John Donald, 208

Waddel, John Newton, 39, 41, 42, 58

Walker, Leroy Pope, 141, 142

Wall, Louisa Herrick (granddaughter of ATB), 212, 213

Wallenstein, Peter, 137

Wallis, Severn Teackle, 194

War Between the States, The, or Was Secession a Constitutional Right Previous to the War of 1861–1865 (1915): reissue of ATB's *Is Davis A Traitor; Or Was Secession a Constitutional Right Previous to 1861?*, 186

Warren, Robert Penn, 7

Washington, D. C., 29, 30

Wayland, Reverend Francis, 76, 77, 78, 79, 88, 96, 109, 111, 233n9

Weaver, Richard M., 182, 186, 207, 219n5

Webster, Daniel, 32, 159, 160, 170, 175–78

Wesley, John, 58, 205

Whedon, Daniel Denison, 205

Whig Convention (Vandalia, Illinois), 28

Whig State Central Committee (Springfield, Illinois), 23, 25

Wight, Orlando Williams, 68

Willard, Samuel, 23–24, 223n3, 224n10

Williams, Langbourne M., 211

Wilmer, Reverend Richard H., 55, 188–89

Wilmington, North Carolina, 151

Wilmot Proviso, 4, 22, 32, 99,

Wilson, Charles Reagan, 4, 186, 187, 208

women: conservative attitudes toward the rights of, 117, 130, 209, 260n56

Woodworth, Steven E., 137, 182

Wyatt-Brown, Bertram, 8, 119, 121, 137

Yankee character: ATB's negative views of, 140, 163

Yankee histories of the Civil War and school histories of the United States: ATB on, 191

Yankee school teachers: distrust of in the South, 41, 54

Young Men's Christian Association, 51

Young Men's Whig Convention and Old Soldiers Meeting (Springfield, Illinois), 25